MISSION

and

MIGRATION

**GLOBAL MENNONITE HISTORY SERIES:
LATIN AMERICA**

By
Jaime Prieto Valladares

Translated and Edited by
C. Arnold Snyder

General Editors
John A. Lapp, C. Arnold Snyder

Good Books
Intercourse, PA 17534
800/762-7171
www.GoodBooks.com

co-published with

Pandora Press
Kitchener, ON N2G 3R2
519/578-2381
www.PandoraPress.com

Photography and Illustration Credits

Front cover: all photos by Merle Good except first and fifth from left in photo scroll courtesy Mennonite Church U.S.A. Archives, Goshen.

Back cover: all photos by Merle Good.

Pages: J. W. Shank, T. K. Hershey, et al., *The Gospel under the Southern Cross* (Scottdale, PA: Mennonite Publishing House, 1943), 8; Courtesy Mennonite Archives of Ontario, 9, 79, 90, 91, 94, 98, 106, 107, 108, 110, 113a, 116, 123, 128, 167, 173a, 229; *La Voz Menonita*, (January-February 1940), 10, 12, 16; Courtesy Mennonite Church U.S.A. Archives, Goshen, 14, 15, 22, 24, 87, 99, 101, 171, 175, 184, 187, 188a, b, 189, 192b, 197, 208, 210, 223, 228, 260; Courtesy Albert and Lois Buckwalter, 20; Walter Schmiedehaus, *Die Altkolonier-Mennoniten in Mexiko* (Winnipeg, MB: CMBC Publications, 1982), 30, 31, 32, 35; Peter Klassen, *Kaputi Mennonita. Eine friedliche Begegnung im Chacokrieg* (Asunción: Imprenta Modelo, 1980), 38; Willy Janz and Gerhard Ratzlaff, *Gemeinde unter dem Kreuz des Südens*. (Curitiba: Imprimas, 1980), 40; Ernesto Unruh and Hannes Kalisch, *Moya´ansaeclha ´Nengelpayvaam Nengeltomha Enlhet*, (Ya´alve-Saanga: Comunidad Enlhet, 1997), 41a; *Luz a los Indígenas y Asociación de Servicios de Cooperación Indígena-Menonita, Album* (Filadelfia: Imprenta CROMOS S. R. L., 1986), 41b; Wilmar Stahl, *Escenario Indígena Chaqueño Pasado y Presente* (Filadelfia: ASCIM, 1982), 42; Gerhard Ratzlaff, *The Trans-Chaco Highway. How it came to be*, trans. By Elizabeth Unruh Leite (n.p., 2000), 44, 104, 105a; Peter Pauls Jr., ed. *Mennoniten in Brasilien, Gedenkschrift zum 50 Jahr-Jubiläum ihrer Einwanderung 1930-1980* (Witmarsum, Brasil: 1980), 46, 55a, 61; Gerhard Ratzlaff, *Historia, Fe y Prácticas Menonitas: Un Enfoque Paraguayo* (Asunción: 2006), 47; Korny Neufeld, *Conociendo a los Menonitas*, 2nd ed. (Asunción: 2005), 48, 113b, 115; Courtesy Mennonite Church USA Archives, North Newton, Kansas, 55b, 59, 63, 64, 65, 84, 85, 119, 186; Peter Pauls Jr., *Witmarsum in Paraná* (Curitiba: Imprimax Ltda., 1976), 57a; Peter P. Klassen, *Die russlanddeutschen Mennoniten in Brasilien*, Band 1 (Santa Catarina: Mennonitischer Geschitsverein e. V., 1995), 57b; unattributed, 58; Courtesy Jaime Prieto, 62, 75, 88, 92, 144b, 169, 173b, 174, 178, 193, 199, 201, 218, 219, 230, 246, 247, 248, 249, 250, 269, 276, 279, 290, 291b, 299, 300, 301, 302 (*La Nación*, March 6, 2005); Johannes Bergmann, *En Uruguay encontramos una nueva patria* (Montevideo: Imprenta Mercur S.A, 1998), 76; Courtesy Eunice Miller, 81; Courtesy MWC, 86, 322, 328; Courtesy Daniel Schipani, 95, 96; Courtesy Linda Shelly, 102, 117b, 220, 261, 314, a, b, 315, 317b, 319, 327, 334, 338 a, b, 345; Courtesy Geschichsarchiv der Kolonie Menno, 105b; Courtesy Becky Oulahen, 117a; Courtesy Angela Rempel, 124; Courtesy COM archives, 126, 144a, 177; Courtesy Erwin Rempel, 129; Courtesy Viola Shelly (Lehman), 134; Courtesy Andrew Shelly, 138, 139, 140a, b, 141, 142, 145, 168; Courtesy Center for Mennonite Brethren Studies, 147, 148, 149, 153, 272, 273, 274; Courtesy Maurine Friesen, 156, 157, 158b, 159; Courtesy Joe Walter, 158a, 160; *El Discípulo Cristiano* (August 1971), 192a; *Missionary Light* (May-June 1965), 207, 212; Courtesy Virginia Mennonite Missions, 211; Courtesy Elmer and Eileen Lehman, 213, 232, 252, 255, 258, 277, a, b, c, 278, 280, 343; Courtesy Henry Yoder, 217; Courtesy Paul and Eleanor Derstine, 222, 224; Courtesy Eastern Mennonite Missions, 233, 265, 270; Cover, *Missionary Light* (July-August, 1979), 238; Courtesy Hugo Hernández, 245; Courtesy MCC, 264, 339; Courtesy Larry and Helen Lehman, 289, 291a; Courtesy Linda Witmer, 292; Courtesy Titus Guenther, 317a; Courtesy *Junta Menonita de Missões Menonitas* (JMMI), 323; Courtesy Tim Froese, 333.

Book Design and Layout: C. Arnold Snyder

Map Design: Cliff Snyder

MISSION AND MIGRATION

Copyright © 2010 by Good Books, Intercourse, Pennsylvania 17534

ISBN: 978-1-56148-690-8

Library of Congress Catalog Card Number: 2010022837

Library of Congress Cataloging-in-Publication Data

Prieto, Jaime, 1958-
Mission and migration / by Jaime Prieto Valladares ; translated and edited by C. Arnold Snyder.
p. cm. -- (Global Mennonite history series. Latin America)
Includes index.
ISBN 978-1-56148-690-8 (alk. paper)
1. Mennonites--Latin America--History. 2. Latin America--Church history. I. Snyder, C. Arnold, 1946- II. Title.
BX8119.L22P75 2010
289.7'72--dc22   2010022837

Table of Contents

Foreword

In July 2009 the fifteenth Assembly of the Mennonite World Conference convened in Asuncion, Paraguay. More than 6000 people joined this six-day Assembly representing Mennonite and Brethren in Christ conferences in more than sixty countries. Two-thirds of those attending were from Latin America and the Caribbean. On reflection, it was striking that this vigorous Assembly took place on a continent where the Mennonite and Brethren in Christ movement first appeared relatively recently, in 1917. First came missionaries from North America and shortly thereafter large scale migrations from Canada and the Soviet Union, and then internal missions by the newly-founded churches and communities. It was thus relatively easy to select *Mission and Migration* as an appropriate title for a history of the Anabaptist-related churches of the southern Americas, which at last count (2009) numbered 169,364 members.

We are pleased to present this third volume of the Global Mennonite History. Jaime Adrian Prieto Valladares, Professor of Church History and Cultural Studies at the Latin American Biblical University in San José, Costa Rica, has spent more than a decade researching and writing this unique historical account. Professor Prieto brought to the task his historical training in Costa Rican and German Universities (PhD, Hamburg) as well as his rich experience in Costa Rican Mennonite congregations and as a regional teacher.

In preparing this volume Professor Prieto not only read available source material, but also travelled to most of the twenty-six countries in which Latin American and Caribbean Mennonites now live in order to establish an historical record where little had been recorded or preserved in writing. Much of the fresh history found in this volume is based on more than 350 interviews with church individuals and groups. This volume includes many photographs and sidebars based on these recorded interviews. We are grateful that these source materials will be preserved in the library of SEMILLA – the Central American Anabaptist Seminary – in Guatemala City. We are most appreciative of the individuals and conferences throughout Latin America and the Caribbean who provided hospitality, opened their archival records for research, and were available to be interviewed during Jaime Prieto's travels.

We owe Jaime Prieto sincere thanks for the time, effort, and unique insight that he has brought to this volume. We are also grateful to his wife, Silva Regina de Lima Silva, a well-known Latin American theologian, and their son Tomaz Sataye for sharing in this long effort. We regret that our series could not include more of the large quantities of data collected for this volume. Copies of the unabridged Spanish manuscript will be placed in research libraries in South and Central America, North America, and Europe.

Because of space limitations, the 80 pages of citations and sidebar credits will not be printed as a part of this volume. The citations corresponding to the printed note numbers in this book are available on line, as are the sidebar credits. See page 350 of this book for more details. A printed and bound version is also available for purchase from Pandora Press.

Co-editor Arnold Snyder edited the original Spanish manuscript to its present dimensions, translated the text into English, wrote the introductions to the three main sections, and is responsible for the design and layout of the present book, with helpful design assistance from Cliff Snyder of Good Books. The English text published here will appear later in both Spanish and French versions.

We are deeply indebted to three readers who helped us in preparing the manuscript for publication: Gerhard Ratzlaff of Asunción, a leading historian of Mennonites in Paraguay; Juan Martinez, a former President of SEMILLA and now director of the Spanish Program at Fuller Theological Seminary in Pasadena, California; and Linda Shelly, long-time administrator of Latin America programs for Mennonite Central Committee and Mennonite Mission Network. Linda Shelly provided invaluable assistance in locating many of the historical photographs that illustrate the volume.

The Global Mennonite History is not a self-sustaining activity. In addition to the wisdom and council of the sponsoring committee and the leadership of Mennonite World Conference, we are enormously indebted to many individuals and groups who have contributed funds not only to this volume but to this entire project. These include United Service Foundation, Mennonite Central Committee, Mennonite Mutual Aid, Good Books, Goodville Mutual Insurance, the Oosterbaan Foundation, Mennonite Brethren Historical Commission, Mennonite Foundation of Canada, Mennonite Historical Societies in Winnipeg, Manitoba, Goshen, Indiana, Lancaster Pennsylvania, and others.

As editors we are privileged to work with many fine historians. We learn much from new information but more importantly from new ways of recovering the richness of the church's story. Jaime Prieto has opened for us new windows to the artfulness of church history. We commend this volume as an invaluable contribution to the Global Mennonite and Brethren in Christ story.

John A. Lapp, Akron, PA.
C. Arnold Snyder, Waterloo, ON.

I

Early Missions and Settlements: (1911-1958)

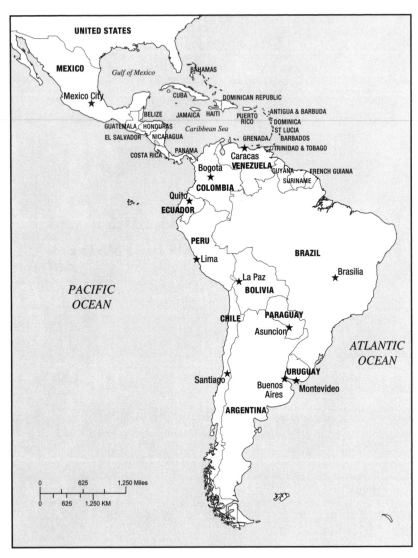

Latin America

Introduction: Early Missions and Settlements (1911-1958)

The territory conquered and colonized by the sixteenth-century Spanish and Portuguese monarchs in the western hemisphere has come to be called Latin America. It has a unique and troubled cultural, political, social, economic and religious history. As the descriptive phrase suggests, the predominant languages spoken today, from Mexico to Tierro del Fuego, are the closely related Iberian Romance languages of Spanish and Portuguese – a sign of the victory of European colonization in the region. Nevertheless, the indigenous reality of Central and South America has not been forgotten, and still provides a visible reminder of pre-Colombian peoples and cultures. Wherever Guaraní, Kekchi, Toba or other indigenous languages remain as the speech of every day life and commerce, the deep and violent colonial history of the region takes the form of a reproachful question posed to the past, the present and the future alike.

The religious legacy of colonization remains a central feature of present-day Latin American reality. The sixteenth-century Spanish and Portuguese conquest and colonization is the inescapable fact that shaped the present reality of the region. Nevertheless, the human embodiment of "latin" America is not predominantly "latin," but rather an indigenous, African, and racially-mixed people who have inherited centuries of Iberian colonization and global immigration.

The sixteenth and seventeenth century cultural battle to "europeanize" indigenous and African peoples was carried out primarily by the Roman Catholic church which chose, in the end, to attempt to eradicate indigenous religious expressions. In this it largely succeeded. The concessions granted to the Spanish crown by the papacy early in the sixteenth century (the "Patronato Real") granted the Spanish

3

sovereigns a virtual control over the colonial church and its clergy. In Latin America the church (with notably few exceptions) functioned as an arm of the Iberian crowns. Just as there were virtually no Protestants in Spain or Portugal, neither was there a significant Protestant presence in Latin America before the late nineteenth century.

The story of the coming of Anabaptist-descended churches to Latin America thus begins in the late nineteenth and early twentieth centuries, in the period following Latin American political independence from Spain and Portugal. This is a fact of significant political and cultural importance. The openness to Protestant missions and Protestant immigrants by the emerging Latin American national governments was a conscious attempt by "progressive" governments to turn away from colonial Spanish policies, economic, political and religious. An obvious step in this direction was to break the monopoly of the Roman Catholic church, particularly in matters of education and public policy. The "liberal" political parties, which espoused the Enlightenment ideals of a pluralist society, the separation of church and state, secular education, freedom of the press, and free trade were the parties that extended a welcome to Protestant missions and settlers.

As will be seen in the pages that follow, Mennonites came to Latin America by entering doors already opened by other "Evangelico" (Protestant) groups. Mennonites were seen as Protestants, and Mennonites readily identified with the Protestant minorities in Latin America, over against the Roman Catholic majority.

From the perspective of the countries who opened their doors, the coming of Mennonite missionaries and settlers always had larger political implications, and not simply religious ones. Mission boards and Mennonite settlers were rarely aware of this larger picture. The more profound political consequences of Mennonite mission and settlement became apparent only on later reflection. The growing awareness of the political and ideological impact of Mennonite presence in Latin America forms an essential underlying theme in the narrative that follows, and becomes even more significant for the Mennonite story in the post-World War II period, as will be evident in the second and third sections of this book.

The first Mennonite church to take root in Latin American soil gathered for worship in 1919, in the town of Pehuajó, Argentina. It was the result of North American mission efforts and represents one major impulse for the planting of Mennonite churches in Latin

America. The model for Mennonite missions in Latin America was provided by the mission efforts of the larger Protestant denominations. Not surprisingly, early Mennonite missions have the "look" and "feel" of the Protestant missions of that era.

The second major impulse for establishing Mennonites in Latin America came with the settling of Mennonite colonists in Mexico, Paraguay and Brazil, in the 1920s and 30s. The Mennonite colonists did not come to Latin America as missionaries bringing the Gospel to a "foreign mission field," but rather came as communities seeking a new life and future for their groups. A second major theme to be seen in the following pages, then, is the parallel development of two rather different Mennonite presences in various Latin American countries. The work of North American Mennonite mission boards eventually led to worshipping communities that, little by little, became "national" churches, with local leadership and control over their church properties and structures. Mennonite colonies also responded, in time, with mission efforts of their own, directed outside their colonies to the indigenous and Spanish/Portuguese- speaking peoples in their respective countries. The beginnings of these developments can be seen already in the initial stages of Mennonite presence in Latin America.

Historical differences among Mennonites complicate the story of Anabaptist-descended Christian groups in Latin America. North American Mennonite missionaries had been formed in the political and religious culture of the United States and Canada, quite different from the Germanic ethnic culture familiar to the conservative Mennonite colonists who passed through Canada on their way South, and the more progressive German-speaking colonists who settled in Latin American directly from Russia. Both English-speaking Mennonite missionaries and German-speaking Mennonite colonists were entering a Latin American culture that had been formed in a way profoundly different from their own. The question of how to express and live the Gospel in a new culture would provide a significant challenge for both groups.

There were, however, further religious and ideological differences among Mennonites that complicated matters even more. The narrative that follows will detail the mission efforts of "Old" Mennonites and General Conference Mennonites (now united in one church conference in the U.S. and Canada) and Mennonite Brethren from North America, to name just the largest Mennonite conferences of the time. In some cases, these different groups established parallel Mennonite churches, with denominational variants, in the same countries. The picture becomes even more complicated after World War II, when smaller North American Mennonite conferences initiated their own mission projects in different Latin American countries, as will be seen in the second and third sections of this book.

On the side of the colonists, the primary division fell between the "church" Mennonites and the Mennonite Brethren – a separation which dates back to a division in Russia in the middle of the nineteenth century. The designation of "MB" is a commonly-accepted abbreviation for the Mennonite Brethren group which broke away from the main body of Mennonites in Russia. There is, however, no such easy designation for the original group, the "church" (*kirchliche*) Mennonites, since in Latin America they tended to identify themselves as the "Mennonite Community" (*Mennonitengemeinde*). In North America members of this group joined the General Conference Mennonites. The distinction between "GCs" and "MBs," well-known in North America, is less applicable in Latin America, where affiliation with the General Conference was secondary and memories of the original separation ran deeper. Some historians have designated the "church Mennonite" group in Latin America as "MGs" (for their self-designation as *Mennonitengemeinde*).[1] For the sake of convenience, we will follow the same practice in this book.

Given the variety of Mennonites and Brethren in Christ who came to witness and live in Latin America, the question "Who or what is a Latin American Mennonite Christian?" is a recurring theme throughout. Are Anabaptist-descended Christians in Latin America more like Pentecostal Christians, like socially-involved Christians, like apolitical Christians who "separate from the world," or like mainline Protestant Christians? The answers to questions such as these – and to the more fundamental, underlying question of how the Good News is to be understood and lived in the various cultures that make up Latin America – continue to be worked out by the Anabaptist-descended Christians who have formed faith communities in the region. By addressing these questions, Latin American Mennonites have made, and continue to make, important contributions to the wider dialogue in which Christians of all cultures are engaged.

The first Mennonite Mission: Argentina (1911-1958)

The historical period between 1880 and 1910 in Argentina (the Conservative Regime) gave birth to the modern-day nation. In this period citizens were granted the vote and an electoral system was established in which both the winning and the losing parties shared power. The country, structured by the ideas of Juan Alberdi, managed its greatest development during these thirty years, placing itself on the vanguard of Latin American development. It had the largest railway network on the continent, enjoyed a great political and institutional stability, and it had a good educational system. Argentina's prosperity depended upon the production of cereals, oils, and meat. Argentina became the second-largest meat exporter in the world, after the United States. The government outlined its policy beginning with three aims of the state: immigration, education, and peace.[1]

Successive presidents favored the immigration of Anglo-Saxon Europeans to Argentina because they were convinced that such immigration would bring about capitalist development and "the triumph of civilization over barbarism." Although there were some Protestants present at the beginning of the nineteenth century, the large scale immigration of Protestants to Argentina took place only in the latter half of the century.[2] The immigrant population grew from 12.1 percent of the total population in 1869 to 25.5 percent of the total population in 1914. The census of 1895 indicates a total of 26,750 Protestants living in Argentina, of which eight out of every ten were foreign-born.[3] The Protestant immigrants promoted the evangelistic work of missionary societies, Bible societies, and publications. Many of the missionary societies founded schools, colleges, institutes and seminaries, some of which became renowned. Religious literature was promoted by denominational presses and publications.[4]

The Argentine state in this period was characterized by an interest in peace. At some distance now from the war that had been waged against Paraguay in the years 1865-1870, there was an expressed will not to enter into armed conflicts with neighboring states. The first Mennonite missionaries who came from the United States could see with their own eyes the political, religious and cultural situation of the various countries of Latin America, and they chose to begin their missionary work in Argentina.

> Once we became aware of the existence of the neighboring continent, where millions of Indians live in ignorance and paganism and where many millions more people of mixed race have lived for centuries in idolatrous superstition, under the name of religion, then our hearts filled with sympathy for them in their need.
> **J. W. Shank**

Foreign missions by U. S. Mennonites began only in 1899, with work in India. This awakened an interest in Latin America missions among a group of persons who were having weekly meetings in Elkhart, Indiana, in 1901. Five years later the Mennonite Board of Missions and Charities was founded in Indiana,[5] although it was not until 1911 that this mission board decided to send Josephus Wenger Shank to South America in order to investigate the possibilities of beginning missionary work.[6] His report was decisive in leading the mission board to send its first missionaries to Latin America.[7]

Josephus W. and Emma E. Shank

In spite of the eruption of World War I, the Mennonite Board of Missions and Charities decided to send two families as missionaries to the Republic of Argentina in August, 1917. Their first contacts in Argentina were with the noted leaders of the oldest evangelical work in Argentina, among whom the Methodists were prominent.[8] The Mennonite missionaries spent the first months of their stay learning Spanish and eventually focused on the area south-west of Buenos Aires in the direction of Toay, more specifically on the towns that were born and grew on the terminal spurs of the Western Railway, such as Pehuajó, Trenque Lauquen and later the city of Santa Rosa.

The first Mennonite church to be established in Argentina was in Pehuajó, along the end of the main line of the Western Rail. The T. K. Hershey family moved to Pehuajó on the twenty-first of January, 1919, and on Sunday the twenty-sixth they held the first worship service in their home. The first believers were of Italian and Spanish origin. They were converted in the first evangelistic campaigns that were carried out in 1919, prominent among whom were members of the Cavadore family. These first converts, along with the missionary family, comprised the first Mennonite church in Latin America. In 1923 work began on the construction of a church, and in August of that same year the church was dedicated to God in a service at which the well-known Baptist preacher and writer, Reverend Juan C. Varetto, preached.[9]

North American missionaries and their children in Argentina, 1930

Trenque Lauquen, which in the dialect of the Pampas Indians means "Round Lake," was a city to the west of Pehuajó, with approximately 9,000 inhabitants. Missionary work there began in September, 1920, when the Shank family moved there from Pehuajó. The first persons to be involved in the worship services were from English families who were connected with the commercial activities of the railroad. The first worship service in Spanish took place in November, 1920. In May, 1921, the first baptized members were received into the church. Albano Luayza was the first national pastor to assume leadership in a Mennonite church. He was an important resource for the work of evangelization, as was also Anita Cavadore, a young Bible reader from Pehuajó.[10]

Santa Rosa was a very Roman Catholic city. The Mennonite missionaries had great difficulties renting a house there, especially because of the threats and the opposition of the local priest. Eventually a place was rented where the first worship service was celebrated in January, 1922. In May, 1925, a special worship service was held to dedicate the church built in Santa Rosa. In spite of being a church whose members lived in constant exodus, the church held its own under the pastoral leadership of Albano Luayza from 1921 until 1939.

Anita Cavadore

Anita Cavadore was the daughter of Italian immigrants who settled in Pehuajó. Along with her sisters, she was one of the first to receive biblical instruction and to be baptized in October of 1919. Shortly after the Shank family moved to Trenque Lauquen in 1921, Anita Cavadore was appointed as an assistant in the mission that was just beginning. Anita was part of the movement of Bible readers, an interesting way of evangelizing the community, house by house, thought up by the North American missionary leadership. The women readers dedicated much of their time to evangelistic tasks, with much love and passion, even though they didn't receive the same salaries as the male pastors. Anita and Emma Elizabeth Shank visited 30 families every week. Anita dedicated nine years to evangelism and to the Sunday school in Trenque Lauquen, and many persons came to know Jesus Christ through her testimony. She demonstrated leadership not only in the local churches, but also at the level of the emerging Conference of Mennonite Churches of Argentina, whose first gathering was organized in 1924. It is not surprising that Anita was elected to the Board of Directors at the convention of 1930.[11]

The first Mennonite churches, situated in larger cities like Pehuajó, Trenque Lauquen, Santa Rosa, Carlos Casares, and finally Bragado, served as points of support for the extension of the Gospel along the length of the railway line. From 1919 until 1933, a total of 21 mission fields were begun by the Mennonites.[12] Fundamentally important in the work of evangelization were the "Bible Van,"[13] the preaching tent, and the publication of Christian literature such as *La Voz Meno-*

nita (The Mennonite Voice), *El Camino Verdadero* (The True Path), and numerous biblical tracts that were distributed to many homes in all the neighboring towns.

September 6, 1930 saw a military coup that initiated the political predominance of military men. From that moment until 1944, the Argentine economy was ordered according to a fascist ideology which organized society by the power of the state. Individualism was suppressed, with people organized into controlled corporations. In this way it was said that order was guaranteed without the property structure being changed at all.[14]

> **Sermon by the Argentine pastor Albano Luayza, 1932: The ten virgins (Matthew 25:1-13)**
>
> Among the many parables that our blessed Lord Jesus told is the one concerning the ten virgins… Five of the virgins were careless. Five were prudent. The ten took their lamps, but only five took oil. Lamps are an instrument and signify the external aspect of religion. The oil signifies the Holy Spirit in the believer, and it is what gives life, or spiritual light.
>
> Those who take religion as something external (like a lamp without fuel), like something inherited from parents, may become members of a church, may do virtuous things, reading the Bible and praying, but since such persons do not have what gives life, they will always remain persons without power.
>
> But, how different it is with the one who took oil in her jar (the jar is the heart). This is a lovely figure: the heart full of spiritual light, and this is what makes such a person shine with brilliant splendour and which "Provides light for all who are in the house"; it is light in the midst of darkness. "You are the light of the world," but, how can you be light if you do not have the seal of the Spirit of God in your heart? …
>
> Brothers and Friends! Do not imitate the careless virgins! Imitate the prudent ones; let your hearts be filled with the Holy Spirit, and then when the Lord comes, or when you go to Him, you will be able to enter to enjoy yourselves with the Spouse.

Following the ideological mark that characterized the North American missionary societies, the Mennonite leaders distanced themselves from the new political situation, but even more so from organizations, such as the Socialist Party, that were attempting to organize the workers. A declaration concerning politics, made by Snyder and Luayza, stated: "Let no pastor or worker in the Mennonite churches take part in any political movement, and at the same time let them not campaign for any particular candidate, and for religious reasons, they should not show preference to the so-called Socialist Party."[15] This attitude in the face of reformist political parties began to change as the military began to take charge of the political direction of Argentina, working along with the Catholic church. At this point the Mennonites expressed their dissatisfaction with the militarization of the country.

The Argentine Mennonite mission had never clarified to the authorities its position on conscientious objection, or its position

Albano Luayza

concerning military service. In 1934 Hershey was of the opinion that as the Mennonites began to settle into the South American countries, there would be "sufficient pressure to present to these different governments what we believe as Mennonites, concerning nonviolence, non-militarization, peace movement, and other doctrines."[16] The Mennonite voice was not long in coming in view of the new situation. In 1935, the Mennonite pastor Luayza criticized an article written by an Argentine military man in *La Prensa* with the title "The importance and the need for military maneuvers." Luayza stated that the arguments and conclusions expressed in that article were the best possible to demonstrate the futility and idiocy of wars: "War signifies the incompetence of humanity in governing itself," he wrote.[17]

The newspaper *La Prensa*, in its publication of March 19, 1937, published a photograph showing a high dignitary of the Roman Catholic church blessing a pile of swords which were to be used by young Argentine marines. In reaction to the intransigent position that the Argentine Catholic church adopted in face of the communists, as a reaction to the civil war taking place in Spain, pastor Luayza responded "There will be no crusade or campaign that will be able to bring peace to the Argentine family, or to the great human family, other than the simple message of the love that God brought to this world by means of Jesus Christ."[18]

Many Argentine citizens are immigrants of Spanish, English, or Italian origin. For this reason the Spanish Civil War did not pass unnoticed by Argentine Mennonites, as can be seen in the variety of commentaries in *La Voz Menonita*.[19] But it was noted Protestant preacher, Juan C. Varetto, an Argentine of Italian origin, who was the great proponent of solidarity with those suffering in this terrible civil war.[20] In mid-1937, Varetto initiated a campaign in which he visited many churches personally, including Mennonite churches, and collected money to be sent to Spain to relieve the pain of many widows, children and homes affected by the civil war.

The great fear of an eventual war of global dimensions is reflected clearly in the commentaries of *La Voz Menonita* from 1933 on. At least two lines of thought can be noted. On the one hand, there are commentaries like those of bishop Amos Swartzentruber and the North American pastor L. S. Weber, who saw this moment of crisis in economic, ethical and moral values as a decisive one, calling the Argentine people to conversion, but they drew away from the human drama that was affecting all of humanity. L. S. Weber was of the opinion that all efforts at global disarmament would not be able to bring about world peace, and thought that hope lay with the salvation of the soul, the sanctification of life, and service to the Lord. He thought that the war was announced as a sign preceding the second coming of Christ, and pleaded that He come to establish a millennium of peace.[21]

On the other hand, Argentine leaders like Felisa Cavadore and Albano Luayza condemned the war, taking their point of departure from significant thinkers in Argentine political life, such as Juan Bautista Alberdi, and from their Anabaptist tradition.[22] At the congress of the Argentine League of Protestant Women, which met in Buenos Aires on May 22-24, 1934, Felisa Cavadore presented a fervent message with the title "The Peacemakers." Felisa began her message by reciting the poem of J. R. Balloch, saying:

> Lord, make me a peacemaker
> I want to be your child
> Beloved Father, God
> Make me, Lord, a peacemaker,
> I wish to be a collaborator
> with Christ.

In this message Felisa Cavadore distanced herself from theological positions such as L. W. Weber's, for having heard the drums of war she thought the opportune time had come to give witness to Jesus' radical message of peace: "Many Christian consciences are still asleep with respect to the war, because they feel disconnected to everything that pertains to

Poem written by the son of an Argentine Mennonite pastor: España, qué haces? (Spain, what are you doing?)

Spain, what are you doing?
Don't you see that the men
of your rich land
have been shot?
They've lost their children,
Their beloved children?

Spain, what are you doing?
Don't you see that the mothers
are losing their children,
children worthy
of sacred love?

Spain, what are you doing?
Do you not see that the children
are left destitute
without father, without mother,
their dreams dead,
when they most needed
maternal warmth?

Spain, what are you doing?
Now your children are dying
to the shouts of war,
What blasphemy roars
inside your borders?

Spain, what are you doing?
Now your people are dying,
bleeding to death,
and Spain will not attain
the peace of yesterday...?
Spain, what are you doing?

political questions, but if Jesus promised to bless the peacemakers, it is because he wanted us to be peacemakers."[23] Argentine Mennonite women repudiated the war with no reservation whatsoever, for in solidarity they heard the groans of the mothers in the places of war: "The clamor that breaks out of thousands and thousands of mothers' hearts, who love as no one loves, ought to be heard. Warfare is the greatest crime of all."[24] Albano Luayza, referring to what was being published in the newspapers concerning the serious war that was threatening the entire world, criticized Benito Mussolini directly:

> ...can Italy wage war in the aid of Christendom?
> No! No! War is anti-Christian. Jesus said "Love your
> enemies," "Do good to those who hate you"... Pray
> God that the group of faithful Christians grow, who
> are capable of dying for the ideal of peace, rather than
> carrying homicidal arms for the destruction of their
> fellows human beings![25]

The Argentine Mennonite churches continued forward with their evangelistic plans throughout the 1930s, opening a Bible school in Bragado to train pastors and church leaders, beginning new mission fields located near the railway lines, but also expanding toward the province of Córdoba, and moving back from the outlying urban areas

Students in the library of the Bragado Bible Institute, 1954.
The Bragado school, which began in 1935, merged with the
Mennonite Biblical Seminary at Montevideo, Uruguay in 1958.

towards the capital Buenos Aires. In 1934 there were 22 congregations with 479 members, 16 missionaries, 3 ordained Argentine pastors, and 3 congregational helpers. After another decade of missionary work 17 new churches and mission fields were added to this list. The majority of these new mission fields were quite small. The leaders were conscious of their enormous economic dependency and reliance on North American missionary personnel They put a twenty-year plan into place with the aim of creating the foundations for an autonomous Argentine Mennonite church with its own administrative personnel, theology, and economic support. [26]

The economic crisis of 1929 had great consequences for Argentine political life. By 1938 it was noted that many members of the rural churches had moved towards the capital for economic reasons. Bishops Swartzentruber and Hershey were charged with making a list of members who now found themselves in Buenos Aires, with the end of visiting them, gathering them together, and if possible, opening a work in that city.[27] Mennonite work began in four locations in the capital as a result of this initiative of caring for rural Mennonite families who had relocated to Buenos Aires. Theological reflection continued, in face of the reality of life in the southern cone. Towards the end of this period, some nationalist tendencies were felt that would culminate in a dissident group led by the young Mennonite pastor, Santiago Battaglia.

Santiago Battaglia, together with Pablo Cavadore, became one of the first two graduates of the Mennonite Biblical College in Pehuajó in 1930.[28] In 1933, Santiago Battaglia was ordained to the ministry and participated in his first ministers' meeting that same month. He soon took on the task of pastoral ministry in Trenque Lauquen.[29] As a good disciple of Hershey and Litwiller, Santiago spoke with great certainty in pastors' meetings in favor of baptism by aspersion.[30] In 1934, in the absence of bishop Hershey, who was on furlough

Tobias K. and Mae E. Hershey

in the United States,[31] Santiago took on the entire charge of pastoral care in Trenque Lauquen and from 1937 to 1938, he functioned as General Secretary of the Conference of Mennonite churches.[32]

When the Hershey family returned in 1937, disagreements began over the pastorate in Trenque Lauquen. The executive council of the

Conference decided to assign Battaglia to another city and assigned bishop Hershey to continue in Trenque Lauquen. Santiago was of the opinion that all were equal in the church, without distinction whatever,[33] and was not disposed to concede. As a result, Santiago Battaglia, accompanied by a good number of the members of the church, separated and formed a new congregation, which they called the "United Brethren Church."

Santiago Battaglia

Bishop Hershey opposed the new group in a variety of ways, which led Santiago to decide to join the Baptist church.[34] In spite of bishop Hershey's efforts to block this, Santiago, his wife Amalia, and twenty persons more were rebaptized by immersion in order to become a new Baptist church. Of this group, only one person was newly converted; the rest all came from the Mennonite church of Trenque Lauquen. Without a doubt this was a hard blow for Hershey, for one of his principal followers had broken with a pastoral doctrine and practice that he had introduced to the Mennonite church in Argentina: baptism by aspersion. In spite of requests to the Baptist convention that Santiago Battaglia should pastor in another city,[35] Battaglia continued as a Baptist pastor in Trenque Lauquen. In 1944, during the Mennonite annual convention celebrated in Trenque Lauquen, Santiago Battaglia sent a greeting to this event with the following words: "The Evangelical Baptist church of Trenque Lauquen greets the Mennonite convention and prays for you, blessings from on high."[36]

The case of Amalia and Santiago Battaglia signals a nationalist expression that would be seen even more clearly in the next historical period, when Argentine pastors became the majority that assumed the leadership of the church, and reshaped the structure of the Conference of Mennonite churches of Argentina.[37] The movement towards the nationalization of mission churches would be repeated throughout Latin America in the coming decades, and is a process that continues to the present.

Juan Domingo Perón won the presidential elections in February, 1946 in spite of the opposition of the United States which had identified his party as a Nazi movement.[38] The government of Perón defended the interests of the wealthy agro-industrial and financial class, while at the same time it tolerated and even stimulated the participation of the working masses in the social and political life of the country. Peronism promoted a national doctrine of justice which assumed a simultaneous hostility to western capital and to Soviet communism.[39] The Peronist era came to an end with the military coup of September, 1955, which removed him from power. The coup was related to the enormous opposition to Perón by the Catholic church, after he had humiliated and outraged the Catholic hierarchy in an all-out struggle for political power. Once a full-scale military repression against Peronism was concluded, elections were held in February of 1958. The president-elect was Arturo Frondizi of the *Unión Cívica Radial Intransigente* (Radical Intransigent Civic Union).

During the first Peronist period, there was government support for Catholic education in the schools.[40] This situation changed in the later years of the Peronist government, when the Minister of Education removed the task of teaching "morality" in the public schools from the Catholic church. In 1952, numerous evangelistic campaigns took place that culminated with the presence of the revivalist preacher Thomas Hicks in 1954.[41] With the president's permission, the preacher held public rallies at stadiums where up to 28,000 spectators could be accommodated. The press featured headlines such as "The miracles performed by Pastor Hicks are due to his faith in God."[42] These campaigns were completely successful in stirring up the urban masses of Argentina in such a way that in 1955 alone, a total of five new Assembly of God churches were established. In this political context, Pentecostalism gave renewed vitality to Protestantism, not only in the great cities like Buenos Aires, but also among the indigenous Toba churches of the Argentine Chaco.

The migrations of entire families from the country to the great city of Buenos Aires had notable effects on Mennonite missions in the 1950s. In concrete terms, the economic crisis meant the end of the missionary work that the Mennonite congregations had initiated in the following places: Maza (1941), Moctezuma (1950), Smith (1951), Francisco Madero (1952), Guanaco (1951), Treinta de Agosto (1953), Comodoro Py (1958) and Carmen de Areco (1959). On the other hand, new congregations were founded in La Floresta (1940), Fortín Olavaria (1942), El Monte (1951), Ituzaingó (1953), Morón (1954) and La Plata (1958).

The active participation of women in the Mennonite church of the previous decades had an impact on the Argentine Evangelical Mennonite Church (IEMA). In 1945 the annual assembly organized the national "Evangelical Chain of Mennonite Women."[43] The "Women's section" of *La Voz Menonita* (*Sección Femenil*) became an important vehicle of communication.[44]

**Reflection by Alicia Battaglia,
"Remember your Creator."**

The government of the old folks appears to be condemned to failure. The world is looking to the youth, because they are possessed of enthusiasm, strength, resolve and manhood. They are the promise of a new order of things. But it is essential that there be faith among the youth so that this new order of things can triumph, for without faith, the days of youth are dead and useless. (...) We are a forgetful race. We forget what is most important for the success of our lives, be they spiritual or material, and we give importance to the passing and ephemeral things of every day, which is to say, we forget what is most sacred. (...) "Remember your Creator in the days of your youth." (...) If we forget our Creator there is nothing good left for us, but rather on the contrary, we do harm to our neighbors and all those who surround us. ... Remembering our Creator is educational, formational, the beginning of something. It is during the days of one's youth that a life is constructed which later becomes permanent. It is during this time that ideas, habits, customs become fixed and during which the heart is shaped. We have need of a good mold during this process, and this mold is remembering our Creator.

In 1947 the bishops of Evangelical Mennonite church in Argentina were still North American missionaries.[45] Nevertheless, a growing Argentine nationalism that was being felt at all levels of society. In January, 1954 a meeting of pastors and workers in the Mennonite church was held in Trenque Lauquen to review, modify and approve new statutes for the organization. The figure of "bishop" disappeared altogether and reappeared as "regional director," namely a person with the pastoral charge of caring for and coordinating the work of the pastors in a given region. In 1955 the Argentine Evangelical Mennonite Church was organized under the new statutes with an elected board of directors; Agustín F. Darino was elected president and Albano Luayza, Vice President.[46]

The new arrangement meant that the board now had to deal with all administrative, representative and pastoral matters, which affected the ability of pastors to work in their own congregations.[47] By the end of the 1950s a generational change was visible, with first-generation leaders needing to retire.[48] This raised the question of pensions and how these older leaders could continue to feel useful within the organization to which they had devoted their lives. On the other hand, it also represented the emergence of a new generation of leaders such as Agustín Darino, J. Delbert Erb, Ernesto Suárez Vilela and among the youth, the leadership of Raúl O. García, Roné Assef and Alicia Battaglia.

The province of the Chaco was considered by the Spaniards to be a place of great misery, but the native groups fleeing the Spanish invasion during the sixteenth century saw the Chaco as a refuge. In the indigenous creation stories, which describe the beginnings of human beings, the principal personalities are women who, descending from the heavens by a cord, meet the men of the earth in order to create children.[49]

During the seventeenth century the Toba, Mocoví and Abipón peoples resisted the continual colonization campaigns of the Spaniards. It was not until 1673 that one group of the Mocoví tribe, tired of the struggle, made peace with the Spanish authorities and accepted the coming of the Catholic mission

Toba poem

When the cicadas announced the ripening of the carob, then the time of happiness began, the time to celebrate life, fertility and abundance.

of the Jesuits in San Javier, near the city of Esteco. Two centuries later, given the interest generated by the anthropological studies of the indigenous peoples of the Chaco by the Scotsman Wilfrid Barbrooke Grubb (1865-1930), Protestant missions among the Tobas of Argentina began by means of the South American Missionary Society and the Anglican Mission.[50]

In January, 1943, the mission board of the Mennonite Church of Argentina decided to send mission workers to the Chaco. Bishop J. W. Shank indicated the urgency of announcing the Gospel to the indigenous peoples in terms of gathering together sheep scattered in ignorance and superstition. He saw the indigenous as peoples who had suffered since the Spanish conquest and who continued their pagan practices and old superstitions while under the control of the Catholic hierarchy.

The first Mennonite missionaries to the Argentine Chaco were bishop J. W. Shank and his wife Selena Gamber, as well as Calvin Holderman and his wife Frances Leake.[51] Shank's trip revealed the great spiritual and material needs of the indigenous peoples, and the words of Isaiah 55:5 became theirs: "See, you shall call nations that you do not know, and nations that do not know you shall run to you, because of the Lord your God." The report submitted to the committee of their Conference on April 26, 1943 led to the decision to begin missionary work in the Chaco.

During this exploratory trip the Mennonite missionaries reached Resistencia, the principal city of the Argentine Chaco, and visited the mission of Misión Id (Go Ye Mission), which at the time was in the hands of the North American missionaries Juan and Carlota Lagar. These evangelical missionaries first came to preach in Resistencia before 1941. Many indigenous people travelled by foot to hear him, and were converted to the Gospel. Juan Lagar and his wife Carlota did not intend to stay, but they did when upon preaching and healing the sick in the name of Jesus Christ, indigenous families began to seek them out.[52] This spiritual revival among the Tobas began at just the same time that they were going through the crisis resulting from the military conquest of the Chaco. Many Tobas had died from a variety of diseases such as measles, and they suffered enormously at the hands of the white people.[53]

The experience of the Holy Spirit meshed well with the traditional religion of the Tobas. They already had a religious conception of the possession of the Spirit, but now that conception was democratized and not only the shaman, but also every one of them could have the Spirit and the symbol of fire. This call began in the Argentine Chaco but it extended into the Paraguayan Chaco, as will be noted in a later chapter. Bishop Shank would witness one of these great spiritual celebrations in Resistencia in 1944 when, by invitation of the Lagars, he was present for the movement of many indigenous peoples who came to participate in the evening services. One of the characteristic

A Toba worship service, Legua 17 (1955)

rituals was to sing while they were marching to be baptized. In one of those services there was a mass baptism of 268 persons.[54]

In September 1943 the Mennonite missionaries already noted were visited by Amos Swartzentruber and T. K. Hershey, and together it was decided to buy forty acres of land for the price of $1,200.00 U.S. dollars. So it was that by the end of 1943 the Mennonite mission concretized their work in Chaco Province, settling the families Shank and Holderman on this compound located to the north of the town of Sáenz Peña, and named Nan Cum, which in the local language means "with the Indians." Calvin Holderman, Selena Shank and Una Cressman collaborated with health care. The first Mennonite worship service among the Tobas took place in November, 1944 in a place called Legua 17, located about 18 miles away from Nan Cum, in an indigenous community which demonstrated great emotionalism and religious fervor. The first baptism of eight persons took place in April of 1945.[55]

When the missionaries Juan and Carlota returned to the United States in 1946, a new leader emerged among the Tobas, the cacique Pedro Martínez, a shaman with healing powers who was disposed to defend his Toba people from the white colonists.[56] He also was a pastor in the Pentecostal Church of God. In the midst of the struggles of indigenous workers laid off in a wage dispute from the sugar mill at San Martín de El Tabacal, other indigenous leaders who also stood up for the workers were Luciano Sánchez and Aurelio López.[57] In 1947, a large number of indigenous people had gathered near Las Lomitas, in Formosa Province, to search for a solution to their problems of having been forced off the land. The local military squadron responded by carrying out a massacre, with support of the local priest and government officials.

In the face of continuing persecution following the massacre, a delegation of indigenous people, in which were found the Cacique Coquero and Aurelio López, travelled to Buenos Aires to speak with Evita and Juan Perón. Although Perón did not come to visit the place of the conflicts, as the Tobas desired,

Bishop Shank reflects on the death of a Toba infant

1. Where is that infant,
   that small child
   of the Toba race,
   whose father is Naño,
   his mother Florita?
2. Over there in the Chaco
   in my house
   I saw that small child
   with his dark eyes
   and happy smile.
   Where is he?
3. He is there in the jungle
   behind the shrubs
   under the trees
   he is resting alone
   his small body.
4. In heaven is heard
   among thousands of angels,
   his gentle voice
   and sweet, which sings
   his glory to God.
   He is with God.

he did send several wagon loads of food and clothing for them. In places like Pozo de los Chanchos, Toba families were provided with a school and land to cultivate. These were some of the reasons why many of the Tobas who were from other churches became involved in the Pentecostal Church of God.[58]

Toba mother and child

For Bishop Shank, beginning a new work among the Tobas was a tremendous challenge which he expressed in his missionary trips, the reading of literature about the indigenous and sharing his writings with the fellowship by publications in *La Voz Menonita*. Bishop Shank could witness the poverty of the Tobas, as well as their pains and struggles.

Beginning in 1949 bishop Nelson Litwiller informed the leaders of IEMA that the Mennonite Board of Missions and Charities had decided that, from a legal point of view, the Mennonite work in the Chaco would be independent of the Mennonite Churches of Argentina. Although there was some bad feeling among the Mennonite leaders of IEMA over this decision taken in the north, without a doubt the intervention of bishop Shank, who invited the Luayza couple to visit the work in the Chaco, facilitated understanding on both sides. In 1950 the Dürksen and Miller families arrived from the Mennonite colony in Paraguay to collaborate for a time on the Nan Cum compound. Later, in 1951, Albert and Lois (Litwiller) Buckwalter arrived. They took up pastoral duties, while Mabel Cressman looked after health matters.[59]

In 1954 the Mennonite missionaries recognized the importance of communicating the Gospel in the language of the indigenous people, and they also noted the limitations of the paternalistic missionary work they were carrying out among the Toba in agriculture, education and health. As a result of this realization the Mennonite Board of Missions sent William and Mary Reyburn to begin a linguistic analysis of the Toba language and to help missionaries understand the cross cultural dimensions of their work. In 1955, in response to the Reyburns' investigations, the Mennonite Mission turned over to resident Toba families the land at Pampa Aguará which previously had been purchased. They also decided to begin the work of translating the Bible into the Toba language and to take on the pastoral task of visiting the churches to share the word of God.

In its beginnings the pentecostal-style revival had been criticized by the traditional churches and by the missionaries because they said it contained syncretistic elements of Toba culture. But the indigenous renewal movement helped the Toba see the need to assume their own leadership in the churches, in a manner consonant with their culture. In 1955 pastor Aurelio López took on an important role in the process of creating a church by his own initiative. He said: "I received a revelation. We wish to make our own aboriginal church. Let us stop following after the white people. When we establish this church I want to take the hand of an aboriginal to be pastor, to organize the church."[60]

The Mennonite church was able to capture the struggles and the spirit of unity of the Toba people. According to Guillermo Flores, a follower of the preacher Juan Lagar, Albert Buckwalter and his wife Lois were the pastoral advisors when the initiative was decided upon by the Toba to organize themselves as United Churches. These Toba churches, stemming from diverse ecclesial backgrounds, organized themselves into a group that gave priority to their cultural identity, rather than denominational doctrine. One of the virtues of the Buckwalters was their painstaking work of accompanying the Toba throughout their struggle for their right to be in charge of their own church, even in the midst of the dangers posed by the government police who wished to intimidate the indigenous peoples.

Nelson Litwiller took on the task of obtaining proper authorization for the Toba churches. In November, 1958 an indigenous Toba church was created under the name United Evangelical Church (*Iglesia Evangélica Unida*).[61] In June, 1960 the appropriate authorities granted the proof of inscription, registered under number 819, to the United Evangelical Church, with headquarters in Legua 17. A board of directors was named to compose the statutes of the church, and in September, 1961 Nelson Litwiller received the inscription documents that listed a total of 28 affiliated churches, 24 in the Chaco and 4 in Formosa. From this date forward, the Mennonites have accompanied the United Evangelical Church and other indigenous evangelical churches as fraternal workers, collaborating in preaching the Word, facilitating translation of the Bible into native languages and preparing an indigenous church newsletter, which is known as *Qad`aqtaxanaxanec* (Our Messenger).[62]

The pastoral and accompaniment mode of the Mennonite missionaries among the Toba represented a significantly new missionary model. In a context in which the Chaco peoples were repressed, and whose lands had been invaded by European immigrants, the Mennonite missionaries faithfully accompanied them throughout the entire process that made possible an autonomous and independent church, based in the distinctive cultures of the Toba, Pilagá, Mocoví and Wichí peoples, which is today the United Evangelical Church.

A third Mennonite group that established itself in Argentina is the Mennonite Evangelical Alliance (*Alianza Evangélica Menonita*), made up of people with diverse experiences emigrating from the Soviet Union. During the 1940s, Mennonites from the Paraguayan colony of Fernheim moved to Buenos Aires in search of work, and

Albert Buckwalter and Roberto Ruiz, at work translating the New Testament into the Mocoví language

remained as residents in that city.[63] Later, in February 1947, a group of 2,305 Mennonite refugees who had fled Russia arrived in Puerto Nuevo, Buenos Aires.[64] The final destination of this and later groups of immigrants was to be Paraguay, and the majority of these people came to live in the Paraguayan colonies of Volendam and Neuland. But, because of the revolution that was taking place in Paraguay in 1947, 150 Mennonites in the first contingent of immigrants were not able to enter the country, and had to remain in Buenos Aires. Six of the families located in a place called Ezpeleta, and the rest settled in other parts of the city. These families eventually decided to continue living in Argentina. MCC, the Mennonite churches, and the Conference of Evangelical Churches of Argentina were very supportive of these refugees in a variety of ways.[65]

At the recommendation of E. C. Bender, Nelson Litwiller established a religious and social center in Buenos Aires, which he led until the end of 1949.[66] During the period from 1945 to 1947, the young Paraguayan Mennonites Martin Dürksen and his wife studied at the Biblical Institute of Argentina and collaborated in provided leadership in the refugee camps. After visiting their country, they returned to Buenos Aires in 1950 to take charge of the religious center there. Baptism was practiced after a person had made a profession of faith, and took place either by immersion or by aspersion, following the same spiritual lines as those practiced in the Paraguayan colonies like Fernheim.

From 1947 to 1954 there was a continual exodus of Mennonites from the Paraguayan colonies of Fernheim, Friesland, Volendam and Neuland to Buenos Aires. Some families settled in Florida, others in Villa de Mayo. This resulted in the organization of a Mennonite church in Villa Ballester, where Martin Dürksen functioned as pastor during the first half of the 1950s. For the year 1954 it was calculated that approximately 500 Mennonites of Russian-immigrant origin lived in Argentina.[67] Since this church emerged thanks to the collaboration between various Paraguayan churches and the North American mission boards, it was decided to call it the *Alianza Evangélica Menonita de la Argentina* (Mennonite Evangelical Alliance of Argentina). Pastor Martin Dürksen had very good relations with the Mennonite Conference (IEMA) and was present at the annual assembly which was celebrated in February, 1957 participating with a message on the topic "The stewardship of time."[68] In 1962, once the church was established and had its own building, MCC concluded its work. This German-speaking congregation has worked together with the Evangelical Mennonite Brethren Conference and the *Konferenz der Evangelischen Mennonitischen Brüderschaft von Südamerika.*[69] The congregation has been continually enlivened by European and North American immigrants in the face of the economic and political upheavals of Argentina.

Pastor Martin Dürksen invited the missionary Mario Snyder to begin a work for Spanish-speaking persons in the neighborhood where the German-speaking church was located. Mario Snyder gathered together 40 persons, including children. From this initial effort would later emerge a Spanish-speaking Mennonite congregation which located in Delviso, on the outskirts of Buenos Aires.[70]

The first decades of Mennonite presence in Argentina witnessed significant changes for the church that was initially planted there by North American missionaries in 1919. By the end of the 1950s the displacement of people from the countryside to Buenos Aires had resulted in a strategic shift, with the closing of many of the smaller churches that had been planted further afield in the earlier decades, and the opening of mission efforts in the capital city itself. By the end of the 1950s, the beginnings of what would become a significant mission work were just visible in the area north of Buenos Aires.

A significant nationalization of the church also took place in this period, with Conference leadership passing definitively from the North American missionaries to Argentine pastors and leaders by the mid-1950s. Mission efforts were significantly extended by the work among the indigenous Toba to the north, resulting in a unique missionary model that accompanied the Tobas as they established their own indigenous churches.

Old Colony Mennonites Settle in Mexico: (1922-1958)

The Aztec and Inca cultures were the most advanced on the continent when the European conquest began. The Aztecs were made up of different Nahuatl tribes who occupied the valley of Mexico. Their advanced culture was based on the systematic cultivation of corn and was polytheistic, based in the worship of nature. Divine beings were represented by drawings and sculptures, temples with platforms were built to honor their gods, they had a system for keeping track of religious events, and a calendar and astronomy that served their ritual purposes.[1]

In 1519 Hernán Cortés left Cuba and came ashore in the port of Veracruz. In the end, Cortés and his soldiers conquered the Aztec empire, created the Viceroyalty of New Spain, and imposed Roman Catholicism on the inhabitants of Mexico. With few exceptions, the church during the colonial period (up to 1808) functioned as an ideological engine of the state, legitimating the coercive action of domination by the state of indigenous peoples, creoles and slaves.[2]

A second foundational period in Mexico's history began with independence from Spain (1810 to 1821). Following independence, the internal wars between Liberals and Conservatives during the period of the Republic (1824-1858) provided the occasion for the United States to annex the state of Texas in 1845. The war between these nations (1846 to 1848) resulted in the loss of almost half of Mexico's territory to the United States. In 1857, under the leadership of Benito Juárez, the foundations were laid for a reform in Mexico that eventually came to fruition in a new constitution that established a separation of church and state, thus breaking the colonial Roman Catholic monopoly.[3] After Juárez's death, General Porfirio Días governed Mexico with an iron hand from 1876 to 1910. During his rule came the investment of foreign capital, the development of the petroleum industry, the construction of railroads, and the establishment of public education. It appeared that Mexico had entered a new era of prosperity. Nevertheless, this prosperity also meant hardship for more than three million indigenous people and the reality that one percent of the population would hold eighty-five percent of the land.

The arrival of the Mennonites in Mexico was helped by the expansion of Protestant societies. Between 1872 and 1916 Protestant religious associations collaborated with the Liberals in the struggle to break away, symbolically and politically, from the colonial corporate and patrimonial society ruled by the Conservatives and the Catholic church.[4] A central historical event for Protestant missions, and which preceded the arrival of the Mennonites in Mexico, was the reform of the old constitution in 1917, which broke the monopoly of the Catholic church and introduced de-clericalization and freedom of education in private schools.

The Baptist Scottish minister Diego Thompson is the first known distributor of Bibles in Mexico when he was sent to travel around the country by the British and Foreign Bible Society in 1827.[5] The first Protestant missionary initiatives in Mexico date from 1852, when Melinda Rankin, a Presbyterian woman from the United States, felt a calling from God to take the message to the Mexican people and undertook the adventure of travelling to the U.S.-Mexican border at Brownsville.[6] The Presbyterians not only founded churches, but also established schools and colleges which offered educational alternatives to more than 20,000 students.[7] Other Protestant churches that became active in Mexico in the first decades of the twentieth century were the Methodists and the Pentecostal "Apostolic Church of Faith in Christ Jesus." The Apostolic Church was a mission movement of Mexican immigrants in Los Angeles who were part of the Asuza revival; they were part of the early forming of the Apostolic Assembly before they returned to Mexico.[8] The Assemblies of God in the United States also took an interest in mission work in Mexico. In short, the spread of different types of Protestantism in the early and mid-nineteenth century grew thanks to the shelter and protection of liberal policies and of General Porfirio Díaz.[9]

General Rafael Obregón took up his post as president of Mexico in 1920.[10] In the climate of political and religious openness toward Protestantism, a commission of Old Colony Mennonite representatives wrote to general Obregón, requesting permission for Mennonite colonies from Canada to be founded in Mexico. On the 25th of Februrary, 1921, president Obregón answered their letter, extending his welcome to Mexico and granting them the basic rights they had requested.

So it was that the exodus of Old Colony Mennonites from Manitoba and Saskatchewan, Canada began on the first of March, 1922. The photographs from this era show a great caravan of wooden wagons in a row, with steel wheels, pulled by one or two horses. The first place where the Mennonites established themselves was 70 kilometers west of the city of Chihuahua, the capital of the state, and 10 kilometers south of the city of Cuauhtémoc,[11] in the place known as San Antonio de los Arenales. The great migration of Mennonites to Mexico, numbering approximately 6,000 persons, took place from 1922 until 1926.

> **Rights conceded to the Mennonite colonists by president Obregón.**
>
> • The Mennonites would be exempt from military service
> • Under no conditions would they be required to swear oaths
> • They would be able to practice their religion freely
> • They had the right to establish their own schools with their own teachers, without any form of government interference.

The Old Colony Mennonites who settled in Mexico descended from Dutch people who first emigrated to Prussia and then to Russia. The "Old Colony" designation points back to the time when Mennonites settled in Chortitza and in Fürstenländer, in the southern part of Russia in 1789.[12] In 1803, when a new settlement of Mennonites came to the banks of the river Molotschna, the new colony came to be known by that same name.[13] Later, between the years 1874 and 1880, another migration took place of approximately 7,000 Mennonites from the Russian colonies of Chortitza, Bergthal and the group known as the *Kleine Gemeinde* to Manitoba, Canada. These came to be called the "Old Colony Mennonites" (*Altkolonier-Mennoniten*). The reason for the migration to Canada was that in 1870-1871 the Russian government proposed substantial changes to the laws concerning immigrants, including the introduction of obligatory military service, to begin in 1881. At the same time the Russian language and Russian school programs were legislated to be introduced into Mennonite schools. The emigrating groups felt these changes compromised their religious principles.

Shortly after migrating to Canada the Old Colony Mennonites experienced a similar situation, when the Canadian government adopted a policy of attempting to nationalize all ethnic groups, with the exception of the French. The Old Colony Mennonites felt that this policy seriously threatened their privileges, especially regarding education, for the Canadian government set out to exert more influence in the schools, introducing education in the English language. The more conservative members of the Mennonite settlements, seeing that their German cultural identity was under threat, decided to emigrate to yet another country where they could maintain their colonies without their culture being threatened. In these years, South America was seen as a place with a great tradition of immigration. The commission of the Old Colony Mennonite church of Reinland, which was charged with finding a new country for settlement, considered Argentina, Brazil, and Uruguay. However, a contact established with the Mexican Consul in Buenos Aires put them in touch with the Mexican authorities.[14] The 200,000 hectares purchased in San Antonio de los Arenales[15] became the epicenter of Mennonite migration to Mexico, above all for immigrants from the Old Colony group.

Not all the immigrant Mennonite groups who ended up settling in Mexico came from Canada and the Old Colony. There is the case of one group of Mennonite immigrants from Russia in 1924, made up of 40 families who, since they did not enjoy the privileges granted to the Old Colony, united with another small group known as the Sommerfelders. They finally joined the larger Old Colony group in

Old Colony Mennonites arrive in Mexico, summer, 1923

order to take advantage of the guarantees granted by the Mexican government to the latter group. Other Mennonite families from Kansas located in Santa Clara and also began to mix in with the Old Colony Mennonites. The Mennonites known as the Holdeman also settled in the region, and attempted to carry out missionary work among the Mennonite settlers.

Klaas P. Heide was a teacher, preacher, farmer, and leader among the first colonists. He was born in Russia in 1859 and was a member of the Old Colony group that migrated to Canada in 1874. In his second experience of migration, from Canada to Mexico in 1922, he represented Mennonite interests to government authorities and landowners with gentlemanliness, calmness, and intelligence, mediating conflicts on all sides.[16] Klaas Heide died in October, 1926. In the last moments of his life he is reported to have said "I am not so worried about the needs of my family. They have what they need. What worries me are my people." Later he added, "But, why should I be worried? The almighty is among us. He will not permit our feet to slip; he who protects us does not sleep."[17] In this way Klaas Heide placed his confidence in God the almighty, who had led them to a new land.

Klaas Heide

Old Colony Mennonites sought to maintain the cultural and faith legacy of their forebearers, not only through the education of their children and youth, but also in the natural landscaping of the lawns, gardens and orchards that surrounded their houses, and in the voluntary distancing of their settlements from larger population centers. The construction and maintenance of their own schools allowed them to maintain their own culture, in spite of the passage of time. The teaching material used in the Mennonite schools in Mexico consisted of just one booklet of forty pages, with one section called the ABC to teach writing and reading; it concluded with readings of the Lord's Prayer, the confession of faith, and the Ten Commandments. The boys and girls carried a small blackboard on which to write and do sums with chalk. Other subjects such as geography, history, social studies, or biology were not dealt with.

The schools were simple buildings in which there was a blackboard for the teacher, and a calendar. Usually the girls sat on one side and the boys on the other, on simple wooden benches, with the older children at the front, the younger at the back. After a short teaching year, from November to March, and later for one month in May, the children were employed in agricultural or domestic activities. The teacher was contracted by the community, and carried out the teaching function alongside his real work as a farmer. Only men were allowed to function as teachers in these schools. The German language used in the schools was not entirely free from the *Plattdeutsch* dialect spoken normally at home.

Learning the A B Cs in a colony school

The small town of Blumenort, founded in Mexico, was similar to the towns in which the Mennonites had lived in Russia. The streets leading to the houses were wide, lined with large shade trees. Near the houses were stables for the livestock, the cows, pigs, geese and chickens. As far away as the horizon stretched enormous fields planted with oats, beans, corn and barley. In the first decades of their stay in Mexico the Mennonites remained tied to their oldest custom of opposition to modern technological advancements. The Mennonite colonies became well-known in Mexico, especially in the state of Durango, for their production of cheeses, butter, eggs, and pork.[18]

The Mennonite families of the countryside were humble and prepared to offer hospitality to strangers. Old Colony Mennonite settlers in Mexico were noted for their simplicity of dress: black or dark blue overalls and straw hats for the men, black or dark blue dresses and a dark veil for the women. The buildings used by the Mennonite community for worship were also plain, with wooden benches and without any adornment whatsoever.

In spite of the close cultural and religious relationship among the colonists, there were differences among the settlers who came to Mexico. Some of the Old Colony Menno- nites were known as Reinländer, and did not accept the Russländer in their congre- gations. For this reason, the latter formed their own congregation in 1938 which was known as the Hoffnungsau Gemeinde. The leader of these families was the immigrant elder Jacob Janzen and the pastor H. P. Krehbiel, who came from Kansas. In 1939 this congregation was recognized as part of the Western District Conference of the General Conference Mennonite Church of the United States. For several decades the pastors of this small congregation were German-speakers who came from the United States and Canada. The Home Mission Board provided teachers for their schools in Cuauhtémoc and Santa Clara.[19]

Words of Farewell of a Father for his Son

Hold your head high,
in face of what threatens you
And never become a slave
Freely share your bread with the poor
And guard their rights.

Do not despise the holy things
And respect the faith of foreigners
And do not permit your Lord and God
To be stolen away by any doubter.

And now one last squeeze of the hand
And one last plea:
Remain true in the foreign land
To the customs of your people!

In 1943 a new migration took place of six Amish Mennonite and Old Mennonite families; they settled in the state of San Luís Potosí, but after three years of enormous economic difficulties, they decided to return in 1946 to Tennessee and Alabama in the U.S.A. In March, 1944, some 20 families of the Old Colony Mennonites from the Manitoba colony in Chihuahua decided to establish a new colony in Agua Nueva, near Saltillo in the state of Coahuila. After the death of their leaders and their pastor Franz Loewen, however, these families decided to return to Chihuahua.[20]

World War II had very little impact on Protestantism in Mexico, but there was a tremendous sending of North American missionaries to other countries after the war. The great majority of new denomina- tions belonged to the conservative fundamentalist stream, with little interest in social questions. After the Second World War, Protestants were granted protection and given greater opportunities to open new churches by the Mexican governments. Mennonite Mission Boards in the United States also expanded their work following World War II, extending missions to the numerous Mexican and Latino immigrants within the U.S.. This story will be told in another volume in this series, but it must be noted that mission efforts to Hispanic migrants also eventually spilled over into Mexico as well.

In 1970 many Mennonite leaders and pastors met for the first time in the conference room of Eastern Mennonite Board and formed the Council of Hispanic Mennonite Churches.[21] The southern district conference of the Mennonite Brethren also developed its work on the border with Mexico.[22] The growth of Spanish-speaking Mennonite churches on the border of the United States with Mexico resulted in the formation of the Latin American Conference of Mennonite Brethren, and its interest in expanding its mission work on the other side of the Rio Bravo.

The Mennonite mission boards made efforts to link their mission work to the Mennonite colonies already settled in Mexican territory, but with limited success. Different ethnic backgrounds, cultures, missiologies and histories played an important role in the misunderstanding between the colonists and the North American missionaries. The mission boards began to see with more clarity that mission work in Mexico should take place among the Mexican population itself.

The Evangelical Mennonite Conference (EMC) of Canada (*Kleine Gemeinde*)[23] sent Cornie and Tina Loewen as its first missionaries to Mexico in 1954, and they established a relationship with Kleine Gemeinde families already settled there.[24] Nevertheless, only one small group of families in Tepehuanes, Chihuahua, who had been expelled from the colony, decided to continue their links to the Evangelical Mennonite Conference of Canada. In 1956 a family of missionaries from that conference moved to Picacho where they established a clinic and collaborated with primary education. From 1959 to 1961 a small church was established in a place known as La Norteña, and missionary work began in Los Ejidos. The Evangelical Mennonite Conference would continue its missionary work in the next years among the German-speaking colonists, later extending its efforts to the Mexican people.

A great drought in the late 1940s and early 1950s and resulting hunger among the Old Colony and Sommerfelder Mennonites in Chihuahua led them to request help from MCC for health and agriculture programs, a request that was met by the Mennonite General Conference together with MCC.[25]

In 1950 the Mission Board of the Franconia Mennonite Conference sent a delegation to Mexico to explore the possibilities of opening a new mission field. After visiting the Old Colony Mennonites in Chihuahua they saw the impossibility of initiating missionary work in Mexico. They recommended establishing a farming colony with the aim of evangelizing neighboring communities. In 1958 the Mission Board decided to send Kenneth and Grace Seitz to Mexico City to work there.[26] The first worship services conducted by the Seitz's took place in Mexico City in the home of Eduardo López and Rhoda Stoltzfus in the neighborhood of San Juan Pantitlan. In this way, in a setting far from the Old Colony Mennonites, a missionary presence began in Mexico City.

Old Colony children drawing water from a well in Mexico.

The Church of God in Christ (Holdeman) also began a small mission in Mexico in the 1950s. This church began in 1948 with several families named Koehn who came from the colonies in Cuauhtémoc. They had come originally from Oklahoma together with their pastor, Henry B. Koehman. After living for a time in Cuauhtémoc, this family began a mission work in Saltillo. In 1958 the mission congregation numbered 24 members and carried on using the Spanish language instead of English.[27]

By the end of the 1950s, the Mennonite colonies of Mexico had located themselves economically in their local communities, but they remained predominantly inward-looking and isolated from their Mexican neighbors socially and religiously, in contrast to what would take place with some of the Mennonite colonies of Paraguay. Mission work among Spanish-speaking Mexican people, just beginning in this period, did not originate with the colonists but was rather the result of evangelistic impulses from Mennonite mission boards from the north.

CHAPTER III

A Mennonite Refuge in Paraguay: (1926-1958)

The coming of Mennonites to Paraguay from Canada, Russia, China and Poland followed the War of the Triple Alliance (1865-1870), which pitted Argentina, Brazil and Uruguay against Paraguay, and resulted in a disastrous defeat for Paraguay. Not only did the country lose territory, but its population was decimated, dropping from the half a million inhabitants it had had in 1865, to 221,000 inhabitants in 1870. In the face of the changed political situation, the country opened up to immigrants and foreign capital, an openness that eventually resulted in the emigration of Mennonite settlers to Paraguay.[1]

Already in 1919 an agent carried out an expedition to the Paraguayan Chaco in search of land for the Mennonites. In 1921 a delegation of Mennonites from Canada arrived to personally investigate the possibilities. The historian Peter P. Klassen has described, with a wealth of detail, the enormous difficulties encountered by this expedition after they entered the "green hell." The railway line entered 77 kilometers into the Chaco, but then ended; the place chosen for Mennonite settlement was still 140 kilometers away, in the middle of the jungle.[2] The powerful company Carlos Casado Ltd., a conglomerate with enormous land holdings in Paraguay, negotiated the sale of 56,250 hectares of land to the Mennonites.

The migrations of Old Colony Mennonites to Paraguay followed the migrations of that group from Canada to Mexico. As noted above, there was concern that the new Canadian laws concerning instruction in English indicated the intrusion of the state into matters of education, and there was concern about the militarization of the country.[3] The reports received from the delegation that travelled to Paraguay in 1921 were encouraging, and a total of 266 families, comprising 1763 persons, decided to emigrate to Paraguay in 1926 and 1927, of whom 168 died in the journey through the jungle, and 335 returned to Canada once they saw the enormous difficulties presented by the Chaco jungle. In the end, a total of 1250 immigrants settled in the Chaco, establishing Menno Colony about 200 kilometers from the Paraguay river.[4]

From the start there was a notable unity in Menno Colony concerning the organization of the colony. Elder Martin C. Friesen was the organizational and pastoral leader of the colony, as well as its pastor. The first baptisms took place on May 28, 1928, in the temporary houses occupied in Puerto Casado before moving to the Chaco. The community organized its traditional activities such as Sunday morning worship, baptismal instruction, times for the celebration of marriage, baptisms, choir singing, activities for children and young people, and Bible studies. The educational system continued as it had been for their grandparents in Prussia, Russia, and Canada; the principal elements were reading, writing, and basic instruction in mathematics.

The Chaco War between Bolivia and Paraguay (1932-1935) was closely related to the coming of the Mennonite colonists to the Chaco. The differences between the two countries had emerged toward the end of the nineteenth century, when the government of Bolivia attempted to compensate for its loss of Pacific coast line by acquiring a fringe of the Chaco virgin jungle. The breaking of diplomatic relations took place

Johann A. Schröder, one of the leaders of the Menno Colony established in Paraguay.

It was 1921, before the emigration of Mennonites from Canada to the Chaco. The delegate Bernhard Töws had just come back from Paraguay when he said the following to me: "Johann, don't sign any contract with the Casado company until the train line has been extended into the Chaco up to kilometer 160. Otherwise the journey of the immigrants will be very difficult, if they have to depend on oxen and carts. On the way there, there is a field of palm trees, which floods every year in the month of May, up to one meter deep." At the time, I didn't listen carefully to the delegate's words, and soon I forgot them. Just a bit ago, one of the pioneers told me the following: "We were travelling along with oxen and wagons, completely worn out, making our way into the Chaco. At the time I was a youngster. One morning we found ourselves with all our tools and belongings facing a large field of palm trees, which was completely covered in water. The night had been very cold, and the water was almost frozen. Our oxen would pull the carts through such cold water only if someone went ahead of them, leading them. Who should get into such cold water? I was disposed to do it, and I went ahead of the first wagon. The caravan followed me the length of the palm field. I lost my health in that cold water." When I heard this story I remembered again the words of the delegate Bernhard Töws: "Don't sign any contract..." And that memory awakens many questions for me today.

in December, 1928 when Paraguayan forces attacked a small fort, taking the Bolivian survivors prisoner. In addition to the dispute over the border in the Chaco War, there were also petroleum interests at stake (Standard Oil) and the North American strategy of exercising its hegemony over the Plata region.

Not only secular historians like Omar Díaz Arce, but also Mennonite writers themselves recognize that the immigration of Mennonites to the Great Chaco had enormous political significance. By selling huge portions of land in the Chaco to the Mennonites, the attempt was being made to locate the colonists inside the "status quo" border line set by both countries in 1907. When the Paraguayan government authorized the coming of Mennonite colonists from Canada to the Chaco, Bolivia reacted immediately, protesting the decision, and the conflict escalated. Mennonite historian Peter Klassen has said "The good and peaceful Mennonites clearly disturbed the peace in the great uninhabited space of the Chaco."[5]

Menno and Fernheim colonies were protected by the Paraguayan army; the Mennonite colonists did not participate in the war, because of their peace convictions. The Paraguayan government took note of this by the proclamation of law 514, passed in 1921, which permitted the Mennonites to settle in the country, exempt from military service. Nevertheless, since they were in a conflictive zone, the Mennonites were caught in many difficult situations where the interests of the armies at war came up against the interest of indigenous groups that lived in the jungle. Peter Klassen's book *Kaputi Menonita* describes the experiences of the war and the peaceful encounter between Paraguayans and Mennonites.

Fernheim colony, which was located next to Menno colony, was made up of 2,000 immigrants who arrived in the Chaco during 1930 and 1932. Many of the immigrants came directly from the Chortitza and Molotschna colonies in Russia, another group came from the Amur region near Charbin in China (1932), and finally a small group came from Poland.[6] With the help of the Mennonite Central Committee 15,680 hectares of land were bought from the Paraguayan corporation, and parcels were sold to the settlers on credit. In addition, the settlers received agricultural necessities on credit: two oxen, two cows, twelve hens, a stove, seeds, and canvas for the construction of their first dwellings.[7]

The Fernheim settlers included members of three different Mennonite groups: the Mennonite Church (MG), the Mennonite Brethren, and the Evangelical Mennonite Brethren (*Allianzgemeinde*). Throughout the early years, members of all three groups worshipped together – with the exception of the first Sunday of every month, when they

worshipped separately – and also cooperated in the mission to the indigenous people.[8] One of the greatest challenges facing the Fernheim community in its early years was re-establishing its spiritual life, for the community had grown cold during the time when the Communist government in Russia restricted religious activities in the colonies. The Fernheim colony also

Isaac J. Braun and his wife, MB spiritual leaders in Fernheim Colony

suffered from the adverse climactic conditions of the Chaco, with the result that 8 per cent of the settlers died of epidemics and diseases. Another great difficulty came with the separation of almost a third of the colony, who decided to move to eastern Paraguay in 1937 to found a new colony known as Friesland.

The settlers at Fernheim colony had some experience with missionary work. During their time in Russia, mission efforts had been directed to Java and India.[9] Interest in local missions began taking shape almost from the moment of founding the colony, and would reach concrete expression with work among the Enlhet Chaco tribe. The Chaco tribes were engaged in fishing, hunting, and gathering wild honey, fruits, and roots. In their agricultural tradition, they prepared small gardens in the springtime which they returned to harvest some time later. Their principal crops were varieties of corn, yuca, pumpkin, watermelon, beans, cotton, and tobacco.[10] Among their implements were wooden spears, bows, arrows, and stone hatchets; they had mastered the arts of weaving and pottery. Land was not privately owned, rather they shared land and agricultural production communally. Their dwellings were made of branches, with roofs the shape of a round dome, covered with wild grasses. The houses usually were located in the forest in a circular or semi-circular arrangement, leaving a large space in the center where the families could gather and participate in the celebrations the gathered community.

The encounter of the indigenous peoples of Paraguay with Christian missionaries dates from the time of Spanish colonization, with the work of the Guaraní settlements (reducciones) carried out by the Franciscans and Jesuits.[11] There also is the case of the peaceful cohabitation of the Enlhet tribe with the missionary W. Barbrooke Grubb, sent to the

Fire in the daily life of the Enlhet people

Chaco in 1889 by the Anglican church in England.[12] The first meeting between the Chaco tribes and the Mennonites took place during the expedition of 1920, when some members of the Enlhet tribe spoke in a friendly manner with a group of six Mennonites who were accompanying Fred Engen, and let them know that they were well disposed to cohabit peacefully with the "whites." After 1926, when the first Mennonite families began to arrive, there was a timid approach on the part of some of the indigenous Chaco peoples already established there, but with the outbreak of the war between Bolivia and Paraguay, many of the Chaco tribes moved into the deep jungle. It would not

First encounter between Mennonites and the Enlhet people (ca. 1930)

be until after the war, in 1935, that some Enlhet families would once again approach the Mennonite colony of Fernheim in search of work, in order to feed their families. For their part, the Mennonites felt some missionary responsibility to look after the needs of the indigenous Chaco peoples.

From the time of their arrival in the Chaco, the Mennonite settlers were surprised at the difficult economic situation of the indigenous people. Upon gathering their harvest in 1931 and in order to celebrate their thanksgiving, the first offerings were gathered with which to begin a mission work among the indigenous peoples. In January 1932, with the participation of the three Mennonite churches of Fernheim colony, a commission for church affairs was formed. The missionary committee set out to establish a mission station near to the colony in order to take advantage of the work of members of the various churches. It was considered a priority to learn the language, to help the sick, and to provide leadership and counsel to the indigenous people in social and economic matters.

The tense situation caused by the Chaco War in the regions surrounding the Mennonite colonies impeded the continuation of this initial attempt at mission work. It wasn't until 1935, after the Bolivian army withdrew from the Chaco in defeat, that evangelistic work was taken up again. At this time the mission committee of Fernheim requested permission from the authorities of the Chaco to begin such a work

Sepe Lhama

among the Enlhet people. The Chaco authorities, who understood the intentions of these Mennonite settlers as an initiative of "Christianization and civilization" of the aboriginal communities, gave a positive response to the request.[13]

The program of evangelization for the indigenous peoples of the Chaco was announced in September, 1935 in Filadelfia, the center of the Fernheim Colony, under the biblical watchword of Ephesians 3:6. The name given to the organization was "Light for the Indigenous Peoples." The first missionaries were Abram Unger, 25 years of age, single and with handicapped feet and hands, and the couple of Abram and Anna Ratzlaff. Abram Ratzlaff was charged with establishing the mission station, and his wife Anna

The testimony of Sepe Lhama

I was born in the year 1914, in the time when the fruit of the algarroba plant was ripening. My father was Yajavay Apmenic. My grandparents gave me the name Lanangvay, which means "invited." When I was a few years old, my mother gave birth to another son. But my mother did not want this child, and killed him shortly after he was born. I got angry with my mother for feeling all alone. Then the people gave me another name, "Sepe Lhama," which means "solitary son." Our parents had their reasons for not wanting to have many children. They said that they did not want to see how they were going to suffer in this life.

When I was still a boy we already had some contact with white men. ... They told us the story of how God created the world and human beings. It was difficult to understand. Later we got word that a group of white people had arrived at the fields where Menno colony now is. Our elders decided to go over there to see what was going on. We saw that they were a different kind of people; they spoke differently from the Paraguayans. They bought potatoes and manioc, and they paid for it with cloth for clothing.

In those days [after the Chaco war] the Mennonites made plans to start mission work among us. Then we invited the missionaries to occupy our great field of Yalve Sanga. They immediately began building a missionary center there. ... The missionary had asked me to be his teacher. I taught him our language. Working in this way, the day came when I recognized my sins, and I was converted. I was baptized on the 24th of February of 1946. My wife was baptized also, three years later.

The mission work continued. We divided the fields up into lots, and we began to plow and sow. It is a lot of work, but it is worth it! Our way of life is less painful now than before. We live in peace and can grow our own food. We have received much help. If we get sick, we have a way of finding a remedy. The biggest help that we have received is the Word of God, which has straightened out our lives and makes it possible for us to walk on the right path.

with setting up the new hospital for the care of the sick. The mission work was begun seven kilometers to the west of one of the Mennonite colony towns known as Friedensfeld number 5, in the place called by the Enlhet people Lhaptana. However, already by October of 1937 it had become necessary to move to a place with better living conditions, called Yalve Sanga (Armadillo Lake). Several Enlhet families began to settle there and, along with the Mennonite missionaries, began to develop a way of life based on more systematic sowing and harvesting. The first baptism of seven members of the Enlhet did not take place until February, 1946.

The Mennonite colony of Friesland was established in 1937 by settlers from Fernheim colony. They had experienced plagues of grasshoppers, ants, and lengthy frosts the previous year. A new period of hunger appeared to threaten the colonies, and when the rainy season began, the grasshoppers and ants appeared again.[14] Faced with this situation many of the Fernheim settlers decided to go to the eastern side of Paraguay, in the department of San Pedro, 45 kilometers from the port of Rosario, where they acquired a property of 7,000 hectares. A total of 140

The only way to markets: the wagon trail between End Station and colonies

families (718 persons) left Fernheim in August 1937 and in September of that year they founded Friesland Colony. Fernheim colony was left with 284 families (1,325 persons).[15]

The departure of these families from the mother colony of Fernheim caused great discontent among its members. P. C. Hiebert, one of the directors of MCC, stated that the attitude of those families who were unhappy with the Chaco was hardly in accord with submission to the guidance of God. For their part, the founders of Friesland referred bitterly to the attitude of MCC as centralized authoritarianism such as was practiced by Russian Communism. They could not understand why MCC could not support their interest in founding their own colony someplace other than the Chaco.[16] The substantial differences between the settlers who remained in Fernheim and those who formed the new colony in Friesland would not disappear until later generations came along who had not lived the conflict directly.

The Friesland settlers included members of both the Mennonite Brethren and the Mennonite Church (MG). Members of the Mennonite Brethren church originally numbered 153 persons who met together for the first time in October, 1937 to select the preacher Kornelius Voth as their spiritual leader. At this same meeting the members decided to continue their relationship with the Mennonite Brethren church in Filadelfia (Fernheim Colony), including continued participation in the "Light for the indigenous peoples" mission work. On the first Sunday of every month this group met before and after lunch to worship and attend to the needs of the church. The other Sundays they participated in worship services with the Mennonite Church (MG) of Friesland.[17] For its part the MG church, with a membership of 166 persons (of whom 22 lived at that time in the neighboring little settlement of Chamorro), gathered together in October, 1937 to organize itself. On that day Abram Penner was named pastor. The members of this church were from the families who had emigrated from Fernheim and had settled nearby, but without forming a closed colony. Over time the majority of the members of this church located within Friesland Colony.[18]

The monthly publication *Mennoblatt* of Fernheim Colony testifies to the influence of the German National Socialist movement which spread among the Mennonite youth. Friedrich Kliewer and Julius Legiehn played a central role in promoting National Socialism among the youth from 1933 to 1935. Kliewer had been born in Poland in 1905, arrived in the Chaco in 1930, and became a teacher in the Fernheim Colony in 1931. Legiehn was born in the Ukraine in 1899 and arrived in the Chaco with his wife and three children in 1930. Legiehn, in an article in the *Mennoblatt*, spoke of the need to cultivate a consciousness of Mennonitism and Germanism. He believed that "God has made a creation of great diversity. And within that diversity is found ethnicity (Genesis 10:4,5; 17:4)."[19] The words of Fernheim leaders such as Jakob Siemens, Heinrich Pauls, and Abram Loewen give evidence that the adherence of many German Mennonites to this ideology was linked to their past, as when they affirmed, "We know and give thanks that God created National Socialism in the time of the great Bolshevik danger for Western Europe. The almighty God has let Adolf Hitler be a great blessing to many nations, and we hope that He preserve our beloved homeland for many years."[20]

From 1936 to 1938, during Kliewer's absence (he travelled to Germany for doctoral studies), a more muted support for National Socialism could be noted in his successor Peter Hildebrand, for other problems in the economic and organizational realm were of higher priority in Fernheim. The teacher Wilhelm Klassen of the *Allianzgemeinde* (Evangelical Mennonite Brethren),[21] opposed the movement that supported this ideology within the colony.

The increasing influence of National Socialism in the lives of Russo-German Mennonites can be seen again in 1938 with the election of Julius Legiehn as *Oberschulze* (overseer)[22] of Fernheim Colony, and with Kliewer's return in 1939 after having completed his doctorate in Berlin. Kliewer married Margarete Dyck, a German Mennonite teacher. They revitalized the National Socialist movement through the youth and the *Mennoblatt*. Opposition to the movement was assumed in part by Nicolai Wiebe, a leader of the *Allianzgemeinde*, for in his view Legiehn and Kliewer were pushing the colony toward a total identification with National Socialist ideology, leaving to one side Anabaptist non-violence.

In April of 1940 three missionaries from Argentina, Nelson Litwiller, Alvin V. Snyder (both Canadian) and Josephus W. Shank (from the U.S.) visited the Mennonites in Paraguay. They arrived at the exact moment when the colony was celebrating Adolph Hitler's birthday and were surprised at the National Socialist spirit that was moving at Fernheim. The missionaries spoke in an attempt to resist and oppose this German ideology, and so entered into direct conflict with Legiehn, Kliewer and others. The Mennonite Central Committee subsequently played a very important role in resolving the internal conflict, promoting voluntary service work and committees for conscientious objectors.

The dream of many Russo-German settlers to return to their German homeland never came to fruition. Furthermore, in 1942 the Paraguayan government broke diplomatic relations with Italy, Japan,

Friedrich Kliewer

and Germany, and with this the National Socialist movement in Paraguay was left isolated. In 1943 and 1944 the National Socialist movement in Fernheim colony ended. Beginning in these years we note the increasing presence of missionaries and missionary societies from Canada and the United States which sought to offer theological and educational alternatives to the National Socialism that had been implanted at Fernheim. In May, 1944, shortly after the expulsion of Kliewer and Legiehn from the colony, the pastors of the Mennonite Brethren church published a resolution which condemned the National Socialist movement.

The Mennonite Brethren church in Fernheim had 401 members in 1940, but tensions caused by the Nazi movement brought division to the MB church which were not healed until 1947, thanks to the efforts of B. B. Janz. In 1952 construction was completed of a church building in Filadelfia for the reunited MBs with a seating capacity of 1600 persons. Following the difficulties that arose when some Mennonite leaders embraced National Socialism, the Evangelical Mennonite Brotherhood (*Allianzgemeinde*) gained strength. In spite of being a small community, it continued participating actively as a member of the mission "Light for the indigenous peoples" and in the establishment of the Leper mission and hospital at Kilometer 81, under the direction of MCC and the Mennonites in Paraguay, begun in 1950. Pastor Gerhard Schartner also was one of the first leaders in Paraguay to support the founding of the Mennonite Seminary in Montevideo, in 1956.

In the 1940s and years following, the Fernheim and Friesland colonies experienced changes in church leadership that strengthened their church communities. The Fernheim community benefitted from young men and women assuming important roles in the community of faith. In Friesland colony, spiritual life was enhanced by work with the youth, systematic Bible studies and other programs.[23] By 1955 the three distinct Mennonite churches of Fernheim colony had the following memberships: Mennonite Brethren (567 members), the Mennonite Church (MG: 350 members) and the *Allianzgemeinde* (Evangelical Mennonite Brethren: 171 members).[24]

The Neuland colony was founded in 1947 and 1948 by families whose religious and educational institutions were totally destroyed following the Civil War in Russia, the persecution under Stalin, the Second World War and the retreat of German troops from the Ukraine at the end of World War II. The immigrants, made up of members of both MG and MB churches, soon formed their own church communities in Paraguay. The Mennonite Church (MG) in Neuland colony was organized in November 1947 and was led for many years by Hans Rempel. It numbered 670 members in 1956. The MB church was founded in the colony in May, 1948 in the town of Gnadental. A sister-church of this congregation was founded in 1949 in Steinfeld, 40 kilometers from

Neuland Church, 1957

Gnadental; it was served by the pastor of Gnadental. The Gnadental church, which at one time had a median attendance of 200 people, saw this drop to 144 by January of 1959. This was due to the emigration of many away from the colony and leadership problems.[25]

Volendam colony was also founded in 1947 by refugees who managed to escape Germany after WWII. The majority of the colonists were part of the Mennonite Church (MG), with a smaller number of MBs represented. By the late 1950s the MG church numbered 800 members; the MB church in Volendam numbered 112 members in 1957.

Joint worship services were held except for the first Sunday of every month, when the MG and MB members met separately. The colony faced great difficulties, among them the departure from the community in the mid-1950s of many members, who left in search of better living conditions.[26]

First colony administration building, Volendam

There were Mennonites living in Asunción for twenty years before a Mennonite church was established there. Peter Fast and his wife Grete were the first to arrive, in October, 1931. Later, many other Mennonites who did not enjoy the difficult life in the Chaco decided to stay and live in Asunción. The first worship services took place in the home of the Fast family. In 1944 MCC opened an office and hostel in Asunción in order to attend to the needs of Mennonites arriving in the city. By 1950 there were about 300 Mennonites of Russian origin living in the city. Finally, in March, 1950 the Evangelical Mennonite Church of Christians in Asunción (*Gemeinde evangelisch-mennonitischer Christen in Asunción*) was founded.

The beginning of work by German-speaking Mennonite Brethren among Spanish-speaking Paraguayans dates to the mid-1950s, when missionaries from the Mennonite Brethren conference in North America began mission work in Asunción. At the same time, there were young people in the churches who were ready to be trained for the task. Hans and Susie Wiens studied at the Baptist Seminary in Buenos Aires, and Albert Enns went to the Mennonite Seminary in Bragado, south-west of Buenos Aires. Dr. Decoud Larrosa, one of the most influential Protestant persons in the capital, said on this occasion: "For 20 years we have anticipated working together with the Mennonites in Paraguay, with the end of winning our people to Christ."[27] It was Larrosa who recommended that the Mennonites locate their work in the section of Asunción called "Hospital de Clínicas," where today the Biblical Institute of Asunción, the Albert Schweitzer College, and the radio station "Obedira" are located. Nevertheless, the place where work began in 1955 was called Las Mercedes. Albert Enns began his work there, disseminating literature and inviting people to come to worship services. His work was well received. At the same time a similar work began in the Hospital de Clínicas area, where a summer Bible school was offered during the summer. In July, 1956, Angel Gagliardi and Cirilo Zayas were the first to be baptized as a result of this mission work.

From the beginnings of the 1940s until the mid-1950s the close cooperation of the Paraguayan governments with the Catholic church could be seen clearly.[28] The governments of the time saw Protestants in the same light as the Catholic church saw them: as foreign agents, traitors to Paraguayan culture.[29] With the takeover by General Alfredo Stroessner in 1954 began one of the longest periods of military dictatorship known in Latin America. He could count on the military and financial support of the United States embassy in his imposition of "order" on the Paraguayan people, who suffered conditions of much poverty and injustice. Stroessner's regime was characterized by political immobility, aversion to political structures and the complete relinquishment of natural resources to foreign companies.

The government of General Stroessner began with the support of the Catholic church, but over time he began to distance himself from it. Protestants, knowing Stroessner's Lutheran background, hoped for support from the new government, and in fact, Stroessner appeared favorably disposed to Protestantism. In Paraguay, as in other countries of Latin America, the Protestantism of the established churches was enriched with the arrival of Pentecostal groups. In Paraguay the arrival of Pentecostals began in 1945 with the coming of the Assemblies of God, which originated in North America, but soon other groups followed from Sweden, Norway, Brazil, Chile and Argentina.[30]

Alfredo Stroessner is still much admired and liked by Mennonite colonists to this day, not only because of his openness to Mennonites, but also because of Stroessner's support for the Transchaco highway, which did away with the isolation of the Mennonite colonies of the Chaco and established direct contact with Asunción.[31]

When the Mennonite colonists headed for Paraguay, they had not the least idea of the geographical conditions they would encounter, or the reality of the indigenous peoples of the Chaco.[32] Nevertheless, there was a strong desire from the start to share the Gospel with the indigenous tribes of the Ayoreo, Enlhet, Nivaclé, Guaraní, Toba, and the Sanapaná. One of the most-remembered stories in the collective memory of the Mennonite colonists is their encounter with Ayoreo people. The Ayoreo tribe resisted the invasion of the Chaco lands with force of arms. In 1947 a group of Ayoreo people attacked the family of P. Stahl, killing four members of his family. The Mennonites saw the urgency of taking the Gospel to these people. In 1958 word came to the colonies that a group of Ayoreo people had taken up arms and attacked a North American petroleum company that had invaded its territory. On that occasion, the young missionaries Kornelius Isaak, David Hein and Cornelius Jacob Amay went to speak with the Ayoreos, taking along gifts. They met with the tribe about 50 kilometers from the location of the U.S. company, in the Cerro León, at which time Kornelius Isaak was mortally wounded by an Ayoreo spear, dying the next day. Years later, in 1963, the Ayoreo people entered into a peaceful dialogue with the colonists, and even came to the Mennonite colonies looking for work. Missionary work among the Ayoreo people was carried on by the New Tribes Mission (*Misión Nueva Tribus*).[33]

The first baptism among the Enlhet people took place in February, 1946 in Yalve Sanga (Armadillo Lake). The coordination of mission work was taken up by the Mennonite Brethren conference of North America in July, 1946.[34] The decade of the 1950s was characterized by internal conflicts between various indigenous groups, by struggles of these groups with the Mennonite colonists, and by government policies that now assigned parcels of land to the indigenous in an effort to change their nomadic way of life.

Beginning in 1936 more and more Nivaclé people began to arrive at the Mennonite colonies to work on the farms. In 1946 Jakob Franz offered to begin mission work for the Mennonites. In 1949, Cornelius Isaak and Gerard Hein began learning the Nivaclé language, and later began teaching it to the young people. An event of great significance for the Nivaclé people occurred between 1951 and 1952, when some groups migrated back to their lands in the Argentine Chaco after the harvests. When they returned to Filadelfia in the Paraguayan Chaco, they brought with them the influence of the spiritual renewal movement that had reached the Argentine Chaco. The missionary Jakob Franz testified that some 300 indigenous peoples were anxious to hear the word of God: "God performed a miracle as well among the Chulupí people."[35] The first baptism among the Chulupí took place in March, 1958 in Filadelfia, leading to the founding of the first Chulupí church, with a total of 21 baptized members. A second church was later founded in "Cayim o Clim" in Neu-Halbstadt.

In 1948 Menno colony extended its territory with the purchase of new land, and founded the Paratodo colony. With the establishment of this and other colonies the Mennonites came into closer friendly contact with the Enlhet people. Some felt a responsibility to let the Gospel be known to the Enlhet. Johan M. Funk took the initiative of teaching them to read and write, and later he became the first missionary among the Enlhet in Menno colony. In 1952 the Mennonite communities decided to begin missionary work among these people, and the *Menno-Indianer-Mission* (MIM: Menno Indian Mission) began. After the first baptisms in 1956 and 1957, the first Enlhet church was founded in Menno colony.

Loma Plata was another place where Enlhet families were already living before the Mennonites arrived. The Enlhet looked for work among the Mennonite farmers who settled there. In 1955 Bernhard W. Toews founded a school for the Enlhet and also preached the Gospel to them. In 1957 the first baptism of Enlhet people took place. Other indigenous tribes such as the Toba and the Sanapaná who were linked to Menno colony later would also form new churches.

When the Paraguayan troops retreated from Bolivia during the Chaco War, the indigenous Guaraní tribes of Ñandeva and Guarayo peoples considered the Paraguayan soldiers to be brothers, since they spoke the same language, and they believed that the Paraguayan troops had come to take them back to Paraguay. These Guaraní families tried to settle in Nueva Asunción, Mariscal Estigarribia, Pedro P. Peña and Fernheim. From 1955 to 1960, some of these Guaraní people migrated to Fernheim colony in search of work, primarily to the towns of Friedensfeld, Gnadenheim, Waldesruh and Filadelfia. In Friedensfeld, where several of these people found employment, they got to know the word of God through Johann Loewen. He would invite preachers who knew both Spanish and Guaraní from the Bible school in Filadelfia to bring the word to the Guaraní who worked in these Mennonite towns. In this way the mission work among the Guaraní was begun.[36]

Guaraní poem for the feast of corn

The universal principle of life springs forth
I will tell you, I will tell you your history
Wisdom springs forth
Our mutual telling
The masculine diadem springs forth
Our mutual telling
The word (thunder) springs forth
Our mutual telling
The adornment of feathers springs forth
I will tell you, I will tell you your history
The cross springs forth, the axis of the world
Our mutual telling
The adornment of the cross springs forth
I will tell you, I will tell you your history

The Mennonite colonists in Paraguay faced unbelievably harsh living conditions in their early years of settlement. Mortality rates were high, and many left the struggling Chaco colonies for more hopeful pastures, both within Paraguay and in other countries. In the midst of these struggles, in the 1930s and 1940s, the pan-German National Socialist movement carried a strong appeal for some colonists who, as strangers in a difficult and strange land, identified strongly with their German ethnic background and culture. All these realities weakened, divided and dispirited the settlers, who nevertheless persevered.

By the 1950s the Mennonite colonies had weathered these social, religious, economic and political storms, and had begun to emerge into economic prosperity. Their religious communities also were strengthened by an early focus on education, church programs and evangelism. What had begun primarily as a search for a secure homeland for Mennonite refugee communities, and had been a struggle for survival, now gained strength and confidence, and began to look outward, further afield, to the people among whom the Mennonites had settled. By the end of the 1950s, the mission impulse had begun bearing fruit: Mennonite churches, planted by the colonists, whose members were indigenous and Spanish-speaking Paraguayans.

In the midst of the positive sharing of the Gospel, however, it remained the case that divisions among Mennonite groups had also been imported by the colonists to Paraguay. Ironically, early stages of mutual cooperation experienced in the difficult times were somewhat reversed with the coming of better times, and this resulted in parallel church buildings, organizations and mission churches, often in the same communities. One of the ongoing issues for Mennonites in Paraguay thus became the matter of church unity. It was a difficult task for diverse ethnic and linguistic groups to work together as members of the same church, but unity also remained a no-less-difficult issue among the colonists who shared a language and a culture and professed the Mennonite faith, but found themselves separated by historical and theological differences. Questions of ethnicity and denominational division continued being addressed in the decades that followed, as will be seen below.

CHAPTER IV

Mennonites Settle in Brazil: (1930-1958)

With its great diversity of climate and geography and the enormous ecological wealth of the Amazon, Brazil is the fifth-largest country in the world, covering an area of 8.5 million square kilometers. One year after the famous Portuguese sailor Vasco da Gama opened the maritime route from Lisbon to India, the commander Pedro Alvarez Cabral changed course in the Atlantic and arrived at what is now the state of Bahia in April, 1500. The visitors were completely won over by Brazil's beauty and fertility, and they would be followed by many more expeditions. The local population, which originally numbered several million native people, was drastically reduced after the arrival of the Europeans.[1]

By 1580 the Portuguese were importing more than 2,000 Africans annually as labor for the sugar cane plantations in the Brazilian north-east.[2] In spite of the enormous cultural influence and the African religions brought by the slaves to Brazil, Roman Catholicism predominated in the colony, promoted by religious orders such as the Dominicans, Augustinians, Franciscans, Benedictines, Oratory congregations, Carmelites, Brothers of Mercy and Capuchins, who controlled the educational institutions of the colony.

The colonial history of Brazil is characterized by Portugal's continual struggle to expand its dominion over the continent and at the same time, repulse the attempts by other empires to usurp the occupied lands of Brazil. The period between 1750 and 1830 is described as a time of crisis for the colonial system and the emergence of an independent Brazil (1822). In 1831 the emperor Pedro I returned to his throne in Portugal, leaving his son Pedro II as governor of Brazil.[3] Pedro II was crowned emperor of Brazil in 1840. The government of

Pedro II, which lasted almost half a century, legitimated a tropical version of monarchical customs. He was forced to return to Portugal in 1889 ending the monarchy. Princess Isabel signed the law for the abolition of slavery (1888), and Brazil was declared a Republic in 1889.

Protestant presence in Brazil began in the nineteenth century; attempts to establish a Huguenot presence in the 16th century came to naught.[4] Nevertheless, there was an early Mennonite presence in Brazil when three Mennonites sailed to Pernambuco (NE Brazil) with the Dutch invasion in the 1640s. Abraham Esau, an agronomist, Isaak Kaufmann, cattle raiser and David Spielman, windmill technician, petitioned governor Mauricio de Nassau to bring more of the persecuted Mennonites of Holland and Germany to Brazil.[5] This tentative Mennonite presence ended when the Dutch were expelled in 1654.

The "Alliance of Friendship, Commerce and Navigation" treaty between Brazil and England in 1810 opened the doors to some Protestant immigrants.[6] Because of the possibilities of establishing large plantations and using slave labor in the time of Pedro II, Brazil became a place of interest for immigrants from the southern United States in the last half of the nineteenth century.[7] With few exceptions, however, the Protestant denominations contributed little or nothing to the abolition of slavery.[8]

Mennonite settlement in Brazil was part of the late movement of Protestant immigration. The difficult revolutionary years in Russia from 1930 to 1931 saw a new exodus of Russo-German farmers, among them many Mennonites.[9]

> "Whoever is fleeing from the homeland can do nothing other than pass through the door that happens to be open at that moment."
> **Benjamin Unruh**

From 1930 to 1931 a total of thirteen ships transported Russo-Germans to Brazil, totaling 1256 persons.[10] By 1934, before the arrival of the last group of immigrants from Harbin, China the Krauel colonies (Witmarsum, Waldheim, and Gnadental) had been populated by 841 Mennonite immigrants, with 454 settling at Stoltz-Plateau in the state of Santa Catarina.[11]

The final group of Russo-German Mennonite immigrants came from the poverty-stricken frontier located between the Soviet Union and China, known as Manchuria. Some of these immigrants were transported to Paraguay; another group of 180 persons arrived in Rio de Janeiro in May, 1934. From the group that arrived in Rio de

Janeiro, the majority was settled in the Stoltz-Plateau Colony, and the rest were located in Krauel Colony.

The Krauel valley, located in the mountainous zone of Santa Catarina, extends 20 kilometers west to east. It was named in memory of the German Dr. Krauel, who explored the area for the first time in 1897. The Mennonite pioneer David Nikkel described the Krauel

Mennonite immigrants sailing for Brazil on board the "Sierra Ventana"

as being located "In the midst of the mountains, to the south, north, and west, locked in by a chain of mountains almost impossible to climb, separated from the world outside, in the middle of the zone where springs of water feed the upper part of the river Krauel..."[12] The mountainous forests of Santa Catarina made the Mennonite immigrants fearful, accustomed as they were to the plains of Russia. For the majority of them it was extremely disappointing not to find land similar to that of their former homeland.

Three important towns were founded in Krauel Colony: Witmarsum, Waldheim, and Gnadental.[13] Some months after their arrival in the heights of the Krauel, the leader Heinrich Martins wrote to Benjamin H. Unruh informing him that each family was working hard, chopping down the forest, and that approximately 350 hectares

Refugees in the Brazilian forest, 1930

**The testimony of
Elisabeth Toews**

.... For us young people it
was very difficult to leave
the Krauel. We had grown
up there, and it was our
homeland. .... I miss the high
mountains, the green forests,
the song of the Sabia and
the old house of my parents,
where we had lived since our
childhood. For a long time I
felt a painful homesickness.
It was lovely living there,
although it was also difficult.
May my old homeland
prosper; I will not forget you!

had been seeded in corn, beans, potatoes, and
manioc. The first cottages that were built had
roofs and walls made of palm leaves, with packed
mud floors.[14]

A church was founded in Waldheim in May,
1930; its 110 founding members had come from
the Crimea in Russia. Its name was "Community
of Evangelical Anabaptist Brethren of Waldheim."
Worship services, youth meetings, and Sunday
schools took place in both Waldheim and Witmarsum.

The settlement would not last. By 1932, many
settlers migrated north to Curitiba to escape the
difficulties of the Krauel Valley, and they sought
homes and employment there. The young people
in particular began to move there in search of
work, so that the more elderly feared that they would soon be isolated in the colonies, far from children and grandchildren. The state
of Paraná was viewed as an alternative, where land was much more
fertile; the Mennonite immigrants who had located there were living
in much better conditions. Others were interested in the dairy business near Curitiba. Life in the Krauel was extremely hard, and there
was little money to be earned, given un-mechanized farm production,
poor roads, and long distances to markets. For these reasons the last
Mennonite settlers left the Krauel in 1945.

Once the valley of the river Krauel had been populated it was necessary to found a new colony, called the Stoltz-Plateau. It was also
located in Santa Catarina, on the slopes of the mountains. The valleys
through which the water ran were fertile, but the mountains were not
suitable for agriculture.

For the first year the 454 Stoltz-Plateau settlers were sustained by
food provided by the German government. The Dutch Mennonite
Relief organization brought life and soul into the developing communities with the gift of a milk cow for each family, money to build
and maintain schools and to help establish cooperatives.[15] The first
harvests were very poor, which forced the young people to move to
the city to seek work and help a little with the costs at home. Shortly
after their arrival in Stoltz-Plateau the families gathered to see who

wished to live somewhere else, but economic conditions did not make it possible to consider buying other land.

Two churches were built in the Stoltz-Plateau Colony. Shortly after the founding of the colony in 1930, Johannes Janzen gathered together seven families of the colony and organized a church under the name of "Evangelical Mennonite Community of Stoltz-Plateau." Since there was no Mennonite Brethren church in this colony, MB families attended this church.[16] In order to be received as a member of this church it mattered not if the person had been baptized by immersion or aspersion; what was considered important was a new

Johannes Janzen

birth in Christ. Ten years later, once the trees had been cut on the hillsides and the springs of the little streams began to dry up, and in face of the infertility of the ground and the poverty of its inhabitants, all the inhabitants of the Stoltz-Plateau had emigrated to Curitiba and other Brazilian cities.

The testimony of Susanna Hamm (1930)

The children sat on the trunk of a tree. We sang and prayed and then I explained how our Savior had been born in a stable like our hut, and how he lay in hay and straw. ... The birth of Jesus seemed a lot like our own childhood here in the cabin, with the great poverty that we were living at that time. ... Then we began to sing. But this time we sang with all the happiness of our hearts and with lungs wide open... The children expressed their joy at being alive, their love and their homesickness in the song.

National Socialism had an impact on the Mennonite colonies of Brazil, as it did also in Paraguay. Already in 1933 there were many visits to the colonies by Brazilian military officials such as Colonel Gaelzer Neto, by German authorities, or administrators of the Hanseatic Colonization Society. Notable among the visits is that of Dr. Jacob Quiring, who stayed at the Mennonite colonies from September to November of 1933. Dr. Quiring was a Mennonite born in imperial Russia who had concluded his doctoral studies at the University of Munich in 1928. Dr. Quiring, who had been associated with B. H.

At home on the Stoltz-Plateau

Unruh in Germany, took up the theme of Mennonitism and the German race in his first writings in *Die Brücke*. The paper also printed writings by Heinrich Schröder, a teacher of Russo-Mennonite origins living in Germany, from where he described, in very sentimental and nationalist language, the funeral of Hindenburg, president of Germany (1934), and also put forward the challenge to the people to maintain their loyalty to the German race (1936). Talea Haijer was another person who wrote for this Mennonite paper. Although she was not a Mennonite, she worked as a nurse in the Mennonite colony of Witmarsum (1935-1938). She wrote: "In reality I cannot separate Christianity and National Socialism. My Christianity obliges me to serve my people. And when I truly serve my people as a Christian, I am a National Socialist."[17]

Another person linked to National Socialism was Ernst Behrends, teacher in Schleswig-Holstein in northern Germany. *Die Brücke* published several of his letters and writings in which he passed on greetings with the well known "Heil Hitler." He was most zealous in providing the Mennonite colonies with literature concerning National Socialism in Germany. His point of view was that the life of the Hanseatic colonies was not necessarily congruent with the attitudes of Nazism. Nevertheless, he defended Quiring as a person who, although he professed Nazism, still was "open and honorable," attentive to the needs of the colonies. In April of 1938 the leaders of the Krauel sent greetings to Hitler on the occasion of his birthday.[18]

The political situation in Brazil changed radically when Getulio Vargas assumed power. In January 1938 began a campaign against the Nazi party in Brazil, the result of which was the deportation of many German Nazi members. The nationalization process continued with all German schools in the country required to use Portuguese as their official language. This caused substantial problems in the Mennonite schools. Worship services were only allowed to be held in *Plattdeutsch* (low German). Although under the direction of the teacher David Enns, a youth organization called the *Deutsche-Brasilianische Jugendring* was founded in 1937, it didn't last long. National Socialism did not spread among the youth of Brazil, as was the case in Paraguay.[19]

The limited relationship that began to emerge with North American Mennonite organizations encouraged Mennonites in Brazil to consider other ways of analyzing their social and communal lives.[20]

One of the major difficulties faced by the Mennonite colonies in Brazil had to do with their internal organization. Brazil did not have the same political conditions as did Russia, in which the colonies organized their communal and religious lives internally, with no connection to the government. In Brazil the struggle centered on attempts to manage the businesses of the colony. On the one side were those who wished to conserve a centralized power in the colonies, and on the other those who wished to act more individually, accentuating private initiatives in the different spheres of life. These disagreements contributed to a disintegration of the colonies. The migration of Mennonite families away from the colonies intensified in 1937, when 88 families – of which 55 were from Auhagen, 31 from Witmarsum, and 2 from Paraguay – settled in Curitiba. It can be noted that the most conservative families, who wished to maintain their traditions, their culture, and their closed communities, were the last to abandon the Krauel.

In 1945 fascist ideologies were in decline and a new period in Brazilian history began when elections were held. In the 1950s an intensive program of industrialization and transportation was promoted, concentrating on economic development in the south-central region of the country. Industrial growth in Brazil permitted the construction of the beautiful city of Brasilia in 1960.

Peter Klassen and family, 1947

The post-World War II Catholic church hierarchy found it difficult to think in terms of social reforms, given its growing anti-Communism. It supported legislation that continued government funding of Catholic educational centers. However, an important sector of the Catholic church did participate actively in agricultural reform and social activism. Among other bishops who supported agrarian reform in favor of rural workers was Bishop Dom Eugenio Salles of Río Grande do Norte.[21] Beginning in 1950 Archbishop Dom Helder Cámara organized the laity, following the French model of social movements, and in 1952 the National Conference of Brazilian Bishops (CNBB) was organized. This latter organization not only intended to evangelize communities but also sought to respond to the social call of the popular sectors, organizing and creating rural unions and educating leaders for communal associations.[22]

In 1950 the traditional Protestant churches such as Baptists, Methodists, Presbyterians and Methodists made up the majority of Protestants in Brazil. The call for social and political change in Brazilian society and changes in international Protestantism created tensions in these churches. Presbyterian youth pushing for participation in the newly-formed World Council of Churches were accused by the government of systematic opposition and Communist propaganda. Suspicion on the part of church leaders grew until in 1962 a supreme council decided to strip the youth organization of its independence.[23] It was in this year that Richard Shaull, the North American missionary professor, left Brazil after having taught for eleven years in Protestant seminaries. Shaull believed that the action of God needed to be described in terms of concrete human situations, rather than being catalogued dogmatically. In parallel with a growing social consciousness among the traditional churches, Pentecostal missions and groups grew rapidly in the large Brazilian cities during this entire historical period. By 1960 the traditional Protestant churches had been overtaken by Pentecostal churches, and had become the Protestant minority.[24]

Peter P. Klassen has described the division and expansion of the various Mennonites groups in Brazil during the late 1940s and 1950s, as they left the original colonies. Among the different groups of immigrants were families who belonged to the Mennonite Brethren, on the one hand, and others who belonged to the Mennonite Church (MG). These Mennonite groups developed in their respective directions.

Many of the Mennonite immigrants who had settled in the original four colonies went to Blumenau, a town in Santa Catarina,[25] in search of employment. It was a city with a tradition of receiving German immigrants.[26] In Santa Catarina, as in all of southern Brazil, an enormous full-scale campaign of nationalization was underway during the Vargas dictatorship in the 1940s, for it was thought that the Italian and German groups who lived there were in tune with fascist ideologies. When the Mennonites arrived in Blumenau the state's objectives were well underway, affirming a unified, mono-ethnic and culturally homogenous nation state among the immigrant sectors who had established themselves there.[27]

The Mennonite Brethren church in Blumenau belongs to the seven founding churches of the German-speaking Conference of Mennonite Brethren Churches in Brazil. In February 1950 the Mennonite group in Blumenau officially associated with the Mennonite Brethren church in Krauel. Beginning in 1957, under the pastoral direction of Hans Kasdorf, this community began its missionary work in the state with the establishment of a home for the elderly, prison visitation, and weekly public gatherings in the plaza.

The move of the Mennonite colonists to Curitiba marks Mennonite integration and assimilation into the economic and cultural reality of Brazil. These Mennonite communities began opening to missionary work and the establishment of local churches. In the first resettlements of Mennonites to Curitiba in 1937 we find 88 Mennonite families; by 1951 this number had reached 200 families settled in Vila Guaira, Boqueirão, Xaxim and Guarituba. The missionary work of the Mennonite Brethren Church in Boqueirão began with the creation of an orphanage in Uberaba, on the edge of Curitiba. In 1947 a home was opened with room for seven orphan children; in 1957, when the orphanage was closed, it had a total of 61 children in residence. The locale continued functioning as a school under the name "Erasmo Braga" with 200 children participating.[28]

Heinrich Koop transporting milk to Curitiba

Vila Guaira became the first stage in the migration of Mennonites towards Curitiba. By 1965 there were 123 families living there, and they were quickly becoming integrated into Brazilian society. The nearby barrios of Boqueirão and Xaxim were also destinations for Mennonite families, most of whom initially concentrated on milk production. Mennonite families from the Krauel as well as from Paraguay also settled in Guarituba on 10 hectares of land. This small dairy farming community disappeared after 1958, after the state passed laws that demanded the pasteurization of milk. Eventually the property was sold, and this small Mennonite colony disappeared.[29]

In March, 1951, seventy-seven members of the former colony of Witmarsum in the Krauel valley announced that they would construct a new Witmarsum on the Fazenda la Cancela in Palmeira, Paraná, on 7,800 hectares of land. While other families from the Krauel valley moved south, these families moved to the north. Some of the religious tensions of Krauel colony also dissolved, since the families that moved south to form the "New Colony" located in the state of Rio Grande do Sul took with them the Mennonite Brethren church, while the Mennonite Church (MG) and Free Evangelical Mennonite church members (*Freie Evangelische Gemeinde*) moved to the New Witmarsum in the state of Paraná. "New Colony" organizational structures were relatively free, while New Witmarsum continued organizing itself in a centralized way.

None of the colonists of New Witmarsum had the right to title to the land, with the aim of strengthen-

Testimony of Melita Legiehn Nikkel

I was born in Russia on August 30, 1924. I was four years old when I had to leave Russia. ... I came to Paraguay with my parents in 1927. ... it was very, very difficult at the beginning. ... My father was a teacher in Paraguay and I began assisting him in the school. ... In 1952 my husband, the teacher Fritz Kliewer, my children and I moved from Paraguay to live in New Witmarsum. My husband was the person in charge of education. Three and a half years later, after returning from a Mennonite conference in Paraguay, he suffered a heart attack and died. His dream had always been to publish a magazine, something he managed to do when he began to publish *Bibel und Pflug*. ... I was married again in December 1967 to a farmer named David Nikkel. After eight and a half years of married life my new husband died of a stroke. He was a very devout man. ... He told me before he died, very peacefully: "... Love God. When can we love God? Only through other persons. We can't subject or apprehend God; we can only love Him by means of our neighbors. Tonight I'm thinking about all the persons I have known, and I believe I have loved them. In this way I have been able to love God."

ing the cooperation between the colonists and guaranteeing the privacy of the colony. No colonist could sell his property, nor settle on the land without the agreement of the colony. In this way the colony managed to maintain the structures inherited from the Mennonite colonies in Russia. By 1955, 74 families numbering 455 persons lived in New Witmarsum.

Curitiba choir en route to Witmarsum

A short-lived Mennonite colony was founded in the city of Clevelandia to the south of Paraná around 1953. It was populated mostly by MB settlers from Paraguay. This colony cultivated wheat, rice, corn, manioc and potatoes. The *Bibel und Pflug* reported innumerable difficulties lived by this community, especially strong rains and floods that prevented its continuation.

The great city of São Paulo became a place that interested the Mennonites. According to a report by Abraham Fast, already in 1933 a young Mennonite woman found employment in that city as a domestic worker in a home.[30] In the 1950s many German industries, such as VW, Mercedes Benz, and Siemens established themselves in the city. This also permitted the establishment of schools, colleges and German research institutes. In 1948 the Mennonite preacher Peter Klassen discovered a total of 112 Mennonites living in São Paulo. The incorporation of Mennonites into the modern world was not easy. In addition to the work of young women as domestics, married men began to take on difficult jobs in factories, which led to their being absent from their homes for long stretches of time.

In 1949 a locale was rented that served as a "Home for young women," following the general lines of MCC which set itself the task of establishing such homes after the Second World War.[31] Such homes were constructed in Buenos Aires, Montevideo and São Paulo and were meant to be meeting places for Mennonite immigrants who came to the large cities. The home in São Paulo became a place where worship services and devotionals were conducted, open to all regardless of whether participants came from the Mennonite Brethren or the

Mennonite church. The first German-speaking church of Mennonite Brethren was established in the barrio called Jabaquara in 1954. It associated with the Mennonite churches in Curitiba, Paraná, and Bagé, Rio Grande do Sul.[32]

In 1950 Colonia Nova was founded 45 kilometers from the city of Bagé, 30 kilometers from Aceguá on the border with Uruguay, settled by 86 families who came from the Krauel valley. The colony specialized in cultivating wheat, corn and cereals. In 1959, when Julius Legiehn visited the site and its surroundings, he reported that 200 Mennonite families lived there, who had come from Krauel, Curitiba, Paraguay, and other places in Brazil.

Mennonite women in Curitiba prepare relief packages for Europe

Colonia Nova is one of the few Mennonite groupings in South America that from its beginnings was associated only with the Mennonite Brethren church. This is due in part to the fact that the MB church that already existed in Krauel moved to Colonia Nova. In 1952 the Colonia Nova church counted 238 members, making it one of the largest Mennonite Brethren churches in Brazil. The church was supported by a series of preachers and Bible teachers from North America, interested in constructing a Bible school; this gave the colony much prestige in the conference of Mennonite Brethren of South America. Among the teachers was Prof. C. C. Peters of Canada who, coming from Fernheim, arrived in Colonia Nova to promote theological education. In 1954 a large dining hall was built in which to hold meetings, and in 1957 a house for missions.

The regional organization of Mennonite churches was an important development for Mennonites in Latin America. Efforts at continental unity can be seen not only among the MBs, but also in the Mennonite Church (MG) shortly following the end of the Second World War. In February, 1948 representatives of the Mennonite Brethren in South America met at Friesland colony in Paraguay to deal with the question of how their churches should relate to the MB churches of North America. Gerhard Ratzlaff, reflecting on the motives that led to this development, suggests that the different ideologies that marked the Second World War brought confusion to the immigrant colonies and contributed to disagreements and divisions within them. The MB church not only needed to seek counsel, but also needed economic support from the MB leaders in North America.[33]

For its part, the MG church in Paraguay and Brazil also was interested in connecting directly to the General Conference of Mennonites of North America. During 1947 and 1948 this conference began supporting MG immigrants in Europe and in South America, helping to purchase land, supporting colonies, and aiding in the construction of churches.

Another important issue dealt with in this period were the tensions that had come to exist between the Mennonite Church (MG), the Evangelical Mennonite Churches of Latin America and the Mennonite Brethren. Like the Mennonite Brethren,[34] the MG church also held a conference at Fernheim colony with the participation of North American, Paraguayan and Brazilian Mennonites in February of 1948. This conference took a broadly tolerant view of differences between its different churches, but distinguished itself from other Mennonite groups. The representatives from Paraguay and Brazil, joined shortly after also by Uruguay, concluded the event by founding the Conference of South American Mennonite Churches (MG).[35]

MG churches began to meet beginning in the 1950s for preaching and conferences, forming the Association of Mennonite Churches of Brazil (AIMB);[36] their churches came from Boqueirão, Vila Guaira and Witmarsum (Paraná). The conference challenged the churches to develop and grow; it promoted theological training of leaders and congregations, missionary work, work in literacy and other social ser-

Mennonite church and community hall in Boqueirão, 1957

vices, and maintained contact between the national and continental churches through the periodical *Bibel und Pflug*. The work of the AIMB was concentrated primarily in Curitiba, Witmarsum and neighboring areas.

The Second World War made it impossible to establish educational centers in Brazil, but in 1950 a Bible school was founded in old Witmarsum which taught Bible and German. In 1950 a Bible school was also established at Colonia Nova by the Mennonite Brethren. In 1960 the school at Colonia Nova moved to Curitiba. Here it was known as the Biblical Evangelical Institute. With the support of MB communities in North America and South America, this center offered a good program of theological education which included biblical studies, music and education. In 1961, Paranaense Bible Institute began at this location offering a three-year course to train pastors and leaders. In 1972, the Bible Institute would be combined with the Seminary which had been in another section of Curitiba, forming the Biblical Institute and Seminary of the Mennonite Bretheren (ISBIM) with 100 students in four courses.[37]

Mennonite settlement efforts in Brazil from 1930 to 1960, unlike the settlements in the Paraguayan Chaco, failed to establish colonies along the lines of the self-governing Mennonite colonies of Russia. Poor geographical locations, along with the integrative nationalistic policies of the Brazilian government, contributed to this result in Brazil. Mennonite settlers in Brazil gradually moved away from their colonies into Brazilian society, which offered better economic opportunities. At first the German-speaking settlers worked at maintaining their own churches and communities in this more dispersed context, including re-establishing their inter-Mennonite lines of division, particularly between the Mennonite Church (MG) and the Mennonite Brethren. As the 1950s drew to a close, churches began to be established and transitions were made to bring the Gospel to Portuguese-speaking Brazilians. North American Mennonite Mission agencies helped move this process along, which led to continuing collaboration between the emerging Brazilian Mennonite churches and those in North America.

II

Consolidation and Expansion: (1959-1979)

Introduction: Consolidation and Expansion: (1959-1979)

The decades of the 1960s and 70s witnessed the consolidation and growth of the Mennonite churches and settlements described in the previous section. These decades also saw the establishment of many new Mennonite communities, mostly by way of mission efforts, in eighteen new Latin American countries in the Southern Cone, the Andean Region, the Caribbean, and Mesoamerica (Central America). This second major section of the story of Mennonites in Latin America will follow regional geographical lines of division. In the case of many individual countries, such as Uruguay, Colombia, Peru, Bolivia, Puerto Rico, the Dominican Republic, Jamaica, Cuba and Honduras, the arrival of Mennonites predates 1959. For organizational reasons, we will tell the story of these Mennonite communities within the historical framework of the two decades from 1959-1979.

The geo-political dynamic shaping this historical period is the Cold War, which emerged immediately following World War II. The East/West division, physically present in Europe, moved into the Western Hemisphere in 1959 when Fidel Castro overthrew Fulgencio Batista's dictatorship in Cuba. Castro's subsequent political and economic alliance with the Soviet Union set the stage for confrontation with the United States. The 1960s saw the emergence of "liberationist" political parties and revolutionary and guerilla movements in Latin America. The Liberal/Conservative politics that had dominated Latin American republics since nineteenth century independence were now complicated by the threat of socialist revolutions from within, overtures to revolutionary parties from the Soviet Bloc, and United States resolve to keep Latin America free from Soviet influence.

In this tense situation, the United States helped organize an attempted invasion of Cuba (the "Bay of Pigs") and after a tense stand-off with the Soviet Union over missile bases in Cuba, enforced an economic embargo of the island. The U.S. also systematically backed military regimes in Latin American countries, and occasionally contributed to their establishment, as in Guatemala and Chile, "maintaining order" in the region and resisting revolution from the left. The occasional armed conflicts that previously had taken place between Liberal and Conservative forces in Latin America now gave way to guerilla movements and systematic repression by military dictatorships (funded and supported by the United States) against what were perceived to be "revolutionary" movements – oftentimes simply efforts by workers and peasants to organize better working conditions or fairer distribution of land. Although particulars varied from country to country, the worst of the military regimes that ruled Latin American countries in the 1960s and 70s suspended or rigged elections, and terrorized their political opponents with para-military death squads, the assassination of prominent religious and political leaders and the "disappearance" of thousands of people. The revolutionary movements were not free from acts of violence and terror, although the proportion of atrocities was strongly weighted on the side of the military regimes. The narratives that follow will briefly note national distinctives in this tense regional climate.

Paralleling the dramatic political shifts that occurred in this period, the Roman Catholic church underwent its own revolutionary changes under Pope John XXIII (1958-1963) – changes that, in Latin America, put the Roman Catholic church on a collision course with the emerging right-wing military dictatorships. The Second Vatican Council (1962-1965) brought drastic changes to Roman Catholicism world wide. The militant Catholic triumphalism of the past gave way to a public recognition of the right of all people to religious freedom, the encouragement and pursuit of ecumenism within Christianity, and the toleration of non-Christian religions. Changes in worship were also revolutionary, with the abandonment of the Latin liturgy and the promotion of vernacular Bible translations and lay Bible study. "The Church" was defined at the Council as "the people of God," rather than in clerical terms, and lay movements of all kinds were encouraged.

The results of the Second Vatican Council for the Roman Catholic church in Latin America were particularly dramatic, given its colonial history and its traditionally conservative political stance. Latin American bishops met together regularly at the Council in Rome. They came to recognize that they shared a unique Latin American reality that demanded their united attention and were encouraged by the Council's emphasis on the social responsibility of all Christians. In particular, Pope Paul VI's encyclical, *Populorum Progressio*, noted that the poverty of the masses was the result of injustice that should be overturned. The second general conference of Latin American bishops (CELAM) that met in Medellín, Colombia in 1968 passed resolutions that called unjust social and economic structures "sin," defined God as a "God of justice" and called Roman Catholics to embrace a Christian love leading to social justice, here and now. The bishops pledged to help build a more just society by supporting families, cooperatives and other organizations of the poorer masses. In response to the conservative call for "law and order" being sounded by military regimes fearful of Communist takeover, the Medellín resolutions rejected a definition of "peace" as an "absence of violence," arguing instead that "Peace is a work of justice." The fundamental violence to be addressed, the bishops asserted, is the structural violence that maintains people in poverty.

Before long, the Roman Catholic church was "taking the side of the poor," with clergy helping organize rural cooperatives, urban unions, leading lay Bible studies and working with the poor to improve their living conditions, in the name of Christ. In the Cold War rhetoric of the time, the Roman Catholic church was suspected of supporting leftist revolution. Many socially-committed clergy and laity became victims of the political violence of the right.

In this radically new political and religious situation, Latin American Protestantism was pulled in different directions. Progressive Roman Catholics were now open to ecumenical dialogue and collaboration – a confusing development in light of the unrelenting hostility of previous decades. Roman Catholics began distributing vernacular Bibles and leading lay Bible studies, previously the exclusive domain of Protestants. A few Protestant leaders supported an engaged Christian social activism, but the most far-reaching Protestant expressions in the region were pentecostal and charismatic, emphasizing spiritual salvation and eternal life, not changes to society. Some governments encouraged Protestant proselytizing as the properly "apolitical" Christian response.

As we will see below, the Mennonite and Brethren in Christ churches, who entered Latin America as Protestant denominations, were caught in the middle of these conflicting currents, and responded in different ways to the regional and national dynamics faced in these decades. What did it mean to be an Anabaptist-descended Christian in the turmoil of the 1960s and 70s in Latin America?

Southern Cone

The Southern Cone

Mennonite Settlement and Missions in Uruguay: (1926-1958)

The cycles of nomadic and planting cultures[1] that populated the territory of the "eastern band" (today Uruguay) date back ten thousand years.[2] The Guaraníes and the TupGuaranies eventually dominated the region. In 1516, the Spaniard Juan Días de Solís arrived at Río de la Plata (La Plata river) only to be killed by the group of Guaraní who occasionally settled on the coast. Evangelization by the Catholic church in Uruguay was a slow process, since this was a region that possessed no precious metals, goods, or a large indigenous population. The eastern band was the last area to be colonized, but just as in the rest of the continent, the Catholic church became the protagonist of religious, civil and political life through its Catholic hierarchies.[3]

The laws established after independence, at the beginning of the nineteenth century, stimulated the immigration of European colonists and facilitated the arrival of Protestants to the southern cone. Between 1867 and 1874 approximately 150,000 Europeans migrated to Uruguay. The process of secularization and the separation of church and state[4] culminated in a new constitution in 1917, and permitted the expansion of Protestantism in Uruguay.[5] From an economic point of view, the Second World War was favorable to Uruguay, for it could export products such as meat, wool, and wheat at very good prices in the international market.[6] Along with an increased presence of missionaries from North America, groups of Protestant immigrants continued to arrive from Europe, because of the Second World War. The first Mennonites to come to Uruguay were part of this stream.

Although the Mennonite missionaries in Argentina had explored expanding their work to Uruguay as early as 1946, and had even proposed concrete steps in that direction,[7] the first Mennonites to live in Uruguay arrived in 1948, and came as refugees from West Prussia and Poland.[8] Their traditional Anabaptist values had been challenged by Nazi ideology, and with the beginning of the Second World War the congregations that were located in the free city of Danzig were joined to the German *Reich*. With the onset of war, the majority of Mennonites in Poland emigrated towards Germany and settled in Warthegau, Germany. The Mennonites of Lemberg, Danzig and East Prussia, were forced to flee later, as the German armies were being defeated in 1945. These latter Mennonites fled in great caravans in the cold winter of 1945, along with some 12 million other Germans from the east.

Poem by Ernst Regehr:
"Farewell to Rosenort, 1945."

Surrounded by cold, by our miserable luck,
death came into our midst.
It joined us, rode into the caravan,
and took our loved ones from us.
The elderly died as well as the children,
We buried them quickly at the edge of the road.
Grenades and bombs exploded loudly,
I cannot believe that God wishes this to be.
We were not able to mourn any one of them,
We had to continue on without pause.
The road, interminable, loaded with pain,
Interminable the sorrow that resounded in our hearts.
We walk by faith, without understanding what is before us,
Teach us to say with real conviction,
not just with our lips, but in our hearts:
"May your will be done" – and not mine,
so that in this way my heart might be stilled.
And even though my paths are rough and full of thorns,
I know that you will guide me to the best end.
And although I still cannot understand
why I had to be separated from my homeland,
"May your will be done," Lord, do not leave me helpless,
and do not let it happen that when I die, I be displaced
without a heavenly home.

The Mennonite Central Committee worked to locate places where Mennonite refugees could settle permanently, and Uruguay was one possible prospect. Pastor Nelson Litwiller managed to convince the Uruguayan Ministry of the Interior to accept these Mennonite refugees from Europe.[9] When the steamship "Volendam" left Bremerhaven, Germany, it carried 751 Mennonite refugees from Danzig, and East and West Prussia as well as from Kazun and Wymischle, Varsovia and Galicia.

During the sea voyage, in October, 1948, a small group of Mennonite Brethren from Wymischle and Kazun, from the province of Varsovia, Poland, met and decided to form a congregation. With the agreement they signed on board ship they formed the first MB congregation in Uruguay, and soon after settling in the country, they joined the South American MB conference.[10] Other Mennonite refugee groups who came later had small numbers of MBs, such that by the end of the 1960s there were around 80 Mennonite Brethren church members in Uruguay.[11]

When the Vollendam reached the shores of Montevideo, the refugees were received by pastor Carlos Gattinoni and a beautiful choir from the Methodist church. Many of the Mennonite young women soon went to work as domestics in private homes. The first land which the refugees managed to obtain was called "El Ombú"[12] and was located 295 kilometers north-east of Montevideo. It was a ranch of approximately 1,100 hectares in the department of Río Negro. With the help of MCC, the ranch was bought and paid for in April, 1950. The

The Volendam

colonists cultivated corn, wheat, and grains for oil such as linseed, sunflower, and peanuts. They also raised milk cows, horses, chickens and pigs. In 1951, 80 families and 12 single people lived in El Ombú, of which 40 worked in Montevideo. In January of 1952 a primary school was founded on the colony.

In October 1951, 430 more Mennonite refugees arrived from Danzig, Poland, and Russia. With the help of MCC a ranch known as "Brabancia" was purchased located 70 kilometers from El Ombú, or 360 kilometers north-east of Montevideo. This farm was given the name of Gartental. The settlers organized themselves as an agricultural cooperative and cultivated wheat, barley, oats and sugar beets. In March of 1952 a school was started in the colony with the first church congregation founded in 1953.

The third colony founded by Mennonites was called Delta, located at kilometer 93 in the direction of Colonia. This colony was founded because of the lack of space for Mennonite families at El Ombú. With the economic help of Prussian Mennonites in Kansas, U.S.A., the property was bought in February, 1955 and an agricultural cooperative was organized. The local school began functioning in 1957, and in 1956, a congregation of 97 members was formally organized under the name "Mennonite Congregation of Delta."

The Delta pastoral team. Front row, left to right: preachers Otto Jochem, Helmut Quiring, Heinrich Fröse. Second row (l-r): preachers Waldemar Driedger, Ernst Regehr, Elder Klaus Dück, deacons Willi Jochem and Arthur Quiring, preacher Horst Dück.

The city of Montevideo also became a center for many of these Mennonite immigrants, since they received better salaries there than in other provinces. In 1953 approximately 215 persons lived in Montevideo in rented homes. For this reason MCC rented a building which functioned as a free hostel for Mennonites who came to the city to do necessary paper work or look for work. On Sunday evenings the young people would get together to sing hymns, see movies, or just chat. Eventually a large farm of 250 hectares, known as El Pinar, was rented by Mennonite families for eight years, to be used for meetings of young people and activities of Mennonites from Montevideo.

Another initiative that was born in Montevideo was the Nicolich colony, located 23 kilometers from Montevideo, behind the airport. In 1959, this small colony in the heart of Montevideo had 79 persons who sent their children to the German academy. In October, 1952 a constitutive assembly of the Mennonite Congregation of Montevideo was held in a rented Methodist church. In 1958 this Mennonite congregation was officially registered with the government.

The Mennonite Board of Missions and Charities (MBMC) of Elkhart Indiana initiated work among Spanish-speaking Uruguayans in 1954.[13] The location of La Unión was chosen to begin the work, since there were no Protestant churches in that area of Montevideo.[14] La Unión was an area populated by working families, teachers and small business people. The first public worship service took place in the Martin family home on Christmas, 1955, with 40 neighborhood people in attendance.[15] English classes led to the baptism of Milka Rindzinski in January, 1956, the first Uruguayan to accept baptism.[16] Within two years, ten more members were baptized. In these early years, the *Luz y Verdad* radio programs that originated from Puerto Rico were very useful means of evangelism.

The Protestant churches in Uruguay in the 1950s used mass evangelistic campaigns to promote the Gospel.[17] The Mennonites collaborated with these efforts and also initiated their own tent evangelism campaigns for several years, beginning in 1956, with some success. A small church was begun in Sauce, for example, thanks in part to Mennonite tent campaigns held in 1957. The town of La Paz in the department of Canelones, which had no Protestant presence, was visited several times, culminating in a series of tent campaigns from 1956 to 1958.[18] More than 70 persons made professions of faith, leading to the first baptisms in 1958 and the assignment of a full time pastor to lead the La Paz church a year later. It was a dynamic congregation, with many enthusiastic youth contributing and participating in the life of the church.[19] But there were also less successful ventures. The tent campaigns and professions of faith in the town of Pando did not lead to a permanent church, nor did the evangelistic visits to San Gregorio or Camino Maldonado, although those who came to the Gospel did find other church homes.

In 1953, at the urging of Nelson Litwiller, the MBMC decided to establish a regional Bible school, recognizing that the theological school in Argentina had succeeded in training native leaders and that continued efforts in this direction were needed. Given the 18,000 Mennonites in Latin America, and the geographical and political accessibility of Uruguay, Montevideo was the preferred location. The Evangelical Mennonite Seminary opened in 1956 in the MCC offices in Montevideo, with 19 German-speaking students and 6 Spanish-speaking students.[20] By 1963 the seminary had trained 130 students from 8 countries, the majority from Paraguay, Argentina, Uruguay and Brazil.[21]

As part of its mission, the Mennonite church supported two medical clinics, the first in the Plácido Ellauri neighborhood (popularly known as *cantegril* or "precarious dwellings"), originally run by the

Baptist church. The Mennonite church assumed responsibility for the Policlínica del Cantegril in 1960; it continued to be served by the Baptist doctor Néstor Figari.[22] The clinic offered free medical care to needy people in the surrounding neighborhoods. A second clinic opened in La Paz in 1959, administered by the Mennonite church of La Paz; it was known as *La Esperanza* (Hope). It opened in response to the Asian Flu epidemic of that year. Many persons came to know Jesus Christ and the Mennonite church through the offer of medical assistance.

The political context in Uruguay changed radically in the 1960s and 70s, beginning with the deregulation of the monetary system in 1959 and the acceptance of the Alliance for Progress.[23] A socialist liberation movement appeared in 1966, countered in 1967 with the beginning of a "constitutional dictatorship" under military leadership. An outright military dictatorship came to be imposed which, by the 1970s, routinely utilized arbitrary arrests, torture and the "disappearance" of dissidents. This regime remained in place until 1981.[24]

The Roman Catholic church underwent dramatic changes at the same time that military repression was emerging.[25] The renewal impulses of the Second Vatican council and the liberationist emphases of the conference of Latin American bishops in Medellín (1968) led to a pastoral emphasis on the poor, actions of solidarity with workers and peasants, and prophetic condemnation of human rights violations.[26] In 1962 the ecumenical movement "Church and Society in Latin America" (Iglesia y Sociedad en América Latina – ISAL) located its headquarters in Uruguay. ISAL was strongly critical of U. S. colonialism and supported liberation movements.[27]

Ecumenical religious life in Uruguay in the time of dictatorship ran in two divergent streams. On the one hand there were those who sympathized with ISAL, who tended towards socialism and criticized the Uruguayan dictatorship. This pro-human-rights movement gained strength in ecumenical circles in the 1970s, but some clerics, Protestant and Catholic, who leaned in this direction were arrested, tortured and even killed.[28] On the other hand, beginning in 1968 there was a significant upsurge of charismatic-pentecostalism, especially through the preaching of the Argentine Juan Carlos Ortíz and the spread of his ideas through his book "Disciple."[29] Ortíz emphasized speaking in tongues, the challenge of being a community of disciples of Christ, and the palpable love that should identify such a community. In the same way that human rights issues joined certain Roman Catholic sectors with some Protestants, so also the charismatic experience broke denominational lines.

The Mennonite colonists who came to Uruguay following World War II remained largely untouched by the political and religious upheavals of the 1960s and 70s. Their churches, which numbered around 750 members by 1960, continued to grow steadily from within, but the most significant changes were economic. The rural colonies of El Ombú, Gartental and Delta organized a cooperative in 1960 known as UCAL, and soon afterwards formed a dairy cooperative known as CLALDY. New buildings for the cooperative were constructed in Young in 1966, and with the help of loans from MEDA (Mennonite Economic Development Associates) for modern equipment, this cooperative was producing 2,000 liters of milk daily by 1968.[30] Financial aid from the German government helped finance further investment in the dairy cooperative in the early 1970s, and also helped finance the construction of schools in Gartental (1957), Delta (1958) and El Ombú (1963), which continued instruction in German for the children of the colonists.[31] By the 1960s, instruction in Spanish had begun in these schools.[32] Delta colony undertook mission work, establishing the Iglesia Menonita Rincón de Cufré, five kilometers from the colony. Language remained

The school (foreground) and church in Gartental

a problem in reaching native Uruguayans, but students from the seminary in Montevideo were able to help.[33]

At the end of the 1950s, the 200 Mennonite colonists who lived in Montevideo worshipped in seven different locations in the city, but met for instruction classes and baptisms at the MCC building.[34] In 1968 a very active women's organization formed, and the Montevideo congregation also supported the work of the Evangelism Board from its beginnings in 1960. The Mennonite colonists also made efforts to fraternize with the Spanish-speaking Mennonite churches of Uruguay, celebrating joint worship services in the 1970s and helping with a variety of charitable works.[35]

A favorite song of the youth of El Sauce church

March on, oh youth:
Never lose sight of Jesus Christ!
Struggle for the good:
This is the Christian's by-word in prayer.
Trust in the Lord
For victory. You will sing a new song.
March on, oh youth
Following the footsteps of the Savior.

The Mennonite Brethren of Uruguay numbered 160 members in 1960, which declined with the economic difficulties of the decade. Thanks to the missionary efforts of Jakob P. Neufelds of Canada, who took over the mission home in Montevideo, by 1979 there were 5 MB churches in the country, with 176 members.[36] Translation from German to Spanish remained a problem that was gradually overcome. In 1971 Amalia and Walter Presa became the first national pastors in Peñarol, Montevideo.[37] By 1975 the language most used in MB congregations was Spanish. In 1978 a Bible School was established to train church leaders.

The Spanish-speaking churches founded by the Mennonite Board of Missions (U.S.), which organized as the Conference of Evangelical Mennonite Churches of Uruguay (CIEMU), experienced modest growth and some exceptional difficulties in the 1960s and 70s. The small church of La Unión closed its doors in 1963, with members joining the congregation of La Floresta, that was being established on the grounds of the Seminary. The Mennonite church of El Sauce was also small, with only 11 members in 1964; nevertheless in that same year it established a clinic to serve the community which continued to function throughout the 1970s, serving around 10 people per day. By the end of 1967 the El Sauce church had 40 members.[38] The church continued to support Bible studies and other evangelistic efforts,[39] extending work into Villa Juárez and Santa Rosa.[40] The congregation also collaborated with the Catholic church in helping the victims of floods in the town of Fray Marcos in April, 1970.[41]

The congregation of La Paz received pastoral leadership from several seminary students and pastors. In 1967 the church had a membership of 35 persons[42] rising to 49 members in 1970. In 1959, a community clinic had been established, served by Dr. Néstor Figari, who also served the clinic at Timbúes.[43] It was still functioning in the 1970s, open one day a week. After some difficult years, new era seemed to begin in the mid-1970s with the completion of a new church building and more pastoral changes.[44] The church began a remarkable ministry when it bought a small farm four kilometers from La Paz. Under the leadership of pastor Álvaro Fernández, the farm developed into a home for poor and needy children.[45] By 1977, twenty-five needy children were being given food, clothing and care, and of these, eleven lived at the farm full time. The women of the church made and mended clothing for the children. In 1977, Álvaro Fernández resigned his pastoral post to work full-time with the children,[46] but the church continued on with a strong youth group and outreach activities.[47]

The Mennonite church in Timbúes, located in a poor neighborhood of the city, continued to support a clinic, but grew slowly. In 1968 the church had 22 members, although in that same year more than 40 youth began attending. The church's activities in the 1960s concentrated on the work of the clinic, work with youth, and work with the poor of the neighborhood.[48] Church membership was diverse, from university students to the illiterate, from people who made a living gathering litter from the streets to middle class professionals. By 1970 around 60 youth were active, from all areas of the city.[49] Many of these young people became increasingly aware of and concerned about the socio-economic situation of the poor.

By 1971, and the return to the Timbúes church of Daniel and Eunice Miller,[50] the congregation (*Comunidad Cristiana de Timbúes*) was working actively with the poorest people of the neighborhood, especially in el cantegril de Plácido Ellauri, guided by Daniel and Eunice's vision of being a non-traditional, Christian community guided by Jesus' teachings in the Sermon of the Mount. The church

Daniel and Eunice Miller

provided food for some families and helped people obtain their identity papers and civic credentials. Since many of the youth of this neighborhood were arrested by the police – often for no reason at all – the church represented them and worked to get them released from jail. Problems arose when some of the youth came for purely political reasons, with no interest in the life of the church as such. Pastor Walter Isnardi hoped that the coming of the Millers would help.[51]

Military repression was particularly intense in large, poor neighborhoods such as Timbúes. Daniel Miller had to appear repeatedly before the police, protesting the arbitrary detention of the youth. The police tried to intimidate him, on one occasion saying "Don't come back again, or there will be consequences. We'll put you in jail too." On one occasion the church was searched by the police and later they searched the Miller household and arrested Daniel Miller. While in prison he suffered forced lengthy periods of having to stand with his arms outstretched, and he was repeatedly threatened and psycologically tortured while being interrogated, with police demanding to know what he was doing in the Timbúes neighborhood. Finally he was released on April 19, 1973 after more than three days in prison.[52] There would be others who also paid a high price for their faith and solidarity with the youth.

Miguel Brun, "The church and the student revolt" (1968)

Many youth who, for a long time had placed their hopes in conventionally legitimate means, have been frustrated by the growing intractability of social problems. ... The rebellion of youth is not directed simply against this or that government, but rather is opposed to the present conditions of life, the organization and the order that perpetuate the status quo. ... [The youth] dream about creating a new humanity, and they wish to be educated to that end. ... If students feel that the church is part of the degenerate world, they will not wish to listen to the church, and will fight against it as one more appendage of the old society. On the other hand, if the church preaches "a new heaven and a new earth," if the church is capable of dreaming with them and strives to work prophetically to promote a world of truth that is liberating, a world that comes as close as possible to the Kingdom of God, the youth will see the church as the group that best articulates their hopes, and they will love her. ... The church should pay attention to the students as the prophetic voice that calls for a new order. And the students should be able to see the church as the arm of God, reaching out to lead and comfort them.

The church worked to explain that "the difference between a revolutionary and a Christian is that the Christian does not simply react to an intolerable situation, but rather responds to a word of Christ." Consequently, "in the face of the problems of life and in society, Christians work as hard as they can to find solutions." The fundamental conviction was that "the word of Christ makes a difference, and has to make more of a difference still."[53] Nevertheless, the difficulties encountered did curtail programs and membership. In 1972, the church numbered 41 baptized members, of whom 18 were active.[54] In 1975, Daniel and Eunice Miller returned to the U.S. for health reasons.[55] Beginning in 1976 the Timbúes church became embroiled in an unfortunate and divisive struggle over control of a small farm, the "Chacra Emanuel," bought by the church with money donated by the Evangelization Board and the U.S. mission board. The conflict finally was resolved, with considerable outside help, in 1979.[56]

In 1961 the Mennonite Seminary moved to the "La Floresta" neighborhood of Montevideo, which led to the founding of La Floresta church at that location. Seminary staff and some families from the recently-closed church of La Unión made up the core membership. In 1964 the church had 14 members, with a Sunday school participation of 20 persons.[57] Activities of the church ebbed and flowed with the Seminary year, and membership never did expand greatly, in spite of community activities such as English classes, Sunday school, a women's group and a summer vocational school for neighborhood youth. The situation did not improve when the Seminary closed at the end of 1974 and moved to Paraguay. In 1979, leadership was shared by members of the congregation.[58]

A church was not established in the town of Las Piedras in the 1960s, in spite of the presence of some baptized members in the community. However, in the 1970s, youth from the La Paz church began working in Las Piedras again. In 1979, pastor Álvaro Fernández moved the children's home to Las Piedras, where it was named "Hogar de Siquem."[59] In that year, 50 homeless children were given shelter. The children's home was supported by donations from German, Spanish and English churches, as well as by the Evangelization Board of Mennonite churches of Uruguay.[60] In 1979, 45 people from both the Home and the community attended Sunday services in Las Piedras.[61]

Biblical reflections of pastor José Pedro Laluz, El Sauce church

Why do you cry for me? Luke 22:61-62. We are currently on the eve of Holy Week, a time when, in different Christian churches, believers re-live the events of the passion of our Lord. ... There are even some who come to weep at the death of Jesus on Good Friday, as if all had come to an end with the death of Jesus on the cross of Calvary. .... The tears should not be for Jesus, but rather for ourselves: for our sin, our doubting of His love and his message, for our egoism and indifference in the face of the pain of others. We should also cry for those who are oppressed by the "forces of this world," for those who die in misery in the midst of a world of wealth. We should cry! But not for Jesus. Rather, in order that our tears clean our spirits still contaminated with evil.

The town of Villa Joaquín Suárez is located 20 kilometers northeast of Montevideo. In spite of evangelistic efforts and the brief existence of a small church in the 1960s, neither the town nor the church prospered. In 1971, the congregation numbered 7 people, all members of the same family.[62]

The Evangelization Board of the Mennonite Churches of Uruguay was organized in 1960 with the aim of preaching the Gospel to all creatures (Mark 16:15). The Board worked closely with the mission boards in Elkhart, Indiana and Newton, Kansas.[63] In 1963 Milka Rindzinski, a member La Unión church, was named as representative for the Spanish-speaking churches on the Evangelization Board. Not only was she the only woman on the Board, she would exercise her leadership gifts faithfully for many years.[64]

In 1965 the Spanish-speaking Mennonite churches began investigating obtaining legal standing and incorporation, in order to manage property and deal with the government on a variety of issues. At the time, the Seminary was the only organization with such legal standing.[65] In 1970, under the leadership of John Driver, the CIEMU was proposed, organized, and began functioning.[66] Obtaining legal standing for the Conference became more urgent with the closing of the Seminary in Montevideo, but the situation had not yet been resolved by the end of the 1970s.[67]

In their worship services, the Spanish-speaking churches tended to sing short, rhythmic, and happy choruses. One of the first collections of these hymns was by the chorister Israel Colón González, in which 116 choruses were copied on mimeographed sheets.[68] In 1978 a printed song book was prepared for the Mennonite churches of Uruguay.[69]

Julia Campos teaching a seminary class, 1964

The Evangelical Mennonite Theological Seminary (*Seminario Evangélico Menonita Teológico*: SEMT) was legally incorporated and recognized by the government of Uruguay in 1960.[70] By 1968, courses were being offered in a wide variety of subjects, from Christian education, to Bible and music, taught by 14 professors.[71] In 1962 publication began of the *Rincón Teológico* ("Theological Corner"), in mimeographed format, which

connected pastors, pro-
fessors and others inter-
ested in the work of
SEMT. This publication
published reflections
on relevant theological
and pastoral themes,
and published updates
on the activities of pro-
fessors and alumni. It
ceased publication in
its old form with the

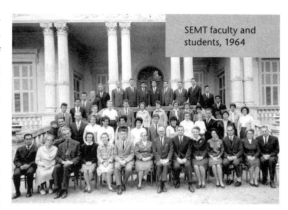

SEMT faculty and students, 1964

closing of the Seminary in 1974, although the Conference worked to
resume publication in 1975.[72]

The work of Seminary teachers Miguel Brun (Pastoral and Dogmatic
Theology), Daniel Miller (Christian Education and New Testament) and
Julia Campos (Christian Education) with youth in the poor neighborhoods of Montevideo created difficulties for them and, by extension,
the Seminary. Miguel Brun was also arrested by the police. According
to Eunice Miller, Miguel Brun's case was far more difficult, for many
youth had confided in this pastor and psychologist. It is probable
that on being arrested, some of these youth mentioned his name as
their spiritual counselor, which may have led to his arrest and torture.
He refused to reveal personal information, even under torture, and it
proved difficult to obtain his release; on being released he immediately
sought exile in France.[73] Julia Campos chose exile in Mexico when it
appeared that her arrest might be imminent, and many youth also
left the country because of being targeted. Such difficulties may have
contributed to the closing of the Seminary in Uruguay.[74] The SEMT
board decided to move operations to Paraguay in 1974.[75]

With the closing of the Seminary in Montevideo, the need for
theological education had to be addressed in new ways. Milka Rindzinski played a central role, coordinating a continuing program of
theological education with CIEMU.[76] Part of the Seminary library was
purchased for this purpose,[77] and intensive worshops were programed
for 1976 and 1977, with courses offered in evening classes.[78]

Women such as Milka Rindzinski and Anelore Fast played a
fundamental role in the pastoral and administrative work of the
Mennonite church in Uruguay. There was an active Women's Group

that involved women from the various congregations. It sponsored youth camps and managed to begin broadcasting the radio program *Corazón a corazón* on Uruguayan radio. Periodic meetings of this group included worship and group study on a variety of themes and topics.[79]

Milka Rindzinski

The first Latin American Mennonite Congress that met in Bogotá, Colombia in 1968 encouraged the publication of material for Latin American churches.[80] Milka Rindzinski was named to represent the Uruguayan church on the publication committee that was formed.[81] She was involved in securing the publication of John H. Yoder's *Textos escogidos de la Reforma Radical* which, along with J. C. Wenger's work on the history and doctrines of the Mennonites, became the most important publication from the Anabaptist tradition in Spanish.[82] The second Latin American Mennonite Congress was held in Montevideo in July, 1972 at the SEMT. It opened with reports on the work of Mennonite churches in each country, and with commentary on the socio-political events in Latin America. Along with presentations by Henry Dueck, Daniel Miller, Daniel Schipani, A. Darino and Armando Hernández, Edward King of Honduras presented a variety of literacy materials.[83]

The radio ministry of JELAM, which prepared the popular program *Luz y Verdad*, was embraced and promoted by the Mennonite church of Uruguay in the 1970s. The Delta Colony supported the broadcasting of JELAM programs on two radio stations.[84] In addition, the programs *Comentando*, produced in Argentina, and *Corazón a corazón* were promoted by Eckhard Regehr and Rubén Lira.[85] Milka Rindzinski represented the Mennonite church of Uruguay at the JELAM conference in Costa Rica in 1972; Beatríz Barrios did the same at the meetings in Bogotá, Colombia in 1976. In 1979, JELAM published one of the first collections of addresses

Poem from the eleventh gathering of Mennonite women, 1968

Lord, keep me in your hands, and guide me;
Be my guide to the end of my days.
I will not take even one step without you.
I will give my life to you until its end.
Protect me in your mercy,
And I will have your peace in joy or in sorrow.
For I wish to walk with you always.
And trust in you with the simplicity of a child.

of all the different Spanish-speaking Mennonite churches in Latin America.

The Mennonite church in Uruguay was ecumenically involved with other Protestant churches in the 1960s and 70s, participating notably in the WCC-sponsored consultation on youth in the church in 1960, and providing leadership in the formation of the Union of Protestant Youth of Uruguay (UJEU) in that same year. This organization, with the participation of approximately 1,700 youth from Lutheran, Waldensian, Methodist, Pentecostal, Salvation Army and Mennonite churches, was a demonstration of ecumenical unity and mutual respect. A program of leader exchanges, publications and congresses was projected.[86] Milka Rindzinski was named secretary of the board of directors; she served from 1960 to 1962, and participated by presenting an addresses at the second UJEU congress in 1962, in which several Mennonite youth took part.[87] Norberto Woelke and Daniel Miller also participated in UJEU commissions in its early and formative years. In 1970, the Uruguayan Mennonite church failed to send a representative to the UJEU meeting,[88] but in 1971, pastor Walter Isnardi, who worked among the youth in the poor neighborhood of Timbúes, was invited to participate in an ecumenical youth gathering in Chile.[89]

Uruguayan Mennonites also collaborated with other Protestants in the Billy Graham crusade which was held in October, 1962,[90] as well as having a representative present at the Billy Graham evangelism

Seminary Building in Montevideo, 1961

congress held in Bogotá.[91] H. James Martin, executive secretary of the Evangelization Board, invited Frank Byler to represent the church at this congress, expressing confidence that he would "as much as possible express our moderate position in the face of extreme voices of ecumenism, propagated by the WCC, on the one hand, and the fundamentalists of organizations (such as Billy Graham's), on the other, both of whom claim to be the official voice of the Latin American Protestant churches."[92]

The beginnings of the Mennonite presence in Uruguay encompass both the establishment of Mennonite colonies of German-speaking refugees, and mission efforts among Spanish-speaking Uruguayans by North American Mennonite mission boards. By the 1960s and 70s, two pastoral and theological directions become visible in the Spanish-speaking Uruguayan Mennonite churches. Daniel Miller represented the ecumenical wing of the church, concerned about the youth and the social issues of a country in the grip of a military dictatorship. B. Frank Byler represented the sector of the church that was influenced by the ecumenical charismatic movement that emerged in Uruguay following the leading of the Argentine preacher Juan Carlos Ortíz.

Beatríz Barrios

Byler would appeal to the pouring out the Holy Spirit at Pentecost (Acts 2: 32-33) as the fundamental experience of evangelization. Under the influence of Juan Carlos Ortíz,[93] the charismatic experience of the Holy Spirit impacted other persons in the CIEMU at the end of the 1970s and early 1980, such as the pastor Beatríz Barrios[94] and the missionary James Martin.[95] On the side of the Mennonite colonies, a slow but steady integration into Uruguayan society can be noted, with fluency in Spanish becoming more and more common, as well as increasing collaboration with Spanish-speaking churches outside the circle of the colonies.

CHAPTER VI

Mennonite Churches in Argentina: (1959-1979)

Political life in Argentina in the 1960s and 1970s was marked by political authoritarianism and military dictatorship. The military coup of 1966 foreshadowed the future, with its repression of political dissent and debate. By 1969 a leftist guerilla movement had become active, mobilizing the radical political left. There was a brief return to electoral politics and Peronist rule, from 1973 to 1976, but the military coup of 1976 proved decisive. By the end of that year there were an estimated 17,000 political prisoners, 650 documented political assassinations, and a very long list of people tortured and "disappeared."[1]

By 1962 the Roman Catholic church in Argentina was beginning to move in the opposite direction, towards ecumenism, social justice, structural change and liberation, in response to reforming currents spreading from the Second Vatican Council. In spite of the significant emergence and work of Catholic organization of students and workers, and the impressive number of bishops and priests that supported fundamental reform, the conservative wing in the church slowly regained power.[2] Progressive Catholic currents were neutralized by political repression and ecclesial opposition and censure. After 1976, the list of martyrs grew long: Fr. Vernazza,[3] Mons. Angelli, bishop of Rioja, the priests Gabriel Longville, Carlos Días Murias, Alfredo Kelly, Duffau, Leaden, Sor Alice Domon and Leonia Duquet, Francisco Suárez, the catechist Mónica Mignone, the Protestant teacher Mauricio López[4] and many others who had taken up the teachings of Vatican II and Medellín.[5]

The Argentine Evangelical Mennonite Church (IEMA) extended its work in Buenos Aires in the 1960s and also established mission work in the province of Río Negro in Patagonia. The work in Buenos Aires expanded with the coming of Mario and Barbara Snyder as missionaries in 1960. They settled in Villa Adelina and began having meetings in their home, including showing films for interested persons.[6] In 1961 the evangelist R. Ciri held evangelistic meetings, in which members collaborated in various ways. By 1962 a locale was rented and the church grew with several baptisms. In 1964 Néstor Comas was commissioned pastor of the Mennonite church of Villa Adelina, a post he would hold until the end of the 1980s. In 1967 a church building was completed, and in 1969 the church had 40 baptized members.[7]

Mario and Barbara Snyder

A new Mennonite church was founded north of Buenos Aires at a place called Kilómetro 30. It began in 1964 with worship services held in the home of Boris Janzen. Alicia Neufeld, a member of the German-speaking Mennonite colony of Boulogne, worked in this emerging congregation from 1961 until her death in 1967, supporting it with pastoral work.[8] In 1967 a church was built for the congregation, at which time the church numbered 6 baptized members, with seven new members added in the following two years.[9] The plan had been to have Mario and Barbara Snyder assume leadership of this church on their return from a furlough in the U.S. in 1965, but Barbara's sudden death in that year delayed Mario's return.[10]

The IEMA also grew with the addition of two established churches that joined the Mennonite conference in 1973. The first to join was the Iglesia Jesucristo Rey, located in Buenos Aires and pastored by Rogelio Perugorría who studied in the Mennonite Bible School in Bragado. It was an independent church that supported its full-time pastor. The second was the Iglesia Nazarena Apostólica, also in Buenos Aires, pastored by Roberto Luis Romero and his wife. This church was also financially independent and was building its own place of worship.[11] Not all churches survived long-term, and these two eventually ceased to exist. The Buenos Aires churches would receive substantial leadership from Mario Snyder, as will be seen below.

Extending the presence of Mennonite churches into Patagonia was contemplated already in 1959 and proposed by pastor Ernesto Suárez Vilela.[12] An exploratory trip in 1963 led eventually to the city of Choele Choel being chosen as a good place to begin establishing a church, located as it was in the center of an agricultural area on the Río Negro river.[13] The Sieber family moved there in 1969 and began public worship services in November of that same year. In 1971, Diana and Rafael Stábile were chosen to begin working alongside the Siebers in Choele Choel.[14] When the Siebers returned to the U.S. in 1974 for a short furlough, there were 17 families relating to the church.[15] That same year the annual convention of the IEMA was held in Choele Choel for the first time.[16] More than half of the delegates were under twenty-five years of age, and a renewed communal and missionary interest was evident. Abat de Comas thanked the Lord for "the blessing of renewed children and the presence of young people interested in the direction of the church."[17] Among the projects projected for the following year was extending the work to neighboring towns such as General Conesa, Valcheta and later, Viedma. The educational project continued to take shape, with a projected extension of helping primary students with learning disabilities, adult education, a home for youth, and help for persons in transition who were seeking better economic situations. These changes were to proceed at a prudent pace.[18]

The assembly in 1971 was significant for setting a new organizational direction for the Argentine Mennonite church. It was decided to abolish the office of bishop, whose pastoral functions would be assumed by secretaries of different national zones, and a new confession of faith was approved.[19] At the 1973 assembly it was decided to coordinate the work of the church by organizing into zones within the five provinces in which there were Mennonite churches.[20] The secretaries responsible for each zone were to help their churches by offering courses and guidance in matters of stewardship, evangelism, worship, music, peace, and the training of leaders.[21]

Amos, former bishop of IEMA, and Edna Swartzentruber, retired in 1964 after 40 years of mission service

The Argentine Mennonite church had grown: in 1974 the IEMA counted 1,136 baptized members in 31 different churches.[22] Beyond its work at the regional level, the national organization continued working through national committees dealing with youth, steward-

ship, evangelism, Christian education, Peace and Service, and the
Mennonite women's organization.

The youth were especially involved in church affairs in the 1970s.
In a series of meetings, youth leaders from the churches asked that
more time be given to work with youth, and furthermore, that pastors give more serious attention to the youth and their ideas.[23] At the
annual assembly in 1973, a group of youth leaders and delegates challenged the directors of IEMA for ignoring their request for changes
in the persons responsible for organizing youth retreats. In response,
the acting organizers resigned and were replaced by Mario O. Snyder,
J. Delbert Erb and Erhard Enns, to the satisfaction of the youth representatives.[24] The stewardship committee of the IEMA focused on
preparing instruction material for the churches in the form of printed
study lessons and offers of small group retreats and counseling.[25]

By the 1970s the energetic evangelistic efforts seen in the early
1960s had faded, and there were efforts to address the problem. Was
the decline in enthusiasm due to
a lack of confidence in antiquated
methods of evangelism?[26] At the
annual meeting in 1971, the role
of missionaries also came up for
discussion. Some thought that it
would be best if the missionaries
would focus on education, music,
and leadership formation. Others
were of the opinion that missionaries, by definition, should dedicate
themselves to missions, and that it

The Mennonite Church in Bragado

was a waste of resources to pay missionaries to pastor already-estab-
lished churches. On the basis of this discussion, the IEMA annual
assembly of 1971 resolved to a) communicate to the churches in the
north that in the future, missionaries should no longer be sent as
pastors of local congregations, b) but that this question should not yet
be considered closed. c) That missionaries in the future should always
collaborate with neighboring congregations, and d) that the work of
leaders should be planned and coordinated with the Seminary.[27]

At the following annual assembly in 1972, pastor Agustín Darino
reported that matters had not improved, and that the churches were
not evangelizing with methods old or new. The matter needed con-

tinuing attention and forums for discussion dealing with the questions: a) Is evangelization relevant today, and why? b) How should it be carried out? c) What should be the content of the message? d) How important is the state of the congregation in carrying out successful evangelism? It was reported that Ricardo Perugorría was investigating how to carry out evangelism in Buenos Aires, and that congregations would receive a report in due course.[28] These concerns were important in leading the IEMA to begin working in Río Negro province. The involvement of several Mennonite leaders in the charismatic movement would soon give renewed energy to evangelization in the Argentine Mennonite church.

The committee for Christian Education was under the leadership of pastor Mario O. Snyder in 1972 and 1973. A national survey of leaders and pastors made it clear that two areas that needed urgent attention were the preparation and education of leaders, and vocational orientation for youth. The directors of IEMA decided to name "secretaries of Christian education" for the various regions.[29] This arrangement led to the teaching of a variety of courses in the regions, such as "Getting to know the Bible" (11 lessons), "The Theology of the Old Testament" (22 lessons), "Pastoring adolescents" (weekend retreats with youth leaders), plus leadership training workshops, classes on baptism, the Lord's Supper, the biblical bases of nonviolence, and church renewal.

The committee in charge of peace issues and service was involved in the early 1970s in the practicalities of facilitating Argentine youth to serve with MCC in Bolivia and supporting teaching on nonviolence and service within the churches. Agustín Darino, the head of this committee, was particularly active in several congresses held in the southern cone on the themes of peace and justice, such as the MCC-supported conference on peace and nonviolence, held in Medellín, Colombia in 1974.[30] In 1973 two Mennonite youth, Ricardo Perugorria and Dionisio Byler, protested the government's policy of obligatory military service and refused to render military service. They were supported by the Mennonite church in their stand.[31]

Throughout the 1960s and 1970s the Mennonite Women's Association (*La Cadena de Mujeres Menonitas*) was led by dynamic and changing leaders. The organization strongly encouraged and participated in the missionary and evangelistic work of the IEMA.[32]

Coloring these developments was a new economic reality. In October 1970, the secretary of the Board of Mission in the U.S. announced that financial support by the mission for pastoral work would be reduced to zero over a period of five years, ending in the fiscal year 1974-75.[33] One of the problems faced by the IEMA was the fact that several congregations, such as the ones in América, Ramos Mejía, Floresta, Cosquín and Pehuajó, were without pastors. It was suggested that one way to resolve the "leadership crisis" would be to appeal

Nelson Litwiller (r) introduces Albano Luayza, who will bring the morning message, Pehaujó, 1969

to members of congregations to use their spiritual gifts in pastoral leadership.[34] Churches such as la Mechita and América were not in favor of each church paying pastors directly. Bragado, Morón, Floresta, Ramos Mejía and Córdoba, on the other hand, thought each church should reach its own agreement with its pastor concerning salary. Trenque Lauquen, Tres Lomas and Pehuajó were of the view that a common fund should continue, which could be accessed to help churches who were having difficulty paying their pastors. These diverse opinions led to the approval by the assembly of the following resolution: "That the Board of Directors (of IEMA) continue studying the problem, and that the system of a common fund be continued, with no other system implemented for now, except to the extent that different congregations address the problem in a natural evolution of the case."[35]

The financial crisis continued to be the focus of the 1973 assembly, since the reduction of funds from the U.S. had affected the common fund, which received contributions also from all churches, including those not able to pay a pastor.[36] In view of the impending end of contributions from the north, the board of directors asked certain churches (América, Arrecifes, Carlos Casares, Cosquín, La Plata, Morón General Villegas, Trenque Lauquen, Tres Lomas and Salto) to make arrangements with their leaders and pastors, progressively assuming their full support.[37] The deficit of $12,283.00 that had accumulated as of December, 1974 would be covered by the final payment from the Mission Board. In February, 1975 it was agreed to reduce support to pastors Eduardo Alvarez, Rodolfo Arregui, Lucio Casas, Amer Oyanguren and José R. Palacios. The churches in which they worked would have to take on the financial responsibility for their pastors.[38]

The movement of the Spirit in Argentina had different sources. On the one hand there was the preaching and speaking in tongues in the ministry of the Pentecostal pastor Juan Carlos Ortíz at the end of the 1960s, which shook up Protestantism in Argentina.[39] On the other hand, the charismatic movement which began to revive the Argentine churches of the Free Brothers (*Hermanos Libres*), such in the case of pastors Alberto Darling and Jorge Himitian, and the case of the Baptist pastor Alberto Motessi in the 1970s, had a direct influence also in Mennonite churches.[40] This influence was evident at the IEMA assembly in 1971, when the recently-appointed pastor Ricardo Perugorría spoke on the topic of "The Church and its Ministries," saying that what was needed were "ministers called and filled by the Holy Spirit."[41] An important leader of the Mennonite church in Argentina, Nelson Litwiller, was influenced by the charismatic renewal at the University of Notre Dame in 1972.[42] At the Mennonite convention of 1973 the theme was "The Era of the Holy Spirit," with principal presentations by Augusto Ericcson, a pastor from the Argentine charismatic renewal.[43] In the Morón and Ituzaingó churches, pastor Mario Snyder and the young Oscar Luis Figueron experienced spiritual renewal themselves, and joined the movement with pastors such as Juan Labbozzetta and Ivan Baker.[44]

> **Nelson Litwiller's sermon to the IEMA convention in 1976**
>
> It is my prayer that the unity of the Holy Spirit and the love in Christ prevail in this congress... Therefore I would like to emphasize that ... I recognize and accept and affirm each brother in the spiritual experience he might have had. I believe that the experience in Christ which each one has had is a valid experience ... and is the result of the work of the Holy Spirit in our respective lives.

A formative experience took place at the IEMA assembly, held at Choele Choel in 1974, when a sermon by Dionisio Byler was interrupted by a power outage caused by a frightening fire close to the locale. The events that followed were dramatic: "In this

Mario and Egda (Schipani) Snyder and children, wedding day, 1967

way several of those present humbled themselves before the Lord and received liberation and the filling of the Holy Spirit. The worship service continued in a great spirit of adoration and praise, until around one in the morning. At the conclusion of the service, we were told that the wind had shifted, preventing the spread of the fire which had consumed the entire sawmill. Glory to God."[45] In 1974, in meetings with church workers led by B. Frank Byler and Daniel Schipani, the theme was "The Holiness of the Church."[46]

The impact of this charismatic renewal movement was strongly-felt in 1977 in the Morón church pastored by Mario O. Snyder.[47] This caused so much tension with some of the national leadership that there was a danger that the church would leave the Conference.[48] Nevertheless, the church remained within the Conference and was the motive force for a renewal in the IEMA as a whole.[49] This can be seen in the sermon preached by pastor Raúl García, president of the IEMA, at the annual assembly of 1978. On that occasion he summarized the events of the past four years, highlighting the new renewal currents. He stated,

> the Lord with his Spirit blows where He wills, as He wills, and when He wills. All that is left for us to know is how to adjust the sails of our vessels properly so that we don't block the blowing of the wind; nor should we ourselves try to blow more than the wind does, negating the free passage of the wind of God... May the Lord find us in the right place, open to the wind of the Spirit.[50]

Raúl and Anita (Swartzentruber) Garcia and family

As noted in the previous chapter, the Evangelical Mennonite Theological Seminary (SEMT) in Uruguay also served Argentine pastors of the IEMA. In the 1960s and 1970s, pastor Raúl García was IEMA's representative to the Seminary in Montevideo, maintaining the necessary contacts. In 1970 and 1971, in the sabbatical absence of rector Ernst Harder, Raúl García headed the board of the Seminary, while John H. Yoder coordinated the teaching faculty.[51] In 1971 there was the expressed desire to more closely coordinate pastoral educational activities of the IEMA with the resources of the SEMT; there was some hope of opening a school in Río Negro.[52] In 1972 and 1973 the Seminary in Montevideo opened an extension in Buenos Aires which was called the "Evangelical Mennonite Center of Biblical Studies" (*Centro Evangélico Menonita de Estudios Bíblicos*: CEMEB). For 1973 a total of seven courses were planned, offered over two semesters. In the end, however, the lack of students led to the offering of just two courses taught to 9 students by John Driver in the first semester. The question arose as to how viable the program in Buenos Aires was, considering how few students took advantage of the offerings. John Driver concluded that a modest seminary program could be offered semester by semester, and that congregations in the interior could be offered the same materials that had already been taught in the capital. Studies in the churches would establish contacts between pastors and teachers.[53]

In light of the imminent closing of the Seminary in Uruguay, a "pastors' institute" was organized in August, 1973, with John Driver in attendance.[54] The proposal elaborated by this commission, for consideration at the 1974 annual assembly of the IEMA, was that congregational theological education should be under the direction of each pastor and the elders of local churches. They were to instruct by the light of the Word and the life of the Spirit, offering courses on weekends, fostering a communal life between teachers and students, centered in Christ and His Word, and an active ministry of the power of the Spirit and the Spirit's gifts. Courses were planned for Buenos Aires, to the west of the province of Buenos Aires, and in Córdoba and points further to the west.[55] A few Mennonite pastors continued studying at the Biblical Institute of Buenos Aires.[56]

Albano Luayza, the first Argentine Mennonite pastor, died in August, 1977. Carmen Palomeque wrote the following, remembering him and his work.

I knew Don Albano as a child. His ardent preaching spoke directly to me as a child, and impacted me for the rest of my life. Sentences and situations were indelibly imprinted like permanent guideposts. There was the suggestive invitation "Come here, Nicodemus, I was waiting for you!" There was the vigorous "Here is the boy!" (John 6:9) that he preached when the passing of the years had left its physical marks, but not on his spirit. His message was invested with power and authority: the power of the Spirit gave him strength, and his authority was backed up by a life completely and integrally consecrated to the service of just one cause. ... Together with his incomparable companion, Doña Querubina, he faithfully served not only the Lord, but also his large family and his neighbors. ... His vibrant voice now has been joined to the chorus of the redeemed, while its unforgettable echoes resound among those of us who knew and loved him.

Finally in 1974 the SEMT closed operations in Uruguay and was moved, initially, to Menno Colony in the Chaco of Paraguay. The Mennonite Brethren, who initially wished to participate in a joint project, decided to establish their own seminary in Asunción. In Argentina it was thought that the SEMT should be located in Asunción, and that the CEMEB in Argentina should promote distance education programs by extension. In this context, Frank Byler was invited to return to Argentina to work with biblical Studies by extension, offering practical education and leadership formation courses at the congregational level, as well as offering seminars and conferences.[57] In December 1975 a meeting was held in Paraguay and consensus was reached that the new theological institution that would replace the SEMT would be located in Asunción. Raúl García, as representative of the IEMA, supported the decision and asked for its approval.[58] For its part, in 1977 the IEMA named J. Delbert Erb, Frank Byler and L. Brunk the persons in charge of the CEMEB.[59]

One of the most important contributions of the IEMA to the Mennonite and Protestant churches of Latin America in the 1960s and 70s was the translation and publication of important theological and historical works from English into Spanish. Ernesto Suárez Vilela was

the Mennonite pastor who most distinguished himself in this, working closely with the Protestant Publishing houses *La Aurora* and *Certeza*, which had head offices in Argentina.[60] Along with translations of biblical commentaries, he also translated John Christian Wenger's *Glimpses of Mennonite History and Doctrine* (*Compendio de Historia y Doctrina Menonitas*) and Millard Lind's *Responses to War* (*Respuestas a la Guerra*).[61] After several years of teaching service at the SEMT, he returned to Argentina from Montevideo with his family in 1971,

Ernesto Suárez Vilela

and then lived behind the Floresta church in Buenos Aires.[62]

Ernesto Suárez continued editing the *Discípulo Cristiano* (Christian Disciple), sixty percent of whose costs were covered by the mission boards of the U.S. Plans were made to downsize the publication and to include bulletins from other Latin American churches. Publication of the *Discípulo Cristiano* ceased in 1972, replaced by *Cuadernos Menonitas*, a less expensive publication with a more limited circulation.[63] Under Ernesto Suárez's direction, the first number of *Cuadernos Menonitas* appeared in 1973 in an edition of 1000 copies.[64] In addition

Ernesto Suárez Vilela also published several important books for the Spanish-speaking Mennonite churches,[65] and also contributed to the radio programs *Comentando* and *Luz y Verdad*. Many of his talks were later collected and published in a book called *Reflections of a Latin American Protestant*.[66]

The IEMA maintained a good working relationship with the German-speaking Mennonite colony of Boulogne in Buenos Aires, as demonstrated by the letter from pastor Sieghard Schartner, who personally participated in annual meetings of the IEMA. In that letter he asked for IEMA collaboration in supporting work with children in the neighborhood of Viso.[67] The IEMA also continued contact with the work in the Chaco through the Mennonite missionaries active in the region, who occasionally participated and spoke at annual meetings of the IEMA, sharing information on the growth of the indigenous churches and the progress of the translation of the Bible into the Toba language. In 1977 the annual conference heard details of the sending of Dennis and Connie Byler to the city of Formosa, where they were to investigate the possibility of opening a mission work among Spanish-speaking people of that city, as well as to help with Bible teaching in the indigenous churches.[68]

Toba worship service, Argentine Chaco

The Argentine Mennonite church also collaborated closely with the *Luz y Verdad* radio broadcast, as well as with the Executive Board of Mennonite Broadcasts (JELAM). In 1970 the Mennonite pastor Dan Nüesch produced a radio program for JELAM called *Comentando* (Commenting), a program that provided commentary on social, moral and religious events in the modern world.[69] It was meant to reach a non-believing audience with radio spots aired gratis by radio stations, as culturally-relevant programs. Mennonite Broadcasts used the first 40 programs taped early in 1971 in several Latin American countries, and projected this as a daily feature in the future. They were expected to be used in Argentina as well, along with the *Luz y Verdad* and *Corazón a Corazón* (Heart to Heart) programs.[70]

JELAM was organized in 1972 to administer Mennonite radio programming in Latin America. It became independent from Mennonite Broadcasts, which nevertheless continued providing the bulk of operating capital.[71] Daniel Schipani participated in the organizational meetings for JELAM held in Puerto Rico and Costa Rica. Armando Hernández of Colombia was named president, and moved to Puerto Rico to administer the new organization. The "radio commission" of the IEMA was the Argentine link to JELAM.[72] By 1973 *Comentando*, *De Corazón a Corazón* and *Luz y Verdad* were being broadcast on Argentine radio stations, and tapes of these programs had been sent to Uruguay for broadcasting on a radio station in the interior of that country.[73]

In 1975 the television program *Hay que vivir* (One has to live) was broadcast on channel 9 in Buenos Aires. It was broadcast on a Friday in prime time, and aimed to counter-balance immoral programming with directly biblical teaching. The program, led by Dan Nüesch without JELAM sponsorship, was aired for fourteen consecutive weeks. A lack of available funds led to the discontinuation of this program. Nevertheless, the program also aired in Bahía Blanca, Córdoba and in the interior of the province of Mendoza.[74]

During the 1960s and 70s the IEMA continued as an active member of the Federation of Argentine Protestant churches (*Federación de Iglesias Evangélicas de Argentina*: FIEA), with Mennonite pastors often participating on the board of directors of that organization. Work with the FIEA included collaboration in helping churches affected by flooding in Argentina[75] and continued relationships with organization such as the World Council of Churches, the Protestant Commission of Christian Education (*Comisión Evangélica Latinoamericana de Educación*

Cristiana: CELADEC),[76] the Protestant Latin American Union (*Unidad Evangélica Latinoamericana*: UNELAM)[77] and an ecumenical committee for loans.[78]

An indirect contribution of the Mennonites to inter-confessional education was the naming of Juan T. N. Litwiller, son of the well-known missionary Nelson Litwiller, as rector of the Protestant Superior Institute of Theological Studies (*Instituto Superior Evangélico de Estudios Teológicos*: ISEDET) from 1969 to 1971. Under his direction the seminary initiated new directions, such as encouraging a spirit of community in theological work, team teaching and group work in theological education, offering the first complete post-graduate program in Latin America. Sadly, Juan T. N. Litwiller died unexpectedly in 1971 from medical complications following corrective surgery. He had been in a traffic accident several years earlier.[79]

Baptism in the Toba community of Miraflores, Argentine Chaco

The Mennonite church in Argentina in the 1960s and 70s worked hard to consolidate its member churches and to renew a spirit of evangelism and outreach among its members. There were significant new church-planting efforts that took root in the region of Patagonia and north of Buenos Aires. National leaders were the driving force behind the church in these decades, with missionaries providing valuable support for the educational and evangelistic programs of the church. By the middle of the 1970s, the Argentine Mennonite church had become essentially self-supporting, no longer dependent on the mission board for meeting conference budgets.

The most significant energy for growth came from the charismatic/pentecostal currents that brought challenge and renewal to Argentine churches. These dynamic spiritual movements gave a growing edge to the Argentine Mennonite church, while solid work in publication, education, and broadcasting continued, to the wider benefit of the Spanish-speaking churches in the region. In the midst of the political upheaval that wracked Argentina over these decades, Mennonites predominantly remained the "quiet in the land," tacitly accepting the earlier missionary policy of preaching the Gospel of salvation and helping those in need, but overtly siding with no position that could be labeled "political."

Worship in the Mennonite church, Choele Choel

The Mennonites in Paraguay (1959-1979)

Political life in Paraguay in the 1960s and 1970s was defined by the dictatorship of Alfredo Stroessner, who ruled continuously from 1954 until he was deposed in a coup in 1989. In 1968, after his third fraudulent electoral victory, considerable opposition to his regime began from labor unions, the "agrarian leagues," university students and especially from Roman Catholic seminarians and bishops who, under the influence of Vatican II and Medellín, made common cause with the peasants and students suffering military repression. Some clergy were expelled from the country; others were placed under arrest. It came to such a point that the bishops asked that Catholic Relief Service to suspend aid to the government. Its view was that in addition to creating a begging paternalism, the government was using those very funds for political ends against the people.[1]

In spite of attempts to better relations between the Catholic church and the Stroessner regime, the Catholic church was virtually alone in denouncing its crimes and injustices. In 1975 around 800 peasants were incarcerated and authorities of the Catholic University protested the detention of anthropologist Miguel Chase Sardi. The military responded by searching the Jesuit High School Cristo Rey, supposedly seeking guerillas; it accused the priests of being communists. The Episcopal conference explained in a pastoral letter that conscienticizing and liberating education should not be confused with Marxist doctrine. The letter revealed the levels repression had reached, and protested the use of torture and the use of violence against those who simply opposed the regime, as well as attacks by police against secondary schools and Catholic diocesan seminaries.[2]

Although the new constitution implemented by General Stroessner in 1967 maintained that the official religion of the country was Roman Catholicism, a separate article guaranteed freedom of conscience and the right to profess, teach and spread any religion freely, as long as that religion did not run counter to "good morals and the public order." During Stroessner's rule Protestant churches enjoyed wide freedoms, and attained their highest rates of growth. During the great evangelistic campaign of Luis Palau in 1976, for example, Paraguayan television channel 9 broadcast the entire event free of charge. Rogelio Duarte's analysis is that this opening to Protestantism was, in part, a result of the regime's confrontation with the Catholic church but also was possible because prejudice against Protestants had diminished considerably and Paraguayans generally regarded Protestants with more respect.[3] Historian Rodolfo Plett has noted the new and numerous Protestant groups who came to Paraguay in the 1960s and 70s, and the list is impressive.[4]

Clearing brush for the
Transchaco Highway

The Mennonite colonists in Paraguay also experienced dramatic growth in this time, both in the Chaco colonies and especially in the capital. An event of great significance for the economic development of the Chaco colonies was the completion of the Transchaco highway in 1964. The highway reaches from Asunción and traverses the entire Paraguayan Chaco, past the Mennonite colonies, reaching the border with Bolivia. The project began in 1955 when General Stroessner established a comission for building the highway. An agreement was signed with the U.S. for building the highway in 1956, and MCC was put in charge of the project. Harry Harder directed the project, which was carried out with the help of many Mennonite Voluntary Service youth. When the road reached the Mennonite colonies in October, 1961 it was more than 400 kilometers long. In September 1964 the road had been completed to the Bolivian border.

The Transchaco highway became the principal means of communication and transportation for the colonies, and turned Menno, Fernheim and Neuland colonies into the most productive centers in the Chaco. The development of the Chaco dairy industry would not have been possible without the highway. It led to the Mennonite colonies eventually producing more than 50 percent of all dairy products in Paraguay.[5]

Grading the Transchaco Highway

The Mennonite Brethren of Paraguay continued building in the 1960s and 70s on their beginnings in the colonies and their presence in Asunción, in spite of some emigration of colonists away from Paraguay.[6] The Filadelfia colony experienced a migration of members out of the colony to Brazil, Canada and Germany, beginning in the 1950s – a movement that continued for more than 20 years. Nevertheless, by the end of 1979 the church numbered 1,046 members in seven local churches and had a program in place to prepare pastors and leaders.

The Bible School established by the Mennonite Brethren in Friesland continued functioning until 1969, when it numbered 43 students. It was an important institution for the development of leaders. In the 1970s the Mennonite Brethren decided to begin mission work among the Paraguayans in a small town called Estanislao (Santiní), located about 50 kilometers away from Friesland colony. The first missionaries were Harold Funk and Alfred Klassen; they managed to establish a worshipping community with its own organizational autonomy.

Neuland colony experienced a crisis in the later 1950s, as many members moved away from the colony. The Gnadental church moved to Neu-Halbstadt in 1963 where a new church was built. The completion of the Transchaco highway gave new economic life to the Neuland community, and had the same positive effect on Volendam colony. The sale of soya and wheat improved to the point that the

The agricultural cooperative, Menno colony, 1960s

process of emigration was contained, and the MB church could count on a regular membership. In 1975 the MB church began evangelistic work in the towns near the Volendam colony.

In 1954 Albert Enns came as a missionary to minister to the German-speaking Mennonites in Asunción. There had been individuals and families living in the city since the 1930s, but no church had formed. In 1961 Jakob H. Franz, mission secretary for the Mennonite Brethren of the U.S., came to live in Asunción and helped found the first MB church in 1963. The church was made up of young people who came to the capital to study, professionals, missionaries and business people who came and went.

Dedication of the Mennonite Church of Asunción, 1963

The Mennonite church of Asunción (*La Iglesia Menonita de Asunción* [MG]) is led by a board of directors composed of the president, the pastor of the church, ordained preachers, deacons, the treasurer, the secretary, the youth representative and delegates to the mission and the Seminary (CEMTA). The aim of the church is to "Encourage the knowledge of Scripture, spread the Word of God and the Gospel, as well as communal edification and cooperation in the Kingdom of God."[7] In 1979 the church had 102 baptized members.[8]

In 1975 the MBs and MGs joined efforts in founding the Concordia school in Asunción. Besides teaching the courses required by the government, the school taught Bible classes and gave classes in the German language. Half of the students were not from Mennonite families.

There were many reasons for the formation of the Conference of Mennonite Brethren of Paraguay (*Die Vereinigung der Mennonitischen Brüdergemeinden Paraguays*). MBs had a common interest in leadership training through the Bible School in Fernheim, in the mission to the indigenous people of the Chaco, the leprosy mission in Friesland and mission work in Asunción. The MB conferences in the U.S. and Canada supported the process throughout. In July 1961, at a conference held in Filadelfia, it was decided to form the Conference of Mennonite Brethren of Paraguay. Along with that action, the gathering centered on missions. By 1977 there were 973 baptized members in seven Paraguayan German-speaking MB churches.

One of the major projects carried out by the Mennonite Brethren of Paraguay was the Biblical Institute of Asunción (IBA). Instruction began in 1964 with evening classes. The following year a building was purchased and classes began to be offered under the direction of Hans Wiens. Another important institution founded by the MBs was the primary school *Colegio Alberto Schweitzer* which began functioning in 1966.

The religious practices of Mennonite Brethren changed somewhat in Paraguay. The Mennonite Brethren in Russia would celebrate the Lord's Supper once a month, and they practiced the holy kiss and foot washing as ways of cultivating their spiritual life. In Paraguay, the Lord's Supper and foot washing were celebrated once every two months, and the holy kiss was no longer practiced. The principle of allowing marriage only with another believer was relaxed as well. If persons from the Paraguayan MB community married outside the church, they could continue participating in the faith community in the hope that their partners would come to an experience of faith. The struggle to maintain purity in a community has not been an easy one. Rather than imposing prohibitions, the desire has been to emphasize the importance of giving a good Christian testimony in one's manner of life.

The various indigenous peoples who came to the Mennonite colonies in search of work also came to accept the faith and church structures of the Mennonites. Among those groups were the Ayoreos, who began seeking contact with the non-native population in 1963. It was, however, the Silesian Fathers who organized missions among the Ayoreo in Teniente Martínez and María Auxiliadora, near the Paraguay river. The organization *Misión Nuevas Tribus* sent

Mennonite family in Yalve Sanga, 1963

Roberto Goddard, who lived with the Ayoreo in Cerro León, to found a church in El Faro Moro. In the 1970s many Ayoreos lived and worked in the Mennonite colonies; their missionary center was established in Campo Loro.[9]

Many of the Enlhet (Lengua) tribe who came to Menno colony to work received the Gospel and were baptized in 1956 and 1957. Because of the large migration of the Enlhet to the Mennonite colonies, they moved to a thousand-hectare section of land known as Lhacmotalha (New Life) procured for them by Menno colony. The Enlhet organized their own churches there. In the 1970s, several groups of Mennonites joined to continue work with the Enlhet and later also with the Tobas.[10] From the joint mission effort between Menno colony and the Evangelical Mennonite Conference of Canada came several indigenous churches of Tobas, Enlhet and Sanapaná.[11] The missionary Dietrich Lepp and pastor Nito Acevedo worked for ten years translating the Bible into the Enlhet language, with the help of the International Bible Society. The New Testament was published under the title *Tasic Amyaa*.

In 1963 the Bible school in Yalve Sanga held classes for the first time, with 16 students, and beginning in 1975 a Bible Institute was founded there with the support of 20 local indigenous churches and the following missionary organizations: *Luz a los indígenas* (Light to the Indigenous People), *Conferencia Evangélica Menonita* (Evangelical Mennonite Conference) and the *Comité Mennonita de Acción Evangélica y Social en el Paraguay* (Mennonite Committee for Evangelical and Social Action in Paraguay). In 1978, given the several congrega-

Lengua baptismal class, Loma Plata, Menno Colony, with Eleanor Mathies and Mr. and Mrs Bernhard Toews (1963)

tions in Campo Largo, Yalve Sanga, and the district of Filadelfia, the "Conference of Evangelical Churches of Lengua Brothers" (*Convención de las Iglesias Evangélicas de los Hermanos Lenguas*) was formed.[12]

Mission work also reached the Nivaclé (Chulupí) tribe. The missionary Gerardo Hein, assisted by pastor Siyinjoyech Friesen worked for ten years with the help of the International Bible Society to translate the New Testament to the Nivaclé language. They worked throughout the 1970s, and published the New Testament under the title *Nava Isis Ya`clishay*.[13] In 1972, five Chulupí congregations had been established in the Chaco. They formed the "Conference of Evangelical Chulupí Churches" (*Convención de las Iglesias Evangélicas Chulupí*).[14] According to the information provided by the anthropologist in residence R. Rempel, by 1979 the Enlhet and Nivaclé conferences had a combined 17 indigenous churches in the Chaco, with a membership of 3,500 persons.[15]

Testimony of Pedro Cardizo Vocanal

After I had worked for a time in the Mistol Marcado zone, I moved to Jojiyuc, in the area of Gral Díaz. From there I moved to the Mennonite zone. In Cayin ô Clim, Neuland colony, I met a group of countymen and I settled among them. I immediately began preaching there. At just that time they were suffering a epidemic of measles, and many had gotten sick. We had some meetings, we sang the songs, I taught them about God in heaven, and we prayed for the sick. The following day the children had been healed.

The Lenguas, Tobas and Sanapaná who worked at Menno colony organized to form their own indigenous churches. Also participating in these churches were the Maskoy people of the eastern districts, as well as the local Guaraní Ñandeva people of Fernheim colony and Laguna Negra.[16] The indigenous groups would later unite as the "Conference of Evangelical United Churches" (*Convención de las Iglesias Evangélicas Unidas*).[17]

Economic, social and educational development went hand in hand with evangelization. The Mennonite colonies, together with MCC, the government and the indigenous peoples established institutions that brought about this development. Soon after the first baptism in 1946, the Enlhet had asked the Mennonites for their own land to cultivate. By 1953, 50 families of Yalve Sanga were working their own farms on land given to them by the Mennonites, on properties of half a hectare. This proved to be not enough land for the indigenous families. Therefore in 1960 it was agreed to assign each family a plot of 5 hectares, horses and agricultural machinery, and thus was born the first village of 22 families called Naoc Amyip.[18] This new model of

Lengua farmers attend an agricultural course, Yalve Sanga

agricultural colonization continued, and new villages were established between 1957 and 1960. In 1961, the first Enlhet founded the village of Samaria. Likewise the Enlhet of Menno colony south founded the settlement of Nueva Vida. The indigenous who worked on Menno colony north also requested the opportunity to cultivate their lands in Loma Plata and the Enlhet and Sanapaná who worked in Pozo Amarillo founded Nueva Esperanza.[19]

The Mennonite colonists experienced a difficult moment when they were threatened by an armed uprising of 700 Nivaclé people. In the midst of a great drought and a dispute with the Mennonites over potable water, the Nivaclé demanded their right to be independent and to have their own land to cultivate. They recounted the low salaries and bad treatment they had received from their employers. Under the leadership of Chief Manuel and the supposed promises of the Defense Ministry, at least 500 Nivaclé left the Mennonite colonies and moved west, in search of new lands that would be given to them. Some of them died on the way, and others returned to the Mennonite colonies in very poor physical condition.[20]

There were several responses to this difficult experience. The first was the presence and the work of the Mennonite anthropologists Jakob A. Löwen,[21] Calvin Redekop[22] and Hendrick Hack[23] that attempted to better understand the culture of the Chaco peoples. In the second place, MCC helped implement a colonization plan, aiming to organize the indigenous population living in the area of the Mennonite colonies economically, socially and culturally. This plan finally was approved in 1967. Thus was born the The Indigenous-Mennonite Association of Cooperative Services (*Asociación de Servicios de Cooperación Indígena-Menonita*: ASCIM), whose objective was to "provide development services, so that indigenous families reach an economic level that gives them security against hunger, disease and marginalization."[24]

Another important historical and anthropological contribution was provided by Walter Regehr who, in the face of the controversy generated by the Barbados declaration[25] and the fight for indigenous Chaco peoples by the anthropologist Miguel Chase-Sardi,[26] held to the thesis that the hunter-gatherer communities needed a large land area in the Chaco to exploit its resources and allow them to recover properly.[27] Although it is true that at certain times the indigenous people came to the Mennonite colonies to work for a salary, it is also the case that at the same time, a program was developed through which the indigenous received their own farm lands and were enabled to administer their own agricultural production. By 1980, 8 indigenous colonies had been organized in the central Chaco, covering an area of 69,000 hectares.[28]

Raising livestock was promoted on the indigenous settlements, along with a cooperative, the latter of which failed in the end. ASCIM developed programs such as the "Center for Agricultural Training" (*Centro de Capacitación Agrícola*) and a school in home economics for women. In 1952 a hospital was built in Yalve Sanga and later, clinics were built on different indigenous colonies. ASCIM has also led the fight against tuberculosis and intestinal parasites with a program begun in 1970, and also introduced indigenous schools in collaboration with the Ministry of Education and Culture, with bilingual programs in Spanish and the various indigenous languages. In 1959 the J. F. Estigarribia school of Yalve Sanga was founded with 30 students from Paraguayan families. The director was Abram Klassen. In 1960 two Enlhet students enrolled, and in 1961 two Nivaclé students followed. By 1976 the school numbered 152 students, many of whom were indigenous.

Indigenous agricultural colonies

Name:	Year Founded	Ethnicity
Yalve Sanga I	1955	Enlhet
Yalve Sanga II	1961	Nivaclé
La Esperanza	1962	Enlhet/ Sanapaná
Campo Largo	1963	Lengua
Campo Alegre	1964	Nivaclé
Pozo Amarillo	1966	Enlhet/Toba
Paz del Chaco	1979	Enlhet
Nicha Tôyish	1980	Nivaclé

The new social, economic and public health situation led to great growth of the indigenous population. For example, in 1957 the Enlhet population in the central Chaco was 2,600 persons, and the Nivaclé people numbered 900 persons. By 1978 the combined population of these peoples totaled 12,000 persons.

According to Jacob Löwen, this interesting model of missionary work came to be thanks to the presence of the Mennonite settlements (who incorporated all these functions in their common life), along with the Lengua and Chulupí, which overcame limited traditional missionary objectives (spiritual salvation) and forced the mission to appeal to MCC and other agencies to help them establish what is probably one of the best examples of missionary work, focusing on the complete and integrated human being.[29]

According to Löwen, it appears that the indigenous people were attracted to the Mennonites and their way of life, and wished to immitate them in at least three essential ways: a) They wished to be Christians, building even larger churches than those of the Mennonites, and being very active in choral festivals and other religious activities. b) They wished to establish schools, so that parents and children would receive an adequate education. c) Above all, they wished to have their own farms and all the necessary farm machinery, just like the Mennonites, and to live next to them.[30]

By the end of the 1970s, this model of missionary work continued to present great challenges. For the indigenous people, the challenge was maintaining their culture, their economic base of support, and their dignity as children of God in the Chaco. For the Mennonite colonists, the challenge was how to maintain and move away from their ethnocentrism, recognizing their daily life in the changing context of Paraguay, of following Jesus Christ and achieving more just and loving relationships with the peoples of the great Chaco.[31]

As noted earlier, the Spanish-speaking mission to the capital city bore fruit with the first baptism in 1961 by the missionaries Rodolfo and Hilda Plett. Their work took root in the Bernardino Caballero neighborhood, and was extended over the next years to San Isidro, Santa Lucía and San Antonio. In 1964 the Asunción Biblical Institute

Testimony of Pedro Berardo

An unforgettable event took place in the city of Villeta. One evening, while preparing for a meeting with the first people who had arrived, suddenly the lights went out in our sector. People commented that this not a random occurrence, but something prepared beforehand so that our evangelistic campaign would fail. According to some, it was the work of a person with significant influence in that place and the surrounding area. Immediately brother Enns and I went to the nearby city of Guarambaré to fetch an electric generator, while brother Alfredo Klassen calmed the people who were arriving by the light of moon and also did some wiring to adapt to the generator. That evening the meeting began at the scheduled hour, and we had as many people as we had had on previous nights. Once more the Lord won the victory, and we saw his loving and powerful hand.

(IBA) was established, and the Albert Schweitzer Mennonite primary school followed.[32]

In 1971, with the participation of the first four Spanish-speaking Mennonite churches (Dr. Francia church, B. Caballero church, San Isidro church, and the San Antonio church), the Spanish-speaking "Evangelical Conference of Paraguayan Mennonite Brethren" (*Convención Evangélica de los Hermanos Menonitas de Paraguay*) was formed.[33] In addition, a regular publication was published called *La Voz del rebaño* ("The Voice of the Flock") with a print run of 1000 copies.[34] The Conference also established committees to prepare and nourish programs in evangelism, education, youth, women's society, and finances. Beginning in 1973 a mobile missionary team called "Messengers of Christ" (*Mensajeros de Cristo*) was organized; it had great success in establishing new churches.

The bookstore "El Sendero" opens in Asunción, 1964

The Bibical Institute of Asunción (IBA) began giving classes in 1964 in the Dr. Francia church, but by the next year it had obtained its own property. Theological education through IBA was supported jointly by the Conference of Mennonite Brethren of Paraguay together with the Board of Missions and Services of Hillboro, Kansas (BOMAS). Professors from the Mennonite Seminary in Fresno, California also collaborated by offering classes. By the 1980s, 60 percent of the students came from Spanish-speaking churches, with 40 percent coming from German-speaking churches. The Alberto Schweitzer school was supported jointly by BOMAS and both German- and Spanish-speaking Mennonite Brethren conferences. When the school began in 1966 it counted 12 students; by 1979, enrollment had grown to 512 students.[35]

This city block in Asunción houses the Biblical Institute of Asunción (IBA), the OBEDIRA radio station, and the Alberto Schweitzer school

By 1983 there were eleven Spanish-speaking churches functioning, primarily in the capital. They were the result of the missionary work of the Mennonite colonies.[36] There were, in addition, 28 more churches known as "extended churches," referring to the fact that they were congregations in the process of becoming autonomous churches, and the fact that not all of them had their own church buildings.[37]

In addition to the churches already mentioned that originated from the first colonies, there have been other Mennonite churches established in Paraguay. Until 1960, the youth activities of the Evangelical Mennonite Brotherhood (*Die Evangelisch Mennontische Bruderschaft*: EMB) in Filadelfia colony were carried out in conjunction with the Mennonite Brethren. In that year, the EMB youth began to take charge of their own activities and began to take on leadership roles in their community. Because of membership growth within the EMB, a church was built in Filadelfia in 1963. In that same year the EMB participated as a founding member of the *Comité de Misiones Menonitas de Paraguay* (Committee of Mennonite Missions of Paraguay).[38]

The Mennonite colony of Tres Palmas is one of the most unique in Paraguay. It was founded in 1967 by families originating from other Mennonite colonies, such as Bergthal, Menno, Fernheim, Neuland, Asunción, Friesland and Volendam, as well as from other countries such as the U.S., Mexico, Brazil, Uruguay and Bolivia. The colony is located 20 kilometers from Bergthal colony, from which came the first founders of Tres Palmas. In 1984 this colony had 300 inhabitants. The church is known as the Evangelical Mennonite Community (*Evangelische Mennonitische Gemeinde*); it has a congregational church government and baptism is by aspersion.[39]

The Beachy Amish came to Paraguay from the United States in 1967 and founded the Luz y Esperanza colony. A total of 125 colonists bought 2,147 hectares of land next to the Sommerfeld colony.[40] Their reason for coming to Paraguay was their desire to maintain their community life and also to do mission work. An important contribution of this group was the construction of a nearby hospital to serve the Paraguayan people who live in the vicinity.[41] The Conservative Old Mennonites (Mennonite Christian Brotherhood) founded another colony called Agua Azul in 1969, 375 kilometers north-east of Asunción, on a farm of 1,900 hectares, located near the highway that runs to Saltos de Guairá in Brazil. A third colony, called Ríos Corrientes, was founded nearby on 1,500 hectares of land. When the Ríos Corrientes colony was founded in 1975 the community numbered 152 persons.[42] These colonies do not allow the use of radios, but they use automobiles and modern agricultural machinery. They maintain their faith and also carry out mission work among the Paraguayan people. For this reason, some members of these communi-

Beachy Amish church in Luz y Esperanza colony

ties are Paraguayan, and worship services take place in both Spanish and English. They maintain fraternal relations with the Mennonite Church of Eastern Pennsylvania. The Conservative Old Mennonite colonies came to be known as the Mennonite Christian Brotherhood (*Hermandad Menonita Cristiana*).[43]

Another kind of Mennonite colony was established in 1969, when 14 families of Reinländer Old Colony Mennonites immigrated to Paraguay from Mexico. They established the Río Verde colony 350 kilometers north-east of Asunción on 20,526 hectares of land. The original settlers were joined later by families migrating from Belize and Canada. The reason for the migration was the growth of families and the need to find new land on which to live and work. These colonies have made great economic advances. They use modern agricultural machinery to cultivate soya and beans, and they also are involved in dairy production. The Old Colony settlers also work in sawmills and as blacksmiths and carpenters as well as running businesses that provide other colonists with the necessities of life.[44] These groups still emphasize "separation from the world," and for this reason they do not use automobiles, motorcycles, digital clocks or radios. They share a Prussian origin with other Mennonite colonists, and their churches and schools attempt to reproduce the institutions established by their ancestors in Prussia and Russia.[45]

Near the Río Verde colony the Santa Clara colony was established by Sommerfeld Mennonites who emigrated from Mexico. They also were in search of land to accommodate their large and growing families. The Santa Clara colony was founded in 1971 when the settlers bought 2,700 hectares of land in the jungle. The colony began with only 14 families.[46] This group of settlers is more open to the surrounding world; their clothing is more modern, and they allow the use of automobiles.[47]

Durango colony was established in 1978 by German-speaking Old Colony Mennonites from Mexico. The colony was located 310 kilometers south-east of Asunción on 13,400 hectares of land. Out of a total of 1,921 inhabitants, 649 belong to the Old Colony church of Mexico with the rest being children and non-baptized youth. Agricultural production has concentrated on soya and wheat, but the raising of poultry and pork has also been introduced. The cooperation of the families within this colony has provided them with an important economic base and provides solid social security.[48] The Durango congregation in noted for being much more traditional than others colonies. Their tractors, for example, are not allowed rubber tires, but rather only steel wheels.[49]

Alongside the Mennonite Brethren conference, the other Mennonite conference of original colonists, the *Mennonitengemeinde* (MG) conference joined with the Evangelical Mennonite Brotherhood (EMB) group and Mennonite mission boards in the United States to promote active mission work in Paraguay. In 1963 an organization was established for this purpose, which later (1976) came to be known as the "Mennonite Committee for Evangelical and Social Action in Paraguay" (*Comité Menonita de Acción Evangélica y Social en Paraguay*: COMAESP). The expressed aim of the Committee was to "win persons for the Lord and His Kingdom and to be of service to the Paraguayan people."[50] COMAESP took on the responsibilities of mission work among the indigenous people in Menno colony and carried out mission work in Villa Hayes in eastern Paraguay as well as the Mennonite Hospital at Kilometer 81,[51] a hospital serving Paraguayans suffering from leprosy (Hansen's disease).[52]

Hospital personnel and patients, Km. 81, 1960s

Mission work expanded from the leprosy hospital at Km. 81 to a place called Itacurubí de la Cordillera, 87 kilometers east of Asunción. Through the work of Ernst Wiens and his wife, an "Evangelical Mennonite" church was founded there in 1964 with a small group of people who accepted baptism. This church later extended to a place called Kariy Loma, where a small farm was rented for preaching and work with children. Another extension of the Itacurubí church was Cariy Potrero, where the Centeno couple, who were recent converts, began to organize

Hospital at Km 81 (2009)

meetings and worship services in their home. They later reconstructed an old farm building, adapting it for preaching and worship services.[53]

A work began also in Tororó, 100 kilometers from Itacurubí, begun by brother M. Torrales who wanted his sister and other relatives to hear the Word of God. After writing letters, he visited personally to preach and teach in the Guaraní language. The first meetings took place in the house of the mayor of the little town of Julián Estegarribia. Later, sister Matilde Villasantí opened her home for worship services. In spite of her advanced age, she learned to sing praises to God with great joy.[54] Hospital work also led to church planting. The Mennonite church in Boquerón, for example, began with contacts with patients from the Hospital Km. 81.[55]

The work in Cambyretá began in 1956 with the educational efforts of Isaak Thiessen, who taught Paraguayan, Brazilian and German students from various churches, in both German and Spanish. He also offered religious services and Sunday school in German.[56] With the support of COMAESP the school in Cambyretá expanded in 1963 numbering 80 students. A Mennonite church would be founded in this place in the 1980s.[57]

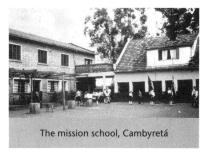

The mission school, Cambyretá

Pastor Juan Federau was responsible for the establishment of a church in Colonia Tuyango, located near Itacurubí del Rosario. The church continued growing slowly in spite of intense opposition from Catholics and two fires that destroyed their place of worship. Juan

Federau was also responsible for beginning missionary work in Villa Hayes, capital of the department Presidente Hayes. In 1964 Federau began with summer Bible schools, followed by Sunday schools. The work came to include the town of Costa Guazú, 7 kilometers away on the Transchaco highway. In 1969, 130 persons regularly attended services and Sunday school.[58]

A Mennonite school was founded in Villa Hayes beginning in 1964. After obtaining approval from the Ministry of Education, instruction began with 33 students. In 1968 the president of the Republic was present to inaugurate several public works, among which was included the school, *Escuela Evangélica Menonita del Cerro*.[59]

Further mission work carried out under the auspices of the COMAESP resulted in a Mennonite church at Benjamín Aceval (1974), near Villa Hayes, Eusebio Ayala (1978) and Cruce Loma Plata (1978). This last town is located 413 kilometers from Asunción along the Transchaco highway. Although the families making up the church are scattered at some distance from one another, it continues to grow. Finally, mission work in Asunción itself began in 1972 with the preaching of Argentine pastor Juan Angel Gutiérrez. He began services in a rented house, but later a modern church was built on Venezuela street.

On the heels of the closing of the Seminary in Montevideo, Uruguay (SEMT) in 1974, a Seminary was established in Asunción in 1977 called the Evangelical Mennonite Center of Theology Asunción (*Centro Evangélico Menonita de Teología Asunción*: CEMTA). CEMTA initially was adminstered by the missionaries, and manifested a passion for evangelism and missionary work.[60] Its aim was to eductate Latin American Mennonite pastors and theologians.[61] The course of study offered initially included Biblical studies, evangelism, ecclesiology and doctrine.

Sunday school at the mission in Filadelfia, 1964

The decades of the 1960s and 70s saw significant advances for Mennonites in Paraguay, economically and as a faith community. When the Transchaco highway connected the colonies with Asunción in 1961 it opened up important markets for their agricultural products and encouraged even more production and consolidation. Now survival was no longer the issue; rather prosperity had became possible. The Mennonite colonies soon became important economic contributors to the Paraguayan economy as a whole. In this new situation, mass emigration from the colonies ceased and church communities stabilized and grew in the colonies.

The 1970s especially saw significant expansion of mission efforts among Spanish-speaking Paraguayans by both MB and MG groups. Not only were new churches planted, but the educational efforts of both MB and MG expanded significantly beyond German-language instruction to include more and more offerings in Spanish. In addition, the establishment of ASCIM and the help of MCC provided a more holistic and integral model of mission to the indigenous people, whose communities and churches flourished in this period. In addition, new colonies were established by new conservative Mennonite immigrant groups, who saw Paraguay as a land hospitable to their community needs.

The Paraguayan experience of these decades focused for Mennonites the question of "ethnicity" and the Gospel. In many of their historical experiences, Mennonites have encountered the world as an immigrant, German-speaking "ethnic" sub-culture living within larger cultures. In Paraguay, the "ethnicity" of the Mennonite immigrants unavoidably came to be recognized as one ethnicity among very many other local ethnicities, indigenous and Spanish-speaking. Preaching the Gospel outside Mennonite communities thus raised fundamental questions about what it meant to be a Mennonite Christian. As being "Mennonite" was defined less and less in ethnic, cultural and linguistic terms, the Mennonite church as a whole sought to define itself as a particular path of faith within the larger Christian community. The educational institutions established in Paraguay played a significant role in this self-reflective process.

The Mennonites in Brazil (1959-1979)

The social-political context of Brazil in the 1960s and 70s is marked by the arrival of military dictatorship in 1964, a situation which lasted until 1985. This period has been one of the bloodiest in Brazil's history, marked by military repression, torture of dissidents, incarcerations and the silencing of all opposition, which nevertheless saw a slight opening around 1979.[1]

In the 1960s and 1970s, the Catholic church made commitments to the peasants and rural workers' unions (located primarily in NE Brazil) with a movement for mass education as envisioned by Paulo Freire. This church movement promoted Base Christian communities and the 1968 initiatives of the Episcopal Conference of Medellin,[2] and was strongly combated by the military government.[3] The activist wing of the Catholic Church along with the progressive leaders of the CNBB (National Council of Bishops of Brazil) confronted military oppression with great courage and moral authority. In the face of violence, Dom Helder Camara became a prophet of nonviolence, calling for peace and a firm stance against all injustice.[4] The historian Enrique Dussel calls the years from 1974 to 1979 a time of blood and hope. The Catholic church of Brazil was a prophetic voice that gave many martyrs for the Gospel and the struggle for justice.[5]

Brazilian Protestantism of this era is marked by the rapid growth of Pentecostal churches.[6] By 1965 the number of Pentecostal members numbered just under 67 percent of the total of Protestant believers in the country.[7] In the 1970s and 1980s, neo-Pentecostal churches flourished, with their syncretism of popular rites, practices and cosmologies of Catholic, indigenous and Afro-Brazilian origins.[8]

The Mennonite colonies formed German-speaking churches wherever Mennonites migrated for job opportunities in the 1930s to 1950s in the states of Santa Catarina, Paraná and São Paulo. Boqueirão became the geographical center from which Mennonite churches were established in Curitiba. Already in 1936, Mennonite Brethren and MG Mennonite churches were established there, with the two groups building a church in 1946, which they shared.

The Mennonite Brethren of Vila Guaira belonged to the Mennonite Brethren of Boqueirão but celebrated Sunday worship, choir singing, youth meetings and Sunday school with the Mennonites (MG) in Vila Guaira; general assemblies and celebrations of the Lord's Supper took place in Boqueirão. In 1962, MB members in Vila Guaira built their own church and separated from the MG and the Boqueirão MB churches. A generational tension can be noted in the establishment of two worship services on Sundays, one in German and one in Portuguese. In 1966, the Mennonite Brethren in Boqueirão separated from the Mennonite Church (MG) and built their own church; the MB churches in Guarituba, Vila Guaira and Xaxim followed.

The MB church of Xaxim was born of a division that took place in Boqueirão in 1959 when 37 persons decided to form an independent congregation under the leadership of Peter Hamm. The Xaxim church established new churches in Jardim Urano (1967) and later in Jardim Itamarati, Jardim Tranquilo, Agudos do Sul and Mandirituba. The Mennonite Brethren built two more churches in Boqueirão, in 1962 and 1970, and a small church was established in Jardim Acacia in 1971.

In the 1950s, the Mennonite churches (MG) began meeting regularly and formed the Association of Mennonite Churches of Brazil (AIMB) in 1952. This organization was concerned with church growth, missionary work, social services and communication through the periodical *Bibel und Pflug*. AIMB's work was concentrated in Curitiba, Witmarsum and surrounding areas.

The Association of Mennonite Brethren Churches of Brazil (German-speaking) (AIIMB) was formed in 1960. The stated aims of the Association were the promotion of mutual aid and the preservation of healthy doctrine. The AIIMB had 13 congregations with 1,879 members by 1986. In 1966, the Brazilian Convention of Mennonite Brethren Churches (CIIMB) was formed. This was a Portuguese-language organization with similar evangelistic aims as the AIIMB. By 1987, the CIIMB had 27 congregations with a total of 1954 members. In 1995, the two MB conferences united under one organization with a new name: Conference of Brazilian Mennonite Brethren Churches (COBIM).

The Mennonite Church (MG) and Mennonite Brethren groups had worked together in Witmarsum in Paraná since their arrival in 1951, collaborating in worship, Sunday schools and youth work. After the departure of some Mennonite Brethren members, the two groups collaborated even more closely, building a church in 1963 and four years later forming a single church organization (*Evangelische Mennonitengemeinde*) which allowed for baptism by both aspersion (MG practice) and immersion (MB practice). Mission work extended social aid to neighboring communities with churches founded in Pugas and Palmeiras. In time, a second Mennonite Church was founded in Witmarsum for the Portuguese-speakers who lived in the colony. The

Dedication of the new Mennonite church in Witmarsum, 1963

Mennonite Brethren of Witmarsum extended their mission work to neighboring Campo Largo in 1969.

As noted earlier, a house was purchased in São Paulo to support German-speaking Mennonite youth who had moved to that city for employment. By 1954, a group of eight was gathering for devotional meetings and sharing the Lord's Supper. The MB church was formally organized in 1960, building a church and pastoral home in Jabaquara in 1964. This congregation worked closely with Baptists, other Mennonites and the Evangelical free church with whom the Lord's supper was celebrated monthly in German. The congregation was well organized, with an abundance of leaders and mission initiatives. Through the biblical education of children in 1973, a new Portuguese-speaking church was established in a neighborhood known as Diadema. The generational cultural shift from the older German culture to complete integration of the Portuguese culture of Brazilian society is evident in this church.[9]

A small MB church was planted in 1963 in Santo Amaro, south of São Paulo by the missionaries James and Lois Wiebe. The first baptism was celebrated in 1966 and the church continues under the leadership of Brazilian pastors.[10] North American mission efforts also resulted in a church founded in 1967 in Campo Belo, close to the airport of Congonhas, with a church building completed in1981. Through the efforts of the church of Campo Limpo, another MB church was founded in Embú on the edges of São Paulo in a poor and heavily-populated neighborhood.[11]

In the Curitiba area, the Women's Union of the Vila Guaira and Boqueirão churches (MG) promoted mission and social work, especially under the leadership of Lilian G. Heinrichs. The young people took on the task of taking the Gospel to prisoners in the jail located in the barrio of Ahú, beginning already in 1959; the women would prepare and deliver gifts for the prisoners during Christmas and Holy Week. By 1980, it was calculated that more than 10,000 prisoners had been reached with the Word of God.[12]

The Mennonite Association for Social Assistance (AMAS) was founded by the AIMB in 1970 as a nonprofit welfare agency. It works closely with MCC, International Mennonite Organization (IMO) of

Osvaldo de Freita and Erwin Rempel baptizing in Goiânia

Europe and funding from the Children's Aid program of Germany. AMAS is supported by the AIMB churches and Mennonite business enterprises, operating several day-care programs and schools, and a professional training program. AMAS also was involved in discussions with federal government politicians which led to an alternative service program in lieu of military service in 1988.[13]

The settlement in Bagé, Rio Grande do Sul, Colonia Nova, encountered difficulties in 1959 because of an exclusive dependence on wheat cultivation. A further church split resulted in the settlement under the leadership of Gerhard Wall. The division was eventually healed and Bagé became a mission field with four MB churches built by 1995.[14]

For Mennonites involved in dairy production, cooperatives presented a good alternative. Franz and Jacob Kröker, along with other families from Paraguay, gathered together to buy a 2,000 hectare parcel of land in Lapa, 75 kilometers from Curitiba. The land was divided into 48 sections and was occupied in 1968 by 32 families of German origin of whom nine were Mennonite. In religious affiliation, the settlers represented the Church of God, Mennonite Brethren, Lutheran and Reformed. They managed to live well together, constructing a community center and a building for sports and special events. The community also built a primary school (in Portuguese), grades one to four. The Lapa community developed well in the context of Brazilian society.

The Mennonite Board of Missions and Charities began a missionary outreach in Brazil in 1954, sending two couples who began work in Goiânia, Goiás and in the city of São Paulo. A year later, two more couples were sent to work in Valinhos and Sertãozinho, São Paulo. The Amazon Valley Indian Mission, an independent Mennonite missioning venture, sent an evangelist couple, a community service couple, a teacher, a lady-evangelist and a nurse to Araguacema, Goiás, in 1954. This work was transferred to the administration of the Mennonite Board of Missions and

Testimony of José Fernandes Brito

José Fernandes Brito was armed and looking for his enemy in the interior town of Araguacema. When he did not find him, he entered the Mennonite Church where the missionary pastor was preaching. José was half drunk, but somehow realized his estrangement from God, and he made the decision to follow Christ. José was serious, and he studied the Bible diligently. He was intrigued with the Anabaptist history he learned from the missionaries. He was led to become a lay-leader and then, a pastor. Even though his formal education was equivalent to third grade, he came to be recognized as a wise pastor and counselor by the people.

Charities in 1959. Three schools, a clinic and five churches were formed in this region of Brazil.

In 1957, the *Associação Evangélica Menonita* (AEM) was formed as a legal entity of the Portuguese-speaking Mennonite churches

Sunday school children in Taguatinga

in the state of São Paulo. The AEM's expressed purpose was to establish new churches modeled on those described in the New Testament, to create Bible schools for training Christian workers, to develop agricultural, educational and charitable institutions and to distribute Christian literature through book stores.[15] Literature work was begun in 1957 with a bookstore established first in

Campinas with more later in Brasilia, Taguatinga and Ribeirão Preto. In 1965 the AEM organized its own publishing house, the *Editora Cristã Unida*, Campinas, São Paulo. Around 50 titles were published under AEM auspices, with more titles published under the "United Press" imprint, after the missionary David Falk bought the company in 1997.

Interaction between the AEM and the German-speaking Mennonites of Curitiba of the AIMB prompted several meetings in 1964, and in January 1965, the AEM and AIMB leaders met in Campinas, São Paulo to draft an agreement of cooperation. The German AIMB sent youth, seminary-trained leaders (who studied in Montevideo, Uruguay) and funds to expand the work in Brazil.[16] In 1967, Pastor Peter Pauls, Jr. of the Witmarsum AIMB church served as president of the AEM a number of years. The AEM and AIMB worked together to form Portuguese-speaking churches in Paraná and Santa Catarina. Working together with the German-speaking Mennonites was a vital factor for a stronger conference and greater sense of denominational self-identity in the immense cosmopolitan country of Brazil.[17]

The Commission on Overseas Mission of the General Conference Churches of North America, began helping the mission venture of the AEM in 1975. Prayer support, missionaries and funds were given, with a church planting project developed in NE Brazil, Recife, where MCC had been working in community development since 1970.

Some youth from AIMB and AIIMB/COBIM churches also worked with MCC.

The Holdeman Mennonite Church (called officially "The Church of God in Christ, Mennonite") originated in 1859 when John Holdeman separated from Old Mennonites in Ohio. Holdeman emphasized a new birth, a holy kiss, marriage only within the community of faith, church membership only for the converted, footwashing, nonresistance and non-swearing of oaths.[18] Over a number of years 250 Holdeman Mennonites came to Brazil, beginning in November, 1968. They bought 2,800 hectares near Rio Verde, Goiás which they dedicated to agriculture and evangelism. Although open to Brazilians, Holdeman cultural norms are strictly enforced, with men required to wear beards and dark overalls, and women required to wear the prayer veil. Alcohol, smoking, television or listening to popular music on the radio are all forbidden. The colony maintains its own school, and English and Portuguese are both used in school and church.

The Witmarsum Colony in Paraná was founded in 1951 with 38 families. Twenty-five years later, the colony had a large dairy cooperative for milk and cheese production, grain elevators, churches, primary and secondary schools, paved roads, electricity and telephones, a clinic and 7,500 hectares of soy beans and rice under cultivation, besides dairy, beef and poultry production. The colony invited President Ernesto Geisel and the Governor of Paraná to the three-day twenty-fifth anniversary celebration. Twenty-two people accompanied the President, including federal senators, cabinet ministers and congressmen. President Geisel complimented the Mennonites on their hard work and on the high level of development of the colony.[19]

In 1988, members from both churches (AIIMB and AIMB) in Witmarsum founded the *Associação Menonita Beneficente* (AMB) for social and spiritual welfare. The project serves hundreds of people living around the Witmarsum Colony.[20]

The Mennonite World Conference assembly, held July 18-23, 1972, was the first such meeting held in Latin America.[21] Around 1,800 people registered for the event, which saw 2,000 participants take part in the public events.[22] The heightened role of women as participants and study-group leaders was notable at this assembly, as was the election of Million Belete of Ethiopia as president of MWC – the first third-world person to hold this office.[23] One of the most controversial declarations was put forward by a group identified as the "Anabaptist

MWC Assembly paricipants in Curitiba

Latin American study group" which conveyed concerns about the political and economic situation and the violation of human rights in the Southern Cone.[24] The declaration condemned the inequitable distribution of land in Paraguay and El Salvador, the cold-blooded murders of indigenous peoples in Brazil, Colombia and Paraguay, and the torture, jailing and murders carried out by political and military forces in Argentina, Paraguay, Bolivia, Brazil and Uruguay. The declaration desired "a new outbreak of the Holy Spirit, who can show us that being silent in the face of these injustices means that we accept them; that [the Spirit] help us to open our eyes and see the oppressed, to identify ourselves with them, to work for their liberation, even if it costs us our privileges, while at the same time loving those who oppress."[25]

The German Mennonite immigrants since their arrival in Brazil have placed great emphasis on education. The *Colégio Erasto Gaertner* was founded in 1936 in Curitiba when 18 primary students began receiving instruction; secondary education was introduced in 1956. By 1979, the school had a total of 850 primary and secondary students and 43 teachers, of whom 28 were from the Mennonite community.[26] In 1957, the Mennonite Brethren established the *Erasmo Braga* primary school in Curitiba in the building that had formerly housed an orphanage. This school underwent several changes but eventually was forced to close in 1980 for lack of economic support. The buildings were first used to house a Biblical Institute and later, the *Instituto e Seminário Biblico dos Irmãos Menonitas* (Mennonite Brethren Seminary and Bible Institute: ISBIM).[27]

In 1960 the North and South American conferences of the Mennonite Brethren Church developed a plan for theological education of church leaders and members for the churches of Brazil, Paraguay and Uruguay, the Evangelical Theological Institute (*Instituto Teológico Evangélico*: ITE). The Biblical Institute in Vila Guaira of Curitiba became the location for a three-year educational course. By 1969 the ITE had 130 students, who helped in the development and formation of MB congregations. In 1968 the MB church of Paraguay decided to create its own theological center. This led eventually to the unification of the ITE (German-speaking) and the *Instituto Bíblico Paranaense* (Portuguese-speaking) and the formation of the ISBIM in 1972, a more advanced seminary located in Uberaba, Curitiba.

The Mennonite Church (MG), by contrast, decided to educate its youth in the biblical and pastoral fields at the Evangelical Mennonite Theological Seminary (SEMT) in Montevideo, Uruguay which had opened in 1955. As noted above, in 1974 SEMT was moved from Montevideo to Asuncion, Paraguay and renamed the Evangelical Mennonite Center of Theology Asunción (CEMTA). Students from the Brazilian Mennonite church (MG) study at CEMTA, but given the difficulties of language, some Brazilian Mennonites choose to study at the ISBIM of the Mennonite Brethren in Curitiba. Other Brazilian students and pastors study at the Baptist seminaries in São Paulo and Curitiba or travel abroad for further study.

Goianorte Mennonite Church, 1977

Mennonites from all conferences in Brazil during this historical period continued to expand their German-speaking churches, but also increasingly reached out to the Portuguese-speaking population with evangelistic efforts. The growing integration of German-speaking and Portuguese-speaking Mennonites led eventually to the formation of unified conferences and educational institutions, and the beginnings of integrated church and community work.

Although the political situation in Brazil was strongly polarized, and the liberationist currents ran strong in the Roman Catholic church of Brazil in these decades, the Mennonite church did not move in this direction, concentrating rather on evangelism and biblical and theological education.

Andean Region

The Andean Region

CHAPTER IX

Mennonite Missions and Growth in Colombia (1943-1979)

Mennonite churches in Colombia were formed first by mission efforts of the North American General Conference Mennonites, who were soon followed by Mennonite Brethren missionaries. The churches formed by the General Conference Mennonites went on to form a conference called the "Evangelical Mennonite Church of Colombia" (*Iglesia Evangélica Menonita de Colombia*: IEMCO); the Mennonite Brethren formed their own conference, called the "National Conference of Mennonite Brethren of Colombia" (*Conferencia Nacional de los Hermanos Menonitas de Colombia*: CNHMC). This chapter will tell the story of these two Mennonite conferences sequentially.

The first contacts with Protestantism in Colombia are linked to the liberators Simón Bolivar and Santander who, at least at the beginning of their careers demonstrated a marked anticlericalism and were affiliated with Free Masonry.[1] The liberal reforms implemented by General José Hilario López during 1849-53 granted religious freedom. Nevertheless, the battle between Conservatives and Liberals continued until 1861, when the armed movement of General Tomás Cipriano de Mosquera descended upon Bogotá and toppled the Conservative president. Once in power, General Mosquera made a request to the Presbyterian Church of the United States that it send missionaries to Colombia.[2]

The Presbyterian Church began its evangelistic work by creating American Schools and founding churches.[3] Nevertheless, Protestantism did not really establish itself until the Liberal period from 1930 to 1946. This period was characterized by the industrialization and modernization of the Colombian state, in which the state utilized all the means possible to encourage foreign investment and suppress

133

the peasants who were demanding land.[4] The historian John Sinclair has affirmed with good reason that at this time Protestantism still projected a foreign image, reflecting the ideals of a conservative North American middle class. Protestantism did not manage to identify with the more humble sectors of the country, for it did not engage the social problems that were destroying society.[5]

Seen from another point of view, the Liberal period from 1930 to 1946 can also be described as being religiously tolerant: it permitted the establishment of twenty new Protestant missions in Colombia. The missions created theological institutions for the education of pastors, as well as community services such as medical clinics, publications, and print shops. A mutual collaboration also developed between Protestant organizations to such a point that eleven new missions took up unfinished work left behind by other Protestant denominations. The first Mennonite missionaries in Colombia, supported by the Presbyterian Church, began their mission work through educational service.

Mary Hope and Gerald Stucky with their children Tim (infant), Judith, Peter and Paul, 1951.

When China's doors closed to missionaries, the Mission Board of the General Conference Mennonite Church looked to Latin America as a possible mission field. William C. Voth and Gerald Stucky undertook an exploratory trip through several countries of Central and South America, from September 1943 to March 1944. William C. Voth contracted typhus in Bogotá, and for this reason they had to stay in Colombia for three weeks. These weeks were important, for they allowed Stucky to come into contact with Presbyterian missionaries, and in the end it was recommended to begin Mennonite mission work in Colombia.

Mennonite mission work began with an educational project for the healthy children of parents with leprosy (Hansen's disease). The first missionaries were Gerald Stucky and his wife Mary Hope Wood of Indiana, along with Janet Soldner and Mary Becker of Kansas. They arrived in Colombia in September 1945. The place chosen to establish the school was a six-hectare farm located in the Andes mountains, 80 kilometers west of Bogotá, near the towns of Cachipay, Anolaima, and La Esperanza. This farm, with coffee and banana plants and one house, was first rented and then bought from a German by the name of Luis Haderer. In March of 1947 the project of forming a small boarding school began, initially with nine children enrolled.[6]

Conservative governments from 1946 to 1950 moved closer to the Catholic church, suspended institutional guarantees and imposed martial law. Jorge Eliecer Gaitán, leader of the Liberals and supported by the popular sectors, became leader of the parliamentary majority and was a clear candidate for winning the elections of 1950-1954. But on the 9th of April, 1948, Gaitán was assassinated, unleashing a wave of violence in Colombia – the so-called "Bogotazo."[7] In June 1948 the bishops of Colombia met to condemn Communism and Liberalism in their pastoral letter, emphasizing that the social doctrine of the Catholic church was the only possible way to resolve the social problems of the country.[8]

The spiral of violence involved Liberals and Conservatives, Catholics and Protestants, conservative Catholic clergy and Communists, peasants and land owners.[9] There was a great effort on the part of the Catholic church to obtain political power and restrict religious liberty. It was an easy conclusion to draw that Liberals, Free Masons, Communists and Protestants were the enemies of the Catholic religion, and that it was necessary to combat them. Led by certain priests and their laity, a kind of popular xenophobia was unleashed against

Mary Hope's Testimony

I was born in Michigan, United States, in 1916. [Our family was] involved in the life of the Presbyterian Church. When our grandmother would visit us, she would tell us many missionary stories from Iran. This motivated me strongly toward mission work. I did my theological education with the Presbyterians in New York, and that is where I came to know the Mennonite student Gerald Stucky, whom I married in June of 1943.

During his stay in Bogotá, my husband Gerald Stucky came into contact with the American Leper Society which was looking for someone to open a collegiate or school that would take healthy children of parents who had leprosy. ... In 1947 we began a school in Cachipay with a total of 23 children. ... We lived happily with the boys and girls, like one big family. ... Many of these children today are doctors, nurses, lawyers and in many other professions. We sowed the seed and tried to live as a family, for we knew that God is faithful.

North American Protestant missionaries, who were depicted as foreign agents.

Both Armando Hernández[10] and James C. Juhnke[11] document a series of attacks and acts of aggression by Catholic priests or representatives of state institutions carried out against North American and Colombian Mennonites because of their evangelistic work, although none of these attacks resulted in loss of life. Only with the plebiscite of 1958 did Liberals and Conservatives agree to share power, and avoid confrontation and conflict between their parties. The new political situation which began in 1958 and culminated with the reforms of Vatican II would provide a space for better relations between Catholics and Protestants. The nonviolence of the Mennonites and their commitment to serve Colombian communities allowed them later to extend their missionary work to other cities.

Part of a song Mennonite missionaries heard sung in Anolaima

Protestant liars
Your church is not of Christ
It is of Zwingli and Luther
and Calvin, another minister
Chorus:
We don't want Protestants
coming to Colombia to corrupt;
We don't want Protestants
polluting our homeland and our faith.

Hundreds of pastors
are invading our homeland now,
they are marauding wolves
given to us by foreigners.

You do not love the Virgin
who is Christ's mother;
In hell you will find Satan,
your father.

The social and political situation in Colombia grew turbulent in the decades of the 1960s and 70s. Alternating liberal and conservative governments responded with violence to the deep social inequalities in the country, especially the desperate situation of the peasantry.[12] By the mid-1970s, guerilla movements such as the Revolutionary Forces of Colombia (FARC) and the National Liberation Army (ELN) had emerged, representing the new Latin American leftist movement.[13] The Roman Catholic priest and sociologist Camilo Torres grasped the political, ecclesial and economic contradictions that particularly oppressed the poor of the country.[14] His theological reflection on "efficacious love," written shortly before his death in February, 1966 as a member of the guerilla movement, was his response to the political options he faced. His radical option for armed revolution made manifest the breaking apart of the Constantinian union of Church and State that had found its best expression in Colombia.

The second conference of Latin American bishops held in Medellín in August, 1968 was a fundamental event for the historical life of the church in Colombia and Latin America. Under the influence of the Second Vatican Council, the documents from Medellín address topics such as justice, education and peace, and locate themselves in the nascent movement of Liberation Theology. The document on peace clearly affirms that peace is the fruit of justice, and that the current situation of non-peace is one of conflict, tension, and war which belongs in the category of sin. The Medellín documents formed the basis for for critical theological reflection in all of Latin America.[15] Organizations such as the Priests of Golconda (Cundinamarca, 1968) and Priests for Latin America (SAL, 1972) began theological and socio-economic reflections on the Colombian reality. Many members of these organizations suffered repression, exile and even death when they sided with the peasants and the poor of the country.

The alternating liberal and conservative govenments of Colombia in the 1960s and 70s pursued policies based in military repression and opposition to agrarian reform. The result was social disintegration and institutional crisis. Masses of people found themselves in the midst of violence, and participated less and less in elections. Violence and oppression were woven into Colombian daily life during this historical period.[16]

Although the earlier difficult period of religious intolerance had passed, Colombian Protestant churches in the 1960s still felt its repercussions.[17] Colombian Protestant churches began to nationalize by means of the "Evangelism in Depth" revival program (*Evangelismo a Fondo*) promoted by the Latin American Mission.[18] Churches were founded from cell groups meeting in homes, leading to the building of churches and mass-evangelism campaigns. Pentecostal churches contributed greatly to the growth of Protestantism.[19] The Assemblies of God, for example, held a well-attended "Faith in Christ and Divine Healing" campaign in Cali in 1968, which led to the building of a church and regular worship services. By the end of the 1970s, preach-

Camilo Torres on revolution

As a sociologist I have wanted love to become efficacious by means of technology and science. Upon analyzing Colombian society, I have come to the recognition of the need for a revolution so that the hungry are fed, the thirsty given to drink, and the naked clothed, to achieve the well being for the majority of our people. I believe that the revolutionary struggle is a Christian and priestly struggle. Only by means of this struggle, facing the concrete realities of our country, can we realize the love human beings should have for their neighbors.

ing campaigns, healings and miracles were promoted by popular preachers such as Yiye Ávila, Jorge Raschke and T. L. Osborn, and pentecostalism was promoted by numerous radio broadcasts.[20]

In the 1970s the charismatic movement shook the religious world of Colombia and all Latin America. It established a bridge between Protestants and Catholics by virtue of shared experiences of the Holy Spirit. In spite of some openly ecumenical efforts in the early 1970s, however, most Protestant charismatic groups distanced themselves from the Roman Catholics and became independent churches.[21] Another characteristic of Protestant churches in this period was a continual division because of doctrinal, organizational or personality differences.[22] Still, some Protestant theologians reflected on the social realities of Colombia, and took concrete steps to address social issues.[23] The Mennonite church founded MENCOLDES in the mid-1970s to work on social issues from a nonviolent perspective, opening an important perspective for Colombian society, and the Lutheran church of Bocayá worked to establish economically independent farming communities.[24]

Entering into the 1960s and 70s, the mission work of the General Conference Mennonites expanded and was consolidated in a functioning national organization, the "Evangelical Mennonite Church of Colombia" (*Iglesia Evangélica Menonita de Colombia*: IEMCO). At Cachipay, the location of the original Mennonite work in Colombia, a church was founded with the help of students and graduates of the Mennonite school in 1953. By 1960 it had its own national pastor,

Cachipay student body, 1964

Luis A. Rodríguez, a graduate of the Alliance Biblical Institute in Armenia, and had 24 members. The next two decades, however, were tumultuous, with an internal conflict leading to a church split in 1963, followed by another division two years later, as well as external conflict with local Pentecostal groups.[25] Some tensions arose between the local church and the national organization in 1969, resulting in three prominent members leaving the church. Nevertheless, mission work was carried out in the neighboring towns of La Florida and Tocaima. By 1971, some issues had been resolved, and evangelistic work resulted in eight baptisms that year.

Cachipay teachers, 1961: (bottom to top): Lucía Contreras, Margarita Romero, Virginia Terreros, Arnubia Días, Miriam Blanco

Evangelistic work also extended to the town of Peña Negra, near Cachipay, in 1971 with services in the home of Cachipay church member Alfonso Castro.[26]

The years 1977 and 1978 were difficult for the Mennonite church in Cachipay because of heavy debt and a scarcity of members. The new church council named in 1979 focused on three areas: leadership of worship services, evangelistic work, and administration.[27]

The school founded at Cachipay in 1947 to provide care and education to children of parents with leprosy soon expanded to serve children of Mennonite families, and then began serving other children of the area as well. The school met the requirements of the Colombian ministry of education, while also being established on Mennonite doctrines and principles. Its philosophy of education emphasized social solidarity, living in peace, respect for life, and seeking solutions to social conflict.[28] The school came to have an enrollment of 70 to 80 children who occupied various buildings containing school rooms, a dining room, a dormitory, a laundry, a chapel and a workshop. It ceased to function as a boarding school in 1966, becoming a day school.[29] In 1972 there were 60 children enrolled.[30]

The *Cristo vive* (Christ lives) church in Anolaima, after its founding in 1952, grew in the 1960s and constructed its own church in 1968. This church was notable for the work done with poor families.[31] When

Disney and Jaime
Caro, 1964

Eliécer Góngora and his wife Arcelia took up the work in Anolaima in 1975, the church counted 42 members, but internal conflict resulted in some members leaving the church. Nevertheless, these members later returned to the church with an offering, with which a church debt was retired.[32]

The church in la Mesa began in 1951 with the establishment of a school (later called the *Colegio Americano Menno*) along with worship services in the home of the missionaries Laverne and Harriet Rutschman. In spite of strong Catholic opposition, a church was functioning by 1963.[33] Its first pastor, Jaime Caro, emphasized evangelistic campaigns. The "Evangelism in Depth" program as well as the ALFALIT literacy program were both supported by the church. By 1971, the church numbered 32 members. Nevertheless, the church in la Mesa had its share of division, pastoral changes, and cases requiring church discipline in the 1960s and 70s.[34]

The *Colegio Americano Menno*, founded in 1955, offered an alternative to Protestant families who faced religious discrimination when trying to enrol their children in local public schools.[35] Vernelle Heen Yoder was the first director of the school, which was closed several times by municipal authorities. In 1956, Luis Rodríguez continued teaching his students at home when the authorities put obstacles in the way.[36] By 1959 the school counted 20 students, and in 1965 the government granted the school its license and gave the school official accreditation.[37]

Students at Colegio Menno, ca. 1960

In 1964, twenty years after founding the school at Cachipay, Gerald and Mary Hope Stucky decided to collaborate with some ex-students in opening a church in Ciudad Berna, a suburb of Bogotá.[38] In May, 1967 more than 400 people celebrated the first worship service.[39] In 1971 Antonio Arévalo became pastor of this church.[40] The 1970s saw impressive growth in this congregation, which came to number 250 members, with around 400 people attending regularly. Pastor Arévalo was strongly influenced by pentecostalism, emphasizing speaking in tongues, the filling of the Holy Spirit, praise songs, hand clapping, halleluyas, and audible, simultaneous congregational prayers. A group of church leaders who had been raised in Colombian Mennonite schools were not in agreement with this style of worship. This led to a doctrinal crisis within the church and the departure of some of the founding members. A nucleus of ex-students in fact began a new work further north, in an area called Chapinero – what would later become the Teusaquillo Mennonite church.[41]

The Berna church offered an important ministry to the community in the 1970s, founding and running a day care service for poor families in the Policarpa Salavarrieta neighborhood. Gloria Figueroa's leadership in this effort was notable. The church also established a medical clinic, where care could obtained for a very small price.[42] Pastor Antonio Arévalo led the church until 1981, when he left to work

The church in Ciudad Berna, 1969

in New York with a hispanic congregation. His place was taken by Angel Cañón who had been pastor at the Mennonite church of Teusaquillo.[43]

The Mennonite church of Ibagué began in 1965 when missionaries Glendon and Rita Klassen were seconded to the Presbyterian church as workers in a teachers' training school in that place. At the time there were 10 Mennonite students attending the school, and soon the group began gathering for Sunday school and evangelization efforts, with the first baptisms taking place in 1966.[44] The Mennonite church of Ibagué was founded officially in January, 1968. By 1973 the congregation had assumed full responsibility for financial support of its pastor, and in October, 1979 a new church building was dedicated to God.[45] In 1970 members from the Mennonite churches of Berna and Ibagué began evangelistic work in the city of Girardot. Two years later a locale was acquired for church services and the congregation was officially inaugurated. The congregation continued to grow for the rest of the decade.[46]

The Mennonite church of Colombia recognized the importance of preparing leaders and pastors, and sent students to various institutions for further theological education. In 1970, Luis Rodríguez became one of the first to study theology at the *Instituto Bíblico Alianza* (Alliance Biblical Institute) in Armenia. In 1976, IEMCO decided to collaborate with the Institute by sending the missionaries Lawrence and Lydia Wilson to accompany Mennonite students there.[47] This work set the foundations for a Mennonite church in that city in the 1980s, following a successful evangelistic campaign.[48]

When Gerald and Mary Hope Stucky returned from a furlough in the United States in 1973, they began meeting with ex-students from Cachipay and other interested persons in their home in Bogotá. The group grew to 40 people and, following baptisms and weddings the group decided to form the Mennonite Community of Chapinero in 1977.

In the 1980s the Chapinero congregation joined with a former Presbyterian congregation that shared its interest in both spiritual and social action. Following a visit from the Puerto Rican preacher Angel Bahamundi, who brought spiritual healing and revival to the group, the congregation decided to name Angel Cañón as pastor of the Mennonite church. Shortly after, a building was purchased to serve as the administrative center for the Mennonite church. It was remodelled to contain offices, worship and study space and a bookstore. The

Teusaquillo Center

Chapinero congregation, today known as Teusaquillo, located in this new building.[49]

The Mennonite church of Facatativa, a city west of Bogotá, began in 1976, with the spiritual healing of Pedro Olaya after he requested prayer from Mennonite church members. Meetings began to be held in his house, and pastor Antonio Arévalo of Bogotá was invited to lead the group. This congregation was very active in prayer and made strong links with other Protestant churches of the city. A successful evangelistic campaign of personal evangelism, evangelistic cell groups, audiovisual presentations and courses led to the growth and establishment of a Mennonite church in the city.

By 1968 the Evangelical Mennonite Church of Colombia (IEMCO) had taken over governance of the Colombian Mennonite church from the Mennonite Mission in the U.S.: missionaries now worked under the direction of the national church, and titles to all properties were transferred to IEMCO.[50] The entire process took place without internal struggles, thanks to the wisdom of the missionaries and national leaders of that time.[51]

At the local level, IEMCO recognized the autonomy of every congregation. Local congregations were to be run by church councils and would choose their own pastors, deacons, secretaries, treasurers and Sunday school superintendents. At the national level, IEMCO held yearly general assemblies with representatives of all churches, and named the board of directors. Mennonite distinctives were emphases on the church, love, discipleship, and the authority of Scripture.[52] By 1980, IEMCO was made up of twelve organized congregations, with two more in formation, and numbered a total of 856 baptized members. Among its ministries, it had established a home for the elderly poor, a bookstore, a foundation

Guiding principles of the Chapinero Community

1. We believe that Jesus Christ is our Lord and Savior.

2. We will strive to make the life and teachings of Jesus the norm of our conduct.

3. We agree to form a visible church (the Body of Christ), called the Mennonite Community of Chapinero, and with God's help, give and receive support: to serve one another mutually, to seek fraternal communion, and to seek the Kingdom of God and His justice.

4. We will strive to learn and to grow in the Christian life, offering our gifts to the service of the church.

Aims of IEMCO, as published in its constitution, 1968

a) To glorify God the Father; to exalt Jesus Christ the Lord and Savior; to honor the Holy Spirit.

b) To form local churches to the extent that the Lord opens the way.

c) To preach the Gospel to all creatures, carrying out in this way the Great Commission of the Lord.

d) To edify the church, which is the Body of Christ the Lord, and to offer mutual help to believers.

The *Hogar Cristiano La Paz*

for social and economic development and a Mennonite center for biblical studies.[53]

The *Hogar Cristiano La Paz* (Peace Christian Home) was a project that originated in 1968 with the concern of Mennonite women from several congregations about the needs of poor older people living in Bogotá. Oliva de Bastidas, one of these women, was instrumental in renting a facility in 1973 in the Calvo Sur neighborhood of the city and, supported by the Berna church, offered the services of the home to the elderly in the churches.[54] The aim of the home was "To provide a home, love and protection to as many elderly as possible, who have insufficient resources, and who have no other way of receiving adequate help or attention."[55] By 1979 a three-story house had been purchased to continue this mission.[56]

Oliva de Bastidas

The *La Luz* (The Light) bookstore had its beginnings in 1972 as a travelling and home bookstore run by John Wiebe.[57] Once the Mennonite Center was established in Tesauquillo, the bookstore located in its own space, becoming the second-most important seller of religious books in the city, following the Catholic bookstores.

Grandmother Graciela Chacón

Grandmother Graciela Chacón, 86 years of age, was found by Oliva de Bastidas on a sidewalk near the church, on a July day. She was a spectre of humanity, surrounded by stray dogs who took away the food she received as handouts. Bothered by this lamentable situation, sister Oliva waited a good while, to see if someone would come for her. Eventually a poor woman came and took her to a small lean-to near the church, where grandmother Chacón had a bed and a trunk, which probably held some identity documents. When sister Oliva asked for permission to look into the matter, the other woman denied her permission, and became very agitated. Sister Oliva then came with a policeman to help her investigate what was going on. Inside the trunk she found a certificate of citizenship and other documents that proved grandmother Chacón to have been a teacher who had also been a school director. This led sister Oliva to investigate what had become of her pension, for she also found payment receipts. She discovered that the woman who had come for grandmother Chacón in fact was cashing the checks, keeping the money, and turning the grandmother out into the street to beg. The pension office told sister Oliva that if she could house the grandmother in the home for the elderly, they would transfer the pension there. With some difficulty, sister Oliva managed to take grandmother Chacón to the home, where she was cleaned up and cared for. A bed, mattress and bedding was donated for her use by a furniture factory, and she slowly recovered her health. After some time, sister Oliva took her to the national pension offices, well-dressed from head to toe, and able to speak for herself. The director of pensions and the doctor who had treated her were completely surprised at the transformation, and were very thankful for the care and attention given to her. Grandmother Graciela Chacón lived at the home another eight years, before passing away at the age of 94.

The Colombian Mennonite Foundation for Development (MENCOL-DES) was founded in 1975, receiving legal government status a year later.[58] As an arm of IEMCO, MENCOLDES was created to respond to individual and communal needs. The board of directors was composed of equal numbers of members from the Mennonite church and the Mennonite Brethren church. The first executive director was Luis Correa, member of the Mennonite church of Teusaquillo.[59] Financial support was provided by MEDA and MCC as well as by World Vision, OXFAM and Bread for the World, among others. MENCOLDES programs focused on improving agricultural production, community organization, health programs, and providing credit sources for small industries and businesses. Agricultural programs were concentrated in the department of Chocó. By 1980, 74 lines of credit had been advanced for a total of $1,650,000.00, with 95 percent of the money lent to members of the two Mennonite conferences.[60]

Luis and Fanny Correa, 1968

The need to educate national leaders led first to the teaching of distance education courses, directed by Armando Hernández and by the missionaries George and Margaret Ediger.[61] This led to the foundation of the *Centro de Estudios Bíblicos* (Center of Biblical Studies) which began functioning in 1971 in the towns of Anolaima and la Mesa, offering classes at both the licentiate and bachelor levels. Classes in theology were also offered at the Mennonite church in Bogotá in 1972, in which 32 students participated, and course offerings expanded into other churches from there.[62]

In the 1960s and following, the Colombian Mennonite church strengthened its connections with churches in other countries. In February, 1968 the first Latin American Mennonite Congress was held in Bogotá. The aims of the Congress were to provide an occasion for church representatives to get to know one another and the work being done in other churches, to examine what work could be done collaboratively (such as publications and evangelism), and to strengthen the work of the church in Latin America into the future.[63] Messages, talks and devotionals were offered by Mennonite church representatives from a wide variety of Latin American countries.[64]

Approved recommendations of the Latin American Congress, 1968

• We recommend that the Mennonite churches identify with the suffering people and work to eliminate the causes of misery and injustice, initiating social programs or participating in ones already in place, as circumstances dictate.

• We recommend that Mennonite churches, along with other pacifist groups, seek the possibility of finding legal alternatives to military service, for reasons of conscience.

• Given some changes of attitude and procedure towards Protestants in the Roman Catholic Church following Vatican II, we recommend that dialogue take place with Roman Catholics, as long as it can be done without compromising our biblical principles.

In spite of the fact that the majority of participants in this event were North American missionaries, the meeting took place in a new ecclesial, political and social Latin American context, and marks the beginning of a new Latin American consciousness which would continue to grow in the Latin American Mennonite congresses which were to follow.

In 1971, a meeting of Mennonite representatives took place in Bogotá in which the foundations were set for the creation of JELAM. Colombian pastor Armando Hernández was named Executive Director of JELAM and moved to Puerto Rico in 1973 to take charge of the radio programs produced and distributed by JELAM. In Ibagué the local radio station agreed to broadcast the *Luz y Verdad* programs on Saturdays and Tuesdays.[65]

The interest of the Mennonite Brethren in missionary work in Colombia began with students at the Bethany Biblical Institute of Saskatchewan, Canada.[66] In 1943 the Mennonite Brethren of North America decided to send G. W. Peters and his wife to visit South America. They in turn recommended continuing the missionary work begun by Plymouth Brethren missionaries in 1929 at the station of la Cumbre, in Cali, Colombia. The first missionaries were Daniel Wirsche and David Wirsche in 1945. This initial Mennonite Brethren mission work in the del Valle region of Colombia, which includes the city of Cali, soon would extend to the region of el Chocó in the western part of the country, and to the city of Medellín.

At la Cumbre the Mennonite Brethren continued the educational work begun by Ana E. Woolf with her little school for poor children. The Los Andes school opened in 1947, but was closed after three days by local authorities. It was not allowed to open until the following year. In 1949 there was so much public disturbance that classes were suspended for a time, and in 1950 the school was closed again by local officials. Much pressure at other levels had to be applied in order to be able to re-open the school.[67]

After the Wirsches visited the Pacific coast, it was decided to begin a work in the Chocó, more specifically in Istmina, where a house was rented that belonged to the Chocó Pacifico Mining Company. The Chocó is a region in western Colombia whose towns are populated primarily by indigenous people and descendants of Africans. The first baptism in Istmina took place in 1949, and a church of African-descendants began to form. Opposition by the Catholic church to the missionary work of the Mennonites was so strong that, by order of the priest and with the collaboration of the local authorites, the chapel was closed in December of 1947. It was only opened again following great efforts and discussions in Bogotá.

Jacob Loewen with native students

Thanks to the work of the anthropologist Jacob Loewen, mission work among the Noanama indigenous tribe began, with the aim of translating the Bible for this tribe, composed of about 2,000 persons. Here also, persecution by the authorities reached such a point that Loewen had to transfer his linguistic work to Cali. In 1957, Loewen travelled to the United States and decided to continue his linguistic work with the Embera-Wounaan tribe on the border between Panama and Colombia (see chapter 21).

The clinic that was built in Istmina in 1947 faced opposition from the Catholic brothers and the authorities. It was closed and re-opened several times, but continued to provide its medical service to the community up to the early 1960s. In 1964 the clinic attended to 3,338 patients, but by June of that year the clinic was closed for good.[68] With the opening of the Hospital Universitario del Valle, the Mennonite Brethren decided to collaborate by providing two missionary nurses to work in that center. The hospital paid their salaries, while the mission board provided their housing. Gertrudes Woelk and Esther Wiens worked in the emergency ward and along with testifying to co-workers and patients, they also provided medical assistance to members of the San Fernando church. In 1968, after four years of service, they reflected that it had been a positive experience, and projected plans for expanding their work in the future by opening clinics in the area for teaching basic health principles.[69]

Part of the strategy for gaining local acceptance for the Mennonite church, in face of Catholic intransigence, was to include education in the mission of the church, a pattern that was repeated in many of the mission locations established by the Mennonite Brethren. The school in Istmina, which opened in 1951, had to be closed because of strong local opposition. It re-opened in 1960 with 18 pupils, but closed again in 1964 for lack of teachers.[70] The bookstore *El Faro* (The Beacon) began operating in 1960 as an extension of the mission in Istmina, providing religious literature for the region.[71]

The church in la Cumbre, which became the point of origin for many new churches in the surrounding area, first had to withstand a vigorous anti-Protestantism in the late 1950s and early 1960s, fomented by local Roman Catholic priests. Stone throwing directed at both the church and the school was commonplace, and statues of the Virgin del Carmen were placed at the entrances to la Cumbre as a sign of protest against Protestants. People were encouraged to make

The testimony of Antonio Mosquera

I was born by the San Juan river in a village called San Antonio, very close to Istmina. I was raised there as a country child, by the edge of the river. I had the privilege of playing constantly on the river, in a canoe, swimming, fishing, and playing in the town square with other children. ... When I was a boy I would travel by canoe to study at the school of Istmina. I was six years old when I got to know the first missionaries who arrived in Istmina in 1946. They were John and Ana Dyck. ... They would come to my house to evangelize in the evenings, carrying a gas lantern for light. Ana would teach us to sing songs accompanied by her accordion, and taught Bible lessons to the children using figures. The sound of the accordion was a rare thing; it was unknown in that little town. ... As a child, I was impressed by the stories of God opening the Red Sea, and the stories of Jesus feeding the multitudes. For these reasons I preferred going to Sunday School instead of the mass.

At that time, public education was controlled by the Roman Catholic clergy, and they had a very strong influence in schools and colleges. I began being punished at school for attending the meetings of the Mennonite Brethren. They would not allow me recess and would make me kneel on the floor on toasted kernels of corn, with my hands in the air. The teacher would see me ready to cry at being so tired, and even then would not let me lower my hands. ... My father told John Dyck what I was going through, and he recommended that I switch to the Mennonite Brethren educational centre in la Cumbre (Cali). This is how I came to the "School of the Andes" in la Cumbre to finish my primary schooling.

special prayers before these images.[72] Added to this was the difficulty the church had in raising enough money to meet the needs of the church and the school. Nevertheless, the testimony of these believers continued, and attendance grew to 90 persons or more in 1961, with evangelistic efforts to surrounding towns, such as Sabaletas, continuing as well.[73]

Educational efforts eventually bore fruit. The Mennonite primary school in la Cumbre, *Colegio los Andes*, faced economic uncertainty in 1961, but managed to survive and was licensed by the Ministry of Education the following year. After fourteen years of operation the school had graduated 66 students, of whom 36 went on to secondary education; of these, only three had received their high school diploma. The need for high school education led to the offering of first year courses at la Cumbre in 1964.[74] By 1966 a Mennonite high school had been established and moved to Cali where it came to be called *Colegio Américas Unidas*. By 1969 this secondary institution had 63 students enrolled. Of these, 38 were children of Protestant families, and of these, 19 were from Mennonite families. By 1970, half of the student body was Mennonite.[75]

Colegio Los Andes, 1959

The Mennonite church of San Fernando in Cali not only continued to grow as a congregation,[76] the church property also became the location for the new Cali Biblical Institute in 1960.[77] Students were to live in residence and assigned a pastor as supervisor.[78] The program counted twelve students in 1961; the following year 25 students were enrolled.[79] In spite of help from the mission, covering costs was difficult for the students, but there was immediate benefit to local churches, as students collaborated with evangelism, distributed tracts and helped with worship services, youth groups and Bible schools as part of their curriculim requirements.[80] In June, 1963 five young people graduated after having completed three years of biblical studies; another 20 youth were involved in both day and night courses.[81] By 1974 there were six instructors giving classes in the Biblical Institute: Víctor Plazas, Carlos Osorio, Américo Murillo, Oscar Murillo, Jesús Ramírez and Gabriel Mosquera.[82]

Mission efforts in the Chocó region continued following the active evangelistic pattern set by the early MB missionaries. John Dyck, for example, visited La Isidra, Suruco, Andagoya, Andagoyita, Primavera, Bebedo, Condoto, Las Mojaras, Novita, Tado and other small communities.[83] One of the earliest MB churches in the region was in Noamaná, organized in 1955, where a school was started in 1960.[84] In the 1960s, MB churches were founded in Andagoya, Basurú, Boca de Suruco (where the Sinaí church established two mission stations in Primavera and Giguales[85]) in Platinero, Condoto (one of the first mission communities in the Chocó) and San Pablo Adentro. There were evangelistic efforts in Raspadura and Belén de Docampadó as well as in the towns of Nóvita, Certegui and Ánimas.[86] In 1974 the Istmina church initiated a new evangelistic work in the town of Misará.[87]

The Mennonite Brethren churches of the Chocó were organized regionally, meeting in an annual assembly of church delegates which consulted on church issues and elected a board of directors. This board later met

Testimony of José Vicente Castillo

In 1959 the Catholic priest of San José would preach against the Protestants; he taught people to hate them. As a parishoner, one of the things José Vicente Castillo did was to put down nail mats so that when the vehicle of the Mennonite missionaries passed the tires would go flat, and they wouldn't be able to come to the town. But one day José Vicente himself was travelling along the same road on a bicycle and blew out his own tires, took a nasty tumble and suffered injuries. He got up and removed the nail mats, thinking to himself that if God were not with these people he wouldn't have had the accident. After his conversion, José Vicente himself became a Mennonite pastor in that town.

on a monthly basis to deal with pastoral, administrative and other issues. Under this supervision, a women's organization was formed and particular attention was paid to the needs of the numerous youth in the regional churches.[88]

In the late 1950s and early 1960s the Mennonite Brethren were very active in planting churches in the del Valle region around Cali, among which were churches in Cisneros, Villa Hermosa, San José, Jiguales, Río Blanco, Dagua and Yumbo.[89] These churches were typically small, with one of the largest being the church in Cisneros which had reached a membership of 60 persons by 1969.[90] These small churches also initiated primary schools in connection with the church, sometimes with as few as six students as was the case for the primary school operating in Dagua in 1964,[91] but also sometimes growing to a significant size, as in the case of the primary school at Yumbo which registered 94 students in 1968 with two teachers giving instruction.[92]

Churches in more rural areas encountered continuing opposition from local Roman Catholic priests and parishoners, in varying degrees of intensity and severity.[93] In some cases, ferocious local opposition led some members to leave the church,[94] but in general, evangelical fervor continued in spite of the opposition. Perhaps the most difficult problem faced by these small churches was posed by their limited financial resources. They were all supported in some measure by the conference and mission board, but even so they struggled to help support their pastors and teachers and to meet church expenses.[95] Nevertheless evangelistic efforts at opening new churches continued, often supported by students from the Biblical Institute, with churches planted in Villa Colombia, Barrio Alfonso López, Barrio Popular, Vivienda Popular, Siloé, Digua, Maracaibo (with 62 baptized members in 1968), Belén, Chigorodó. In addition, preaching and evangelistic efforts took place in many other locations.[96] The Mennonite Brethren Churches located in the del Valle region were organized regionally and met once a year, with representatives from the churches in attendance. This regional committee was in charge of pastoral and administrative oversight for the churches of the region.

Beginning in 1968 the city of Medellín became the target of new mission efforts. The plan was to have missionaries open new works which would be carried forward by national leaders. No doubt the United Biblical Seminary, in which Mennonite Brethren participated, provided an impetus for mission efforts in Medellín.[97] By 1973 a small congregation had been formed in the neighborhood of El Salvador in Antioquía, and plans were made to construct a church building there, as the church continued to grow.[98]

The national organization of the church, the National Conference of Mennonite Brethren of Colombia (*Conferencia Nacional de los Hermanos Menonitas de Colombia*: CNHMC) was formed in 1953. The designation for the national organization was changed in the early 1970s to the "Association of Mennonite Brethren Churches of Colombia" (*Asociación de Iglesias de Hermanos Menonitas de Colombia*: AIHMC). Conference business was carried out by an executive committee named by the annual assembly of congregational representatives. The San Fernando Mennonite church in Cali, which housed the Biblical Institute, became the center of activity for Mennonite Brethren in the 1960s and 70s. The *Pregonero* became the official printed journal for the conference. In spite of some difficulties in the 1960s and the suspension of publication in 1973, the paper was reorganized and continued to report on church events.[99]

In 1960 the National Conference of Mennonite Brethren of Colombia counted 183 baptized members.[100] At an evaluative meeting of pastors and church workers in 1966 it was noted that economic difficulties were predominant, with many small churches having few resources, often carrying debt for church buildings and unable to generate enough income to pay their pastors. Some proposals were made at that time to address the situation, and they had a positive effect.[101] By the early 1980s, the MB Conference in Colombia had come to include 24 churches with a baptized membership of 1,100 persons.[102]

The National Conference of Mennonite Brethren of Colombia collaborated in a series of interdenominational efforts with other Protestant groups in the country, as well as with the Evangelical Mennonite Church of Colombia. Both Mennonite conferences were founding members of the Evangelical Confederation of Colombia (CEDEC) when that Protestant body was formed in 1954. This group, which included Baptists, Adventists and Lutherans, lobbied for religious liberties and joined together to pray for change.[103]

Two interdenominational educational institutions also served the Colombian Mennonite church. The teachers' college in Ibagué (*Escuela Normal Presbiteriana de Ibagué*) was run by the Presbyterian church in Colombia. Both Mennonite conferences collaborated by providing teachers and sending students to be trained there. Students did practicums at the *Colegio Americano*, located in the same building. The school offered courses in Bible, Christian Education, Doctrine and Church History. Mennonite graduates were pressed into service teaching in Mennonite instititutions such as the *Colegio de los Andes* and Istmina.[104]

The United Biblical Seminary (*Seminario Bíblico Unido*), which was operating by the mid-1960s, was a wide-ranging interdenominational effort in which both Mennonite conferences participated.[105] By 1968 the seminary began concentrating on distance education, and came to be located in Medellín, with vice-rectors in Cali, Medellín and Bogotá. In Cali, the Seminary used the premises of the Mennonite Brethren in San Fernando. The Seminary offered certificates and diplomas for Sunday school teachers, a diploma in theology and a bachelors degree in theology.[106] The Seminary also offered ten-day workshops for interested churches and their members.[107] In 1973 the Mennonite Brethren approved affiliation with the Biblical Seminary of Medellín, and the following year nine MB students were enrolled.[108]

Colombian Mennonites also participated in interdenominational evangelistic efforts. A notable case occurred in 1960 and 1961 with the Billy Graham crusade, for which Mennonite churches provided support through prayer and logistics.[109] The influence of "Evangelism in Depth" and the Navigators was notable in these and other evange-

San Fernando Church in Cali

listic efforts, particularly among the Mennonite Brethren. The emphasis of these groups was to strengthen the Christian life of members by means of prayer, fasting and learning to follow Christ, as well as promoting evangelism in and for the church and Bible school by organizing groups, workshops and retreats.[110] According to a report by Herman Buller, MB participation in the "Evangelism in Depth" program brought about a real enthusiasm for evangelism, although it also had some limitations.[111]

Beginning in the 1970s, the work of MEDA and MCC also began to take concrete shape in Colombia. The initiative was to provide loans for cooperatives, for rural development, provide commercial loans and also logistical help and education in administration.[112]

The ultra-conservative, Catholic nature of Colombia in the 1940s and 50s made it a challenging task to establish Protestant and Mennonite churches in the country. Nevertheless a Mennonite church presence was well rooted and growing by the 1960s and 70s.

The Mennonite churches of Colombia placed a notable emphasis on education, beginning with the boarding school for children in Cachipay. Local churches, no matter how small, generally attempted to establish a local primary school in conjuction with the church. In addition there were efforts to carry out secondary education for community and church members and to provide Bible school and seminary instruction for pastors and leaders. Mennonites in Colombia collaborated closely with other Protestant groups in these educational efforts, and demonstrated their general concern for the educational well-being of Colombians.

A positive result of these concerted efforts in education has been the emergence of a strong national church leadership in the Colombian Mennonite churches. Control by national leaders over the General Conference and Mennonite Brethren churches evolved naturally in these decades, and saw the emergence of national conference organizations. The national conferences became owners of church property and took over the planning and coordination of activities for the Colombian Mennonite church, as well as responsibility for church budgets – a mark of the mature and capable national leadership of these churches.

In the midst of the political crisis of violence brought on by Cold War tensions, with a militaristic doctrine of "national security" on the one hand and a growing leftist guerilla movement on the other, the Mennonite churches of Colombia worked to integrate their positive response to charismatic renewal and the need of the poor and marginalized of the country for material assistance. With the help of MEDA and MCC, and following in the Anabaptist tradition of discipleship, Colombian Mennonites founded MENCOLDES as a faith response to the social, economic and political crisis. The intentional combination of charismatic evangelism and social action is a notable mark of the Colombian Mennonite churches.

Mennonite Missions in Peru (1946-1979)

The conquest of the fabulous empire of the Incas, known as Tawantinsuyo, by Francisco Pizarro from 1531 to 1535 has been called one of the greatest feats in the history of humankind.[1] The Incas, or "sons and daughters of the sun," had conquered and unified many nations as they extended their empire from the north of Ecuador to the middle of Chile, from the Pacific Ocean to the high plateau of Bolivia and the jungle region of Peru.[2]

From the moment in which Brother Vincente de Valverde, the chaplain of Francisco Pizarro's army, demanded that the Inca Atahualpa convert to Christianity and submit to the King of Spain, the Christian religion became a pretext for conquest. From 1535 to 1556, greed, hatred and murder characterized the actions of the Spanish conquistadores and soldiers and the clerics who accompanied them. By the beginnings of the 17th century, all the church institutions needed to consolidate the church were in place: dioceses, monasteries for men and women, the tithes, three universities, primary schools and hospitals.[3]

The abuses and arbitrary measures carried out against the indigenous peoples resulted in a series of uprisings during the colonial period, including the failed armed uprising of José Gabriel Tupac Amaru, who occupied Cuzco in November, 1780. Tupac Amaru's demands in favor of all Americans led the Creole ruling class to no longer support Bourbon power in the Americas. Several prominent clerics prepared the way for the emancipation of Peru from Spain.[4]

The barest beginning of Protestantism in Peru is marked by the arrival in June, 1822 of Baptist pastor James Thompson in Lima, at the invitation of the liberator General José de San Martín.[5] However, the

155

real opening for the establishment of Protestant missions in Peru came with the recognition of religious toleration in the constitution adopted in November, 1915.[6] Protestantism was nationalized and institutionalized in Peru from 1930 to 1960, during which time numerous new missionary organizations arrived, especially of holiness and Pentecostal currents, strongly influenced by North American fundamentalism.[7]

Among the missions which settled in Peru in the 1940s was the Summer Linguistic Institute (Wycliff Bible Translators), of special interest for the study of Mennonites in Peru. In 1945 the Peruvian government approved the establishment of that institute, with the promise that it would initiate the colonization of the Amazon jungle.[8] The bilingual schools administered by the Institute broke the Catholic monopoly. The base for this linguistic work was constructed in Yarinococha, a lake accessed by sea planes and close to the city of Pucallpa.[9]

The Ashaninca peoples live in the Peruvian jungle; their language belongs to the linguistic family of the Arawak or Arahuaca, and the word Ashaninca means "our people," in the sense of "countrymen." There had been many Franciscan missions among these people, but rebellions were also common.[10]

In the Ashaninca village of Poyemi

The Protestant mission to the Ashaninca peoples was begun by the Adventists in 1920.[11] The Krimmer Mennonite Brethren Mission joined the work in May, 1946, when Sylvester and Mattie Dirks began to collaborate with the Wycliff Bible Translators (WBT) among the semi-nomadic Ashaninca in the eastern part of the central Peruvian jungle. At that time approximately 30,000 indigenous people lived in small villages along the river systems of the jungle. During their time with the WBT, the Dirks' were supported economically by the Krimmer MB Mission.[12] Their work emphasized the phonology and morphology of the language of the Ashaninca, for the Peruvian government did not allow the WBT to evangelize. Living near these indigenous peoples were around 12,000 Spanish-speaking Peruvians who lived in small towns similar to Atalaya and Santa Rosa.

In 1949 the Dirks' left their linguistic work, but requested permission from the Peruvian government to continue working among the Ashaninca peoples in agriculture, health and evangelization. They returned in June of 1950 to do this work and acquired 110 hectares of land in the Department of Ucayali, near the rivers Urubamba and Ucayali. Now located again in Atalaya, they chose a place called "El Encuentro" to serve as the center of operations for the missionary activity of the Krimmer MB church. From 1952 on the Dirks' carried out Bible studies every Thursday and Friday.

Sylvester Dirks helped the Spanish-speaking community as well as the indigenous community with the application of DDT and giving injections when members of the community fell ill. The missionaries communicated equally with the Ashanincas as with the Spanish-speaking Peruvians who lived in the small towns of the region. Given the cultural and linguistic differences between the two groups it was felt necessary to request another missionary couple. The Mennonite Brethren Board of Mission and Service collaborated with this church project of working with Spanish-speaking Peruvians by sending the missionaries Joe and Jan Walter (1954) and Johnny and Harriet Toews (1958). They worked in education, contributed to the health clinic and in pastoral and biblical work in Atalaya, Santa Rosa and San Pablo. Paul and Maurine Friesen arrived in El Encuentro in 1960 to join the Dirks in ministry with the Ashaninca.

The 1960s and 1970s were marked politically by populist governments which generated high expectations for developmental policies, encouraged by the Alliance for Progress.[13] The "Bishop's Pastoral Letter on some aspects of the social question in Peru," published in 1958, is a milestone in that it identified commitment to social justice as a Christian duty. This commitment took concrete form in the agrarian reforms inaugurated by

Paul Friesen with Ashaninca men

Ashaninca dwelling

Fernando Belaúnde in 1964, when the Archbishop of Cuzco, Mon. Carlos M. Jurgens ordered the redistribution of 13,000 hectares – owned by the Catholic church – at a time when the peasants simply occupied the land out of desperation. The Peruvian government put social and agrarian reforms in motion, supported by the bishops of Peru, reinforced by the calls for justice from the Episcopal Conference of Medellín. In this context, the priest Gustavo Gutierrez, advisor to the National Union of Catholic Students and also to the bishops gathering at Medellín, published his book *The Theology of Liberation* (1971), a theology written from the reality of Latin America which came to be known world-wide.[14] After 1975 there was a return

Learning to read

to repression and torture of peasants, union members and political detainees, under the militaristic "National Security" policy. In many dioceses of the Catholic church, lay people, priests and bishops took up a prophetic role of denouncing these developments.[15]

The translation work in the Amazonian jungle of Peru among more than thirty different ethnic groups was extremely controversial during the 1960s and 1970s. There were demands for justice on the part of creoles, peasants and indigenous people.[16]

In 1961 the Mennonite Brethren Mission Board decided to relocate the Dirks family with the Summer Institute of Linguistics so that they could continue their translation work with the linguist Willard Kindberg; their translation of the Gospel of John into Ashaninca was concluded in 1964. The Dirks family returned again to El Encuentro in 1964, where they evangelized for three more years. When the Dirks family returned permanently to North America, there

was a desire among the Ashanincas to take leadership and the church project continued.

In 1954 Joe and Jan Walter came from the United States to work with the Spanish-speaking community in areas around El Encuentro. The Swiss Indian Mission was looking for a place to start an indigenous Bible Institute and began in El Encuentro for one year. Members of five different tribes studied at this place in periods of six to nine weeks. In 1968 the Mennonite Brethren Board of Missions and Services continued working in that project of biblical education, sending

Ashaninca family doing Bible study

Paul Friesen as a teacher. In 1969, for example, of the fifty students in the Institute, sixteen were Ashanincas studying with Paul Friesen.

In 1963 there were fifteen baptized members, and by 1968 twelve church communities had been established. It was precisely because of this interest in forming church communities as alternatives to the Catholic church that opposition emerged.

On the other hand, the cultural resistance of the Ashanincas to the formation of denominational churches must also be mentioned. It is notable that the Mennonites worked to follow a pastoral method similar to the one followed in the Argentine Chaco. In 1968 they supported the emergence of the Ashaninca Evangelical Church Association and its related organization of community development known as the Ashaninca Development Committee. These were regional associations that gathered together members, not by denominational origin, but by cultural identity.[17]

From 1946 to 1979, Mennonite work in Peru concentrated on linguistic and evangelistic work among the indigenous peoples of Peru. The struggle of the Ashaninca people to preserve their culture, language and way of life, highlighted methods of evangelization. Mennonite missions in Peru have been notable for their cultural sensitivity, having worked hard to encourage the establishment and growth of locally-led indigenous churches. Mission work in Peru was modest in scope, but in these decades slowly expanded to reach out to Spanish-speaking Peruvians as well.

Mennonite Colonies and Missions in Bolivia (1946-1979)

Bolivia is located in the center of South America, comprising an area of more than one million square kilometers, but with no access to the ocean. The territory was originally part of the Inca empire which fell to the Spaniards in the sixteenth century.[1] Catholic doctrines spread at the hands of soldiers and the preaching of the priests. The Franciscans and Dominicans were the predominant orders.[2] Sporadic uprisings were suppressed by the Spaniards.

Independence from Spain came in 1824, after 15 years of struggle. Simon Bolivar was declared the first president of the nascent republic in 1825; the nation still carries his name.[3] One of the ideals of Simon Bolivar was religious freedom; nevertheless, his recommendations were not heeded. The second article of the constitution says literally: "The Roman Catholic Apostolic religion is the religion of the republic; all other public forms of worship are prohibited."[4] It would not be until 1905, when the liberals came to power, that article two of the constitution would be amended by the changing of the word "prohibited" to "allowed."

The historian Peter Wagner has pointed to the period from 1895 to 1919 as the time of the entry of missions to Bolivia,[5] but from 1920 to 1939 persecution of Protestants continued, although this did not stop Protestant missions from continuing to arrive in Bolivia. The period from 1936 to 1945 saw the reconstruction of Bolivia after the Chaco War and also marks the arrival of pentecostalism in the form of the Assemblies of God church in 1946. By 1967 the Assemblies of God had established 50 churches in Bolivia, with 4,255 members. The Holiness Church of God, another Pentecostal group, grew strongly among the Aymaras in La Paz after 1946.

April, 1952 marks the beginning of a military revolution in Bolivia which led to the nationalization of mines, an agrarian reform, and universal suffrage.[6] This new socio-political context opened the door wider for Protestant churches. The peasants were anxious to open their communities to anyone who could offer support in health and education. The churches now began facing more directly the problems experienced in the communities.[7] It was in the midst of this historical reality that the arrival of Mennonites to Bolivia began, not through missions, but rather via the immigration of farming colonies from Paraguay.

The Mennonites in Paraguay were the first to take advantage of the privilege to colonize the country, first offered by the Bolivian government in 1926 and 1930 but not open in reality until 1953.[8] In March, 1953 the new government of Bolivia reactivated agrarian reform and offered opportunities to colonists. Several persons from Fernheim colony visited the country, and were able to meet with the Director of the Ministry of Agriculture in La Paz, who informed them that the laws privileging colonists were still in force. Peter Regier reported concerning the climatic and soil conditions that "there are obvious agricultural possibilities because of the fertile soil, which is well populated; there is no frost in winter, and in summer the temperature remains under 38 degrees (10 degrees less than in the Paraguayan Chaco). The crops are sugar beets, cotton, corn, coffee, manioc, sweet potatoes, citrus fruits, and many more."[9] The report also mentioned the favorable prices being paid for crops in Bolivia.

A second investigative trip visited Villa Montes, for talks with a textile factory. This cotton firm was disposed to extend credit to 20 Mennonite families for a period of 10 years, under the following terms: the Bolivian Cotton Company would offer 20 interested colonists a land holding of 60 hectares each, $2,600.00 U.S. dollars, and one tractor for each five families. All this was offered on credit, at no interest. The first two years would be free of payment, but thereafter the debt would be divided among the eight remaining years and would be paid annually with a specified cotton quota. The Mennonite families did not believe they had the resources to undertake such a debt, but they hoped they could count on the support of the Committee for Aid to Colonists in North America.[10]

In January, 1954 the first Mennonite families moved from Paraguay to Bolivia with 5 wagons and 15 horses. Peter Regier wrote in his report that two wagons and a team of horses had been left in Villa

Montes. He thought that letting the people continue to see the horses was good advertisement for the new Mennonite colonists. There were three men from Fernheim who had managed to buy 1800 hectares; the cotton firm had helped them with the financing. They were committed to selling their cotton to the firm for the market price for as long as their debt lasted, after which they would be free to sell the cotton elsewhere.

In 1955 Peter Regier reported that the Mennonite colony in Bolivia had grown and that it was now inhabited by 100 persons; he also reported that in January, 1955 it had once rained for 16 hours without stopping. When Frank Wiens of MCC visited Bolivia he reported that the Mennonite colony of Santa Cruz was composed of 7 families who had come from Fernheim. He also reported that delegates from another 50 families from Menno colony in Paraguay had arrived to investigate the possibilities of settling in La Paz. Wiens spoke with government authorities and they were disposed to allow the establishment of more Mennonite colonies in Bolivia. He believed that the Mennonite families living in Bolivia were poor both spiritually and materially, and even though there was a preacher, attendance at worship services was very weak.

In one of the reports written by Nikolaus Kröker for *Der Bote* during 1954 and 1955, in which he compares economic conditions between Paraguay and Bolivia, there is a good description of the conditions found by the Mennonite colonists in Santa Cruz:

> Now we find ourselves in Bolivia and it is going pretty good. The Algodonera company has kept its word so far. We have already made the first payment of a loan on the land. There is a house on the land where we can live. The land is measured and there are building sites on both sides of the road. There is extra land at both ends of the colony. The company wants all of the land fenced in, and we have already begun on this work. The land where the building sites are is nearly all open land and is very fertile.[11]

Nikolaus Kröker was pastor to the families who moved to Santa Cruz. His writings show him interested in letting people know about the good geographical location of the Tres Palmas colony, which would facilitate the sale of its products.[12]

The reasons for the migrations from Paraguay to Bolivia were economic. The Mennonite colonies were closed societies that were strongly oriented to the sale of their products. In the case of the Mennonite colonists in the Paraguayan Chaco region, the cost of exporting agricultural produce was very high and earnings small, since transporting their products to the city was expensive. The Transchaco road had not yet been built. Furthermore, the first Paraguayan colonies were settled on land that was not well suited to agriculture[13]

On the 8th of July, 1956 a great celebration was held in the Mennonite colony of Tres Palmas with the inauguration of the new school, as well as thanksgiving for the harvest. Present at the celebrations was the German consul of Santa Cruz, the German ambassador in La Paz, and a personal advisor to the president of Bolivia.[14] The Mennonite colonists soon were able to obtain credit from the North American organization "U.S. Point Four," re-negotiating their initial debt and furthering themselves economically. It is not hard to understand why, a short time later in 1957, another group of 25 Mennonite conservative immigrant families – originally from Canada but at that time in Menno colony in Paraguay – re-located about three miles from Tres Palmas. In 1958 there were 189 inhabitants of the Mennonite colonies in Bolivia.[15] These original colonists prepared the way for more colonists who would come to Bolivia in the 1970s, as well as preparing the way for the founding of church organizations.[16]

Year of arrival, place or origin, and population of the Mennonite colonies in Bolivia, 1961-1983[29]

Colonies	Arrival	Origin	Persons	Number of Families
Bergthal	1961	Paraguay-Canada	297	50
Swift Current	1967	Mexico-Belize	2,510	300
Riva Palacios	1967	Mexico	5,500	1,094
Sommerfeld	1968	Mexico	366	61
Santa Rita	1968	Mexico-Belize	1,385	196
Las Piedras	1968	Canada	840	130
Reinland	1968	Paraguay-Canada	240	30
Rosenort	1975		350	–
Morgenland	1975	Paraguay-Canada	217	31
Valle Esperanza	1975	Mexico	1,486	180
Colonia Norte	1975	Mexico	357	50
Nueva Esperanza	1975	Mexico	1,200	200
Nueva Holanda	1982	Canada	490	70
Tres Cruces	1983	Mexico-Belize	550	69

In the 1960s and 1970s, the government of Bolivia experienced a series of elections, military coups and counter-coups which, however, did not impede the spread of Protestant churches.[17] In fact, in 1957 the bishop of the Methodist church reported that president Hernán Siles had invited the Methodists to establish as many churches, schools and medical centers as possible.[18] This is how a great surge of Methodist churches came to be established among the indigenous population

Felipe Flores stands out among the Aymara leadership. He studied in Protestant schools and became a professor in the Methodist college. Because of his political involvement, he reached the highest strata of the Nationalist Revolutionary Movement, and was named secretary of the National Confederation of Farm Workers of Bolivia. He also founded the Bolivian Social Evangelical Movement (MOSEB) and was elected to the national legislature where he served until he was assassinated in 1965.[19] By 1965 there were more than thirty-five Methodist congregations extending from La Paz to Cochabamba, Santa Cruz, Sucre, Potosí, Bei and Tarija, with a membership of 4,000. Eighty-five percent of the membership were Aymara- and Quechua-speaking people.[20]

The Bolivian Baptist Union also flourished, with thirty-nine congregations and a total of 3,435 members in 1967. In 1968, Justino Quispe was elected president of the Bolivian Baptist Union. He was an Aymara who had studied at the Baptist Seminary. He led the Aymara department of the "Evangelism in Depth" program that managed to gather together more than 7,000 people for the Protestant Aymara Congress. In 1967, this Bolivian organization began to attain economic independence, for the Canadian Baptists decided to no longer support this convention.[21]

The 1960s and 70s saw inter-confessional organizations emerge.[22] Especially important in Bolivia were the programs "Evangelism in Depth," the literacy program ALFALIT and the Caravans of Good Will, promoted by the Latin American Mission. The movement promoted by the World Council of Churches, known as "Church and Society in Latin America" (ISAL) took a clear position of critique concerning the social situation in Bolivia at this time of military dictatorship.[23] The important role played by the Methodist church must be recognized, and is clearly described in the "Manifesto to the Nation" signed by bishop Mortimer Arias in March, 1970. This document spoke of the liberating face of God in the Bible, expressed its agreement with the withdrawal of troops from the mining districts, and spoke of the need for educational reform and the nationalization of national wealth.[24]

Agrarian reform in Bolivia continued to attract immigrant groups, including even more German-origin Mennonite colonies from Paraguay, Canada, Mexico and Belize.[25] The primary reason for the immigration of these colonists was the attempt to maintain their families, communities, churches and education in accordance with their traditional structures. Virtually all of the Mennonite colonies located within a radius of 300 kilometers south, north and east of the city of Santa Cruz de la Sierra. Most of these Mennonite colonies were very conservative, emphasizing specific rules of conduct.[26]

Bishops of the Old Colony settlements of Santa Rita, Riva Palacio and Swift Current

What we are expressing here covers more or less our tasks and our work in the field, to provide our daily needs, such as we learned from our forebears so that we can be an honest farming community. This is how we wish to live, using tractors that do not have rubber tires, nor using electricity. We have no cars or trucks. We do not need them, and we prefer that the rest of the population use them. This is how we were taught by our parents in accordance with what Paul says in 2 Timothy 3:14: 'But remain in what you have learned and believed, knowing from whom you learned it.' If someone has soya, corn or any other load that needs to be transported, we use national companies to do it. We farm with our steel-wheeled tractors, and when we need to travel, we use horses and buggies. If we need to shop for food or go to visit the doctor, we go to Santa Cruz.

For these conservative Mennonites, "worldly things" had a negative effect on communitarian life and were unnecessary for the spiritual health and well being of the Christian community.[27] There were, however, other Mennonite colonies in Santa Cruz that were less conservative and permitted the use of vehicles, rubber-tired tractors, telephones and other modern devices.[28]

The great majority of the Mennonite colonies were made up of families who had many children (eight to ten) and had well-defined geographical boundaries as well as political and ecclesial autonomy. The Bolivian government granted them freedom to practice their religion, exempted them from military service, and allowed them to administer their own schools. The Mennonites were seen by other Bolivians as a hard-working and honest people, with a great capacity to cultivate new land, but at the same time there was wonder at the refusal of these people to participate in the development of culture and society. Little is known within the colonies about what is happening outside. Medical care is provided by people within the colonies who are self-taught.[30]

With respect to the role of women, it can be noted that in the colonies that came from Paraguay, women play a less traditional role than in the colonies originating in Belize or Mexico. The patriarchal character of the colonies means that the women play a subordinate role, dedicating themselves to home responsibilities such as child care and farm tasks such as milking the cows or feeding the chickens. When one visits the homes

Mennonite farmers return from Santa Cruz

of the colonists it is typical to find the head of the family sitting next to the visitors, after which are seated the men, and then the daughters and the mother. In many cases the women will sit down to eat after the men have been served and have eaten their meal.[31]

The church occupies a central place in the life of the colonies. It is the bishop who applies the community norms. Bishops normally are persons named to that position for life; they exercise much power, given that they are charged with maintaining order in the colony and the church, and they settle disputes or differences internally, without recourse to the Bolivian judicial system.

The Mennonite Central Committee began playing an important role in Bolivia in the 1960s and 70s.[32] MCC began its work in Bolivia in 1955 when Frank Wiens, then director of MCC in Paraguay, went to work in the Point Four Program in Bolivia on behalf of the colonists. This was a program of United States aid to the new agrarian policies of the Bolivian government. The MCC program was an alternative service program for conscientious objectors in the United States. The first Mennonite PAX men came to Tres Palmas in Santa Cruz, Bolivia to work with the colonists in agriculture.

The role of bishops and pastors

In this way the guides or superiors, together with the pastors and the souls entrusted to them, proceed as the Savior has commanded in the Gospel of John 21:15-17: 'Pastor my sheep, care for my lambs' and according to 1 Peter 5:1-6. And so the entrusted souls are taught according to the Gospel, or said another way, with the divine Word of the Bible of God, and the children are also taught the Word of God in their schools with our own teachers. By means of reading, writing, sums and the rest, they are taught what they need to know in order to seek first the Kingdom of God, according to Matthew 6:33, and after that, what they need to know in order to live a farming life so that they can earn their daily bread and live in religious obedience.

In 1960 the Bolivian government approved the MCC project of creating a clinic in Tres Palmas. The clinic worked on behalf of poor families and the families of the colonists, providing general health care, promoting general hygiene and combating malnutrition, contagious infections and parasites, looking after emergencies and providing maternity care. The buildings were completed in 1962. Several rooms were dedicated to patient care, with some rooms used as lodging for young MCC volunteers who came to serve in various projects. During the 1960s between 500 and 600 patients annually were attended in this clinic. Serious cases were referred to the hospital in Santa Cruz.

Cuatro Ojitos was another place where young MCC volunteers helped with agriculture, community organization, music, English and mathematics. MCC also collaborated with Heifer Project International (HPI) which provided poor families with farm animals.[33] HPI began its work in Bolivia at the request of the Methodists, and began its work there when the Aid Institute of the United States sent veterinarians to inspect animals on the colonies. From 1960 to 1967, HPI distributed 82 heifers, 110 pigs and 3,400 chickens among the colonists and poor families.

From the very start, the work of MCC took place in an ecumenical context. MCC volunteers worked with the Committee for Social Action of the Evangelical Churches of Bolivia, the Canadian Baptists, ALFALIT, and HPI. Others also worked with Wycliff Bible Translators, Andes Evangelical Mission, Union Evangelical Churches of Cochabamba and the Evangelical Union of South America. In 1962, Ervin Kauffman and Gary Gingerich, for example, worked with the Rural Institute Montero of the Methodist church, an organization that taught young people mechanical and agricultural skills.

Through the work of MCC, a Sunday school began for local children. In 1965 MCC volunteers also got involved in the Caravans of Good Will, a

The Tres Palmas school with teacher Susie Froese, 1962. The school building was also used for worship

program of the Protestant churches of Bolivia which provided health and agriculture services along with doing community development and literacy work. 1965 was declared the year of evangelization by the Protestant churches. Tres Palmas and many other communities were impacted by the "Evangelism in Depth" program.

Beginning in the 1970s a new dynamic emerged for MCC, for it was now in a position to initiate and supervise its own programs. In 1968 there were 28 Mennonite volunteers; by the 1970s that number had grown to 40 persons. By 1977, all volunteer workers were under the direct coordination of MCC. MCC offices moved to the center of Santa Cruz, and the work of

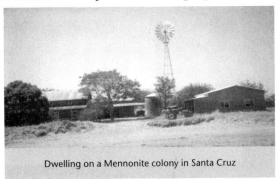

Dwelling on a Mennonite colony in Santa Cruz

MCC concentrated on just six locations. The clinic in Tres Palmas was sold to the colonists and the work of community development was given a new direction, with the colonists and Bolivians themselves being involved in the programs from the very start.

In this new phase, MCC nurses developed a program for training health promoters in Bolivian communities. This included health education, nutritional instruction, infant care, vaccination, health education in the schools and the promotion of the use of latrines. The program extended was so successful that private organizations requested MCC's help. In 1977, USAID provided money to the Bolivian Ministry of Health for promoting these kinds of projects. In Caranda in the region of Montero, where such projects were promoted, the Mennonites had already been training health promoters. The MCC-trained promoters worked in the government system. Although this functioned well for a few years, the funding from USAID was not sustained.[34]

Another important project developed by MCC was the program for the control of tuberculosis, a work which began in the mid-1970s in the region of Cotoca. The program involved nurses travelling to various locations, providing information about TB and vaccinating against it. During the 1970s ten teams were trained in hygiene, nutrition, child care, small animal husbandry, the role of women, women's clubs and educational activities. Villages and towns also were selected where volunteers would come to help in community development. This work began in Tres Palmas and from there was extended south and to the Cotoca region. Later work included villages east of Montero near Okinawa and between Cotoca and Okinawa, east of Warnes.[35]

Thanks to conjoint work between MCC and MEDA, production projects were supported in the colonies of La Merced, El Progreso, Santa Fe and Yapacani. These programs received financial support from USAID and ecclesial organizations such as Bread for the World. It is true that MCC came to Santa Cruz in order to work with the Mennonite colonists, and that Mennonite missions began their work thanks to MCC involvement in Bolivia. But there is no doubt that the reassessment by MCC at the end of the 1960s concerning its work in Bolivia permitted a reformulation of its work as one of mutual support with Mennonite missions. MCC workers started Sunday schools and Bible schools that formed the base for future churches.[36]

Contacts were made with both the General Conference Commission on Overseas Mission (COM) in Newton, Kansas, and the Mennonite Board of Missions (MBM) in Elkhart, Indiana. From COM Andrew Shelly and Ernst Harder visited Bolivia in 1962, and the possibility of beginning church work in Bolivia was noted in MBM correspondence in October, 1964.[37] In March and April of 1969 the missionary Nelson Litwiller, acting for the Mennonite Mission Boards of Newton and Elkhart, visited Bolivia to explore possibilities. In dialogue with missionaries in the field, he advised that Mennonite mission work should begin in Santa Cruz. Litwiller arrived in Santa Cruz in March, 1969 and met with the Secretary of the Methodist church, Mortimer Arias, whom he had gotten to know during his time at the Mennonite Seminary in Montevideo, Uruguay. Two days later he also met with Roberto Lemaitre, settlement director for the region.

Litwiller visited several regions in Santa Cruz, and also visited several Mennonite colonies. Finally, he also visited Montero and Cuatro Ojitos, where the work of MCC volunteers was much appreciated by the Methodists, Baptists and the Evangelical Christian church.[38] Litwiller believed that church planting should begin in the state of Santa Cruz for the following reasons: he saw the need to relate church planting to the work of MCC; he believed that the fundamental end of mission and service was the establishment of the church; and, in his view, the work of MCC should be linked to the life that church ministry would offer. It would be necessary, he concluded, to turn away from dualist conceptions that put service on one side, and missions on the other.

For Nelson Litwiller, the future for Mennonites in Bolivia could be assured only if an indigenous church could be founded that was independent in its governance and finances. He believed it was important that there be a leader who was a writer, an eloquent preacher, someone skilled in personal relations, a good diplomat and a good administrator who could direct a possible local council of Mennonite churches. He believed that the Mennonite churches of the southern cone should unite to support the founding of the church in Bolivia. In practical terms, Litwiller suggested that the center of operations be Tres Palmas, Santa Cruz, a location where MCC had worked in community development since the 1960s.[39]

In April, 1971 José and Soledad Godoy arrived in Tres Palmas to begin mission work, under the direction of the Argentine Mennonite church and the mission boards of Newton and Elkhart. The Godoy family had worked previously as pastors of the Mennonite church in Salto, Argentina. The work of the Godoy family in Santa Cruz was coordinated well with MCC.[40]

From June to August, 1973 the Newton missionaries Harriet and Laverne Rutschman arrived in Tres Palmas to assist the Godoy family.[41] The Rutschmans' report suggested more participation by local leaders, and a less paternalistic approach.[42] They were more in agreement with a missional model open to the work of MCC, than to the traditional model of missions which was committed to planting new Mennonite churches. They recommended working in cooperation with the Catholic church whenever possible, and that if a new Mennonite church were planted, that it should be in Santa Cruz in an un-evangelized neighborhood.[43]

José Godoy baptizes new believers in Los Tajibos, 1973

The first Mennonite churches in Bolivia were established in Los Tajibos, Cosorió, Las Gamas, La Cruceña, Don Lorenzo-San Julián and El Ví, all places where MCC had been doing community development, literacy work and helping poor families with health centers. The first families to settle in Los Tajibos[44] were mostly "Chiquitanos,"[45] originating from San Antonio de Lomerío.[46] Juan Jiménez Sumami, for example, is a Chiquitano who was born in the province of Ñumplobechabe in San Antonio de Lomeríos. He had participated in the war Bolivia waged against Paraguay in 1933, responsible for transporting an artillery piece and loading the shells that were fired against enemy soldiers.[47] The Great Chaco War unleashed a great migration of Chiquitanos between 1933 and 1936. The Chiquitana familial system disintegrated, new Chiquitana communities emerged in the distant zones, and the large landowners took advantage by expanding their holdings, using the tribal leaders to exploit the labor of the indigenous.[48]

Analecto Chubé was the first Chiquitano to come to Los Tajibos. He was fleeing the authorities who were attempting to force him into working on one of the plantations of San Antonio de Lomerío. Benito Opimí also resisted and confronted the police who were trying to force him to work for the great landowners. He fled with his wife and their four children. They travelled 340 kilometers, following the path of Analecto Chubé, until they finally managed to get to Tajibos.[49] Juan Jiménez Sumami, his wife, their eight daughters and two sons emigrated to Tajibos in 1949 for exactly the same reasons.[50] These were poor indigenous families who, fleeing the forced servitude of the San Antonio plantations, emigrated in search of better living conditions. The migration of these families took place in connection with the construction of the railroad, which originated at the border with Brazil, ran through Corumbú and reached Santa Cruz.[51]

The testimony of Amalia Jiménez Chube

My parents left San Antonio with my eldest sisters and left us there with my grandmother. My grandfather was sick; he had an infection on his foot that spread to his whole body. The people of San Antonio were afraid of him. They removed him from the town, and took him three kilometers away. My grandfather stayed in those hills. We went with him, looked after him, and cooked for him. ... I was seven years old and (my sister) was five years old when we came to Tajibos. My grandfather was abandoned because he only had two sons and both of them had migrated to Los Tajibos; in time he died. My grandmother died later. My one sister, who can speak chiquitano, stayed with my grandmother until she died. It is said that my grandfather died in a fire, that his little house had burned, with him being helpless and sick, and unable to do anything.

Volunteers from MCC arrived in Los Tajibos in 1960. They built a clinic and their medical team looked after the poor Chiquitano families. This is how Nicolas Opimí Huasase and Amalia Jiménez got to know the Mennonites.[52] Through the literacy program ALFALIT, Juan Jiménez and his daughter Amalia learned to read and write Spanish. Nicolás Opimí

An ALFALIT writing class under the direction of Francisco Paxi

remembers the development projects brought by the Mennonites, which promoted raising chickens and cows among the poor families of Los Tajibos. To this day the nursing work of Frieda Schellenberg and the presence of Dale Linsenmeyer, the director of MCC in Santa Cruz, Bolivia, are remembered fondly.[53]

In 1971, when contact between the Mennonites and the Jiménez and Opimí families began, there was strong opposition from the Catholic church. As the Bible studies and worship services began taking place in the Opimí house, the family was rejected by the populace and the priest; their detractors also labeled them Communists. One day some Catholic church members of Los Tajibos brought police from Santa Cruz to the little school, to accuse the people there of being Communists. The police found no such a thing, and finally said: "We want no more problems. Work together. You can practice

Nicolás Opimí Huasase

your Catholic religion in your church, and you worship as you wish, for today there is freedom of religion."[54]

The Jiménez and Opimí families were Catholic, but when José Godoy established a Mennonite church there in 1971, they and the Peña family became the first members of the Mennonite church. Later an Assemblies of God church was established there too, with the intention of unifying both congregations. Although fraternal relations were maintained between the Assemblies of God church and the Mennonite church, the families mentioned above decided to keep their Mennonite identity.[55]

This church was noted for the sense of community among its families and for its profound spirituality; it became one of the most active and stable Mennonite communities.[56] The main worship service and Sunday school was held on Sundays; during the week the young people would gather to read the Scriptures and to sing hymns. There was a great desire to construct a church building for the congregation. Juan Jiménez and Ignacio Peña donated a building lot 25 by 180 meters from their own property for the construction of the church. The community gathered together first to prepare the lot. In April, 1976, they decided to work together making bricks, twice a week. In order to do this they had to travel three kilometers with the cart to

The *Dios es Amor* (God is Love) church, Los Tajibos

bring the necessary water. By July of the same year they had already made 3,000 bricks.[57]

The community of San Lorenzo/San Julian began to form in July, 1971 when Gerald Mumaw of MCC began to help the community of San Julián in the little school they had begun.[58] A small group began reading the Bible together, and then met every two weeks on Fridays to sing praises with a guitar and to give thanks to God for all things.[59] Until the late 1970s, when the construction of a church building began, the San Julian community gathered in the homes of member families for worship.[60] The community known as La Cruceña, located close to the Canadian Mennonite Colony of Reinland, was first contacted by MCC. When José and Soledad Godoy arrived as missionaries, they held services in La Cruceña every Friday evening.[61] In August, 1976, nineteen persons were baptized into the La Cruceña church.[62] Shortly after the Godoy family returned to Argentina, the Cruceña community formed a leadership council responsible for the well being of the community, worship services, visitation of the sick, Bible studies and church finances.[63]

Baptism in Las Gamas

The Mennonite community of Las Gamas also received pastoral leadership from Soledad and José Godoy, with added pastoral help from Beatríz Barrios, until 1976 when the Godoy family returned to Argentina.[64] That same year a church building was constructed in Las Gamas. Likewise, the Mennonite church in Cosorió emerged under the leadership of José and Soledad Godoy.[65] The Mennonite community remained small, although at the beginning of 1976 it managed to build a chapel with missionary funds.

The establishment of the Evangelical Mennonite Church of Bolivia (IEMB: *Iglesia Evangélica Menonita Boliviana*) grew from MCC Bible study groups and formally began with the coming of the Godoy missionary family and then the formation of a Mission Council at the end of 1973. At least three different groups participated in this Mission Council, giving leadership to what would later become the Evangelical Mennonite Church of Bolivia.

1. Members of MCC, who brought the daily life of Bolivian communities to the discussion by means of their projects of development, health, agriculture and education. Given the kind of social work they carried out, these were persons who were most open to ecumenical dialogue, including dialogue with the Catholic church.

2. The missionaries Soledad and José Godoy, who brought an easy identification with the Bolivian people, also brought a strong evangelistic focus and worked to establish churches. They were more prone to distance themselves from the traditional Catholic church, and even oppose it.

3. Laverne and Harriet Rutschman supported the emerging Mennonite communities, and had a growing concern for theological education and the development of local church leadership.

Documents from 1973 to 1976 give witness to the tension and the cooperation that existed between these different participants. It was a period of great creativity because of the new dynamic and developmental concept adopted by MCC, by the evangelistic impulse of the Godoys, with the baptism of some 50 persons, and the contributions of the Rutschmans in the field of liturgy and theological education, not only within the emerging Mennonite communities, but also in the Baptist Theological Seminary.

The division of labor between the Mennonite mission boards of Kansas and Indiana and the Mennonite church of Argentina continued until the planned five years of work by the Godoys was completed. Although there were attempts to renew the contract with the Godoys, the Mennonite church of Argentina was not able to take on the missionary salary, which had been covered up to then by the U.S. mission boards. Soledad and José Godoy returned to their country early in 1976. At this same time, Beatríz Barrios, who had worked for one year with the Mennonite churches of Bolivia, returned to her country of Uruguay.

The final report by Laverne Rutschman, written just before his departure from Bolivia to begin work in theological education in the Latin American Biblical Seminary in San José, Costa Rica, represents an important missiological reflection. The report reaffirmed the principles of the Great Commission: the necessary proclamation of liberation of the human being from sin (1 John 1:9), from death (Romans 6:23) and from all forms of injustice (Luke 4:18).

Laverne concluded his reflections by pointing to the need to have the lordship of Christ be affirmed and practiced in all its fullness, with eyes opened by the Holy Spirit.[66]

We don't know if these reflections were shared with the Missionary Council after Laverne and Harriet left Bolivia in October, 1976, but there was a greater participation of other Bolivian church leaders once the Godoys and the Rutschmans concluded their missionary work. The educational seminars that took place in Santa Cruz, with the participation of members from different Mennonite congregations, brought a greater awareness of what it meant to be Anabaptist in

Laverne and Harriet Rutschman

Reflections by Laverne Rutschman

• How important is it to establish another imported denomination (Mennonite)?

• What should be the relationship between Mennonites and the Catholic church, with whom there is an excellent level of cooperation in the development programs of MCC?

• Given that there are "ethnic Mennonites" in Bolivia (the reference was to the colonies), it is important to ask: "What does it mean to be Anabaptist-Mennonite in an ethical and theological sense?"

• Given that MCC's development programs are building bridges with the Catholic church, what of the relationship between missions and MCC?

• What of the danger that the "new converts" will separate from their larger communities, and that the new congregations will become places of refuge, rather than salt and light for the earth, as Jesus indicated?

• How will the church incarnate the problems of social injustice lived by the Bolivian people, without making an arbitrary division between body and soul?

• Who are the national leaders? (This indicated the danger of a church leadership remaining under the missionary model copied from outside.)

• How to interpret the text of Matthew 10:34? Should the Gospel divide the nuclear family from the extended family, because of individualist interpretations of the Gospel?

pastoral and theological terms, and impressed a sense of community and belonging on this emerging organization.

In June, 1980 a congress of representatives from the Mennonites churches and MCC gathered to organize the Mennonite church of Bolivia, naming an ad hoc committee to investigate how to obtain legal standing and to write a first draft of statutes. The committee was also to investigate how things were going in the Mennonite congregations of Bolivia.[67] With these concrete organizational steps the first historical period of the Evangelical Mennonite church of Bolivia came to a close.

The historical background of the second Mennonite conference in Bolivia, namely the Evangelical Anabaptist church of Bolivia, goes back to the Canadian Mennonite colonies that were founded in Santa Cruz, already noted in this chapter. In 1937 a group of these churches organized in Manitoba, Canada under the name of Rüdnerweide. In 1959 the Evangelical Mennonite Mission Conference was organized in Manitoba; in 1988 it had a total of 24 member churches and worked with MCC in mission and services.[68]

In 1969 some brothers from the Mennonite colonies in Bolivia initiated correspondence with the Evangelical Mennonite Mission Conference in Canada. This led some members of this conference to visit the Canadian Mennonite colony in Santa Cruz in 1972. They later initiated a ministry in a place known as Choroví, located near the Mennonite colony. A medical clinic was established in Choroví primarily to serve members of the Mennonite colonies and with the aim of establishing a Mennonite church. It turned out that the people interested in founding a new Mennonite congregation were the Bolivian farmers. In 1974 a Mennonite congregation was founded five kilometers from the Choroví clinic in the Zafranilla neighborhood, thanks to the ministry of the missionary Juan Banman.

The second congregation that was founded was known as La Fortaleza. The background to this congregation goes back to 1984, when the Piraí river flooded, and the new neighborhood of La Fortaleza was

Benita Porceles Chumacero, member of La Fortaleza church

founded, near Palmar del Oratorio, seven kilometers south of Santa Cruz. A small church was built there; in 1990 it had 150 members. In 1986 the *Colegio Evangélico Anabautista* was built and four years later 176 children from the neighborhood were attending this school. The Evangelical Anabaptist church of Bolivia held its first national convention in July, 1988 in Santa Cruz. Present were Bro. Lorenzo Giesbrecht, president of the Evangelical Mennonite Mission Conference of Canada, and delegates from the Safranilla and La Fortaleza churches. In 1988, La Fortaleza church had 72 members; its pastors were Daniel Gómez and Jaime Suárez. Around 200 people attended church services regularly, including children. Discipleship was developed in different groups. The discipleship group led by Vida Gómez and Jaime Suárez reached out to the "Los Ambaybos" neighborhood in the las Pampitas zone, where it visited with a family named Días. Adit Sosa visited Villa Fátima and Villa Santa, where Dora de Gómez ran a Sunday school attended by around 100 people. La Fortaleza church also organized a men's group and a youth group. This church collaborated with World Vision and 170 children attended a program for disease prevention; their mothers received nutritional education.[69]

A third congregation of this conference was born in Los Ambaibos through the missionary work of the La Fortaleza church; it is located six kilometers east of Santa Cruz. The Los Ambaibos congregation had twenty members in 1990. In 1989 another church was established in Los Angeles, eighteen kilometers from Zafranilla. In 1997 this church had twenty members.[70]

The Mennonite presence in Bolivia began with the establishment of German-speaking, conservative Mennonite colonies in the Santa Cruz area. The success of these colonies encouraged more settlement of this kind to take place throughout the 1960s and 70s, as well as in subsequent years. The presence of MCC in Bolivia was initially directed in support of the Mennonite colonies, but soon expanded beyond them into more generalized development work in the country, and eventually provided an entry for the establishment of Mennonite churches. The Mennonite presence of colonies and MCC development work was joined by more formal mission efforts to Spanish-speaking Bolivians beginning around 1970. These efforts were notable for the presence of missionaries from the Argentine Mennonite church, working in conjunction with Mennonite missionaries from North America in places where MCC had been helping poor and displaced persons. The churches founded as a result of these efforts came to form the Evangelical Mennonite Church of Bolivia. They were joined after 1970 by churches of the Evangelical Anabaptist Church of Bolivia, with Canadian "Rüdnerweide" roots.

The Bolivian experience provides something of a microcosm of key cultural and missiological tensions faced by the Mennonite church in Latin America generally. It is worthwhile reviewing the thoughtful questions posed by Laverne Rutschman in 1976, as he pondered the various Mennonite communities and forms of life and witness present in Bolivia: the "closed" model of German-speaking colonies; evangelism in a spiritualistic mode; witness through social action and community development; the possibilities of ecumenical relationships; the need for national leadership. These various modes of expressing the Mennonite faith bring into focus some of the fundamental challenges faced by Latin America Mennonite churches – to different degrees in different countries.

Caribbean

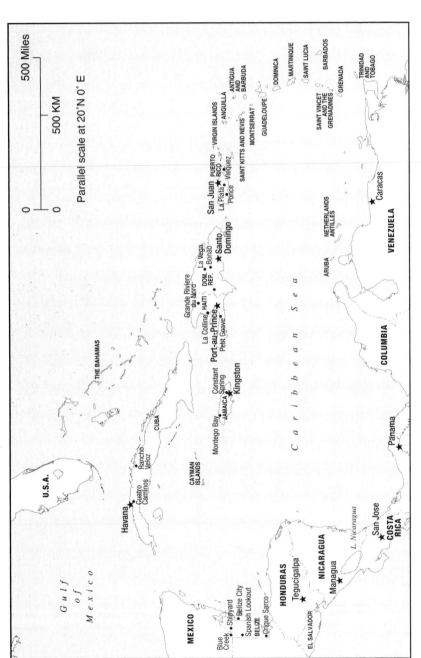

The Caribbean

The Mennonite Church in Puerto Rico (1943-1979)

When Christopher Columbus arrived at Boriquen on the nineteenth of November, 1493, the beautiful island contained around 60,000 indigenous inhabitants. The merciless exploitation and extinction of the indigenous peoples around the middle of the sixteenth century led to the introduction of African slaves, in order to sustain the Puerto Rican economy, which was based on the cultivation of sugar cane. Puerto Rican society was based on the owner-slave relationship until slavery was abolished in 1873. The nineteenth century concluded with occupation by the United States in 1898, following strenuous battles against Spain.

José Martí, the apostle of liberty in the Caribbean, said that "changing masters does not mean liberty," and this is precisely what occurred with the new relationship.[1] In 1917 the Congress of the United States, against the will of the chamber of delegates of Puerto Rico, imposed United States citizenship in the document known as the "Jones Act," which would rule the country until 1952. Puerto Rico continued as a colony, subject to the naming of its governor, secretary of justice, education, and auditor by the federal government of the United States. In July 1967 a plebiscite was held in which 60.5 percent of the population voted in favor of remaining a "Free Associated State"; the rest of the population supported the proposition that Puerto Rico become another state in the Union. Efforts by the governor Rafael Hernández (1973-1976) to change Puerto Rico's status were rejected by U. S. president Gerald Ford.

The U.S. conquest of Puerto Rico reduced the power of the Catholic church, since church and state were now separated, religious teaching was eliminated from the schools, and cemeteries taken over by the liberal state. Immediately following the landing of the Marines in Puerto Rico, Protestant missions began planning and planting churches.[2] The Federation of Evangelical Churches of Puerto Rico was organized by 1906, becoming the first council of Protestant churches in Latin America.[3] Protestant missions contributed greatly to the "Americanization" of Puerto Rico, a process that had theological as well as cultural connotations, although some Protestant churches got involved in the workers' movement.[4]

Puerto Rico was strongly affected by the economic depression that began in 1929 and which led to a crisis in the sugar industry. Pentecostalism grew quickly in the 1930s, turning away from the middle class orientation typical of the traditional churches, expressing itself instead in the language and culture of the masses, the marginalized, and the rural people of the country.[5] With its apocalyptic message announcing the imminent second coming of Christ, and with divine healing, glossolalia and the manifestation of the Holy Spirit, the Pentecostal churches symbolically condemned the established order without, however, engaging the political, economic, and social foundations of the establishment.[6]

The Popular Democratic Party under the direction of Luis Muñoz Marín, and the "New Deal" of U.S. president Roosevelt led to the transformation of Puerto Rico from an agrarian society into an industrial society in the 1940s. The Mennonite church arrived in Puerto Rico in the midst of this process. Conscientious objection to war service by peace churches in the United States resulted in the creation of the "Civilian Public Service" (CPS) to administer non-military work brigades.[7] In 1943, under the sponsorship of the CPS, the Service

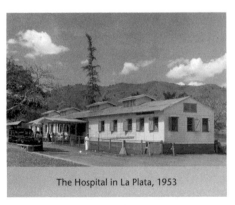

Commission of the Brethren, the Mennonite Central Committee, and the Friends Service Committee opened service units in the Puerto Rican towns of Castañer, La Plata and Zalduondo in order to work in programs in health, community development and agriculture.[8]

In the valley of La Plata a notable medical service began immediately (construction of

The Hospital in La Plata, 1953

latrines, nutrition, and medical clinics), along with work in agriculture channeled through 4-H clubs (family farms), recreational activities for young people (volleyball, basketball, softball, ping-pong, dominoes, checkers and badminton), and construction of libraries and community centers for popular education. The Mennonites thought that the local populace was full of superstitions with roots in the Catholic church, and that many local people carried superstitions inherited from their indigenous ancestors. They recognized that local people often preferred to visit a local shaman rather than seek medical help. In the Mennonite description, the Puerto Rican people embodied a combination of superstition, religious fatalism, ignorance and distrust of strangers.

The agricultural project in the La Plata valley extended to the towns of Aibonito, Cayey, Cidra and Comercio, eventually involving 362 small farmers working approximately 4,600 acres of land. All this work was done "in the name of Christ," the MCC slogan used during the Second World War in aiding the needy, under the firm conviction that God's power was needed to transform lives, but that at the same time, one needed to attend to psychological, physical, mental and economic needs.

The small clinic that opened in 1943 was extended in 1944 and 1945 to the communities of Toita (Matón), Buena Vista (Cayey), Rincón (Nogueras) and Pulguillas to treat poor people suffering from malaria, cancer, and malnutrition. With the end of World War Two, the CPS program ceased, and so did the work of the dispensaries in various communities, such as Rincón, Buena Vista and Toita; the same happened with community development programs. Nevertheless, the Mennonite General Hospital continues to function in Aibonito to this day. From July 1943 until 1951 a total of 146 Mennonite workers from the United States supported the projects in Puerto Rico. Puerto Rican volunteers such as Juan Bautista, Fermina Gutiérrez, Everisto Rivera, Longino Arroyo Matos and Ramona Vázquez de Santos, also collaborated in these projects.[9]

From the start of work in Puerto Rico there was a strong interest in establishing Mennonite churches.[10] The director of MCC, Orie O. Miller, said so during his visits to Puerto Rico in those first years. In 1944 Bibles and New Testaments were distributed in the region, and it was recommended that the chapel of the North American workers be used as a worship center for the community. In 1945 the first

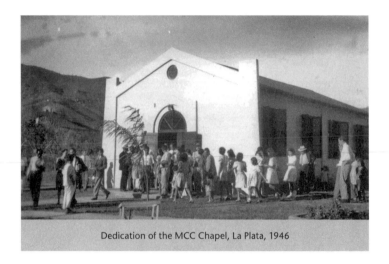

Dedication of the MCC Chapel, La Plata, 1946

Sunday school was held in Puerto Rico. The first Mennonite chapel was completed in March of 1946.

In April, 1947, Lester T. Hershey and his wife Alta arrived to assume the pastorate at La Plata, where they were received with great enthusiasm. The first Sunday school began with nine children. By May, 1947, 22 persons had accepted the Lord, of whom twelve were later baptized. Initially worship in Spanish was held at 8:30 AM, after which a service in English was held for the workers from the United States.

The first Puerto Rican Mennonite church was called *Iglesia Menonita el Calvario* (Calvary Mennonite Church). In its first year the church carried out a variety of evangelistic activities and participated in joint services with neighboring churches. Programs included Sunday school, prayer meetings, and evangelistic meetings, Bible study on Monday nights, and Christian education for the congregation on Friday nights. There was a spirit of community that led to cooperation between families in the cultivation of produce. Already in its first year the church participated in the radio program "The Voice of Calvary."

In 1947 Lester Hershey travelled to Barranquitas a Orocovis, in search of a new area for evangelism. The crossroads of Palo Hincado caught his eye, and in November 1948 a fifteen-day evangelistic campaign began there led by T. K. Hershey, Paul Lauver, and Lester Hershey. The campaign resulted in 30 confessions of faith. In January and February, 1949 a biblical institute was founded with the participation of young people from La Plata, Rabanal, Pulguillas and Palo Hincado, and a year later twelve people organized the Mennonite Church of Palo Hincado. The church of Palo Hincado began to support the work of the Baptists in the area of Cuchilla. The first conference of the Mennonite Church of Puerto Rico took place in La Plata in March, 1949 with the participation of delegates from La Plata, Pulguillas, Rabanal, and Palo Hincado. The main speaker was Alberto Espada Matta of the Christian and Missionary Alliance Church of Puerto Rico.

Mission work began in Pulguillas on the property of Don Antonio Emanuelli with the pastoral work of Paul and Lois Lauver, who arrived in December, 1945. The chapel was built in 1946 and could seat 200 people. By July, 1948 the congregation numbered 31 local people. In this same year 167 children and adults visited

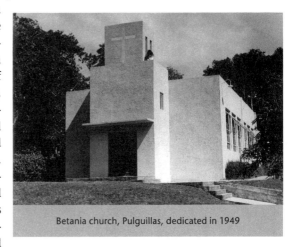

Betania church, Pulguillas, dedicated in 1949

Sunday school, and a women's group had been organized. In 1948 Beulah Litwiller opened the Pulguillas Christian Day School, the first educational center of the Mennonites in Puerto Rico. In 1949, Lester Hershey became co-pastor of the church in Pulguillas, along with Paul Lauver, and a year later the the church was named Bethany Mennonite Church. This year saw the second annual conference of the Mennonite Church of Puerto Rico, and evangelistic work began in Coamo Arriba.

Toward the end of 1947, when Lester Hershey was travelling by horse on his visitation work, he passed by a path that led to the municipality of Rabanal de la Cidra. He thought of establishing a Mennonite church there. The first worship service was held that year, and one year later the Good Shepherd Mennonite Church was dedicated. The work at Rabanal was supported Melquiades Santiago and Angel Rivera. In 1949 the first ten members were received into the congregation and the women of the congregation organized. The first

Lester Hershey (on horse) and Robert
Yoder at the mission property in
Coamo Arriba, 1951

summer school was held in 1949 with the participation of 93 children, and in 1950 a kindergarten was started at Rabanal under the leadership of Marjorie Shantz and Linda Reimer. In this year there were 15 church members and 73 persons attended Sunday School.

Radio Evangelism became an important communication vehicle, not only in Puerto Rico, but with wide-spread influence in Latin America. In 1947 Lester Hershey began a radio evangelism program on a station in Ponce, with a three-minute program entitled "The Voice of Calvary." In February, 1948 the fifteen-minute program became a half-hour program, and the name was changed to "Calvary Hour." The recordings were made in the studios of the Bethany Church in Pulguillas, with Lester Hershey in charge of the messages. Initially the recording equipment was poor, with recording done on large and heavy disks. In 1951 the program managed to obtain high quality tape recording equipment. In 1954 the radio ministry changed its name to *Audición Luz y Verdad* (Light and Truth Program). Fidel Santiago was an active Puerto Rican lay member who collaborated initially as the announcer for *Luz y Verdad*.

In 1955 the program began to mail out correspondence courses for Bible study. On one occasion, a Guatemalan wrote a letter that said: "Thank you for the course... It taught me my responsibility to God. . . . I am distributing tracts in the name of the Lord, and this has been a blessing for me... Before I wasted my time in the streets, but now

Luis Figueroa, radio technician
for *Luz y Verdad*

I am serving the Lord."[11] As the decades of the sixties came to a close, *Luz y Verdad* was being broadcast over 29 radio stations in South America, Central America, the Caribbean islands, the United States, Monaco, and Spain.[12]

Post-war changes saw the relocation of a great mass of immigrants to the cities or to North American ghettoes. During the first years of the decade of the 1950s, the emi-

Lester and Alta Hershey

Sermon by Lester T. Hershey

Reading in a certain pamphlet the other day, I read the following words which made me stop and think: "The Bible contains the word of God." Could it be possible that there are parts of the Bible that are not inspired? ... If there are, how would we know which are inspired by the Holy Spirit, and which are not? ...thanks be to God, we can be certain that "all Scripture is inspired by God and is useful for teaching, for reproof, for correction, for instruction in justice, so that the man of God become perfect, completely prepared for every good work" (2 Timothy 3:16, 17). This is the reason why it is absolutely forbidden to add or subtract any idea or teaching from the Scriptures.

gration of Puerto Ricans to the United States reached a level of 50,000 persons per month. This figure dropped to 20,000 per month in the 1970s, and in the years 1982-1983 had reached a figure of 35,000 persons a year. In the face of this social-political reality, some Christian leaders took the side of the poor, and as a result entered into conflict with the system. This Christian initiative crystallized in the "Christians for Socialism" movement, made up of more than 300 leaders, pastors, and lay persons of Catholic and Protestant churches, who would meet together to reflect on the implications of faith for the Puerto Rican people.[13] Those who agreed with this movement joined in days of protest over the presence of the United States Marines on the island of Culebra, and the protesters became more united through public liturgies held with the fishermen on the island of Viequez (1977).[14]

For its part, the Catholic hierarchy identified with the conservative wing of the Latin American episcopate, dismantled the grass roots pastoral work that was taking place in Coamo and in the area of La Perla, and condemned the "Christians for Socialism" movement. There was little resonance in Protestant ranks, where instead there was a tremendous growth in pentecostal, charismatic, and apocalyptic groups, whose rise was aided systematically by the media of radio and television. Many of these churches were closely tied to U.S. funda-

The testimony of Angel Luis Miranda

I grew up as a child in the mountains of Puerto Rico. I am oldest of a family of eleven. ... my mother was one of the many patients who came to the new Mennonite Hospital in La Plata. My father was so impressed by the services rendered by the doctors and the staff, that he was moved to say, "Some day I'll become a Mennonite."

In 1946, my family moved from the Aibonito area to Palo Hincado, Barranquitas. About three years later, the Mennonite Church began a mission outpost in our new "barrio" in a ... building that was meant to be a bakery. ... My father, upon learning that "cultos" were held in the bakery building, decided to go on his own. I remember how some of the people that attended used to say that they were getting spiritual bread instead of physical bread. My father was so pleased that the following Sunday decided to take his whole family and ... when the invitation to accept Christ came, he and a few others raised their hands. ... I didn't understand what he was doing. Later on, however, after a series of Bible studies in my house, I also made my decision to accept Christ. I was rebaptized at the end of 1949. In this sense, I would say that I became a real Anabaptist. ... By the time I was sixteen, I was already involved in teaching Sunday school, preaching and visitation. ...

In the fall of 1958, I accepted a teaching position at the Academia Menonita Betania in Pulguillas, Puerto Rico, ... located just a few miles from my birthplace.

mentalist groups with an openly pro-American attitude. In the sector of traditional Protestant churches the leaders also aligned themselves with a conservative theology that did not permit participation with those sectors of the populace that hoped for social changes and who affirmed the national culture.[15]

The Mennonite missionary David Helmuth, director of the Mennonite Biblical Institute in Aibonito, thought that Puerto Ricans ought to decide their own future, and that this also had something to do with the local leadership within the Mennonite church. He suggested that missionaries dedicate themselves more to preparing leaders, and that Puerto Ricans begin assuming responsibilities on the Executive Committee of the Mennonite Convention.[16] And in fact, this took place: national pastors began assuming leadership during the decade of the 1960s, to such an extent that for the annual assembly of 1979 all the leadership posts of the Evangelical Mennonite Convention of Puerto Rico were in the hands of national pastors and lay persons.[17]

Although there was a massive emigration of Puerto Ricans to the United States,[18] the Puerto Rican pastor José Luis Miranda agreed with Helmuth in prioritizing the social importance of the internal migration within Puerto Rico.[19] Helmuth indicated the social problems that resulted from rapid industrialization: 9 percent of the families in Puerto Rico enjoyed 45 percent of the income of the entire island. According to the official statistics, the per capita income had risen to $1,200.00 dollars per year. Nevertheless, 43 percent of all families had incomes of under $2,000.00 per year and 77,000 families received less than $200.00 per year. There were other problems in addition: the ecological damage that resulted from the removal of sand from the beaches for construction projects, the 500,000 cars that crowded the streets, and a drug problem that affected some 17,000 addicts. In face of this hard reality, Helmuth called the Mennonite church to a ministry of love and compassion, to attend to these needs.[20]

The Vietnam war put the issues of peace and the relationship of the United States to Puerto Rico back on the table. Helmuth thought that the Spirit of God was awakening the church from its slumber and passive peace testimony. There were draftees in Puerto Rico who were refusing military service. A ruling had established that the drafted Feliciano Grafals met the requirements for being a conscientious objector. He based his decision on the fact that the legal relationship between the two countries was not sufficiently clear to extend military conscription to the island, without there being a previous and specific agreement by the Puerto Rican people. Helmuth lamented that the Mennonite churches had let down the other denominations by not taking a leading role as a peace church in confronting this problem and the issue of violence in Puerto Rico.[21]

This ambiguity was felt among the members of the Mennonite churches: they had received an Americanized gospel, but at the same time had inherited the theological foundations of a peace church and the testimony of North American Mennonite youth who had refused to join the U.S. army. The same differences of opinion that were present at the macro-political level also were present within the Puerto Rican Mennonite church at the end of the 1970s, when there were pointed protests over the presence of United States Marines on the island of Viequez.

At the beginning of the 1970s there were nine Mennonite churches in Puerto Rico; the majority of pastors were missionaries from the United States and Argentina.[22] By 1980 the Conference of Mennonite churches of Puerto Rico numbered 950 baptized members who gathered in 17 different congregations.[23] The Mennonite General Hospital established in Aibonito offered a variety of excellent medical services during these decades, with highly qualified North American and Puerto Rican personnel.[24] Its board of directors was made up of Mennonites and non-Mennonites and the hospital was well integrated in

Luis Eliér Rodriguez, chaplain at the Mennonite hospital in Aibonito

the local community. In the 1940s the hospital was oriented primarily toward service to poorer families, but then began to meet the needs of middle class people, with costs well below that of other private hospitals. Medical care was not used as a means of proselytization for the church. Although there was a chaplain who cared for the spiritual needs of the patients, pastors and clergy of other denominations were welcome to be present.

The Betania Mennonite Academy in Pulguillas continued its educational work. Instruction was in Spanish, with English introduced as a second language. The school had begun with the primary grades, but in the 1970s the new elementary and intermediary grades were introduced. The Academy was attended by children from rural areas as well as from nearby urban areas. At the end of the 1970s there were approximately 250 students enrolled. The positive relationships established between teachers and students led to many of the students identifying with the Mennonite church.

A second important educational institution was the Mennonite Academy of Summit Hills, which attracted students primarily of the urban middle class of San Juan. Instruction here was conducted

Betania school buildings, Pulguillas, ca. 1965

primarily in English, with Spanish as the second language. Enrollment at the beginning of the 1980s stood at 450 students. In addition to the traditional courses, there were also courses offered in fine arts, typing, home economics, art, music, driver's education, physical education, and health. The Academy came to be recognized in San Juan for its high educational standards.

The Mennonite broadcasting that began in Puerto Rico in the 1940s had far-reaching effects. In the 1960s Lester Hershey dedicated his time to the weekly radio program *Luz y Verdad*, which he led until his retirement in 1977.[25] Free Bible courses were offered by correspondence under such topics as "The life of Jesus Christ," "The Church of Jesus Christ," "The great salvation offered by God," "The Sermon on the Mount" and "Christian freedom."[26] In 1965 a new 15-minute long weekly program for women began, known as *Corazón a Corazón* (Heart to Heart), hosted by Marta Quiroga, wife of a Mennonite pastor in Argentina.[27] Also produced in the 1970s were two dubbed color clips for all television stations in Latin America;

Radio message by Marta Quiroga de Álvarez: "What is your life about?"

What is life about? What is life for? Have you ever thought about this? I have.

I think that life is made up primarily of little things: the laugh of a child at play, the warm greeting of a friend, the smell of food when one is hungry, the firm faith in God of a child, revealed in simple and sincere prayer, a song...

The melodious singing of a little brook, frothing as it leaps, while its path deepens through the meadow or a stand of trees, a prayer...

Jesus also directed our attention to small details. Do you remember when he said, "Look at the birds in the sky!" And later, "Consider the lilies of the field." In other words, he is asking us to pay attention to the beautiful things that are within our reach.

Marta Quiroga de Álvarez (front center) and her family

a second program for women, broadcast in Mexico from Monday to Friday (5 minutes long), directed by María Torres de Dorantes; the program *Comentando* (Commenting) for intellectuals, with Daniel Martínez of Argentina as the primary spokesperson (5 minutes daily); and "The greatest week in history" for Holy Week (5 minutes). In 1971 there were 3,717 listeners enrolled in the correspondence Bible study courses. Of these, 2,650 graduated in the different courses offered.[28]

In 1971 a meeting took place in Bogotá, Colombia with Mennonite representatives from Argentina, Mexico, Honduras, Costa Rica, the Dominican Republic, Puerto Rico, and Hispanic members from the United States.[29] This gathering led to the creation in Puerto Rico, the following year, of the *Junta Latinoamericana de Audiciones Menonitas* (JELAM) (Latin American Board of Mennonite Broadcasting), supported financially by the North American mission boards who were doing mission work among Hispanic people.[30] JELAM played an important role in continuing to spread Christian literature and evangelistic radio programs to all of Latin America and the Hispanic world in the United States and Spain, encouraging coordinated action among Spanish-speaking Mennonite church conventions.[31]

Puerto Rico's unique status as a "Free Associated State" in the political ambit of the United States led to the first Mennonite presence on the island: U.S. Mennonite conscientious objectors came to Puerto Rico to do their CPS service in the 1940s. From this beginning grew social, medical, educational and evangelistic programs, carried out initially by North American missionaries. Church membership grew steadily over the decades, and by the 1960s and 70s, leadership of the Puerto Rican Mennonite church was in the hands of national pastors.

The pioneering radio evangelism work of Lester Hershey, based in the church of Pulguillas in central Puerto Rico, would have a wide and positive impact across Latin America, as has already been noted in the previous chapters. From this small broadcasting start, JELAM emerged in 1972 as the regional inter-Mennonite vehicle to coordinate, produce and help finance Mennonite broadcasting in Spanish for Latin American audiences, led and administered by the Colombian Mennonite pastor, Armando Hernández.

Mennonites in the Dominican Republic (1944-1979)

CHAPTER XIII

Before the Spanish conquest, the Minor Antilles of the Caribbean were shaped by the Carib and Tain cultures.[1] The Caribs made frequent incursions onto the larger islands, causing much chaos. On the Major Antilles islands the Tains developed their fishing, hunting and agricultural way of life, cultivating corn, potatoes and yuca.[2] On Christopher Columbus' second trip to the New World, in November 1493, he anchored in front of Española (today the Dominican Republic and Haiti) and founded the city of Santo Domingo. The island became not only the first Catholic diocese of the continent, but also the base of the first phase of the conquest of Latin America.[3]

The quick anihilation of the indigenous population of the Caribbean through forced labor in the mines and epidemics resulted in the wide-spread importation of African slaves. Already in 1568, the African slave population reached 20,000, who were put to work primarily in the production of sugar cane. Because of its geographical position, "Turtle island" became the object of constant struggles between Spain, the Netherlands, France, and England. The French invasion during the years 1640 to 1653 was the result of this military ambition. Although Spain recovered the island in 1654, the French returned to fight for the island, and from 1655 to 1697 they occupied and held the western part (Haiti today). The formation of the border between the French and Spanish colonies was a long and painful process that lasted until 1789.

In 1822 Jean Pierre Boyer, president of Haiti, invaded the Dominican Republic and declared the abolition of slavery in that country. He promised government land to all freed slaves who wished to pursue agriculture. Protestantism came to the Dominican Republic thanks to Jean Pierre Boyer's offer, when 6,000 freed African descendants from the United States emigrated to the island in 1824, settling on the peninsula of Samaná. Among them was the pastor Isaac Miler of the African Methodist Episcopal Church (U.S.), who was charged with caring for the spiritual life of 200 persons who came from the city of Philadelphia. The Methodists, following the anti-slavery tradition of John Wesley, dedicated themselves to preaching the Gospel and teaching the African descendants to read and write.[4]

The presence of Protestant missionaries began to be felt in earnest toward the end of the nineteenth century, as the North American economic and political influence began to grow in the island.[5] The North American military occupation of Haiti in July, 1915 and of the Dominican Republic in May, 1916 aimed to watch over the destiny of the Caribbean and Central America in order to "teach them how to govern until they attain the required maturity." Concurrently, Protestant missionary efforts expanded, with numerous churches beginning work in the Dominican Republic in the early decades of the twentieth century.[6]

General Rafael Trujillo inherited the army created during the United States occupation. His rise to power, based in terror, began in 1930. The hierarchy of the Catholic church provided no obstacle to his economic and political pretensions, in spite of the violations of human rights and the terrible scandals that took place. The Catholic church received economic and institutional benefits until 1954, when a concordat was signed between the Dominican Republic and the Holy See in Rome. During his rule, Trujillo carried out a process of "Dominicanization" of the border region with Haiti, which ended in the massacre of 1937, when the Dominican military murdered 20,000 Haitians. In spite of the fact that a Jesuit mission had been established in this border region, there is no evidence that it ever criticised such cruelty. With this historical reality as preparation, the Mennonite church began its work less than a decade later, exactly in this border zone with Haiti.[7]

In May 1961 Trujillo was assassinated by his own military, leading to elections, but an unstable political situation. In 1965, 42,000 U.S. Marines invaded the Dominican Republic in support of right-wing forces, a move calculated to prevent the emergence of second Cuba in the hemisphere.[8] Protestant missionaries in the Dominican Republic in the late 1950s and 1960s generally steered clear of political matters, in order to avoid problems with the regime, at times criticizing the Catholic church and praising Trujillo for allowing freedom of religion.[9] The "Evangelism in Depth" program played a key role in unifying Protestant churches during the political unrest of 1965.[10] In spite of the armed conflicts and the invasion by U.S. Marines, a campaign of home visitation blanketing the entire country began in July of that year, accompanied by public campaigns and mass professions of faith.[11] The prolongued crises and the response of aggressive proselytism allowed Protestant organizations to unite and grow in the Dominican Republic, and the Mennonite church likewise grew.

The government of Joaquín Balaguer (1966-1978) established order by dismantling the left-wing opposition and gaining the support of the United States, which provided massive economic help through its AID program and also supported the Dominican sugar industry. But when Balaguer attempted to perpetuate his rule in 1978, the U.S. government intervened and did not permit him to seize power.[12] Nevertheless, the 1970s saw an impressive growth in Protestant churches in the Dominican Republic, in part because of the close relationship Balaguer's regime established with the U.S. The largest growth came in the Seventh Day Adventist church and the Pentecostal churches.[13]

Mennonite mission work in the Dominican Republic was initiated by the Evangelical Mennonite Church (U.S.A.; today called "Fellowship of Evangelical Churches") in 1943.[14] The first Mennonite missionary in the Dominican Republic was Ms. Lucille Rupp who arrived in August of 1945 and stayed first in the border zone with Haiti known as Dajabón, where the Missionary Church was also beginning its mission work, before moving her work further south.[15] In February 1946 Omar Sutton and his wife Laura arrived to take charge of the Mennonite work on the border between the Dominican and Haiti; they decided to establish their center of operations in El Cercado.[16] The first church services were assisted by Arquímenes Sméster, a Dominican national who was a recent graduate of the Biblical Institute in Santiago and a member of

A load of charcoal is transported

the Free Methodist Church. He helped them with translation and with the sermons. One of Omar Sutton's important contributions to the community was the construction of the first rural aqueduct, which greatly benefitted the families of El Cercado.

The first years following the arrival of the Mennonite missionaries brought strong Catholic opposition. In one of the letters sent by the Bishop Ricardo Pittini to the dictator Trujillo he said that "salaried ministers are running about the country, inundating it with Bibles, magazines, pamphlets, and flyers which always distill their subtle poison and furthermore direct vulgar attacks against our Catholic religion and in particular against the Dominican devotion to Our Lady of Altagracia."[17] Although the missionaries and the first Protestants experienced tensions with the Roman Catholic priests, thankfully the problems did not reach the extremes they did in other countries, such as Colombia.

The first person to join the Mennonite Church was Ismenia Ramírez who, according to her own testimony, had been asking God to send messengers with the Gospel.[18] The first Mennonite church in the Dominican Republic was established in April 1948, when thirteen persons were baptized at El Cercado.[19] Later the Gospel spread to other towns such as Elías Piña, El Llano, Las Matas Farfán and La Racha.[20]

In 1950 and 1951 several missionaries arrived and work of the church was considerably strengthened; in 1951 the first annual conference of established churches took place in El Cercado.[21] The organization officially adopted the name "Sureña Evangelical Church." In addition, the Sureña Evangelical Church took up the evangelistic

The Testimony of Ismenia Ramírez

Ismenia came to know the Lord at 80 years of age (1940) while she was visiting a daughter who lived in Barahona. When she returned to her home in El Cercado, Ismenia couldn't find the words with which to share her faith. Ismenia Ramírez had no Bible, nor did she know how to read, but she learned how to pray. For the following six years she asked the Lord to send someone who would speak to her people about the way to salvation. ... Imagine her joy when in March 1946 Omar and Laura Sutton and Lucille Rupp arrived at El Cercado. Ismenia rarely missed a worship service until her death at the age of 102 years. In 1949 Ismenia's mother, Ramona, made her profession of faith in Christ, just before her death at the age of 115 years. During the last years of her life, Ismenia spent much time in prayer. She prayed for the young Dominican church, for the missionaries and for those who sent them. She also prayed for her family and friends who were not yet saved. Praise was a prominent part of her prayers. Only eternity will reveal how far Ismenia's prayers reached.

work that the Evangelical Dominican Church had carried on since 1929 in San Juan de la Maguana, with a transfer of the properties of this mission to the Sureña Evangelical Church. From the start, the youth played an active leadership role in the fledgling convention of Mennonite churches. An annual young people's retreat has been held regularly.[22]

Sureña Evangelical Collegiate commenced its educational work in 1956. Later it was named the "Lucille Rupp School," in honor of its first director. Another early institution was the bookstore *El Heraldo*, founded in 1958, which played a very important role in distributing evangelical literature in San Juan.

Song sung at the Fifth Annual Conference (1955)

Sing victory
The word of the victor
Sing victory
We will triumph by faith and love
If trials and troubles come
We will look to our Captain
Who is the Saviour
He will guide us to victory.

In 1957 the conference was made up of eleven Mennonite churches, with 178 baptized members; the majority of these churches were led by Dominican pastors.[23] By 1969 the number of churches had grown to fourteen, of which one church (Lavapié) did not manage to continue functioning.[24] The majority of these churches were located in rural areas, and had very limited financial resources. There was a pressing need for ministerial preparation of church leaders who often had to serve two or more churches. Most local churches depended economically on the conference for support. The thirteen churches functioning in 1969 numbered 456 members, with a total of 652 persons attending Sunday school.[25]

Mennonite pastors, Dominican Republic

The revolutionary political climate in the Caribbean, given the drastic changes that had occurred in Cuba, led to a reconsideration of the organizational structure of the church. In 1964 it was proposed to change the name of the conference from "Sureña Evangelical Church" to "Evangelical Mennonite Church of the Dominican Republic" (EMCDR: *Iglesia Evangélica Menonita en la República Dominicana*) and to transfer the holdings of the mission board to the local leadership of the conference.[26] In addition the conference organized committees responsible for Christian Education and Stewardship and Evangelism.

The 1960s and 1970s saw an increased focus on education at all levels. In 1960 the Lucille Rupp School erected a building in San Juan de Maguana. The school, which had begun with 36 students, had 450 children enrolled by the end of the 1960s.[27] This number held firm throughout the next decade, and the school enjoyed a very high spiritual and academic reputation.[28] Given that students were accepted from both Protestant and Catholic families, the school contributed to the removal of bad feelings between the two denominations. The Omar Sutton School was in operation in the capital of Santo Domingo already in 1964. By 1970 it had 100 registered students and was being administered by the local church of Santo Domingo.[29] Four years later the school had registered 150 students, from Kindergarten up to the first year of High School.[30]

The first Institute for the preparation of leaders and lay people was held in 1963, with thirty-one participants. In 1965 and 1966 the training of leaders was done by means of the "Evangelism in Depth" program,[31] with Mennonites also participating in the interdenominational Theological Seminary of Santo Domingo which provided training for pastors.[32] Further seminary courses were offered from 1968 to 1972. The "Seminary by Extension" program began functioning in 1973, with courses offered on a semester basis in San Juan de la Maguana every first and third Saturday of the month, along with periodic intensive courses. There were 17 students enrolled in the initial year.[33] Theological and pastoral education entered another phase in 1975 with the formation of a united seminary in collaboration with the Free Methodist, Missionary and Antilles Mission

Hymn and theme for the twentieth annual assembly of the EMCDR, April, 1973

Throw yourself into the battle
Throw yourself into preaching
Walk on the roads
Of the air, earth and sea
There are souls without Christ
Going to eternity
Take them the message
Of joy.

The Buen Pastor (Good Shepherd) church, Santo Domingo

churches. The first course offered was an intensive seminar held at the Evangelical Institute in Santiago in 1975.[34]

In the area of communications, the Evangelical Mennonite Church's bookstore *El Heraldo* in San Juan de la Maguana met with considerable success. This led to the opening of a second bookstore in the capital in 1963, called *El Manantial*.[35] By 1970 this bookstore had also proven to be economically sound, which led to the purchase of a building to house the growing enterprise in 1973.[36] The bookstores were important sources of Christian materials, especially for the Sunday schools.[37] The church periodical *El Vínculo* began publishing twice yearly in the mid-1960s, and in 1973 a second publication called *Tu*

Pastor Manuel Sepúlveda

Our primary goal is winning lost souls for Christ. Outside of this goal the church has no reason for being. In its interior life, the church offers itself daily to God; but in the world, it ought to live for those who have not yet heard or received the Gospel. Therefore the church ought to seek constantly for how it can grow numerically, as well as in the grace and knowledge of its Lord and Savior. It is urgent that we motivate our youth ... and to seriously ask why our youth are not interested in the ministry. ... We feel that it is necessary to study Mennonite theology, which has not been sufficiently studied until now. ... It is important that these classes be oriented towards evangelism, Sunday school, and Mennonite doctrine and history. ... We want to share with each one of you the need to awaken in each one of us the message of the church and its mission in the world. And we should not only think and be preoccupied, but rather we should also act, moved by the Holy Spirit and instructed in human knowledge, to the glory of God.

Informador began to appear, the latter with the aim of helping the executive committee of the conference communicate with the church membership.[38] A radio ministry was initiated in 1959 with a program called *La Senda de Vida* (The Path of Life); in 1968 the church in Santo Domingo also began to broadcast a fifteen-minute program called *La Iglesia en Marcha* (The Church on the Move).[39]

In the area of social assistance the Evangelical Mennonite Church collaborated with the local interdenominational agency called "Committee for Social Services of the Dominican Church," particularly in the distribution of clothing and food in the wake of hurricanes and other natural disasters. The Committee was also involved in the literacy program of ALFALIT, in which members of the Mennonite church also participated.[40] The San Juan medical center began functioning in 1970, and by the end of the year had attended some 2,000 patients, with many patients receiving eye care and hundreds of children vaccinated. In 1974 the Mennonite Medical Center moved to San Juan de la Maguana.[41] VS and MEDA initiatives also began in the 1970s, with a focus on agricultural aid, nutritional programs and loans.[42]

Evangelistic activities remained central in the EMCDR, particularly after the concentrated efforts of the "Evangelism in Depth" programs of 1965 and 1966. Earlier work with the Bible Society continued in the 1970s, with EMCDR members distributing Bibles, New Testaments, and printed biblical excerpts.[43] The "Promotion Committee" of the conference gained renewed energy in 1970 when Darío Platt became chair. Among the innovations he introduced was the use of film as an evangelistic medium, but he also organized Bible conferences and public baptisms in local churches.[44] Throughout the 1970s the Women's Association and the Youth Association of the Evangelical Mennonite Church also promoted church activities.[45] These varied ministries proved fruitful. From the 11 Evangelical Mennonite churches operating in 1957, that number had grown to 32 churches in 1978, and conversations had begun with the home church in the U.S. about the possibility of opening a Mennonite mission in Venezuela.[46]

A new impetus came to the EMCDR with the parallel interest and activity of the "Divine Beacon" (*Faro Divino*) National Mennonite Council, which has pentecostal origins. On a visit to the United States Hilario de Jesús, a Dominican pentecostal pastor, came into contact with José Santiago, secretary of the Eastern Mennonite Mission board.

When Santiago in turn visited Hilario in the Dominican Republic in 1974, Hilario de Jesús convened three other pastors and together they decided to associate with the Mennonites. Eastern Mennonite Missions supported these churches economically and by sending missionaries to help in a variety of ways. The Central Church of Bonao became one of the most active churches of this new Council, soon establishing five new congregations. The church in La Vega was also active in mission work and church planting.[47] A follower of Hilario de Jesús, Carlos V. Barranco, became an important leader for these churches, later serving as president of the Council.

The *Faro Divino* churches are noted for their emphasis on the work of the Holy Spirit, and the participation of women in prophetic and pastoral ministries is also notable. Nevertheless, the document that served as the basis for the constitution of the *Faro Divino* churches is the same as that approved in 1976 by the Council of Mennonite Hispanic Churches of the United States. That document recognizes the Holy Scriptures as providing the only rules of conduct for the church of Christ, and also accepts the "Confession of Faith" adopted by the Mennonite General Conference in 1963 as providing guidance in faith and practice. At the general assembly of the Evangelical Mennonite Conference in 1978, members of the "Divine Beacon" churches were introduced for the first time in that setting. They encouraged all present to follow Jesus Christ, and thanked the assembly for its welcome.[48]

Testimony of Ana Marte de Barranco, of the *Faro Divino* church

For us the ministry of the Holy Spirit is foundational in the church, as is prayer and fasting and studying the Word. Because a church without the Holy Spirit of God is handicapped. It is like a table with only three legs: it will fall. It is the Holy Spirit that helps and strengthens us. The Spirit convicts us of sin; the Spirit brings souls. In times past, in this church, there was such a great pouring out of the Holy Spirit that people passing by would come in crying in search of God. They would throw themselves on the floor, asking that we pray for them.

The Mennonite presence in the Dominican Republic was shaped from the start by the mission initiative of the Evangelical Mennonite Church of the United States. The planting of churches was accompanied by further evangelistic efforts, the establishment of schools, bookstores, support for theological education and for pastoral training. By the 1960s, the Mennonite church in the Dominican had moved to national leadership and ownership, with continuing missionary support. The parallel work of the EMCDR with the "Divine Beacon" churches of pentecostal origin – both of whom are now member churches of Mennonite World Conference – provides an interesting example of the multi-dimensional way in which Latin American Mennonite churches may grow.

The Mennonite Churches in Jamaica (1954-1979)

When Columbus first came to Jamaica in 1494, the island was inhabited by the Arawak people. The Spaniards concentrated on raising livestock and growing sugar, but their primary interest in the island was for its strategic location, used as a supply base for Spanish conquests in nearby countries. Beginning in 1509 the indigenous people, subject to forced labor and with no immunity to the diseases brought by the Spaniards, began to die in large numbers until they practically disappeared. It is at this point that the slave trade began.

When the British conquered Jamaica in 1655, the island counted only 3,000 inhabitants, half of whom were slaves. In 1672 the Royal African Company was founded, with a monopoly over slave trade, turning Jamaica into one of the largest centers in the world for commerce in African people. From 1745 to 1770, the rich owners of the great sugar plantations in Jamaica were also the political leaders of Great Britain.[1] Great Britain did not abandon the slave trade until 1807; the slaves finally were emancipated in 1834. In the face of the crisis in sugar prices, large companies moved to operations of mono-cultivation and the exportation of bananas and plantains. Nevertheless, low wages kept the African-descended population in a continually precarious economic situation.

In 1915 Great Britain founded the West Indian Regiment of more than 15,000 Black soldiers from Jamaica and other islands to fight on the side of the Allies. The Black soldiers always received second-class treatment. Because of the racial discrimination they suffered, 18 battalions carried out a mutiny against their superiors in December of 1918. Many of these soldiers returned to the Caribbean and made an important contribution to improving working conditions for other

Blacks in the colonies. After the First World War the more than ten million Africans who lived in Latin America and the Caribbean began to become aware of their African cultural heritage. In Jamaica, Marcus Garvey was one of the most important promoters of the Black Consciousness movement.

Jamaica was severely affected by the Great Depression in many ways; between 1930 and 1935, more than 20,000 Jamaicans had been returned to their country after being deported from various other countries. With the loss of income from outside the country, Jamaica fell into crisis. The Second World War, on the other hand, had very positive effects on the Jamaican economy, for during the 1940s the Caribbean islands were converted into suppliers for Great Britain, producing cotton, sugar cane, bauxite, rice and petroleum. There also was a new wave of emigration to Arabia, Curazao and the United States. In 1941, Great Britain traded land in Antigua, Santa Lucia, Jamaica, British Guyana and Trinidad in exchange for war machinery from the Unites States government. United States presence in the Caribbean began to grow.

During the war years there was a political struggle to free the country from British colonialism. Universal suffrage was granted to the inhabitants of Jamaica in 1944. Industry grew after the Second World War but the promise of the British government in 1947 to help Jamaica and its other colonies toward self-government moved slowly. Britain wished to create a Caribbean federation that would include all the colonies of the East Indies, an attempt that failed completely.[2] Jamaica achieved total independence in 1962.

With the seventeenth-century establishment of British rule,[3] the Jamaican church was divided into fifteen Anglican parishes, but the church did not flourish.[4] The racial question was used both to justify slavery and to exclude Black Jamaicans from the church. The most important fact before 1800 was not the failure of the Anglican church to Christianize the slaves, but rather its failure to influence the lives of the Whites and the non-enslaved in colonial society.[5]

The slave societies of the Antilles were transformed by the arrival of non-conformist missionaries, especially the Methodists whose founder, John Wesley, took a position against slavery. One of the most important features of Methodism was bringing Whites and non-Whites, slaves and free alike into the church. The Moravians and Baptists also arrived in the 18th century.[6] By 1835 the government in

London decreed a transition period from slavery to the incorporation of Jamaicans into society, by means of education. In a context of growing tolerance and cooperation, the non-conformist churches grew greatly.[7] The emancipation of the slaves obliged colonial governments to re-define the relationship between church and state in their territories towards independence and autonomy for the Jamaican church.[8] Interdenominational cooperation improved in 1941 when the Jamaica Christian Council was organized.[9]

The arrival of the Virginia Mennonite Board of Missions and Charities in the late 1950s coincided with the coming of a new era in the history of Jamaica, when the British crown ceded its dominion in the Caribbean to the United States, and the populations were struggling to attain self-government. The Mennonite church in Jamaica emerged with a strong leadership of sisters and brothers who came from the divided Pilgrim Holiness Church in St. Andrew.[10] The first focus of action would be the city of Constant Spring.

Annie and D. H. Loewen, pastors in the General Conference Mennonite church,[11] felt a calling from God to begin a mission station in Jamaica. After arriving in Jamaica in October 1954, they began holding small worship meetings in their dwelling in Constant Spring. One of the first converts was Simeon Walter and his wife Maud.[12] After an exploratory trip in 1955, the Virginia Mennonite Conference decided to support the work of the Loewens.[13]

The church at Constant Spring was known as "Good Tidings."[14] In 1957 broadcasting of "The Mennonite Hour" began, a practical way for Mennonites to become known on the island. "The Way to Life" was another program aired on Radio Jamaica which offered correspondence courses. Warren and Erma Metzler discerned a young populace in search of the truth and lamented that in a country that was supposedly Christian the survival rate for infants was only 80 percent.[15]

Deacon Simeon Walter, at work in his tailor shop

Mission work in Red Hills began when Simeon Walter began travelling on his bicycle to announce the good news of salvation. Beginning in 1955, he visited Red Hills for seven years, leading a Sunday school, dedicating newborns to God, and testifying in the community.

By the end of 1957, 60 persons were gathering for Sunday school at Red Hills, and a provisional shelter was built with cement columns and a zinc roof. The third Sunday in October, 1957 this first improvised church building was dedicated to God, and the first Sunday of that same month a morning worship service was held in which five new members were received.[16] The following year four more young people years were received into the church by baptism.

Mennonites also participated with enthusiasm in the Billy Graham crusade which took place in January, 1958.[17] People flocked to this event. For the Mennonite congregations the campaign meant increased contact with new people and new members in the church who required pastoral care and accompaniment.

Warren Metzler baptizes two converts in Kingston harbor, 1956

Mennonite mission work spread to Retreat, a little rural town that had neither church nor school located seventy miles from Constant Spring on the northern coast of the island. The first visitors to Retreat were from the Good Tidings church.[18] The Metzlers noted that families listened frequently to the "Way to Life" radio program. Continuing visits eventually resulted in the founding of the Church of Calvary in Retreat.

The Hall Green community is tied to the past in the history of Jamaica. In 1839, one year after the end of slavery in Jamaica, a group of ex-slaves took possession of nine acres of land in the Hall Green district of St. Andrews, nine miles north of Kingston. Years later ownership of this property was transferred to an independent Baptist church, for the building of a church and a school. Later, various people who led that church began to annex parts of the property, and to live there. In October 1957, six members of Hall Green Baptist church requested Mennonite guidance for Hall Green, for the leadership of that church had disappeared. In 1958, Nathanael Leair and his wife were received as pastors, on confession of faith, into the Mennonite community.[19]

The members of Hall Green were asked about their preference of belonging to the Mennonite church, or to the National Baptist church. Although some of the older members decided not to change denominations, the church was formally initiated in February, 1959 in a beautiful worship service in which some 200 persons participated. Three persons were baptized and six were received as members in the emerging Hall Green Mennonite church.[20]

The 1960s and 1970s were a time of great social and political agitation. In the midst of a pentecostal renewal and the Rastafarian movement, the Mennonite church established seven new churches and consolidated the Conference of Mennonite Churches of Jamaica.

The workers' struggle and the radicalization of the Jamaican government in the 1960s and 70s led to fear among the personnel of the various North American missions that "another Cuba" would occur.[21]

The 1960s marked a return to African history and culture, and strong ties between the Caribbean and Africa were re-affirmed. Bob Marley and the Wailers did much to popularize "properly Jamaican" music, which evolved into what is known as reggae and spread throughout the world in the 1970s. The Rastafarian movement also continued to flourish on the island, in spite of being repressed by

Rev. David B. Clark, Missionary Church Association of Jamaica, May, 1961

Jamaica is ripe for the Communist picking! Jamaica is the key to all the other British West Indian Islands – are we to sit back and wait for racial violence and Communism to take over? Please PRAY FOR JAMAICA, that the Christian will prove to be a bulwark against atheistic Communism. Our Association has a vital part to play, and we must not fail. It is either Christ, or Communism – there is no middle ground. Either our Churches awake, and profess a living Christ, or else Satan will take over with his super-weapon, International Communism.

the Jamaican authorities.[22] This movement proclaimed that God is Black and that Blacks form the true people of God, on the road to the new Zion, which is Ethiopia. God was said to be in solidarity with this project of liberation of Black peoples.[23] Rastafarianism became a religion of the people, an africanized Christianity.[24]

As in many other parts of Latin America, one of the fundamental elements that permitted "syncretism" of this kind in the churches was the schism that existed between the institutionalized churches and the people. Armando Lampe has pointed to the common aspects that exist between pentecostalism and syncretistic cults, which explain in part the pentecostal revival in all of the Caribbean. The growth of pentecostalism was dramatic in Jamaica. In 1960 only 6 percent of the population was pentecostal; by 1980, the number had grown to 25 percent.[25]

The Good Tidings Church continued to provide strong leadership among the Jamaican Mennonite churches in the 1960s and 1970s. Its facilities were used to offer Bible School programs over holiday times (between July and August), and literacy courses following the

The Good Tidings Mennonite church

Laubach method also were offered.[26] The Good Tidings congregation was noted for its inter-ethnic character. Among its members were Chinese, Blacks, Whites and people who originated in India.[27]

The Alpine Church in Red Hills also continued to be active. In mid-1962 this church had 20 members and another

John R. Mumaw consults with Jamaican church leaders: (from left) Ransford Nicholson, John R. Mumaw, Simeon Walter, Willard Heatwole, Joscelyn Robinson, Ken Brunk.

six persons were receiving baptismal instruction.[28] Hall Green church experienced modest growth in the 1960s and 70s and had built a new church by 1969.[29] In 1961, Eric and Beatrice Robinson of Retreat were converted and baptized. This was a great testimony for the community, for God freed them from alcohol abuse, and on beginning their walk of discipleship, they abandoned their profitable business of selling tobacco and marijuana. Eric Robinson worked as deacon of the church from 1963 to 1976. In 1961 a new Calvary church building was dedicated. By mid-1962 this church counted 11 members and another 11 persons were receiving baptismal instruction.[30]

Community evangelism began in the village of Heartease with Bible studies, Sunday schools and a youth club for young women. A church, later called Bethel church, was first established in an old bar in Heartease, with the first service held in November, 1968.[31] The isolated communities of Joyland and Abram began receiving visits in 1959. A church was built in Abram in 1966; the following year a church was erected in Joyland. By 1970 a church had been founded also in the town of Ocho Rios.[32] Small church communities were also established in Waterloo, Salter Hill just south of Montego Bay and Southfield.

Permanent summer Bible schools were an important resource used by the Mennonites in the evangelization and education of children in Jamaica. Many times these took place out in the open, under the shade of trees.[33] The Laubach literacy method was used in 1966 at the Good Tidings church as well as at the Mennonite church at Abram. In other places, such as Retreat and the St. Mary parish, the Mennonites decided to build secondary schools. This is how Calvary Academy came to be, opening in January, 1969 with a total of 70 students. This school functioned until 1976, during which time it provided many opportunities for testimonies of faith in Jesus Christ.

The Peggy Memorial Home for girls was founded in honor of Peggy Brunk Brydge, daughter of bishop Truman Brunk, who died in a traffic accident in 1958, leaving her six-month-old son an orphan.[34] In 1962 the home had sixteen young women occupants.[35] Later the houses came to be occupied with up to a maximum of 25 resident young ladies. Church World Service provided food and the women made contact with persons in the U.S. for donations to support their ministry. The program ended in 1975 because of a lack of finances and national workers to continue the project.[36] A further help to the needy was the Maranatha school for the deaf, established in 1975.[37]

Radio ministry remained important for Mennonite mission efforts.[38] A separate office was opened in Good Tidings church to handle matters relating to "The Way to Life" radio program. In 1972 between 3,000 and 4,000 persons used the Bible study lessons offered by the radio broadcast. By January, 1979 the Mennonite church of Jamaica began its local radio production, and Keith Allen took over the leadership of all radio programming. In that same year Mennonite Media Ministries no longer continued subsidizing the ministry, and the Mennonite church of Jamaica took ownership of this work.

The faithful grandmother: Florence O'Brien

Florence O'Brien was the first grandmother to look after these girls, which she did for several years. She was a true pillar of the church. She tended to scold people who were careless, but all the same she was jovial, serene, devoted and completely involved in the church. One notable sentence that she often used in her public prayers was the following: "Dear Lord, help us to trust in you, as we trust in our selves." She created a lovely atmosphere in the Home for Girls; the dogs adored her as much as the girls did.

The literature ministry of the Mennonites involved distributing Sunday school materials, tracts and a church bulletin called "The Mennonite Voice." This bulletin was printed bi-monthly, but when financing support from the mission stopped in 1970 the bulletin ceased publication.

Calvary church

The first Annual Conference of Mennonite Churches of Jamaica took place in the Good Tidings church in 1959. In the early years of the organization the program and the leadership of the churches was directed by the missionaries of the Virginia Mission Board, but already at the second Conference there was discussion about the relationship between the Conference and the Virginia board.[39] The first Jamaican pastor to be ordained was Randsford Nicholson, in September, 1968 in a service presided over by bishop Truman Brunk. In February, 1970 the Mennonite Conference of Jamaica was officially and legally incorporated as "Jamaica Mennonite Church, Ltd." Eric Robinson was named president, and the request was made for a transfer of church property titles.

For its part, the executive committee of the Virginia Mission Board approved and made it clear that the Mennonite church of Jamaica now assumed all administrative and spiritual responsibility for the organization. Bishop Truman Brunk concluded his duties as bishop in Jamaica at the end of 1970. In the key year 1976 the Mennonite Conference of Jamaica did not name a single missionary to its executive committee. Twenty-one years after its founding, administrative responsibility now lay in national hands.[40] In January, 1976 the Biblical Institute opened in the Waterloo church in Kingston, offering theological education two times per week.[41] In this new era the Virginia Mission Board continued its financial and teaching support.[42]

The Mennonite Central Committee played an important role in Jamaica in the 1970s, primarily in support for educational centers in Jamaica.[43] Arthur Driedger, director for Latin America for MCC, maintained contact with Mac Taylor, director of the Peace Corps in Jamaica,[44] taking advantage of his experience, for Taylor supervised some 1500 North American young people in his program.[45] Good correspondence was also maintained from the start with Willard Heatwole, at that time missionary of the Virginia Mission Board, who was informed about the first young people from MCC to travel to

Jamaica.[46] The April, 1971 visit to Jamaica by Edgar Stoesz, new secretary for Latin America for MCC, affirmed the work of the Mennonites in coordination with Jamaican authorities and others.[47] When tropical storm Gilda unleashed its fury in October, 1973, MCC coordinated many of the efforts to take clothes, bedding and food to those affected by the storm. MCC also donated money for the Red Cross to take provisions to affected families.[48]

The relationship of MCC with the Virginia Mission Board was maintained, although Stoesz was aware of the fact that MCC was more open to social, political and governmental aspects, to development agencies and ecumenical relations, while the Mission Board concentrated more on the growth of their own churches.[49] In the 1970s, education was MCC's major field of service, such that by 1974 there were already 21 teachers working in primary and secondary schools.[50] Nevertheless, political uncertainty preoccupied Ken and Mabel Zinder, MCC directors.[51] The MCC reports, by contrast with those that came from the churches, are marked by an effort to discern and communicate in their bulletins the difficult social and political life that Jamaica was experiencing. This can be seen in the commentaries concerning the elections of 1976, which finally were won by Manley and the People's National Party.[52]

The Mennonite church in Jamaica saw modest growth from the time of its founding, but contributed important educational efforts with schools for younger children, education for the deaf, a home for girls and in pastoral training. The movement to recover African identity in the 1960s and 70s was not one that was embraced by the Mennonite church. Nevertheless the Jamaican Mennonite church moved steadily towards nationalization in leadership and ownership. When missionary funding was removed in the 1970s, some economic dependency and weakness was revealed.

Parallel to mission efforts, MCC worked at a slightly different vision of giving testimony to Mennonite faith. MCC made a great direct contribution through the young people who worked as teachers, farmers, nutritionists or community assistants in social development projects. At the same time, many of these same workers also participated actively in the various Jamaican Mennonite churches during their time with MCC, and generally strengthened the Mennonite witness on the island.[53]

The Anabaptist-Descended Churches in Cuba (1954-1979)

CHAPTER XV

Christopher Columbus arrived in Cuba on his first voyage of 1492, but it was not until 1511 that the island was integrated into the Spanish colonial system under the leadership of Diego Velázques. The European war of 1791-1815 made it possible to break the Spanish monopoly on trade, and a closer relationship began between Cuba and the United States. In 1898 a second war of independence began, led by José Martí together with slaves and Cubans of African descent. That same year war erupted between the United States and Spain.[1] After Spain's defeat, a series of accords were initiated by the United States with Puerto Rico, Guam, and the Philippines. Cuba resisted the accords and was occupied militarily until 1902. José Martí's dream of liberty died with that occupation.[2] The Liberal period from 1902 to 1929 saw a series of United States military interventions, the breaking of Catholic hegemony and the growth of United States Protestant missions.[3]

The military dictatorships of Machado (1925-1933) and Fulgencio Batista (1952-1959) were marked by the cohabitation of the state with the Catholic church, with priests from Franco's Spain exerting a great influence.[4] An important moment in the life of Cuban Protestantism came with the political involvement of Presbyterian leaders such as Raúl Fernández and Rafael Cepeda who, after the second military coup of Batista in 1952, carried out a plan of church visitations, persuading the Protestants to ally themselves with the struggle against the dictator. Baptist leaders like Frank País and his brother Josué participated in the clandestine struggle in eastern Cuba and, discovered by Batista's police, were killed in 1957.[5] It was under the government of Batista that the missionary work of the Brethren in Christ and the Mennonites began.

The beginnings of the Brethren in Christ church go back to relationships that were established in the 1950s with the Quakers and the Nazarenes in Cuba.[6] The work begun earlier by the Quakers in Cuatro Caminos had been abandoned. Severina Campos remembers that she used to pass by the closed church and think: "Oh Lord, look at the church; would that you would grant the privilege of opening it again, so I could worship you."[7] After some intensive conversations, the church property was sold to the Brethren in Christ. The repaired church was dedicated in February, 1954.[8]

Testimony of Juana María García Morín

I was born in Catalina de Guines, Cuba, on the 4th of February, 1924, 70 kilometers from Havana. My father and mother were humble peasants and lived in El Congo ... where my father sowed sugar cane, and would then cut it and sell it to the mill. I can testify to the work of the missionary Samuel Pain... My family came to hear the Gospel in the services that Samuel and Gladys held in our house. ... When I was thirteen years old I accepted Jesus Christ as my savior... Beginning in 1954 I began working with North American Brethren in Christ missionaries in Cuatro Caminos. I remember the lovely times when we gathered up many children from the neighboring and poor barrios to take them to the school founded by Gerardo and Perla [Wolgemuth]. The yellow "guagua" [bus] would fill up with girls and boys who would laugh and sing happily on the way to the little school. In different circumstances of my life I have experienced the loving nearness of God. For this reason one of my favorite hymns is "Oh, how sweet it is to trust in Christ!"

From 1954 until the triumph of the Cuban revolution the church depended almost entirely on the pastoral work of the missionaries. The Brethren in Christ began to evangelize in the Central Sugar Mill "Portugalete" and in the village of Mella. They also bought a small wooden church in 1958 in the town of Nazareno, and began Bible studies and a Sunday school there.[9] By October, 1960 the work of the church remained in the hands of a Cuban board of directors.

In 1954 the Mennonite Board of Missions and Charities of Franconia, U.S.A., sent its first missionaries to Cuba. Henry Paul Yoder and his family settled in the center of the island in the province of Las Villas, in a place called Rancho Veloz.[10] Cuba was seen as a good place for founding churches because of its "atmosphere of religious liberty." Among the needs that were highlighted were medical services, proper nutrition for children, education, economic help, and the need to found new churches.

The Mission Board outlined a three-pronged strategy: economic self-support, self-administration, and self-propagation of the Gospel.[11]

In 1955 Betty and Aaron King opened a new work and introduced the *Luz y Verdad* radio program, broadcast on a local radio station in the center of the island. Between 1954 and 1958 Margaret Derstine and other single missionaries arrived. They contributed much to the work in little towns such

The main street, Rancho Veloz, pre-revolution

as Sierra Morena, Corralillo, Palmasola and Central Ramona.[12]

As the struggle against the Batista regime intensified even some North American Mennonite missionaries referred to the Batista government as a corrupt dictatorship.[13] In the province of Las Villas, the Mennonite missionaries witnessed first-hand the cruel struggles between the movement led by Fidel Castro and the Batista regime.

A new historical period began in December, 1958 under the leadership of Fidel Castro. Shortly after the triumph of the revolutionaries, relations between the United States and Cuba became increasingly confrontational.[14] The climax of the confrontation came with the presence of Russian missiles in Cuba in October, 1962, which put all of humanity at risk. The final agreement between the super-powers was a compromise in which the United States would not invade Cuba and the Soviet Union promised not to use Cuba as a base for nuclear arms. This is how the revolutionary government in Cuba managed to survive.

Testimony of Aaron M. King

Actual war did not come to Rancho Veloz or Sagua la Grande, where we misionaries live, except for about two days last April when forty died in the general Sagua strike. However, during the closing days of 1958 the threat of war increased and the very air seemed tense with dread expectancy. The rebels were taking town after town after town in this Las Villas province. And while they proclaimed each town as part of the "Free Territory of Cuba," with control over newly taken radio facilities, general communications naturally became tighter and tighter... Around Christmas day three loads of Batista-regime soldiers sped past our house to the radio station, where they quickly disabled the plant to prevent rebel seizure and use of its vital voice. ....

Continue to give thanks with us. Thank God that the war which was costing "thousands of lives and millions of dollars" has ended. Thank Him that we can move about freely in His work once more and that correspondence is beginning to come into the "Luz y Verdad" branch office from both ends of the island. Pray, as one who attends our church services suggested, for peace which the revolution can never give.

The radicalization of the Cuban revolution in a Marxist-Leninist direction had enormous repercussions at economic, social and religious levels. The Catholic church, under the leadership of a largely Spanish clergy who espoused a "Franquista" ideology, was disconcerted, and assumed a confrontationist posture with the new revolutionary government.[15] Although many Protestants initially sympathized with the revolution, many abandoned the new political and social project as it radicalized. Missionaries from North American churches began leaving the country, fearing a Stalinist revolution. It was as if a kind of fever infected the North American missionaries until practically all of them left the country.[16] Around 200,000 Cuban emigrants joined the North Americans in leaving Cuba from 1960 to 1962. The majority of these emigrants belonged to the elite economic and social class, primarily professional men, leaders and executives.[17] The Protestant churches were left without missionaries and without the leadership of a great number of their best pastors, who had been trained in Cuban seminaries and institutes.

This reality was seen in the Cuatro Caminos church (BIC). For example, Locario López, the first national pastor and an excellent preacher and a bulwark during the first fifteen years of the church, became completely involved in union work and the revolution, leaving the church behind for twenty years. The feverish missionary abandonment of Cuba was passed on to the youth. Rubén Perdomo, another young man who was present at the beginnings of the church, left it after five years and never returned. His siblings, Mary and Manuel Perdomo also left for the United States. Almost all the youth who

were companions of Félix Rafael Curbelo in the beginnings of the BIC church of Cuatro Caminos are living today in the United States.[18]

When the last North American BIC missionaries, Howard and Pearl Wolgemuth, left the country together with many other Cuban pastors and North American missionaries, the work remained in the hands of a local Board of Directors. The key person providing leadership to this board was Juana M. García, who was assisted by a young man named Eduardo Llanes. However, he soon departed for the United States. The church continued under

Severina Campos

Juana M. García's leadership along with a team

made up of Heriberto Perdomo Estevez, Herminio Alvarez, Rafael Curbelo Valle,[19] Severina Campos and others.

During the 1960s, the farming couple Francisco Cabrera and Eunice Coca moved to the center of the island to Cuatro Caminos. They came from families with a very long tradition in the Protestant church of Pinos Nuevos. This couple raised five boys, four of whom later became pastors; they also had a daughter born in Havana. The Cabrera-Coca family played an important role because they eagerly shared the Gospel; their coming strengthened the BIC church in Cuatro Caminos in a difficult time of desertion.

The theme of faith and politics in revolutionary Cuba continues to be taboo in many Protestant churches. It was difficult when the Brethren in Christ church lost its school, for it was in this way that the church provided a community service and also testified to its faith. Nevertheless there are anecdotes and testimonies from the brothers and sisters who remained in Cuba that temper the more elevated criticisms of an earlier time.

Pastor Juana M. García dedicated her entire life to supporting her BIC community in a difficult time. She had solid training inherited from the missionaries, and this provided continuity and strength for the length of her ministry. Being aware of her religious tradition, in

The testimony of Félix Rafael Curbelo Valle

I was born in a small neighborhood of Havana. My parents were peasants. I lived in the country on a farm very close to Cuatro Caminos... There are three of us brothers: Carlos, Juan, Rafael and our sister Aída. My brother Juan made contact with the church and was converted. The rest of the family followed. I was about fourteen when I was baptized with my brother, early in 1956. ... When I was fourteen I would study at night, and by day I would work on a farm. In this way I completed grade six. ... I later continued my studies in an institute and at the university I studied agronomy and economics. I did my university work at night. In this way I combined my work in the church, studies, and work in the secular world in order to earn my livelihood; they were years of great sacrifice. In 1960, because of the great exodus that took place in the church, I began to take on official tasks in the church. I have preached very little, but I have taken on various posts, sometimes as vice president or in the preservation and administration of the official documents. This is somewhat hidden work... I've carried it out for forty years, until today.

Juana García leads a
church service

which it is a man who normally presides in the church, she was able to lead and yet be accompanied by a pastor for ritual events such as baptisms, the Lord's Supper or marriages. But the great weight of pastoral leadership for the community of faith rested on her shoulders for all those years. In the 1970s, in the later years of her life, Juana María García decided to marry Julián González, a pastor from the Protestant church of Los Pinos, who had been widowed four years.[20] Without a doubt, the contributions of Julián González to the pastoral and liturgical work of the church were a great help to Juana María García until the time of his death in the early 1980s.[21]

In 1959, when the Franconia board missionaries left, the national leaders of the Mennonite church found themselves in a difficult spot, since the official registration of the church, begun during the government of Fulgencio Batista, had not been concluded. The church had no legal standing, and in the new political circumstances it was not possible to begin that process. As a result, the families remained without pastoral protection for a long time.[22] Mennonite believers in Rancho Veloz, Corralillo, Sagua la Grande, San Vicente and other places of Las Villas continued meeting in their homes to maintain their faith. Vitalina Costa, referring to the long period of approximately seventeen years that the Mennonite families remained without pastoral support, says "We read the Bible as a family. When one knows the Lord, and knows him truly and knows the faith ... it is not possible to forget. It is a small flame that doesn't go out, even though there may be difficulties."[23]

The BIC and Mennonite churches of Cuba experienced first-hand the difficulties of abandonment with the departure of the founding missionaries and most of their trained pastors and leaders. It is a strong testimony that many continued to maintain their faith and practice as an "underground" church in a state that had become less-than-friendly to the practice of Christianity.

Mennonites come to Haiti (1957-1979)

The name "Haiti" comes from Arawak and means "country of the mountains." Christopher Columbus laid eyes on the island in 1492 and it passed into the hands of the Spanish crown. Haiti is located on the western third of the island of Española, and is bounded to the east by the Dominican Republic. The indigenous Arawak population had been annihilated by the middle of the sixteenth century, and many slaves were brought from the coasts of Guinea to Haiti to work the plantations. The Creole spoken in Haiti is the mixed inheritance of native African languages and colonial French.

In 1791 there was a slave uprising in Haiti in which a strong African identity, refined by voodoo, manifested its revolutionary character. The French sent 6,000 soldiers to combat the slave rebellion, but Black troops under Jean Jacques Dessalines defeated the French troops in 1803. Santo Domingo was declared independent and reassumed its original name of Haiti.

Protestants first came to Haiti in 1807, with the arrival of Methodist missionaries. The American Baptist Convention of the U.S. was the second Protestant organization to come to Haiti, in 1823. By 1948 Baptist membership had reached 100,000 persons, located primarily in Artibonite, north, west and south of Gonave Island.[1] The situation changed following the military occupation by the United States, from 1915-1935, when the number of Protestant missions in Haiti increased dramatically.[2] As the 1960s began there were 73 Protestant churches or missions in Haiti. Many of them were independent churches; others represented mission societies from Africa, the United States and Europe.[3]

Mennonites came to Haiti thanks to MCC and Mennonite Disaster Service volunteers, who provided help in the wake of the destruction caused by hurricane Hazel in 1954. In 1957 MCC representatives William T. Snyder and Edgar Stoesz visited Haiti and found a country in desperate need of medical care, and help with agriculture and education.[4] In a subsequent memo of understanding, MCC committed itself to support the work of the Albert Schweitzer Hospital by providing doctors, laboratory technicians, veterinarians and anesthetists. It also committed itself to providing mentors for the rural extension program in Petit Goave directed by Rev. Marco Depestre and part of the British Methodist mission, and authorized exploring a possible collaborative agricultural work with Valle Artibonite.[5] MCC's permanent work in Haiti began in 1958 when Charles Suderman and Marlin Pankratz were sent to work at Petit Goave.[6] MCC's work in Haiti was guided by a developmentalist approach,[7] independent of, but in harmony with the developmentalist programs of the Alliance for Progress.[8] By the end of the 1970s, MCC was cooperating fully with the Albert Schweitzer Hospital, supplementing its various areas of activity in health, agriculture, community development and spiritual care for its workers.[9]

VSers, Grande Riviere (1963). L to R back row: Betty Penner, Paul Derstine, Mary Woelk. Front row: Marilyn and Dr. Glen Miller, Randy Kaufman, Eleanor Yoder. Miller children (L to R): Ken, Korla and Ed.

By mid-1962 the MCC program in Haiti included three areas of work: Petit Goave, Albert Schweitzer Hospital, and the hospital at Grand Riviere du Nord. At Grand Riviere du Nord, MCC collaborated with the Haitian Department of Health in staffing a new 20-bed hospital (1959). By 1962 the Grande Riviere du Nord hospital had 30 beds, and attended 125 persons per day. Some days a mobile clinic was provided to serve the needs of persons living in remote rural areas.[10] Grand Riviere du Nord became a central focus of MCC aid to Haiti from 1959 to 1980.[11]

Haiti became an ideal foreign location for Mennonite colleges. The first seminar on Haiti took place from June to August, 1963, organized by Bluffton College, Goshen College, and MCC. The missile crisis in Cuba had just passed, and the U.S. government had begun its Alliance for Progress program. The seminar offered the opportunity to become acquainted with another culture and a chance to study the economic and development problems of the country, in order to better understand missions to that place.[12]

Beginning in 1963 various Mennonite missions became involved in Haiti
thanks to the initiative of volunteers
who had helped following the disasters caused by hurricanes Flora (1964)[13]
and Inez (1966).[14] The strong presence
of Mennonite volunteers, as well as the
participation of MCC in social projects,
opened the door to a proliferation of
mission efforts by a variety of small
and large Mennonite groups.

Children at the Ecole de Providence,
a project of the Albert Schweitzer
Hospital, supported by MCC

Mennonite Gospel Missions, for-
mally known as "Mennonite Gospel of Haiti," was born in response
to the destruction by the hurricanes of 1964 and 1966, when Mennonite volunteers helped reconstruct homes with churches in the area
of Mirogoane. Fernando Bontrager, one of the missionaries who had
been associated with Son Light Missions for a time, later continued
to work with local Baptist churches and communities.[15] These Baptist
churches are known as the *Misión Evangelique La Redemption d´Haiti*
and in the 1990s began to be supported by Mennonite churches in
Indiana (Midwest Fellowship – Bethel, Sandy Ridge, and North Liberty) who together formed the Bethel Mission Board.[16]

The Christian Fellowship Mission was founded in 1964 by Aden
Yoder, one of the volunteers who aided the Haitian people in response
to hurricane Flora. Through his home congregation, Bay Shore Mennonite in Florida, Yoder was able to intensify the help given to some
Protestant churches around Mirogoane. This group built a church and
a dispensary in Mirogoane and in the mid-1970s, under the leadership of Sanford Sommers, moved to Port-au-Prince with a variety of
missionary efforts. This organization carried projects through teams of
volunteers. Many of the groups of Mennonite missionaries arrived in
Haiti thanks to their contact with Christian Fellowship Mission.[17]

Early in 1966 Eastern Mennonite Missions expressed interest in
working in Haiti.[18] EMM's witness became concrete with the creation
of the *Ecole Biblique par Extensión* (EBEX), which began with the visit
of Wilbert Lind and James Sauder beginning in 1969.[19] In 1969 Lind
led biblical studies for local pastors and Sunday school teachers.[20] On
the basis of Lind's analysis EMM decided to cooperate inter-denomi-
nationally in the education of leaders and pastors in Haiti.[21]

In 1973 the Mennonite missionary James Sauder,[22] together with the pastor and translator Josie Michel,[23] began writing a curriculum for biblical education. The idea was to write the curriculum in Creole to give wide access to the material. In 1975 Josie Michel opened an office for offering the EBEX program, and the program was offered in the central Plateau. When EMM representatives visited Haiti in 1976, they were able to dialogue with thirty members of the Evangelical Council of Churches with the aim of offering a program of biblical education.[24] Later this program led to conjoint work with other denominations who were also interested in the theological education of their pastors.[25]

The Mennonite mission of the Church of God in Christ, Holdeman (*Égliese de Dieu en Christ*) began its work in Haiti in 1963 when it sent people to help in reconstruction following hurricane Flora. This church emphasized planting churches as well as working with Christian Service International (CSI), which contributed health clinics in Mirbalais, Croix des Bouquet, Carrefour and Jeremy and with irrigation projects in Valier and Fond Parisen. CSI also had projects constructing latrines, bridges, roads, cisterns and hand pumps for cisterns. One of the important goals of the Holdeman was seeing that a local church develop its own adequate financing, as well as its own leadership.[26]

The Son Light Mission (Ministries) in Santo began when Mennonites from Virginia Beach, Virginia became interested in Haitian missions in 1970. The first support from Son Light Missions was in Miragoane, and later this support was transferred to other locations such as Santo, where another ministry was established in 1971. In 1982 this organization continued with its ecclesial and educational work, with health work taken over by Son Light Missions, LaColline.[27]

The International Fellowship Haven, Inc. began in 1972, when "Papa" Joe and Mattie Miller began taking mission trips to Haiti. They

Paul Derstine visits hospital staff at Grand Riviere (1990), most of whom had been with MCC in the 1960s

worked mostly with pastor Joseph Vantes Datus of the Church of God in Christ. Their goal was to build one church a year for small congregations, creating a network of 39 churches; these were built over a period of 21 years (1972-1993). The mission also sent pillows, comforters, food and school supplies to Haiti, as well as promoting gardens and other small projects to help the Haitians help themselves. The death of Papa Joe in 1993 temporarily slowed missionary activity. The guidance of the mission fell to Marie Miller who, together with a board of directors, worked to discern follow-up activity.[28]

In 1973 Amos E. Horst began responding to "a vision of poverty from the Lord," trying to respond to Haitian pastors and other Mennonite missions in that country. The Horsts served for seven months in the Blue Ridge home for girls in Leogane, but their primary contribution was in establishing an independent faith ministry. Contributions for this ministry are voluntary and come primarily from the Pinecraft Tourist Church in Sarasota, Florida. Notable among its programs are economic assistance, training for school teachers, evangelism, and aid with implements and food.[29]

The Son Light Missions, Inc. in LaColline began in 1976 with the Son Light Mission from Virginia.[30] Son Light Missions, Inc. expanded its missions elsewhere, but in 1982 the organization split with the New York sector over differences in approach to mission, particularly concerning leadership in LaColline.[31] Son Light Missions became a national church with the creation of four congregations which developed a close relationship with Mennonites in Pennsylvania and Ohio. In 1987 this organization counted 300 members and two primary schools with more than 400 students enrolled.[32] Danny Roes administered the hospital from 1980 to 1987. Many persons who had come to Haiti as volunteers committed themselves to help the community with its health programs. Other programs that have developed have been primary education, support for churches, and food aid.[33]

The Mennonite Communion of Haiti was one of the first independent missions serving in the Mirogoane area in the 1970s. It was organized in 1976 under the leadership of Rodrigue Debrosse, pastoral superintendent of six congregations located in rural south-eastern Haiti. In 1987 these six congregations had a total of 500 baptized members. There were schools in Mussotte and Masson which educated between 500 and 700 students, beginning in 1985. The Mennonite Communion of Haiti receives support from several Mennonite churches in the United States, including the Son Light Mission and independent Mennonite groups in Pennsylvania and Ohio, as well as from MCC. The Mennonite Communion of Haiti is a member of the Evangelical Council of Churches of Haiti.[34]

Blue Ridge International for Christ began in 1977 when Clyde
Bender, a farmer and founder of the Blue Ridge Christian Homes of
Catlin, Virginia began to distribute powdered milk for USAID in Haiti.
In addition to this ministry of aid, Blue Ridge began to send personnel
to Haiti to give educational scholarships to children, support a home
for girls, and provide education for adults. Blue Ridge continued working with the church that resulted from these efforts in the suburb of
Sarthe in Port-au-Prince. The home for girls in Leogane began under the
name Sunnyside Children's Home. It was founded by Amos Horst and
staffed with persons from the Beachy Sunnyside Church of Sarasota,
Florida, before the program was adopted by Blue Ridge Homes.[35]

In 1978 Palm Grove Mennonite Church of Sarasota, Florida sent
Eris and Miriam (Overholt) Labady to Puitsales as missionaries. Puitsales was Eris' community, and Palm Grove was Miriam's congregation, although they worked together in Puitsales. Eric received an
invitation from a church community to develop pastoral leadership
education in a work coordinated by Gospel Light Chapel.[36]

It may be said that native Haitian culture provided a challenge to the
Mennonites, particularly the practice of voodoo.[37] The Mennonite
missionaries who came to Haiti at the end of the 1950s took at least
two positions concerning voodoo: as an enslaving power to be overcome by the greater power of Christianity,[38] or as a major cultural
unifying force that removed tribal differences from former slaves.[39]
Regardless of attitude, there was a common desire among Mennonites
to give testimony to their faith in social development, forestation, and
in health and education work in marginalized sectors. The great proliferation of Mennonite social service organizations and those planting
churches in Haiti reflects the concern of these groups for the difficult
socio-economic and spiritual situation of the country.

Some fundamental questions for the Haitians who came to be
members in Mennonite congregations might be: What impact has
faith in Jesus Christ had on the cultural legacy of your forebears? If
the Haitian people were able to resist slavery through voodoo, and if
it thus extends a civilizing matrix from Africa to America, what does
it mean to follow Jesus as a person of African ancestry? What aspects
of Anabaptist faith can contribute to solutions to the painful problems
which today continue to envelop Haiti?

Settlement and Mission in Belize (1958-1979)

Belize is located on the eastern coast of Central America, bordering Mexico in the north and north-east, Guatemala to the west and south, and the Caribbean Sea to the east.[1] When the Europeans arrived in this area, there was both a Mayan population and Amerindians who originated from nearby Caribbean islands.[2] These aboriginal groups put up a strong resistance to the invaders at the end of the 18th century, and were confined to the islands of Dominicana and San Vincente. The union of these groups with African slaves was the origin of the Black Caribbeans of Belize. These arrived on the Central American coasts of Guatemala and Belize beginning in 1797, after being deported from the island of Ruatan by the English. Many of these people located in Stann Creek, Punta Gorda and the villages of Hopkins and Seine Beight; they are known as Garífunas.

When England conquered Jamaica in 1665, Belize came to be part of the kingdom of Mosquitia which belonged to English bucaneers (Providence Company). From 1859 to 1980 Guatemala continued to claim Belize as part of its territory, without any success whatsoever. Belize continued to be British territory until 1981, when it finally achieved economic and political independence.[3] Multiple migrations have made of Belize a multi-ethnic country, with the population in 1970 made up of Creoles (30.8%),[4] Mestizos (32.9%), Mayas (18.8%), Garífunas (11.5%), Whites (3.7%), and immigrants from India (2.3%).[5]

By the middle of the nineteenth century there were around 7,000 Protestants (Anglicans and Baptists) in the country.[6] In 1847, Spanish refugees fleeing the war in Yucatan (Mexico) came to British Honduras in search of peace and land, and they introduced Roman Catholicism. This Catholic colony settled in Corozal, in the northern dis-

227

trict.[7] From this beginning Catholicism spread until it came to include sixty percent of the Belizean population. The Catholic strategy was to emphasize evangelization among the Black population.[8] At the beginning of the 1970s, when the total population of Belize numbered 88,000, many more Protestant groups were represented. The number of persons who congregated in the 85 Protestant churches numbered 28,238 in total.[9]

Mennonites came to Belize in 1958, with the migration 1,627 Old Colony Mennonites from Mexico to Belize. These were immigrants who had first moved from Germany to Russia, then to Canada, and from there to Mexico. They formed the colonies of Blue Creek, Shipyard and Spanish Lookout.[10]

In April 1959, Paul G. Landis of EMBM, together with Orie O. Miller, director of MCC, visited Belize and met with numerous representatives.[11] They concluded that the most urgent necessities were a center in Belize City where farmers could sell their produce and have access to agricultural help and medical services. In 1960 the first MCC hostel for colonists opened, and in 1961 MCC opened its center for selling produce. The couple assigned by MCC were also asked to be alert to mission opportunities in the city.[12]

Mennonite Center, Belize City

When the devastating hurricane Hattie struck with 200 mile-per-hour winds in 1961, Mennonite Disaster Service of Lancaster decided to send twelve volunteers from Pennsylvania, Maryland, Delaware and Ohio to help in the reconstruction of the affected towns.[13] By March 1962, twenty-eight volunteers were helping in the reconstruction of humble homes that had been completely destroyed by the hurricane.[14] The destruction was such that the capital of Belize was moved to the city of Belmopán. Many houses had to be reconstructed again in the little town of Hattieville. At the beginning of June, 1963, MCC passed over its service program to the EMB of Salunga. Medical services were provided for the clinics in Hattieville and San Felipe.[15]

Later the Old Colony Mennonites continued to be supported with agricultural personnel.[16]

Blue Creek Colony is located 18 miles west of Belize City and was founded by 80 Old Colony Mennonite families. In spite of illness and infant deaths, the families grew rapidly to become 200 families. The Mennonite Mission Conference, which brought together Mennonite families from Bolivia, Mexico and Canada was formed in the 1970s. The Old Colony way of life and worship practices were traditional and conservative. Leaders appealed to members to stay on their lands in accordance with their traditions, or else leave the group and join another.[17]

In 1978 several *Kleine Gemeinde* families from Spanish Lookout Colony moved to Blue Creek to help in the school and the congregation. In 1987, 80 families lived in Blue Creek Colony.[18] The eighty families who formed the Shipyard community located around seventy miles north of Belize City.[19] One of these was the Wall family, who came to the city center to sell their peanuts at the Mennonite center.[20] In addition, Shipyard colony received help from MCC in the form of a clinic and personnel through the PAX program who provided agri-

Clearing land in Belize

cultural help.[21] It was estimated that 1700 persons lived in Shipyard Colony in 1965.[22]

Spanish Lookout Colony was founded in 1958, made up of 75 Mennonite *Kleine Gemeinde* families from Quellen Colony, Chihuahua, Mexico. Their reasons for leaving Mexico were the lack of available land and objections to the social norms of the Mexican state. Spanish Lookout Colony bought 7,500 hectares of land in Cayo District, situated north of Belize river in what was then a jungle. The colony came to produce eggs, chickens, beans, corn, sorghum, milk, cheese and meat.[23] Their products were sold in the Mennonite center in Belize City and in Orange Walk. By the end of 1968 the colony was prospering: it produced 2,000 liters of milk per week. Since the market did not require such amounts, what was left over was made into cheese. The colony also produced some 3,500 pounds of chicken meat and 10,000 pounds of beef per week.[24]

In the 1970s a clinic was established on this colony which was staffed by Mennonites from the Salunga mission. The farmers of this colony continued transporting their produce in simple wagons to the Mennonite center in Belize.[25] The administration of streets, bridges and schools was carried out by the colony. Some of the families later moved to Interlake, Canada, and another 25 families relocated to the Northfield Mennonite settlement in Nova Scotia, Canada. The natural growth of families is what led to the new migrations. In 1987, 1,108 Mennonites lived in this place. Refugees from El Salvador and Guatemala came to the colonies in search of work. The colonies maintained four schools with a total of 75 children enrolled.[26]

The Eastern Mennonite Board of Missions continued developing its work in three areas in the 1960s: it continued to support the center in Belize City, it began work in Orange Walk, located 65 miles north of Belize, and help was provided in San Felipe where nurses Dora Taylor and Ada Smoker ran the clinic recently opened by the government of Belize.[27] With the arrival in April, 1964 of Ella and Paul Z. Martin as directors of the mission work of EMBM in Belize, a new period began in the formation of the church in Belize.[28]

In the 1960s people gathered at the Mennonite center to sing hymns with brothers and sisters of other Protestant churches.[29] The radio programs *Luz y Verdad* in Spanish and "The Mennonite Hour" in English were broadcast,[30] and young people from Voluntary Service carried out religious activities on Monday afternoons for local youth.[31]

The church at Orange Walk

Every now and then all the Mennonite missionaries in Belize City would gather to worship and celebrate the Lord's Supper together.[32] The church in Belize City held services Sunday mornings; Wednesdays the church offered Bible studies and prayer meetings.[33] In 1978 a new church building was inaugurated which comfortably seated 100 persons for worship and school.[34]

Orange Walk had a population of approximately 400 persons in 1966.[35] Mennonites came here to provide Voluntary Service help in agriculture.[36] Part of the local population spoke English, others spoke Spanish and others Creole (a mixture of the other two). In 1964 Dr. Harvey Mast and his family arrived to work in the clinic.[37] There was constant activity in the clinic, where Jesus Christ could also be shared with the patients.[38] By 1968, attendance at worship services at Orange Walk had increased so much that a church was built in the commercial center that had been constructed for the farmers of Shipyard and Blue Creek as an extension of the service already carried out in Belize City.[39] The commercial center was important economically for the sale of produce and crop fertilizers.[40]

Orange Walk, like San Felipe, was visited by the Honduran evangelist Miguel López in 1969. Attendance was good, but there were no new faith commitments. Nevertheless, Miguel López and pastor Ben Stoltzfus personally visited many homes, and hoped that several of these people would draw nearer to the Gospel of Christ.[41] In mid-1978, the new church building of the Mennonite community of Orange Walk was inaugurated. The modern, well-ventilated and lit building was the result of the work of many brothers and sisters who worked to gather the funds and to build the sanctuary.[42]

By mid-1960, San Felipe – originally a Mayan town – had around 400 residents. It was peaceful, the population was friendly, and the language spoken was a mixture of English and Spanish.[43] The nurses Dora Taylor and Ada Smoker would travel from San Felipe to other towns to care for Mayan children, whose houses were built with palm-leaf roofs and dirt floors. One of these families invited them to conduct Bible studies in their home, and many neighborhood children attended.[44] A pre-natal clinic was established in the San Felipe clinic, with medical work coordinated with Dr. Mast through the mobile clinic. After continued Bible studies[45] a Mennonite church began to take shape.[46] By mid-1966 a church building had been built; for its dedication, pastor Miguel López from San Esteban in Honduras came, and carried out a week-long evangelistic campaign. With this began regular worship services, Bible studies, and English classes.[47]

Construction of the church in San Felipe

Don Andrés Wicab and Don José had to transport the construction beams [for the church] in a Jeep. The load was so heavy that the rear wheels sank into the mud. The road the Jeep had to use was only a footpath, like a tunnel traversing the expansive jungle. But the men knew what to do, and with the help of the winch they were soon there with the beams. Andrés Wicab, of Mayan descent, was the designer and builder of the church. The building was beautifully crafted, inside and out with a series of supports lashed together in the form of a "V," the roof adorned with very beautiful geometric figures covered with palm leaves. This artesanal construction measuring 42 by 22 meters was truly a beautiful example of Mayan architecture. The construction of this beautiful church was ... an adventure, an act of faith in obedience to God's leading.

The San Felipe church

Following Miguel López's evangelistic campaign, several persons came to know Jesus and experienced fundamental changes in their lives.[48] Among them was Dimas Quintana, a 60-year-old man who accepted the Lord during Miguel López's campaign. He composed the following song, which was sung by the San Felipe community.

> How content my heart is,
> And happy
> That the Lord receives me
> With open arms.
> In my soul He calls me,
> You come to me.
> What love of my Jesus! [49]

Toward the end of 1967, Ben and Rebecca Stoltzfus and their two small daughters arrived in San Felipe to pastor the Mennnonite church there.[50] In 1969, attendance at worship services and Sunday school had reached 70 persons. The churches in Orange Walk and San Felipe invited the evangelist Miguel López to return again in August, 1969; on this occasion thirteen people responded to the call to follow Jesus.[51] Nevertheless, in his letter of September 5, pastor Ben Stoltzfus noted that not all was proceeding as hoped. A man who had been baptized shortly after was found drinking alcohol in the street, and a young woman had renounced her membership because she wished to marry outside the church, something that caused much conflict in the church. Several members were at the point of leaving the church, including one of the potential leaders of the church. For this reason, Ben Stoltzfus requested prayer from readers, so that the community might continue to go forward. He noted that in spite of the disturbances, a larger-than-usual group had come to the worship service the night before.[52]

The 6th of October, 1969 was a tragic day for the Mennonite church of San Felipe, for their pastor, the missionary Ben Stoltzfus, was shot and killed on the road between Orange Walk and Belize City. He had been on the way to a consultation with Paul Kraybill and Harold Stauffer of MBM. The most likely cause of the murder was robbery. The burial took place on

Ben and Rebecca Stoltzfus and their daughters

the 9th of October in the town of Orange Walk, with the participation of 600 persons.[53] The journal *Missionary Messenger* published an extensive homage to Ben Stoltzfus in its March 1970 issue. Harold S. Stauffer wrote: "The sudden death of Ben Stoltzfus resulted in local leadership needing to assume responsibility more quickly than would have been anticipated. Their response has been one of courage and real dependence on the Lord."[54]

After an interim period,[55] the leadership of the church came into the hands of the Belizean pastors Teodoro Torres and Emilio Novelo in 1972.[56] In this year MEDA, through the Eastern Mennonite Board, began a project of loans to families in the San Felipe church to buy 30 acres of land, so that they could sow corn and rice.[57] Early in 1973, a missionary who had served in Belize visited San Felipe and noted how the pastoral and Sunday school leadership was now completely in Belizean hands.[58] At this time church had 33 baptized members.[59]

The August Pine Ridge Mennonite Church began with missionary activity from the nearby San Felipe church. The evangelist Miguel López preached there in August, 1969. Two persons accepted Jesus Christ during this campaign,[60] and a nucleus for Bible study formed, supported by the San Felipe church.[61]

Outreach continued in the 1970s, with believers from August Pine Ridge and San Felipe churches visiting the little town of San Roman every two weeks. Although the townspeople showed little interest, the visits persisted throughout the decade.[62] Henry Buckwalter began a series of visits and worship services in the village of Georgetown in mid-1977.[63] Georgetown was a bilingual Caribbean village (Garífuna and English) which had first heard the Gospel by means of the program "The Way of Life" (*El camino de la Vida*).[64] The desire to help the residents economically led to the sending of Daniel Hess and Duane Leatherman for several months during 1978, to serve the community. Duane Leatherman helped by teaching music, helping with the school garden, directing prayer meetings and Bible studies on Wednesdays, as well as teaching Bible stories to the children. He also corrected homework and supported the Bible studies that were organized on a weekly basis.[65] In the Cayo Valley, VS youth worked with the farmers to improve the tomato, cabbage and corn crops with fertilizers, fungicides and pesticides. In the little town of Benque they also promoted projects for chicken and pork production. In addition to all this, they also enjoyed working with the Church of the Nazarene which was present in that place.[66]

In August, 1971 a meeting of representatives of eight Mennonite churches was held at the Carol Farm, to begin forming the Conference of Mennonite Churches of Belize.[67] The church had obtained its legal status in 1971, and in 1973 the Evangelical Church of Belize was formed.[68] By 1987 this organization numbered 14 congregations with 400 baptized members. The members spoke English, Garífuna and Spanish. Several of the missionary families were sponsored by EMBM and served as pastors in the districts of Orange Walk, Belize, Cayo and Stann Creek.[69] In addition, the evangelistic programs broadcast by Radio Belize continued to be offered in the 1970s, with very good results.[70]

An Institute of Evangelism was held in 1969 in San Felipe. Members of non-Mennonite churches, such as the World Gospel Union, also participated in this theological education venture. At the end of the institute it was clear that more literature was needed in Spanish for the formation of leaders. It was likewise clear that it was important to implement education by extension by means of intensive seminars, where local leaders would be able to participate.[71]

The Amish Mennonite Aid (AMA) of Plain City, Ohio[72] established its mission work in Belize under the name Pilgrim Fellowship Missions.[73] Following the great destruction caused by hurricane Hattie in 1962, the government of Belize offered the Mennonites the opportunity to serve, based out of Hattieville, which had been reconstructed by Mennonite Disaster Service. The first Amish workers to come arrived in May, 1962 and along with providing their social services, from the beginning demonstrated their interest in Belizeans who were completely without church involvement.

In 1965 Lester Gingerich was ordained to the ministry in Hattieville. Small houses had been built in this place to house the families who had lost everything in the hurricane. Very soon 72 people began congregating in a meeting place, which somewhat alarmed the Roman Catholic clergy. A school was established in the same locale as the church. The death rate in this community was unusually high: in the first seven years, eighteen persons died, mostly elderly people and children, due to unhealthy conditions. As a result, the town was relocated seventeen miles away, and renamed New Hattieville. A Mennonite church was built here in 1974; the old building continued to be used as a school. In 1975, Gilberto Stevens was named pastor, assisting the missionary pastor of the congregation; in 1978 he was ordained full time pastor.[74]

The Hattieville clinic opened to the public in December, 1963. Personnel from the Belize hospital trained nurses for the first few months. In the first years of operation, a doctor from Belize would come to see patients. The Ministry of Social Affairs provided the money for food; AMA provided the personnel that cared for patients and paid the church members who worked there.[75]

In 1967, AMA mission activity extended to the small village of Double Head Cabbage, located about 20 miles north of Hattieville. Two acres of land were bought in the village and a simple building was constructed which served to hold Sunday school, which was attended by 75 to 100 children and adults. The missionaries who came would visit the neighbors and help them plant corn, rice and beans with their traditional tools. They also built a coop with 100 chickens to serve as a model of small industry for the inhabitants.[76] One of the much-appreciated young missionaries was the teacher Anthony Beiler, who drowned in the Belize river on the 20th of July, 1977.[77]

The work of the church reached another town called Isabella Bank, near Double Head Cabbage, whose residents were farmers of indigenous descent. A building was constructed in 1971 that served as the "Harmony School"; it soon had two teachers and 35 students. Sunday school was held every Sunday in the morning, along with preaching services, mid-week prayer meeting and meetings for women and youth. Maurice Lanza was ordained in April, 1978 and became the first national pastor of this congregation.[78]

At the end of the 1970s, help was extended to the 30 families who lived in Crique Sarco, a village in the extreme southern part of

Belize which receives a tremendous amount of rain. The families were primarily descendants of the Kekchi Mayan tribe. Following dialogue, the community leaders saw the need for medical care in the community. In 1977, Dorothy Wingard and Elsie Byler established a clinic. There already was a Protestant church present which welcomed the Mennonites and invited them to worship. Part of process of getting to know the Mayan families was the effort to recover local medical knowledge of plants and remedies used to cure illness.[79]

In 1965 the first group of Amish colonists immigrated from the United States, having bought some land in the Cayo district, southeast of San Ignacio (Cayo). They lived in a very simple way, using horses to work the land. Some differences in doctrine, ideals and convictions, however, led to divisions. Some colonists returned to the United States; others moved to Bartons Creek. By the end of the 1980s the Pilgrimage Valley area had become an agricultural production area; the majority of its residents were North Americans connected with the Mennonite families of the Cayo Christian Fellowship Church in Villa Esperanza.

The small mission organization, "Caribbean Light and Truth," was founded by the Salem Mennonite Church of Keota, Iowa. Its aim is to bring the Gospel to people of the Caribbean. The first missionaries were sent to Belize in 1974. Membership grew so quickly that it was necessary to ordain three new Belizean pastors in 1980.[80]

The experience of Mennonites in Belize has grown from an early establishment of conservative Mennonite colonies, to a wider vision of a church ready and willing to serve the material and spiritual needs of the local people. Both mission efforts and MCC efforts have played a role in this development. The story of Mennonites in Belize is significant, in addition, for the collaboration of Honduran Mennonites in the evangelization of Spanish-speaking Belizians. Mission efforts were extended not only from the north to the south, but from "new" Spanish-speaking Mennonite churches in Honduras to a re-focussing Mennonite church in Belize. The mix of conservative Mennonite colonists with mission-minded evangelists with developmentally-minded MCC and VS workers defines the world of Mennonites in Belize.

Mennonite Presence in the Lesser Antilles (1967-1979)

In the first century before Christ, Arawak people originating from Barrancas in Venezuela, near the mouth of the great Orinoco river, came to the islands of the Lesser Antilles and the Bahamas, up to the Greater Antilles.[1] Christopher Colombus arrived in Trinidad in 1498 and this cultural encounter meant the extermination and absorption of the Arawaks by the Spaniards. In 1625 the English, in their attack on the Spanish empire, took over these small islands for the first time. The period between 1895 and 1940 can be called the time of North American imperialism; it manifested itself in the Caribbean with U.S. control of the Panama Canal (1904-1914).[2] Protestant missions increased in the Lesser Antilles after that date. In the case of the Mennonites, their arrival coincided exactly with the late independence of these islands, especially in Trinidad and Tobago, British Guyana, Grenada and the Virgin Islands.

The Mennonites in Trinidad and Tobago (1967-1979)

The independence of Trinidad from the English took place in 1962.[3] It was in this new context that the mission board of Virginia initiated work in Trinidad, joining several mission organizations in the process.[4] The request that came was for medical help in the fight against leprosy.[5] In 1971 Richard and Martha Keeler received authorization to come to the island as the first Mennonite missionaries. Richard Keeler immediately began work as a doctor in the new program for the control of leprosy for the government of Trinidad. He and his

237

wife also directed the radio program "Way to Life," with Martha answering the questions, doing pastoral orientation, and enrolling new students. The number of correspondence lessons increased from 1,679 in 1970 to 5,915 in 1971.[6] The number of correspondence students continued to increase until by 1976, 29,440 lessons had been processed. The radio program helped so much in providing spiritual direction that Herman Browne, president of the North Trinidad Keswick Convention, stated "What will we do in Trinidad, if 'Way to Life' leaves?"

Dr. Keeler's work in the leprosy program was much appreciated, and many of his patients came to express the love of Christ in their lives and testimonies.[7] Some of them decided to follow Jesus. The number of new patients continued to diminish year by year, such that by 1978, there was only one third the number of patients that there had been five years previous. The number of children with leprosy decreased from 50 percent to 20 percent during the same period. Students were able to continue with their education, and adults with their work. Preventative treatment helped eradicate the disease. In 1978 the majority of patients in Trinidad had been cured of leprosy, an indication of the effectiveness of the treatment being offered.[8]

Two more missionary couples arrived in the 1970s to help with existing programs, evangelize, plant churches and train national leaders.[9] Three Mennonite communities began to form at the end of the 1970s. The first was the Mennonite church in Torrib-Tabaquite which

The Diego Martin community, 1979

emerged as a direct result of the "Way to Life" program. The second was the Mennonite church in Charlieville which came to be thanks to the ministry of the Keeler family. The third was the Diego Martin church which formed as a result of community Bible studies. By mid-1979 a total of 11 persons had been baptized as members of these Mennonite congregations with around 80 persons attending services at these three locations. The oldest Mennonite church member in Trinidad was Alice Moze, who was known for her lively spirit and love of God. Another member was Ruphina Moze who found the Lord in part because of the death of her husband in 1977. In her testimony she would repeatedly affirm "in spite of all my family difficulties, I keep walking ahead with Jesus."[10]

The religious tragedy that struck the Guyanas in 1978 with the notorious case of Jim Jones and the People's Temple had repercussions also in Trinidad, where the authorities began to deny visas to missionaries.[11] The authorities were cordial, but intended to reduce the number of foreign missionaries. It appeared that the doors would be closed to North American missionaries in the long term in Trinidad, which underlined the importance of preparing the national leadership to take up the missionary work in this country.[12] The mission board decided to invest major resources in training national leaders. For this reason B. Charles and Grace Hostetter travelled in January 1980 to Trinidad, to help in the education and formation of leaders.[13]

The small Mennonite presence in Trinidad has grown from a combination of medical aid and radio and personal evangelism, leading to an emphasis on pastoral leadership education by the end of the 1970s, in response to a narrowing of local political options.

Mennonites in Grenada (1976-1979)

The small island of Grenada is one of the "windward islands" along with Martinique, Santa Lucia, Barbados, San Vincente, the Grenadines, Trinidad and Tobago. They are so-called because the prevailing westerly winds would blow the ships travelling to the new world first to these islands, south-east of the Lesser Antilles, after which they would continue their journey to their final destination in the Caribbean or North America.[14] The slow process of de-colonization lasted until 1974, when together with the Bahamas, Grenada obtained its independence.[15] Mennonite presence in Grenada has been limited to MCC presence, with an agricultural project on the small island of Carriacau, a dependency of Grenada.[16] On Grenada itself, MCC's work was located in the suburb of Gouyane, in the south-west part of the island.[17]

Mennonites in the Virgin Islands (1977-1979)

The Virgin Islands, an archipelago of small islands, were seen and named by Christopher Colombus on his second voyage to the Americas in the year 1493. After 1672 control of the islands was shared by Britain and Denmark.[18] In 1917, the Unites States purchased the islands from Denmark, and renamed them the Virgin Islands of the United States.[19]

Mennonite presence in these islands came in 1977, when the Eastern Mennonite Board of Missions decided to send missionaries to share Christian literature. With a central office in St. Croix, the program supplied books to 19 Caribbean islands from St. Thomas to Trinidad, working with representatives of each island. Rhoda Wenger, a missionary with extensive experience in Tanzania and Somalia, developed this program beginning in January, 1977. Catherine Leatherman continued the work from 1978 to 1979.[20]

The Mennonites in British Guyana (1967-1979)

In 1953, British troops intervened in the British Guyanas in order to remove the socialist government of Dr. Cheddi Jagan and proceeded to hold a series of elections over the next decade. This being the height of the Cold War, the United States, in conversation with Great Britain, launched a strong campaign against socialist political parties.[21] The independence of Guayana finally came about in 1966.[22] This country, with so many inhabitants from India and Africa, and with many religious traditions (Hindu, African, Muslim), aroused much interest on the part of Protestant missions, primarily from the United States. The Evangelical Council of Churches organized in British Guyana in the 1970s was made up of the Methodist, Congregational, Lutheran,

Moravian, Presbyterian, Church of God, and Nazarene churches, among others.[23]

This was the situation in British Guyana when Lloyd Weaver, Jr. and Roy Kiser of the Virginia Mission Board visited Trinidad and Guyana in 1967 to investigate the possibility of establishing new mission fields.

In his report, Roy Kiser saw the Gospel as the means for transforming the country. He reported positively the statements of Hudson Chang, director of the Christian Literature Crusade, that in those places where Christian pamphlets were distributed, where Bibles or New Testaments were sold or given away, people would not go along with revolutionary processes, which in his way of thinking were what had produced the violence in the country between 1962 and 1964. From his point of view, there was a dangerous attempt underway to introduce Cuban and Russian communism to the island, and evangelism could prevent its success.[24]

In 1967, through the Mennonite church in Jamaica, Lee Wright, Sammy Barnett and Andy Cornwall were sent to Guyana to distribute Bibles and to evangelize.[25] These young men worked under the supervision of Hudson Chang.[26] Mennonite Broadcasts supplied the young men with 120,000 tracts to be distributed at no cost.[27] Two years later Paul and Evelyn Kratz and their daughter Celah travelled to Trinidad with Roy Kiser to begin mission work there. The Kratz family, who earlier had worked as pastors in a congregation in Staunton, Virginia,[28] were assigned to help with the correspondence courses which were broadcast on the radio, and also to initiate pastoral work.[29] A good number of Guayanese began participating in the courses offered by the radio program "Way to Life," and home visits led to faith commitments.[30] The Kratz family

Roy Kiser describes Guyana

Land of waters, country of jungle,
Wild animals, many fishes;
Britons, Chinese, Amerindians;
Negroes, East Indians.
Mud and mad men.

Eastern religions, western culture;
Populous coastline, unexplored hinterland;
Sugar estates and bauxite mines,
Dikes and diamonds and drainage ditches.

Political crises, spiritual crosses;
Poverty and diamonds, gold and gods:
Hunger for power, pangs of fear.
This is Guyana.

left Guyana in mid-1972 and moved to Trinidad, where they managed the offices of the "Way to Life" program. From these missionary initiatives were born later the various Mennonite churches which gave rise to the Open Bible Mennonite Church.[31]

Mesoamerica

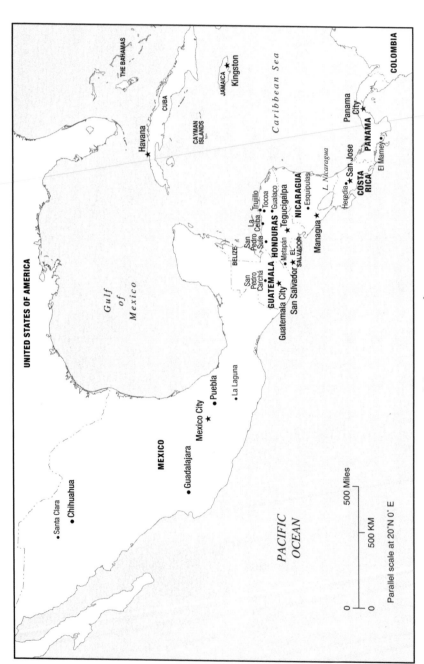

Mesoamerica

Mennonites in Mexico (1959-1979)

The decades of the 1960s and 70s in Mexico featured considerable labor unrest and a financial crisis fueled by government spending and external debt. The historic meeting of Catholic bishops in Medellín, Colombia in 1968 had an influence in Mexico, with bishops Méndez Arceo and Samuel Ruiz becoming proponents of a Latin American theology of liberation.[1] The Protestant presence in Mexico was enhanced during the presidency of Adolfo López Mateos (1958-1964), given that his wife was Presbyterian, but by 1968 student unrest had influenced Protestant seminarians as well.[2]

The 1960s saw the formation of the Latin American Conference of Mennonite Brethren which led to mission churches opening in Nuevo Ideal and San Miguel in Durango, as well as in Díaz Ordaz and Los Ebanos, and later in the city of Reynosa. A further church was formed in 1983 in Lineras, Tamaulipas. The Conference also sponsored a radio program called *La Fuente Viva* (The living fountain) which broadcast from 1964 to 1977. The Conference was noted for its active association of women missionaries, men's groups and Board of Christian Education.[3]

In 1964 the Mennonite Brethren established a congregation in Guadalajara called the Evangelical United Church of Guadalajara.[4] This com-

Baptism, Mennonite Brethren church, Guadalajara

Julián García,
a founding
member,
Guadalajara
congregation

munity, which formed officially as a congregation in April of 1970, held regular public Bible studies as well as scientific lectures and films. In utilizing religious films as a means of evangelization, the missionaries collaborated with groups such as The Navigators. In 1977 the showing of "A Thief in the Night," depicting the events of the last days and the second coming of Christ, had a tremendous effect in Guadalajara. At least 1100 persons watched the film, and 56 persons made decisions for Christ as a result.[5] A church building was erected in 1975 and opened for worship in October of that year.[6]

The Evangelical Mennonite Conference began its work among the Spanish-speaking population in 1956 in a place called La Norteña; a church was constructed in that place in 1961. EMC mission work was extended in Spanish by the broadcasting of the program *Luz y Verdad* and *Die Heilsbotschaft*. In 1966 a new radio program, *La Fuente de Vida* (The Fountain of Life), began to be broadcast. A further important means of communication and evangelization was the magazine known as *El Mensajero* (The Messenger), published from 1963 to 1988. The Evangelical Mennonite Conference also operated a Biblical Institute in Picacho which served to educate leaders and pastors for the churches. Due to the high costs and impracticalities of maintaining a residential theological school, in 1972 the Biblical Institute was

Confession of Faith, Evangelical United Church of Guadalajara

We believe in God, the eternal Spirit, infinite in holiness, power, wisdom, justice, goodness, love and mercy. This only God has revealed Himself as Father, Son and Holy Spirit.

We believe in God as the Father, creator of all that is. He can be known by means of his self-revelation in his works as the source and sustainer of life. He is a God of love who directs all things to the end of his eternal purposes. In his mercy and his grace he adopts as His children all those who repent of their sins and have faith in Jesus Christ as their Lord, Master and Savior.

We believe in Jesus Christ, the eternal Son of God, whom God sent to the world in order to reconcile us to Himself and to redeem us from sin and eternal death. He was conceived by the Holy Spirit and born of the Virgin Mary. According to the Scriptures he is truly God and truly human. He lived a perfect life, holy and without sin. In order to accomplish redemption he suffered crucifixion and death for us and our sins. He arose physically from the dead in order to carry out our justification and ascended into heaven where he is at present, interceding for His people, the believers. He will come again to this world in flesh and soul in order to judge the living and the dead and to give his kingdom to His Father.

We believe in the Holy Spirit, who is one with the Father and the Son. The Spirit carries out the redemption of human kind. He convinces, regenerates, guides, teaches, infuses, enables, comforts, intercedes, instructs and unites all believers into one body, and glorifies Christ. Christ baptizes believers with the Spirit in the process of conversion and fills them repeatedly so that they can carry out ministries He appoints for them.

replaced by a Theological Seminary by Extension. The first urban mission began in 1974 in the city of Chihuahua, and a sanctuary was built there in 1983.[7]

In the mid-1970s, the Canadian missionaries who were doing local church work began having difficulty attaining visas. National pastors began assuming those responsibilities, but not without difficulties: the missionaries had been supported financially from Canada, and now the national pastors had to find their own support in the local churches. Furthermore, local pastors had not been adequately trained or prepared for the responsibilities they now faced. In the end, however, this was an important process in the consolidation of a national leadership for the EMC churches.

Mission efforts by the Franconia Conference Mission Board in 1958 concentrated on the Central Plateau region. The Zúñiga family, among the first converts, became prominent church leaders. The medical doctor Guillermo Zúñiga and his wife were dynamic and active members. Their son, the veterinarian Guillermo Jr., and Guillermo Sr.'s brother, the Mennonite pastor Rubén, shared this commitment to the church.[8] From 1963 to 1965 a VS community service project was carried out in the neighborhood of Colonia de San Juan in Mexico City. The church that was established in that place also produced notable leaders and pastors.[9] The Franconia mission expanded in 1961 by establishing a

Guillermo Zúñiga

church in the Santa Anita neighborhood, and again in 1972 with a new mission effort in Colonia Churubusco. The "Fraternidad Cristiana" congregation that emerged met in the Espartaco suburb in the 1980s. The congregation that sprang up in the Prensa Nacional suburb arose from the home Bible studies held in the home of Catalina Vásquez Zúñiga beginning in 1974. A new congregation was established there in 1976, which immediately expanded with mission work in the San Andrés suburb in the 1980s, where a small congregation began meeting in its own church.[10]

Trique family, Oaxaca

In 1960 the Franconia Mission Board began mission work in the town of La Laguna among the Trique indigenous people in Oaxaca, a state located 300 miles south-east of Mexico City. Two missionary couples worked on translating the Bible into Trique along with Wycliff Bible translators. The New Testament was translated into Trique in 1968. Part of the evangelistic work in this region involved showing religious movies. In 1974 the first ten baptisms took place in La Laguna.[11] The people of the town opposed the new converts, saying that they had given themselves over to the Devil. Pascual Salazar García recalls meeting with townspeople and explaining their faith to them, after which the converts were treated better.[12] In 1976, after fifteen years of work, the congregation numbered 36 baptized members; a church building was erected in 1978.[13]

In 1962 the first Franconia board missionaries came to the city of Puebla and established a Mennonite church there. VS workers came to Puebla in 1967 to teach in an English academy, a program that lasted until 1972, when VS stopped operating in Mexico.

Pascual Salazar García and son

Although the earliest meeting on record took place in 1963, in 1965 the Council of Evangelical Mennonite Churches of Mexico was officially designated as the representative body for the churches established by the Franconia Conference. This Council usually met every month and once a year met with all the churches for fellowship and worship. The Council maintained contact with the parent church in the U.S. though the respective executive secretaries of the Franconia conference. The member churches of the Council are the churches of the Central Plateau and Puebla; the churches in Oaxaca maintained a fraternal relationship with the Council but were not members.

The Franconia mission board developed an active radio ministry in Mexico, broadcasting *Luz y Verdad* programs which promoted Bible study courses by correspondence, and developing a popular radio program called *Corazón a Corazón* (Heart to Heart) which was broadcast over sixteen different radio stations. In 1968 the radio ministry employed eight full time persons, something which caused some consternation among pastors in the church who, following the principles of Franconia missionaries, received no salaries. A fraternal visit for a special seminar by Lester Hershey, international director of the *Luz y Verdad* radio program, may have helped defuse the situation.

In 1960 the Pacific Coast Conference began mission work in the north-west part of Mexico, first in the city of Obregón, Sonora and later, thanks to the conversion and baptism of Francisco Urias, in Sinaloa. By 1986 there were six organized congregations in Sinaloa, as well as eight mission fields, led by three ordained pastors and eight lay leaders. In Sonora there were two organized congregations and three mission stations, led by one ordained pastor, two licensed pastors and one lay leader. By the end of the 1980s these Evangelical Mennonite Churches counted 200 baptized members.[14]

Young members of *El Buen Pastor* church, Mexico City

The expansion of a Mennonite presence into the Spanish-speaking population of Mexico has been the result, not of the evolution of the German-speaking Mennonite colonies (as in Paraguay or Brazil), but rather of mission efforts from the north and from Mexican churches themselves. The evangelization work of the Mennonite Brethren, the Evangelical Mennonite Conference, the Franconia Conference, and the Pacific Coast Conference has resulted in small Mennonite churches scattered across the country, including a Mennonite presence in the capital city.

Mennonite Missions in Honduras (1950-1979)

Seven hundred years before the arrival of the Spaniards to the land of Honduras, a Mayan ceremonial center of major significance was flourishing in Copán, in the eastern part of Honduras, the second-most important for the entire Maya civilization.[1] On his fourth trip to the new world in 1502, Christopher Columbus arrived at the island of Guanaja on the northern coast of Honduras with the usual devastating results for the inhabitants. African slaves were imported beginning in 1543; two years later there were already 1,500 African slaves in Honduras, working as forced labor in the mines.

The independence of the Central American states from Spain took place on the 15th of September, 1821. One of the eminent citizens of Honduras is Francisco Morazán who, after winning the elections of his country in 1834, fought for the unification of the Central American Federation. He dedicated himself to this task until he was shot in Alajuela (Costa Rica) in 1842. Liberal reform began in Honduras in 1876[2] and opened the doors to North American capital and the entry of Protestant missions. The first Protestant organization to enter the country was the Central American Mission in 1896.[3]

The United Fruit Company in particular expanded quickly: by 1924 it owned 87 thousand acres of land in Honduras.[4] Protestantism expanded in parallel, with many churches establishing themselves among the banana workers. Both foreign and national missionaries took advantage of the railway infrastructure in order to evangelize. The presence of United States Marines in the midst of the civil war in March, 1924 marked the road that later would lead to dictatorship.

According to the testimony of Maurice Lehman, Mennonite interest in mission work in Honduras began because of the curiosity awakened in pastor Jacob Brubaker of Lancaster, about the origin of bananas. After an exploratory trip by two mission representatives in 1948,[5] Eastern Mennonite Board of Missions and Charities decided to send its first missionaries to Trujillo. After studying Spanish for several months, George T. and Grace Miller with their daughter and son moved to Honduras, beginning their mission work in November of 1950 in Trujillo, where they were joined by Catarino Clotter. After their first year the Millers confirmed the importance and need for mission work in Trujillo.[6]

Once it was decided to begin work in Trujillo, the Mennonites concentrated on forming churches and at the same time attending to health by means of medical dispensaries, thus combining evangelization and service in a way that would mark Mennonite missions in Honduras. Worship services were carried out in both English and Spanish. Worship services in English were primarily for those of African descent, who still kept this language. By early 1953, 74 persons attended the English worship service.[7] The Mennonite Church of Trujillo was officially dedicated to God in February, 1952 in an emotional and festive service. This was the first Mennonite church to be built in Central America.[8] Towards the end of 1952, James and Beatrice Hess came to do pastoral work in Trujillo and provided a great impetus to the project. James Hess delighted in moving about on horseback to preach the Gospel.[9] By the middle of 1954, with the baptism of four new members, the membership of the Trujillo church reached 60 persons.

When the first Mennonites came to Honduras, conditions were deplorable for the inhabitants of the Caribbean coastline. These places had been exploited by the single-crop plantations of bananas of the

The Mennonite church in Trujillo

United Fruit Company, but in 1930 the "sigatoka" disease ruined the plantations, and in place of what earlier had been an immense banana-growing activity, there remained only the old and abandoned railway lines, semi-covered with vines and the overgrowth from the forest.[10] The American missionary Dora Taylor and the Honduran Tilda Imbott[11] worked for many years as nurses in that place in the clinic known as "La Esperanza" (Hope), where up to 20 patients were attended daily. The medical service of these nurses put them in contact with the people and with the authorities of the place. In 1955 a new medical clinic was opened in Santa Fe, but its work was not limited to physical healing of patients; the nurses also visited boys and girls in poor communities like Tarros, and evangelized in the humble shacks of straw and dirt with illustrated Bible stories.

Mission work in Tocoa, a town located south and inland from Trujillo, began in 1952 when Eldon and Jessie Hamilton began serving the community with a medical clinic. In that same year Aida Padilla, a young woman of thirteen, was converted to Christ and desired baptism, but the church did not manage to establish itself until November, 1955, when 13 persons were baptized and another five were accepted as members of the church in a lovely ceremony in which the Lord's Supper and foot washing were celebrated.

In Tocoa, unlike Trujillo, people were more closely tied to the Catholic church and did not look favorably on the arrival of Protestant preachers. Shortly after the Hamiltons arrived, the bishop of the Catholic church visited the place and a great celebration was held in his honor. Jessie Hamilton, Aida Padilla and later also the missionary Grace Hockman nevertheless provided a great service with their clinic, known in Tocoa as "The little house of consolation." Many poor families were cared for there, whose children had often lost their lives because of innumerable stomach parasites.

The visit of Paul N. Kraybill to Honduras in January 1957, representing the Eastern Mennonite Board of Missions and Charities, brought Mennonite mission work in the rural zones into dialogue with Honduran government authorities, as well as American representatives of the United Fruit Company.[12] On another front, the improvement of some roads and bridges between the ports of Trujillo and Puerto Castillo and towns to the interior, such as Masicales, Tocoa, Saba and Gualaco, permitted the extension of work into the interior of Honduras, specifically in Gualaco. The Hamilton family arrived and settled here in August, 1958.[13]

The political context for Honduras in the 1960s was set by events in Cuba, and a United States policy that aimed to contain the spread of Communism in Latin America.[14] In 1963 the Honduran president was deposed in one of the bloodiest coups known in Latin America. In spite of massive demonstrations and protests against the government by popular organizations and workers, in June 1965 General Oswaldo López Arellano officially assumed power.

The border war between Honduras and El Salvador that broke out in 1969 had its roots in the crisis of the Central American Common Market and the migration of more than 50,000 Salvadoran families into Honduran territory.[15] The war began with the invasion of Salvadoran troops ten kilometers into Honduran territory in July, 1969, and eventually cost the lives of 3,000 people and the loss of homes for 38,000 families. The war was finally controlled by the Organization of American States, although the final peace treaty was not completed until 1980.

Although some Roman Catholic movement towards social reform began in 1957, the conservatism and anti-Communism of the Catholic church in Honduras was reactivated with the triumph of the Cuban revolution in 1959.[16] Following the council in Medellín in 1968, a small change of direction can be noted in the Honduran Catholic hierarchy. Pastoral letters no longer emphasized the dangers of Communism but rather the inhuman conditions in which many Hondurans lived.[17] Honduran Protestant churches grew rapidly in the years 1959 to 1970 and underwent a process of nationalization.[18] The "Evangelism in Depth" program expanded Protestant churches in all Honduran territory, including the isolated rural zones which often had been abandoned by the Catholic church. Membership in the Honduran Protestant churches increased from 4,000 in 1950 to 18,000 in 1967.[19]

Both Catholicism and Protestantism, however, essentially legitimated the existing political structures in their messages and pastoral actions. The Honduran military dictatorships were not questioned by religious leaders in the 1970s. It can be said that for the Roman Catholic[20] and the Honduran Protestant churches, the developmentalist model promoted by the Central American Common Market, agrarian reform, and the programs of the Alliance for Progress all functioned without contradicting their pastoral visions.

The supposed apolitical thought of the North American missionaries sent by Salunga fit well within the developmentalist theories implemented by North American governments in the 1970s, but did not question the military order established in Honduras. During an early visit to Trujillo, Paul Kraybill was clear that the inhabitants of this region needed the liberating message of Jesus Christ.[21] Nevertheless, the Salunga mission worked to offer an integral gospel that paid attention to the spiritual and also spoke to the daily needs of the people by supporting health, community development and agriculture programs. The clinics in Trujillo and Tocoa, for example, which were begun when the Mennonites came to Honduras, continued in the poorest areas of Honduras such as Trujillo and Gualaco, from the 1950s to the 1960s.[22] Later this work would be extended to other towns such as Santa Fe and Concepción.

But political forces remained at work. The Mennonite mission societies operated like other North American missions, developing programs in dialogue with other missions and with local authorities, as well as with ambassadors and North American companies working in the country.[23] Mennonite Voluntary Service (VS) volunteers worked in the framework of "community development" in coordination with institutions such as CARE (social work projects), SANAA (potable water), and USAID.[24] The development projects of the time operated in the framework of the Alliance for Progress, and the Eastern Mennonite Mission Board was no exception in this regard. The mentality of the missionaries was shaped by their United States nationality and anti-Communist background. When difficult political situations arose in a militarized Honduras, the missionaries sometimes accepted the anti-Communist propaganda of the government in its totality.[25] Some missionaries were concerned that they might have to leave the country if Communist forces took over Honduras.[26]

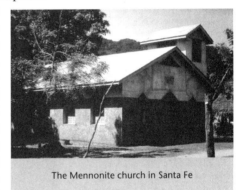

The Mennonite church in Santa Fe

But difficult times also provided opportunities for real witness. During the Honduran/Salvadorian war of 1969, Protestant pastors gathered in Tegucigalpa to pray about the situation. The result was a movement to gather clothing, food and money to help the victims of the war. Only two weeks after the start of hostilities, two tons of powdered milk arrived from MCC Canada to be distributed among the displaced families. Various congregations in Tegucigalpa collected clothing and food for those affected, and members of the Honduran Mennonite church together with VS workers did voluntary work, distributing food, clothing and medicine.[27]

Arthur July

One of the key church members responsible for spreading the Gospel in Trujillo and surrounding areas was a humble Black peasant, of Jamaican origin, named Arthur July. He was a strong man with a wide smile who dressed humbly and wore a straw hat on his head, an English-speaking man with a great sense of humor. He began cleaning the gardens around the clinic in 1952. Although he was never ordained, Arthur July played an important role as a person who accompanied others in their evangelistic and pastoral work. He knew the culture of his people very well and easily communicated the Gospel to them.

In terms of establishing new churches in the department of Colón, the Mennonite congregation of Trujillo became the mother church for new congregations and a laboratory for the training of the first national pastors. Francisco Flores and his wife were the first licensed and fully-supported national co-pastors, beginning in 1964.[28] In 1965, when the Flores family moved to pastor another church, Manuel Medina and Efraín Padilla received pastoral licenses to accompany Norman and Grace Hockman in the pastoral work of the Trujillo church.[29] The first national pastor to take on full pastoral duties in Trujillo was Rafael Ramos in 1970.[30] Arthur July accompanied this work until mid-1972.[31] The expansion of the work of the Mennonites in Trujillo cannot be understood apart from the intense medical and missionary work begun by the nurse Dora Taylor in the 1950s. She gave a very effective apostolic testimony that people could come to know the transforming power of Jesus Christ.[32] She left the country after 13 years, having seen the consolidation of her medical and evangelistic efforts.[33]

Over time, the number of English-speaking people declined in Trujillo, and virtually all worship services were in Spanish.[34] In 1965 the "Evangelism in Depth" program resulted in some life-changing conversions.[35] In 1966, when Manuel Medina and his wife Filomena and their family came as pastors to Trujillo, the church had 55 members, of whom seven were new believers, three of whom had made their profession of faith in prison. Manuel Medina began visiting nearby villages such as Bambú, Río Esteban, San Antonio, Guadalupe, la Colonia and Chapagua, which resulted in commitments of faith and baptisms.[36] Students at the developing Biblical Institute helped considerably with pastoral work in the local congregation.[37]

The Mennonite presence in Santa Fe, a community of predominantly African descendants (Garífuna) located near Trujillo, began with the founding of a clinic there by Dora Taylor.[38] The cultural customs of the Garífuna of Santa Fe were difficult for the North Americans and Spanish-speaking natives to understand. In one of the meetings of the General Council of the Honduran Mennonite churches, which met in 1966, the following motion was approved: That an anthropologist be obtained to get to know the culture, customs, etc. of the Blacks, so that the Lord's work be better carried out among them. Approved."[39] Evangelism and community work continued, with VS workers assigned to Santa Fe to work in agriculture and water projects.[40] Other small churches emerged in the vicinity of Trujillo as a result of evangelization work: the Mennonite church in Bambú, the Mennonite church of Río Esteban, the Mennonite church in San Antonio (fifteen members in 1966), and the Mennonite church of Guadalupe.

> **Missionary Alma Longenecker describes a local celebration.**
>
> This is the Quince, the day Hondurans celebrate their independence. The celebration must be in full swing, judging from the screams of drunken men and the rhythmic sounds of the marimba and drums which provide music for the dancers, while the bell tolls that slow, mournful beat for the man who was stabbed during the night. I ask amid the chaotic noise, 'From what have they been liberated?' They have received their freedom from the rule of Spain, but this confusion reveals that they have not been liberated from the power of Satan.

Mennonites began work in Tocoa in 1952. From this base the message was extended to neighboring towns, and national leadership grew little by little.[41] Francisco Flores and his family were members of this church. They would later become important leaders in the Honduran Mennonite church. One of the activities that maintained the life of the church was the summer Bible school, which involved many children,[42] and evangelistic campaigns added more people to the community of faith,[43] but missionary reports also describe situations where people drifted away from the church with unacceptable conduct, and finally needed to be separated from the church and Sunday school.[44]

In 1965 leadership of the church in Tocoa was in the hands of José Martínez, Amzie Yoder and Efraín Padilla, and construction of a new chapel was being completed. It had a concrete floor, which was a great innovation in those times.[45] The medical clinic in Tocoa, founded in 1952, functioned until 1966, when the government opened a health center.[46]

The Christian Day School in Tocoa was another Mennonite project. It opened in 1957 to educate the children of missionaries.[47] By 1963 the school had thirty pupils and served the larger community until 1965, when it closed because of the difficulty in obtaining Christian

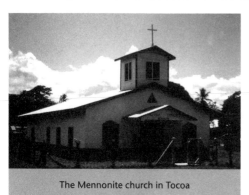

The Mennonite church in Tocoa

Honduran teachers.[48] Community and agriculture service in Tocoa began in 1958, with the arrival of Amzie Yoder, the first PAX volunteer.[49] The PAX unit was located on ten acres of land sown with sugar cane, about two miles from Tocoa; it came to be known as "the home of the gringos."[50] PAX volunteers instructed the peasants in agriculture, helped the school children of Tocoa plant gardens and collaborated in music-making and crafts.[51] Their work was noted for the distribution of seeds, grafts of trees, and the sale and distribution of eggs, as well as instruction on how to improve crops.[52] The Mennonite youth declared, "our work here is in agriculture and community development, but our first priority is Christ."[53]

In the area north of Tocoa several small Mennonite churches were founded through mission activity.[54] In the town of Concepción, located five and a half miles from Tocoa, missionary activity resulted in the founding of a church. Francisco Flores, known affectionately as "don Pancho," was very active in this nascent congregation, coordinating the Sunday schools.[55] The missionary nurse Jean Garber visited the community once a week to attend to medical needs.[56] In May, 1960, on one of trips there on horseback due to the flooding of the roads, Jean Garber heard that the Catholic priest from Trujillo had come to perform a wedding. One of the Mennonite members invited to the ceremony shared with Jean what the priest had said: "This morning I wish to speak about the Gospel... Christ says 'I am the door. All those who enter by another way are thieves and murderers.' The thieves and murderers are the other religious groups... Some of these groups bring medicine with them, deceiving you this way... Stay far from them..." Jean concluded that the clinic was playing an important evangelistic role in Concepción.[57] Further missionary work was carried out in this town, including an evangelistic campaign in 1967. In 1970 the deacon Petronilio Martínez was in charge of the work in Concepción.[58]

The work in Savá, which began in 1961, was notable for the VS workers who provided veterinary tools and products needed by the local ranchers and taught simple ways of pasteurizing milk and making nutritious chocolate.[59] Elam K. Stauffer described Savá as a den of iniquity with rampant alcoholism, open prostitution and thieves who operated openly with no fear of reprisal. The missionaries noted four murders in one report.[60] Francisco Flores, his wife and family moved to the town in 1962 to give leadership to the church there.[61] An evangelistic campaign in 1968 added members to the church. It is interesting to note that some VS workers married Honduran youth, as was the case with Mary Leaman who married Abraham Zúniga of the Savá church. Mary later worked in the hospital in La Ceiba; Abraham pursued studies in education.[62]

Cayo Cochinos is a group of small islands, some 18 miles from the coast and the port town of Farallones, which lies 40 miles east of Trujillo. An exploratory trip in 1962 resulted in visits by James Sauder and Lester Hershey and an evangelistic campaign in July of 1968.[63] Further evangelistic visits reached Orica and La Paz.[64] The village of Colonia de Aguán, which lies close to Trujillo, was visited by missionaries already in 1960. It was not electrified, and early devotional times required the use of a lantern.[65] Evangelistic visits were also made to Tarros, La Chapagua and Taujica, with modest results.

Gualaco is located almost at the center of the department of Olancho, an area with small coffee growing operations.[66] The ministry that developed in Olancho followed the usual strategy based on the preaching of the Word of God, and service by means of medical clinics, agriculture and community development. After ministering in Tocoa, Eldon and Jessie Hamilton and their children arrived in Gualaco in August of 1958. They were the first Protestant family to live in that place.[67] They believed the town was thirsting for the Word of God: "They are a lovable people and it seems sad indeed that for generations they have been living in darkness and superstition, never having the opportunity to hear the Gospel, while at home many have heard often and still do not heed."[68] The veneration of the Virgin of Suyapa, the patron saint of Honduras, and anti-Protestant attitudes became visible in Gualaco the following year, when posters appeared on doors throughout the town that read "Long life to the Virgin of

Suyapa, Queen and Mother of this home. We are Catholics. Please don't bother us with Protestant propaganda."[69]

In spite of opposition from the local Catholic priest and the arrival of a "Holy Mission," many young people in the town were receptive to the Gospel.[70] Gualaco became a key point for the development of the Mennonite church in the department of Olancho, especially after the arrival of James and Rhoda Sauder. From Gualaco the Word of God spread to neighboring towns such as San Esteban, San Pedro, Las Joyas, San Buenaventura, La Boca and Saquay, places where several persons accepted Jesus Christ.[71] There were real tensions between the Mennonite missionaries and the predominantly Roman Catholic population of Gualaco, as the reports from the missionaries reveal.[72] In 1965, Lolo Méndez and his wife converted to Christ. Don Lolo had been an alcoholic, and in time he became an excellent leader. After several months, Don Lolo, his wife and mother were baptized in Gualaco.[73] A chapel was built in the town and was dedicated in 1971.

The clinic in Gualaco was built in 1959 and attended 150 persons per month.[74] Conversions also took place as a result of this work.[75] In addition, volunteers from the PAX program worked on agriculture projects with local farmers who planted corn, rice, beans, and various vegetables, worked on the construction of the clinic, the church and other buildings.[76] The small town of San Esteban is not far from Gualaco and was visited in 1960. After several evangelistic campaigns and growth in membership, a church was built and dedicated in 1967.[77] Voluntary Service personnel worked in San Esteban on livestock and poultry projects.[78]

VS'er John Gingrich with Francisco Domo: the chick project, 1970

La Ceiba, the capital of the department of Atlántida, became the location for the Honduran Voluntary Service offices, beginning in 1961. The city, facing the Caribbean Sea, was at that time the headquarters of Standard Fruit Company and had 200,000 inhabitants. In 1962 Lois and George Zimmerman became VS directors in La Ceiba.[79] In March, 1964 the "Evangelism in Depth" crusade came to La Ceiba, resulting in several conversions and the formation of prayer groups. Further evangelistic work led to growth, and a church began to be built in 1968. By 1969 the church counted a total of 55 members.[80]

Worship in the San Marcos church

The Mennonite mission moved to the capital of Honduras, Tegucigalpa, early in 1964 and a new historical era began.[81] On returning from a sabbatical year in the U.S., James Sauder noted the challenge facing a church expanding from three old rural mission stations (Trujillo, Tocoa and Gualaco), moving into the larger cities like La Ceiba and Tegucigalpa. It was his view that the future of the church lay in the theological and pastoral preparation of national workers, and that the Lancaster Mennonite Conference should facilitate this process.[82]

In January, 1964, shortly after the opening of the central offices in Tegucigalpa, the project *Academia Los Pinares* began, operated by the Eastern Board of Missions and Charities. There were ten students in the first group, and there was no library as yet; by 1967 there were 73 students,[83] and this number had risen to 110 by 1971.[84] Many VSers served in the Academy, teaching English and other courses. The boys and girls who attended the Academy represented many nationalities and came from religious traditions as diverse as Protestant, Jewish, Catholic and Anglican.[85] Even so, teaching included aspects of Mennonite spirituality, such as praying or reading the Scriptures.[86]

The families of children attending the Academy became the point of departure for the Mennonite church of Tegucigalpa. Just as in Trujillo, the church began as a church for English-speakers, with initial worship services in the chapel of the Academy. Shortly after, services in Spanish began in another neighborhood of the city, although the thinking was to try to unite both groups.[87] In 1970, the church in Tegucigalpa counted 36 members.[88]

Shortly after arriving in Honduras, the missionaries and VS workers began meeting yearly to share their experiences and plan future action. In 1961 a council was formed composed of ordained Mennonite missionaries and representatives from Honduran congregations.[89] This was the birth of the General Council of the Honduran Evangelical Mennonite Church (CGIEMH), which permitted the participation of both missionaries and the leaders of local congregations.[90] A smaller executive committee was chosen by the CGIEMH to carry out church projects, and committees oversaw education, the Biblical Institute, the annual conference, and printed materials. A national women's society began functioning in 1968,[91] and the following year a national youth organization came into being.[92] A constitution for the Honduran church was approved in 1969, including the official name: *Iglesia Evangélica Menonita Hondureña*: IEMH (Honduran Evangelical Mennonite Church).[93] Thus was born a national organization that began to minimize the participation of the missionaries and encourage the participation of local church leaders. Nevertheless, changes came slowly. The presidency of the CGIEMH remained in the hands of missionaries until 1972. In 1970, the Mennonite church in Honduras received full legal status, at which point the transfer of properties from the Mission Board in Salunga to the national organization began.[94]

With the creation of a national church organization came also the desire to establish norms for the Christian life and a confession of faith. At the November, 1962 meeting of the CGIEMH it was also decided to adopt the Dordrecht Confession of Faith, to which articles were added concerning the Word of God, the Holy Spirit, Separation from the World, and Ordinances. A short time later an article on citizenship was added that said: "No member shall take on any political leadership post. Matt. 16:13; Jeremiah 17:5; Phil. 3:20; Acts 4:20; 2 Tim. 2:4."[95]

As responsibility for the church began to pass into national hands, financial problems became evident, particularly concerning the sala-

Included in the confessional norms adopted in 1962

a) In conformity with 1 Cor. 11, we suggest that Christian women in our congregations wear a prayer veil of a single color, be it black or of the kind that can be used at all times.

b) We suggest that women's dress be of a color and cut that is decent, with sleeves, and that it cover the body well. 1 Peter 3:1-4; 1 Tim. 2:9-10.

c) That the speech of brothers and sisters be healthy and avoid rough talk or profanity. James 3:1-12.

d) We strongly protest against carnal excesses such as the use and distribution of tobacco, alcohol and lotteries. We also protest against worldly diversions such as dancing, the movies, etc.

ries of pastors, whose numbers increased as new congregations were formed. Many of the smaller churches could not support pastors, a perennial problem for the General Council. A further problem was the higher cost of living for pastors in the cities. In 1967 the Council decided to increase urban pastors' salaries by 25 percent.[96]

Social service programs were central to the Honduran Mennonite church from the start. From 1958 to 1965, Mennonites invested $65,943 in VS programs.[97] The first decade saw 79 VSers coming to Central America.[98] In 1965 the Mennonite Central Committee also located offices in Tegucigalpa and hosted VS personnel.[99] In the 1960s the Mennonites supported social development by participating in the ecumenical organization called the *Diaconía Evangélica Hondureña* (Honduran Protestant Diaconate).[100] In 1968, in view of the growing autonomy of the Honduran Mennonite church, it founded its own organization to address social concerns, the *Comité de Servicio Cristiano* (Christian Service Committee: COSEC).[101] Along with the founding of COSEC came the withdrawal of Mennonites from the larger ecumenical organization. Relations remained cordial with some mutual cooperation.[102]

A systematic national evangelism effort began in 1963 with the "Evangelism in Depth" program, which involved public campaigns, home visits and the establishment of cell groups.[103] There was great enthusiasm for evangelization in the 1960s. In 1966, 80 persons made professions of faith with many of these preparing for baptism.[104] The theme of these evangelism efforts, "God working through each believer," necessitated education in biblical discipleship, something that was promoted by the Committee for Evangelical Advancement.[105]

Evangelistic campaigns continued periodically through 1970, organized by the Committee.

Central American missionaries considered the literacy programs of ALFALIT as having potential to strengthen the church.[106] Honduras had an illiteracy rate of 55 percent. In this context, in the 1960s Anna Mary Yoder began an ALFALIT program in Honduras that became an important tool, enabling people to learn to read and also to get to know the Gospel. In September 1969, Edward King, who had had previous experience with ALFALIT in Bolivia, took over the program in Honduras together with his wife Gloria. The costs were borne by MCC and the Eastern Mennonite Board. One of the purposes of the program was to use the Bible as the basis for learning to read.[107] The program extended to Savá, Trujillo, Ilanga, Tela, La Ceiba, Aguan, and San Pedro Sula and involved 88 volunteer teachers, 46 illiterate people and 32 visits to various leaders, authorities and mayors.[108] ALFALIT had a tremendous impact in Honduras. From February to April, 1971, 1,000 volunteer teachers were prepared and by the end of May, 3,000 adults had enrolled in the classes. The project extended into the First Infantry Battalion of the Honduran Army, as well as into the penitentiary,

Adalid Romero (left) and Francisco Calix, Mennonite pastors in San Pedro Sula, baptize one of 39 new members on the beach in Tela, Honduras

with 800 and 150 students, respectively. In a 1971 evaluation of the program, Edward King noted that there needed to be better cooperation with ALFALIT from the Mennonite churches, and that there should be integration between the churches, COSEC and ALFALIT.[109]

The Mennonite Biblical Institute (IBM) began in the 1960s to educate church leaders from Trujillo, Santa Fe, Tocoa, la Concepción and Gualaco. The Institute originally had no buildings; classes were offered in various places in intensive courses. When the clinic closed in La Esperanza, the building came to be used to house the Institute and classes began there in 1965. The level of education of

Edward King supervising a new volunteer teacher

participants varied between those who had completed primary school and those who had completed only the first grade of their primary education. As a practicum, students would go from house to house, preaching the Gospel.[110] In 1970 plans were begun to move the Biblical Institute to La Ceiba.

From the start, Mennonite missionaries maintained good relations with other Protestant groups. After 1962, shortly after the formation of the CGIEMH, it was decided to officially join the *Alianza Evangélica* (Protestant Alliance). The Alliance promoted evangelism work ("Evangelism in Depth"), represented Protestant churches before the government, and led retreats for pastors, women and youth.[111]

The turbulent decade of the 1970s saw the emergence of two new Mennonite groups in Honduras: the *Amor Viviente* (Living Love) church, and the arrival and settlement of Old Order Amish. In the 1970s Honduras entered a period of political, economic and labor unrest which saw the emergence of a series of dictators who were supported and aided by the military and the wealthy classes of the country.[112] These governments put in place repressive anti-labor policies in the name of anti-Communism; some Christian social action programs fell under the same label. In the 1970s the Catholic church underwent significant internal changes, giving rise to the Christian Family Movement and a charismatic stream, on the more conservative side of the political spectrum, as well as university programs for the formation of Christian democratic leaders and "radio schools" pushing for social and economic changes, on the reformist side of the political spectrum.

The conservative political forces took repressive action against progressive sectors of the Catholic church. The torture and assassinations that took place in 1975 in Santa Clara de Olancho became the defining social-political and religious event of the 1970s. The Colombian priest Ivan Betancur and the U.S. priest Miguel Jerónimo Cypher were church community organizers using Paulo Freire's literacy methods of education in their work. They and nine of their peasant followers were tortured and assassinated, Catholic radio stations were closed and three more priests were arrested. These actions set the political tone for years to come and put an end to the prophetic pastoral work which had begun to germinate in Olancho, Choluteca and Yoro.[113]

A significant parallel development within Honduran Protestantism in the 1970s was the rise of neo-Pentecostal groups, who soon became significant numerically. Rather than being denominational, the neo-Pentecostal groups tended to call themselves simply "Christian" and focused their work among young university students, drug addicts, and people of the middle and upper classes. Their worship services were very public and featured modern instruments and contemporary music. The pneumatology at the center of their theology was focused not on the church, but rather the spiritual power within individuals which allowed them to confront social conditions. A gospel of prosperity often accompanied this pneumatology as well.[114] One of the four most significant neo-Pentecostal groups in Honduras in the 1970s was the *Amor Viviente* church which originated from within the Honduran Mennonite church.

The *Amor Viviente* church was born thanks to the efforts of the Mennonite missionaries Edward and Gloria King, based on their charismatic experiences and personalities. The Kings concluded their literacy work with ALFALIT in 1972, and prior to a year's sabbatical in the U.S. had already set out their plan for evangelism work among university students and the youth and street people of the Honduran cities. Their proposal was accepted by the Honduran Mennonite church and Eastern Mennonite Board of Missions.[115] The Kings began their work in Tegucigalpa on their return to Honduras in 1973, reaching out to young people in poor neighborhoods with Bible studies and recreation programs. The young people who responded and were disciples by the Kings were, in fact, ex-drug addicts who had now been converted to Christ.[116]

The ministry of the Kings was marked by the charismatic expression that impacted both Latin American Roman Catholicism and Protestantism in the 1970s.[117] Edward King liked to go the top of El Picacho, a mountain north of Tegucigalpa, one day a week, where he would survey the city below and spend the day in fasting and prayer for the youth ministry. It was during such a time of contemplation, in 1974, that the name *Amor Viviente* came to him as the right name for the ministry.[118] At the July, 1975 meeting of the General Council of the IEMH it was decided that the Kings would continue working within the Honduran Mennonite church, submitting periodic written reports on their work with *Amor Viviente*, and furthermore that Edward King would mobilize a group of youth who would work in the churches, teaching and strengthening them.[119]

The organization of *Amor Viviente* was strongly centered on Edward King, who chose several of the young men for discipleship training; they became known as "disciples of Edward King." King's intention was to prepare these young men to be the future leaders of *Amor Viviente*. This group met once a week in their various houses for instruction from Edward King.[120] The faith and joy of these young people in following Jesus Christ was manifested spontaneously in the streets and areas surrounding the central park of Tegucigalpa, where they sang, testified and preached openly. Hector Urbina and Julio Sierra became notable preachers, travelling around on city buses, evangelizing and distributing tracts. Two musical groups were formed and a regular coffee house emerged where young people would come to sing and play board games. Edward King would take these occasions to share the Word of God with them.

The testimony of Héctor Urbina

We lived in a time of miracles: when we prayed that God transform someone's life, we always expected something miraculous to happen. I remember my own situation of those days. I looked entirely different then than I do now, with long hair and poorly dressed. As far as my spiritual condition was concerned, I was completely lost, having fallen into the grip of drugs and alcohol. I was desperate, with a great need for love and acceptance... The Lord found me in this condition and led me to the *Amor Viviente* church...

For almost a decade, *Amor Viviente* had no building of its own or fixed location, following Edward King's maxim of investing in people, not in buildings.[121] Nevertheless, the success and growth of the movement led to its institutionalization and eventually to the request and granting of separate legal status by the Honduran government. In 1978 the Honduran Mennonite church approved, and *Amor Viviente* continued as part of the larger organization with financing from the Salunga Mission Board.[122] In 1977 the first two *Amor Viviente* churches were built in Puerto Cortés and Tegucigalpa, and permanent churches were established in Danlí and Choluteca in 1978, in San Pedro Sula in 1980, in El Paraíso in 1981 and in the cities of La Ceiba and Progreso in 1984.[123]

As the movement became institutionalized, it became more strongly organized from within by means of cells or small growth groups who were the responsibility of strong leaders. Different groups were identified: the multitudes who followed Jesus for various reasons; the 120 who formed the base community, and who were committed to Jesus and his mission; the 70 sent out by Jesus, who were close to Jesus during his ministry, and who were charged to witness with word and life; and the smaller group, intimates of Jesus who shared his glory and suffering. In light of this understanding of Jesus' ministry, one can see how the institutionalized *Amor Viviente* movement created its own dynamic for growth and leadership development with a structure concentrated on the leader.

In 1980 Edward King left the pastorate of the Tegucigalpa church in the hands of René Peñalva in order to pastor emerging churches.[124] When Edward and Gloria King returned permanently to the U.S. in 1983, *Amor Viviente* was under the firm centralized leadership of René Peñalva. The church had close to 2,500 members organized into 15 different congregations in all of Honduras.[125]

A Mennonite group notably different from *Amor Viviente* was the Old Order Amish, who came to Honduras in 1968. In December 1968 Peter Stoll, an Old Order Amishman from Aylmer, Ontario purchased a 500-acre farm in Guaimaca, in the department of Olancho. When Dorothy Showalter visited this farm in January, 1969, she reported that it was a good area for agriculture, with many creeks, a variety of fruit trees, livestock and a furnished house.[126] Some of the families who began settling in the area came from Indiana from a group of Old Order Amish who opposed smoking and alcoholic drink. They hoped to establish an orphanage in that place.[127] The Old Order Amish who came from Ontario and Indiana were interested in both establishing a settlement and in evangelization. From 1968 to 1974, 16 families

Vernon and Katie Schmucker of the Amish community, Guaimacas, Honduras

moved to Honduras, establishing their own homes but living in close proximity. They maintained Amish customs, slowly learning Spanish as they cultivated the soil. They established an orphanage, a school for Honduran children, and an English school for the Amish children. These innovations led to change, for there were marriages between Amish and Hondurans, and the mountainous territory did not lend itself to horses and buggies. Motorized vehicles began to be used which led to the return of more conservative families to North America.[128] The group that remained in Honduras then affiliated with the Beachy Amish of the U.S. After 1986 there was a new division among the Amish. More than half of the families met in three congregations and affiliated with the Beachy Amish, receiving periodic visits from their bishop in Indiana. The more conservative group was organized into two congregations and affiliated with the Fellowship Churches.[129]

The planting of the Mennonite church in Honduras was notable for the dual emphasis that was placed, from the start, on both spiritual and physical nurture. Likewise, the founding missionaries carefully prepared local leaders for the Honduran churches, something that benefited not only the local churches, but also other emerging Mennonite communities in Central America. Missionaries in Belize, for example, would request the presence of a Honduran Mennonite evangelist for work in Pine Ridge, San Felipe and Orange Walk in 1969 and 1970, as has been seen.[130] Miguel López of the Honduran church was asked to carry out an evangelistic campaign in Guatemala in December, 1970 and later was asked to do the same in Managua, Nicaragua.[131]

The formation of the *Amor Viviente* church also stands as a remarkable witness to the power of the Gospel and the Holy Spirit to transform lives.

At the same time, the revolutionary currents that arrived full-force in the region in the 1970s raised significant questions about the role of social structures in perpetuating poverty and violence. The apolitical assumptions of the 1950s and 60s were challenged in a

Worship at the 30th anniversary of the Amor Viviente church, 2004

Cold War context of Soviet-supported guerillas and U.S. supported counter-revolutionary governments. How would the Honduran Mennonite Church respond?

The Mennonite Brethren in Panama (1959-1979)

At the time of Spanish colonization, Panama was populated by the Chibcha peoples, who formed an intermediary culture extending from present-day Nicaragua in the north to southern Ecuador, thus locating the Chibcha between the great Maya and Inca cultures.[1] The Chibcha people were skilled potters, basket weavers and workers of gold. The Embera and Wounaan peoples are two of several groups of Chibcha peoples still living in Panama.[2]

The Spanish ports in Panama became important for the slave trade as well as the exportation of Peruvian gold and silver to Spain. Once cargo was transported across the narrow isthmus to the Atlantic ocean, Spanish ships would attempt the dangerous trip to Europe.[3] Panamanian territory was conquered by force in order, as Vasco de Núñez de Balboa said, to preach the Gospel and Christian baptism and to convert the Spaniards into the richest people ever to have arrived in the Indies.[4] By 1610 the population of Panama City was listed as 548 citizens, 303 women, 156 children, 148 Blacks, and 3,500 African slaves of both sexes – testimony to the human misery witnessed by its ports.[5]

Following independence from Spain in 1821 Panama became part of Greater Colombia, a situation that changed when the isthmus became the site of a transoceanic canal. After the French effort to build a canal failed, and tensions between Panama and Colombia escalated, the United States stepped in negotiating a peace between those countries. The following year, 1903, the U.S. and Panama signed a contract that ceded to the U.S. a "canal zone" in return for cash payments and a U.S. guarantee of Panamanian independence.[6]

With the Panama Canal came also the first major Protestant presence in the country.[7] The constitution of 1904 declared the majoritarian religion to be Roman Catholicism, but also proclaimed freedom of religion and called for the Christianizing of the indigenous tribes.[8] Panama soon became the center of operations for the American Bible Society for Mesoamerica and the Caribbean (1892) and in 1916 became the site of the Congress for Christian Action, an important event which gave impetus to Protestant missions in Latin America.[9] Pentecostal missions came to Panama in 1919.[10]

Bible study in Panama

Mennonite presence in Panama came when Mennonite Brethren missionaries, David Wirsche and Jacob Loewen, were denied permission to continue working among indigenous people in Colombia. In the summer of 1959, Wirsche and Loewen took up their translation and educational work among the indigenous peoples in the Darién region of Panama. In El Mamey and Lucas they worked with the Embera people and in Chitola among the Wounaan; a mission to Spanish-speakers was established in Jaque.[11] Jacob Loewen worked as a linguist, translating and producing literature in the indigenous languages; David Wirsche taught the indigenous peoples how to read and write. They were joined by Glenn Prunty and his wife who did pastoral work among the Spanish-speakers in Jaque.[12] By 1960 the first publications of selections from Mark and Acts were ready in the Wounaan language. With the help and approval of indigenous leaders, the literacy process advanced among both the Wounaan and the Embera people.

One of the best early students was Aureliano Sabugara, who not only learned to read, but also taught his people to read their own language.[13] He was a native Wounaan from the Chocó region in Colombia who, as a youth, had lived a life of drunkenness and excess. Around 1959, after a particularly extreme drunken binge, the woman with whom he lived invited him to follow the Gospel. He came to accept the Gospel, and soon joined many other Embera and Wounaan people in emigrating to Panama.[14] After his conversion and move to Panama, Aureliano became an influential banana grower in El Mamey, where he employed several African-descended workers.

Aureliano had unique linguistic resources: his mother tongue was Wounaan, but he had lived among the Embera from the time he was a child, and also was married to a woman of the Embera people. He became a key person for Jacob Loewen's work, travelling with Loewen in 1960 to Kansas to collaborate in the translation of the Gospel of Mark and the book of Acts.[15] On his return to El Mamey, Aureliano dedicated himself to evangelizing among the Embera.

When Loewen and Wirsche returned for their yearly summer visit in 1961 they found a church already built and a membership of

Aureliano Sabugara

33 people. The church was dedicated in July of that year. The following year a church of 50 members had been organized in Lucas by Jesús Reyes, another early convert. In 1963, Glenn Prunty and members from El Mamey visited the small remote village of Chitola; by 1966 the church there counted 50 baptized Embera members. In 1963 the church in Jaque also numbered 50 members.

The 1970s saw a large influx of indigenous people from Colombia to Panama, attracted by the lower cost of living, the relative religious freedom in Panama and the ease with which they could become Panamanian citizens. The Wounaan migrants have been the most ready to respond to the Gospel. By 1973 the Mennonite Brethren church of Panama counted 481 members, of whom the majority (300) spoke Wounaan.[16]

El Mamey church worship service, 1965

Mennonite Presence in Costa Rica (1960-1979)

In 1502, on his fourth voyage to the new world, Christopher Columbus dropped anchor off the coast of Costa Rica. His capture of two indigenous chiefs for transport back to Spain prefigured the kind of treatment the indigenous tribes of the area would receive during the colonial period.[1] During the period of Spanish colonization (1569 to 1821), Costa Rica was simply a province of the General Captaincy of Guatemala, notable primarily for the depth of its poverty. It had few Catholic churches and belonged to the diocese of Nicaragua.[2]

Costa Rica became independent from Spain in September of 1821, and when the Central American Union collapsed, elected its first president. A more tolerant attitude toward non-Catholic groups was a result of independence, as was the encouragement of European settlers, many of whom were Protestants.[3] The first Protestant church in Costa Rica was founded in 1865, an English-speaking Episcopal church known as "El Buen Pastor" (the Good Shepherd) which exists to this day. Episcopal churches were also built for the African-Jamaicans who came to Costa Rica to build the railroad at the end of the nineteenth century.[4] In 1891, William and Minnie McConnel were the first missionaries sent by the Central American Mission, and Protestant churches began to be established, particularly in San José and Alajuela, two of the more liberal provinces.[5] Other Protestant denominations, such as the Methodists, the Latin American Mission, Pentecostal groups and Baptists arrived in the first decades of the twentieth century.[6]

The civil war of 1948 resulted in the founding of the Second Republic and the elimination of the army by constitutional decree. The Protestant Costa-Rican Alliance was created to represent the various Protestant churches of the country and to ensure that religious liberties would be preserved.[7] It was in this context that Mennonite work in Costa Rica began, under the Conservative Mennonite Conference of Ohio.

The Conservative Mennonite Conference (CMC: before 1954 called the Amish Mennonite Conservative Conference) originated in 1910, when conservative Amish pastors and congregations separated from the Old Order Amish. The evangelistic emphasis of the new conference was expressed first in Sunday schools, but later extended to overseas service and missions, with a mission board and the publication of the *Missionary Bulletin*.[8] In June 1960, the CMC and the Salunga Mission Board commissioned Orie O. Miller and Raymond Schlabach of CMC to make an exploratory visit to Central America.[9] They reported that Costa Rica was the country where missionary efforts should be concentrated. In 1961 the first missionaries began CMC's missionary work in Costa Rica, with Susie and Raymond Schlabach working on Bible translation among the Bri-brí people in the Talamanca region and Eileen and Elmer Lehman concentrating on establishing churches among the Spanish-speaking population of the country. A third impulse was the desire to work among the poorest people in the country.

Although the Schlabachs worked primarily in biblical translation, they also evangelized in the community. Raimundo and his wife Luisa were baptized by Elmer Lehman in the Talamanca river in 1969, the first Bri-brí people to receive baptism; this was the beginning of the first Mennonite church in Talamanca.[10] Although parts of the New

Testament were translated into Bri-brí, the work proceeded slowly. In 1978 the CMC Mission Board decided to suspend the work. After almost two decades of work, the New Testament had still not been translated. Most of the Bri-brí people had begun to speak Spanish and it was estimated that completing the translation work would take at least another ten years.[11]

Elmer and Eileen Lehman (on right) with the Carvajal family, 1965

Eileen and Elmer Lehman began work among the Spanish-speaking population in the strongly Catholic city of Heredia in March, 1962, starting with personal evangelism; the first person to accept Jesus Christ was Mayra Mora.[12] Another means of evangelization was the radio program *Luz y Verdad*.[13] The case of Jovita de Corrales is notable. She was converted by listen-

Worship service in Talamanca

ing to the radio program and her husband followed her profession of faith. He became one of the most successful evangelists in the Mennonite church of Heredia, and became the first national pastor.[14]

A third evangelistic method was the preaching crusade. This form of evangelism was used widely throughout Latin America in the 1960s by Kenneth Strachan through the "Evangelism in Depth" movement.[15] The movement maintained that "the expansion of a movement is in direct proportion to the success it has in mobilizing its members to continually spread its beliefs."[16] Elmer and

Eladio and Jovita Corrales

Eileen Lehman participated in Pablo Findenbinder's evangelistic campaign of 1967 which resulted in ten members joining the Mennonite church in Heredia.[17] In that year the church in Heredia numbered 37 baptized members with 125 persons attending services regularly.

The first Mennonite church in Heredia in 1964

The radicalization of the Cuban revolution led to the exodus of many missionaries and Cuban pastors. Among them were the Methodist teachers Justo González and his wife Luisa García. They took refuge in Costa Rica and initiated the ALFALIT literacy program in 1962. This program coincided well with the activities of the Mennonite missionaries, for it aimed to be "an effective instrument for understanding the Kingdom of God."[18] Literacy work reached into many poor rural sectors of Costa Rica and later expanded to Managua, Nicaragua.[19] The development work done by the Mennonite VS workers in the poor zones of Costa Rica was carried out initially with the momentum generated in the 1960s and the Alliance for Progress promoted by the U.S. government. VS agricultural and construction work was concentrated in the Atlántida region of the country as well as in Puerto Viejo de Sarapiquí, Siquirres, and Upala near the Nicaraguan border.[20]

In 1965 Henry and Esther Helmuth came as missionaries to Costa Rica to give leadership to the emerging church in Puerto Viejo, Sarapiquí, a place where VS work and missionary work blended together very well.[21] When the Helmuths returned to Costa Rica in 1970, after two years of study at Eastern Mennonite College, they clearly had been influenced by the charismatic-pentecostal movement that had begun in the U.S. and spread quickly in Latin America. They took up work in Barrio Pilar, Guadalupe, in a populous district of San José,

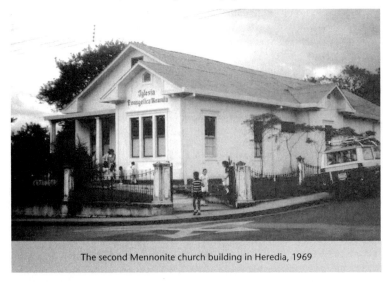

The second Mennonite church building in Heredia, 1969

pastoring the Templo Casa de Oración. Under their leadership, the charismatic movement strongly impacted the Mennonite churches. The CMC confession of faith was translated into Spanish in 1970. When the Conference of Mennonite churches was formally organized in 1974 there were five local congregations in Sarapiquí, Upala, Guadalupe, Heredia and la Pithaya, with many notable national leaders.

Another group of Mennonites, the Beachy Amish, arrived in 1968 when twenty families from Ohio, Virginia, Georgia and Maryland settled on 750 hectares of land near Laguna del Arenal.[22] According to Galen Yoder, they had come to Costa Rica because "where we lived in the United States there already were many churches, and the Bible teaches us that Christians should go into all the world to preach the Gospel."[23]

These Mennonite settlers dressed in conservative style, with the women wearing veils signifying submission to men, who in turn were submitted to God. They did not allow radios or televisions, although they did use modern milking equipment and a Ford truck to transport their goods to market.[24] Costa Ricans were welcome to join the community as long as they were ready to accept the same faith and way of life, which included a prohibition of smoking, dancing, drinking liquor, and swearing but taught love of enemies. Excommunication was employed for those who did not follow community norms. Don

Michael Kropf, Amish Mennonite in Tilarán, near the Arenal volcano

Avelino Ugalde, who lived for many years near Laguna del Arenal, was one person who accepted this Mennonite faith and way of life; he joined the community with his wife and children.[25]

The Arenal settlement was disrupted first by the eruption of the Arenal volcano in 1969, and then by the expropriation of much of the land for the construction of the Arenal hydroelectric dam. Some families managed to stay, but by 2005 other members of the community had relocated to Upala, Grecia, San Carlos, Guatuso and Los Chiles (Alajuela) as well as in Coto Brus (Puntarenas), Sarapiquí (Heredia) and Pérez Zeledón (San José).[26]

Orlando Carvajal baptizing in Puerto Viejo de Sarapiqui

Mennonites in El Salvador (1961-1979)

El Salvador is the smallest country of Latin America measuring 21,000 square kilometers. It is also the most densely populated country on the continent. The dense population is a result of geography, for the highest mountains are located next to the neighboring country of Honduras. The majority of the indigenous population were Nahuatles from the mountains of Mexico and the Pipile people. Between 1526 and 1539 there were unsuccessful wars of resistance by the indigenous who were led by the chief Lempira in Honduran territory. The social structure put in place in El Salvador did not permit the democratization of education; in 1770 there was not a single school in the capital, while countries such as Guatemala and Nicaragua already had universities.

In 1821 independence from Spain was proclaimed by Central American countries (the short-lived "United Provinces of Central America"). With the collapse of the Central American Union, El Salvador became an independent republic. In 1840 the first systematic coffee plantations were established in El Salvador. Coffee became the number one export which gave rise to an oligarchy of coffee growers. The period from 1871 to 1920 saw the rule of liberal governments whose ideology maintained that the state should not intervene in the economic mechanics of market forces.

In 1923 labor and peasant unions began to organize; the government responded by forming the National Guard. The peasant uprising (1932) led by Farabundo Martí had terrible consequences for the country. The military's implacable response led to the slaughter of an estimated 15,000 to 30,000 peasants. From that time on political power in El Salvador was assumed by military governments, with the most important posts assumed by military men, and lower government posts assigned to civilian friends of the military.[1]

The beginnings of Protestantism in El Salvador date from 1896 with the arrival of the Central American Mission.[2] According to a census carried out in 1910, there were 1,018 Protestants in El Salvador.[3] Metapán, one of the locations where the work of the Mennonite churches would evolve later, had a Protestant church early in the century.[4] José Martínez Martínez, a peasant from the village of Zapote in Metapán, today a member of the Mennonite church, recalls that as a child in the 1930s, his parents Maximiliano and Estefanía Martínez would take him to the Central American church.[5]

The Central American church was conservative, not in favor of noisy worship services, clapping hands or any talk about baptism in the Holy Spirit. But between 1952 and 1953 the churches of the region began a campaign of forty-day prayer, with the result that the Central American church of Cañas Dulces in Metapán experienced a great revival in the Spirit. Nevertheless, the persons involved in this revival were expelled and upon leaving, joined the more pentecostal Church of God. The Church of God extended to the center of Metapán and later opened a work in Los Llanitos, in the region of Santa Rita.

In his youth, José Samuel Martínez Martínez got to know María del Socorro Leal Peraza, who belonged to the Church of God. In 1956 they married, and he also became a member of the church in Cañas Dulces in 1962. In Cañas Dulces there were only Protestant churches.[6] The experience of José Samuel Martínez is similar to that of other current members of the Mennonite churches of El Salvador, whose Protestant heritage comes not from one, but from diverse churches with their particular doctrinal and historical roots.

The Mennonite church in El Salvador originates with several Salvadoran families who, in their struggle to survive, emigrated to Guatemala and Honduras beginning in the 1950s.[7] Some families joined Protestant churches in those countries.[8] The situation for Salvadoran emigrant families changed radically with the outbreak of the war between Honduras and El Salvador in 1969. Land in Honduras was reclaimed, and many Salvadorans were jailed in Honduras for not having legal documentation. Finally the exodus of thousands of Salvadorans began, with people returning to their country with nothing.[9] Among the re-settled people were a group of families that joined together in Metapán to form the Mennonite church of El Salvador (IEMES) in 1979.

A second Mennonite presence came by a very different route. In 1961 Orie Miller of MCC, Mark Peachey of the Conservative Mission Board, Jacob J. Hershberger and Norman D. Beachey of the Amish Mennonite Aid (AMA) visited Central America to explore mission possibilities.[10] A recent hurricane in Haiti had also devastated many areas of Belize. In El Salvador Jacob Hershberger met with officials of the Institute of Rural Colonization of the Salvadoran government. They invited the Mennonites to make a contribution in the field of agriculture. In the face of a strong military dictatorship and the influence of the Catholic church, an accord was reached with the Mennonites to collaborate with the Institute, but with restrictions on evangelistic activities.

The first project unfolded in Sito del Niño, twenty miles from the capital, San Salvador, in May, 1962.[11] The Mennonites began working in agriculture and community development programs. Their work took shape with the founding of a 4-H boys' club, on the model of such clubs in the United States. Its aim was to teach children carpentry and cooking. Another project involved importing New Hampshire Red chickens from a business in Pennsylvania. In 1967 the Mennonites supported community development projects that reached various geographical points covered by the Institute of Rural Colonization.

Evangelization as such began in 1968, when Roman and Amanda Mullet came to San Salvador. Santiago Delgado was the first Salvadoran to be baptized by the Amish Mennonites in El Salvador. In September, 1969 Harvey and Kathryn Kaufman came with their children and settled in Texistepeque, to begin evangelistic work. At the end of the 1970s a small school was built for children in the place known as Las Casitas. In August, 1979 there were twenty-two members in the church, and a small church building was constructed in Santo Tomas.[12]

One of the important works of the Amish Mennonites in El Salvador was the establishment of an orphanage, built in 1970 on 40 hectares of land situated near Aguilares, twenty miles from the capital. By 1974 this facility was home to 17 children from very poor homes, many of whom were severely malnourished or had no parents at all. Many of the orphaned children were adopted by Mennonite families in North America. The land provided fruits and vegetables, and the

North American churches provided much support with donations
of clothing and money. The children called the workers "uncle and
aunt."[13]

The Mennonites also came to work at a medical clinic in Zacamil
which had been founded by the Baptists under the name of Ayutica. A
church was established in Zacamil as well as a school attended primarily by the children of Mennonite families. Churches also were established in Aguilares and Texistepeque where in the 1970s around 350
persons would gather for worship on Sundays. The Amish Mennonites
also established a library in Aguilares, which provided an important
service to the community.[14]

In 1975 a Spanish-speaking Christian school in Candelaria de la
Frontera was founded. A church was subsequently built in this place.
In 1978 another school was established in a place known as El Cer-
rón, and a small church was also built there. The Amish Mennonite
organization in El Salvador is called the "Mennonite Mission."

Mennonite presence in El Salvador is not homogenous. It originates,
on the one hand, from churches planted by Salvadoreans themselves,
in a process of re-patriation, and churches planted by conservative
Amish Mennonites. The latter mission efforts have included projects for material improvement and support, as well as evangelistic
efforts.

CHAPTER XIV

Mennonite Missions and Churches in Guatemala (1964-1979)

Approximately sixty percent of the present population of Guatemala is of Mayan descent, a culture that dates back to 3,000 BC. The Mayan civilization reached its zenith between 1200 and 1440 AD, ending finally with their conquest by the Spaniards.[1] In addition to the Mayan descendants of Guatemala today are the African-descended Garífunas of the Atlantic coast, with the balance of the population made up of mixed-race mestizos or ladinos.[2] Beginning in 1821 and independence from Spain, political leadership in Guatemala swung between liberal and conservative regimes.[3] With the government of Manuel Estrada (1898-1920) the country was opened to North American agrarian capitalism, with monopolies in banana production, electrification and rail transport in the hands of the United Fruit Company. Growing social unrest led to the reforming presidencies of Juan José Arévalo (1945-1951) and Jacobo Arbenz (1951-1954). Their opposition to the United Fruit Company resulted in the CIA-led invasion of Guatemala in 1954, cutting short the program of agrarian reform.[4] Revolutionary opposition groups organized throughout the country in the next decades, opposed to a series of military dictators who came to rule the country. Indigenous communities in particular were subjected to military and paramilitary attacks in these years. One of the worst of these was the massacre of more than 100 Kekchi people in the villages of Panzós and Alta Verapaz in May, 1978.[5]

After independence from Spain, Protestant groups began arriving, first the Anglicans and then the Methodists.[6] The indigenous woman Juana Mendía is the first-known native Guatemalan to accept the Gospel, and also the first martyr from Verapaz, dying for her faith in 1843.[7] The period from 1923 to 1981 has been described by historian

Virgilio Zapata Arceyuz as the time Protestant work in Guatemala exploded with the coming of numerous missionary organizations.[8] The guerilla wars, the migration of peasants to the city, the terrible earthquate that rocked the country in 1976, with 22,000 dead and a million people left homeless, were reasons for the expansion and growth of many new Protestant organizations.[9] The Mennonite presence in Guatemala began with the coming of missionaries from the Conservative Mennonite Fellowship of Ohio in 1963, the first of five separate Mennonite mission organizations to work in the country in the next two decades.

The Conservative Mennonite Fellowship (CMF) was formed in 1957 as a response to the perceived apostasy of other Mennonite groups. Among the founding principles were nonresistance and nonconformity to the world, which included the wearing of the prayer veil for women and short hair for men.[10] The CMF's interest in mission work led to an exploratory bus trip in 1963 by 36 persons through Mexico to Guatemala. By 1964 a property was bought in Chimaltengo, Guatemala in the midst of the indigenous population in the highlands. Jacob Coblentz, his wife Marta and their three children moved to Chimaltengo in September of that year, the first of a series of mission workers. Along with running a small business selling chickens, eggs, pastries and fertilizers, they initiated a Sunday school in their home and distributed photocopied Scripture passages. When they returned to the U.S. two years later, three people had accepted the Lord. By 1969 a spacious church had been built, and three years later the first native pastor, Rogelio Pichiya, was selected by lot and ordained to minister in Chimaltenango. A conservative and fundamentalist nature led this group to see their mission as one of confronting local shamans, Catholicism and the liberal attitudes of the ladinos.[11]

Continuing mission work led to the opening of evangelistic efforts in Zaragoza, Las Lomas, and El Tejar. Catholic opposition to these efforts was evident in Las Lomas, when the vehicle of the Mennonites would routinely be left with four punctured tires. In Las Lomas, a small village northeast of Chimaltenango, 1,000 meters above sea level, Mennonite testimony was carried by the young woman Victoria Ramírez. She adopted the conservative dress of the CMF, wearing the prayer veil and long dresses. Victoria gave active testimony to her friends in Las Lomas, and the community slowly opened to the message. Early in 1973 ten persons of that village were baptized into the church.

In the region of Tecpán, which is also part of Chimaltenango, the work of the church spread to neighboring towns, begining with Pamesul. Chus Ajic played an important role in these developments. Late in 1966 he heard the preaching of Joseph Overholt in the park of Chimaltenango, calling for the acceptance of Christ before the final judgment. He engaged in a conversation which led to the first worship service in Pamesul, in his home, on the occasion of his father's birthday. He was a local person of some influence in the Cachiquel community, and the services continued on a bi-weekly basis; they soon spread to the village of Palama. In 1970 a clinic was constructed in Palama, with Norma González attending local patients. The work in Palama expanded with the building of a church and the establishment of a chicken-growing project, which benefitted the quality of life of local residents. At the annual Bible conference at Palama in 1973, the lot fell to Marcelino Cristal and he was ordained to the ministry, assigned to the neighboring town of Paquib, located six hours from Palama. The mission in this region continued to spread, reaching the villages of Zaculeu and Aguas Escondidas.

In the department of Solola, a mission outpost began in the village of Novillero, where the native language was Quiché. From Novillero the Gospel spread to the more remote villages of Pamebazal and Santa Clara. The story of Julio Vásquez, who became a member at Novillero, is a familiar one for this region. At the age of seventeen, he followed his father's example and began drinking heavily. Following his conversion, Julio managed to defeat his alcoholism, and joined a group of ten persons receiving instruction for baptism. The temptation to return to drink was tremendous, since many of his friends constantly invited him to join them. Alcohol abuse was a common problem the missionaries had to confront constantly.

As well as the problem of alcoholism, the missionaries found themselves in conflict with local shamans and healers (witch doctors, so-called), who continued ancient Mayan practices. Likewise the

> **Memories of Victoria Ramírez, as told by Dallas Witmer**
>
> "It was wonderful growing up in Las Lomas! By day she worked long hours with her daddy in their two-acre fields planting corn and beans, hoeing the crop with a twelve-inch *azadon*, or kneeling by the central fire built on the floor of their kitchen clapping out the day's supply of tortillas in perfectly disk-shaped corncakes. When she was wrapped in two blankets on her wooden bed at night she dreamed of playing with her Las Lomas girlfriends, or of wild rabbit chases over the winding trails of the area with her beloved dog."

Mennonites found themselves opposing the celebration of Catholic festivals, which in their view were simply a mixture of pagan traditions and Catholicism. Local customs concerning marriage also posed a problem: the custom was for people simply to live together and begin families, without benefit of matrimony. For their part, the missionaries insisted that baptism could only be given to monogamous marriages. The Quiché people clung to their customs and as a result, Mennonite mission efforts were not very successful in that community.

With regard to the difficult political situation in the country, in which the indigenous peoples were being increasingly repressed by the military governments of Guatemala, the missionaries seemed not to see the problem. The main preoccupation expressed in their writings of the 1970s was the fear that the government might be taken over by revolutionary or Communist groups, which might threaten their ability to stay in the country. This conservative political stance was evident in 1974, for example, when the CMF missionaries expressed satisfaction that General Kjell Laugerud García had assumed power, for that returned the country to "political stability."

In June of 1966, Orie Miller of Eastern Mennonite Mission (EMM), along with Earl Groff, Norman Martin and Omar Martin of the Washington-Franklin Mennonite Conference (later known as Franklin Conference), travelled to Central America accompanied by James Hess, missionary serving in Honduras, to explore the possibilities of opening a mission field. They made numerous contacts and were encouraged, by government and mission people alike, to consider work among the Kekchi in the region of Alta Verapaz. The Washington-Franklin Mennonite Conference wanted to support work in a specific geographic area and went to EMM for direction. As EMM's mission work developed in Guatemala, the Washington-Franklin Mennonite Conference provided financial support. In addition, some of the mission workers and voluntary service workers came from that conference.

In 1967 a second delegation, including two potential missionaries, Larry Lehman and Richard Landis, made another trip to Guatemala and felt God's call to the Kekchi living in Alta Verapaz. Their vision was to initiate programs that met the needs of the people, particularly in agriculture and health. In addition, missionaries were to be trained to understand the indigenous culture so that the Gospel could be communicated and a church established. It was decided that a twofold work would be initiated: one in the capital city, and a second among the Kekchi community in the province of Alta Verapaz.

In January 1968, Richard and Lois Landis and two agriculture VS workers, Wilmer Dagen and Ray Kuhns, moved to San Pedro Carchá in Alta Verapaz among the Kekchi people, initially concentrating on learning the language and culture of the people.[12] Soon the VS workers began teaching

Larry and Helen Lehman and son (left) with co-workers, 1970s

agriculture and working in communities around Carcha; Richard and Lois Landis relocated to Guatemala City to begin church planting and coordinate the missionary team.

Missionaries reported that the indigenous people of the area lived in idolatry and superstition, and mistrusted the white missionaries.[13] The rituals and customs of the Kekchi proved difficult to fully comprehend. One of their central rituals involved the blessing of a new dwelling, when the community would all gather there with a priest. The ceremony involved sprinkling the floor in all corners of the dwelling with *boj*, a local fermented drink, and the blood of a rooster. An elder would then place a candle in each corner of the dwelling, with a large candle in the middle, filling the house with light. Then the elder would kneel before an image of the patron saint of the home and request a blessing for the family. The ceremony concluded with a communal meal. The purpose of the ceremony was to forbid entry to evil spirits and to bless and welcome the saints. The missionaries were not aware that in this ceremony, the Mayan priest was recreating the world in a symbolic way, exactly as the rite was explained in the *Poph Wuj*, the ancient Mayan sacred text.[14]

The missionaries continued learning the language and the people, presenting slides and films and conducting Bible studies in small groups. In May, 1971, a young Kekchi man named Pablo Tzul Cacao, came for Bible study and accepted Jesus Christ. He was the first to be baptized and became the first church leader in San Pedro Carchá; later he would become the first Kekchi ordained pastor, and a very effective evangelist among the Kekchi people.[15] Through a succession of missionary leaders and Guatemalan pastors, the church in this town grew and by the 1980s counted 50 baptized members with an average attendance of 110 persons.[16]

By 1971 the work of the Mennonites had begun spreading to other towns in the area through efforts of Pablo Tzul and other indigenous evangelists, the missionaries, and the work of Mennonite VS workers, among whom was a registered nurse who began a clinic in Cojaj. A church emerged in this way in Cojaj, numbering 24 members in 1972.[17] With the help of MEDA, a cooperative was organized to pro-

Pablo Tzul preaching

Pablo Tzul Cacao

Pablo Tzul came to know the Mennonites in 1969 through VS workers who had come to San Pedro Carchá to help the native people with agricultural projects. He became good friends with them and would help in translation from Spanish to Kekchi. When his father realized that he had become friends with the Mennonites, he gave Pablo a tremendous beating. Nevertheless, Pablo continued his friendship with the Mennonite young people, and finally was baptized in 1972. His encounter with Jesus led him to re-interpret his Mayan culture; he came to communicate the Gospel in the language and culture of corn of the Kekchi. He became a great apostle among the Kekchi people thanks to his simple dress and life style, the cloth embroidered by his wife and daughters in accordance with traditional culture, as well as his simple home, his passion for dynamic and symbolic rituals concerning the sowing and communal harvesting of corn, and his great gifts as a pastor and evangelist. His work among the Kekchi people continues to this day in the villages and towns of Alta Verapaz.

duce and sell typical Kekchi embroidered blouses, which in turn were sold through MCC in North America and local markets. This cooperative helped 120 local women earn money needed to meet basic family needs.[18] The VS workers lived in Cojaj while supporting the young church. They also initiated development projects such as garden plots, literacy, and a community water project.

The evangelistic efforts of Pablo Tzul and other indigenous leaders, at times combined with the development work of VS workers, led to the opening of small churches in Chirukbiquim, Sacsi Chiyo, Se'hol, Chelac, Caranilla, Chitana, Sequib, Sa mes chá, Santa Cecilia, Sa' Sis, San Pablo Chitap, Seq'uixpur, Pocola, Chicak, Cobehá, Ya'almachak,

Worship in the Kekchi Evangelical Mennonite church, Alta Vera Paz

Caribe, Montecristo, Cancab, Tanchi, Chityo, Sechactic, Tres Calles, Chicojl, and Cahabon.[19] By 1979 Mennonite missionaries continued carrying out an active ministry, with Kekchi leaders involved as pastors, evangelists, health workers, and literacy and agriculture workers.[20]

Early in 1970, the missionaries Richand and Lois Landis moved to the Colonia Mirador of Guatemala City where they worked to combine Voluntary Service programs with evangelization and church planting. A small church soon emerged as well as a social assistance program that provided basic foodstuffs and basic health care. By 1983, the Buen Pastor congregation numbered 70 baptized members, with a total of 136 participants. Continued evangelistic

The Ancla de Fe (Anchor of Faith) church

activity produced the Mennonite churches of Puerta Estrecha, Roca de Salvación, and Barcenas Villa Nueva.[21]

The beginnings of the Casa Horeb church are linked to the El Calvario church which was founded in 1947 as a neo-pentecostal church. Following the earthquake in 1976, El Calvario received material aid from North America, including help from MCC, establishing a Mennonite contact with members of this church. In 1979 a group of El Calvario members, including Gilberto Flores, Hector Argueta, and Mario and Leonor Méndez left El Calvario to begin another church, called Casa Horeb. The first pastor of this congregation was Gilberto Flores.[22] Close contacts with Mennonite churches followed, and in 1982 Casa Horeb joined the Mennonite conference.[23] This church and its members would play an important role in the development of the Mennonite church in Guatemala.

The latent ethnic tension between indigenous and Spanish-speaking Guatemalans became a live issue in the Nueva Jerusalem church in San Pedro Carchá. As the capital city of the department of Alta Verapaz, in a predominantly indigenous region, San Pedro Carchá nevertheless continued to grow with the arrival of more and more Spanish-speaking Guatemalans. This was reflected also in the leadership of the Nueva Jerusalem church: after the work of Kekchi evangelist Pablo Tzul came a succession of Spanish-speaking pastors who provided leadership for the San Pedro church. This created significant problems for the Kekchi and Spanish-

Testimony of Leonor Méndez

I was born in Guatemala in 1949. My parents were artisans, weaving typical cloth. Later my father, who came from Guaguatenango, moved to Guatemala City. I was four years old when he divorced my mother, and I came to live with a stepmother. I lived a violent childhood. My stepmother would beat my brother and me, and refused to give us food. Once, when I was eleven, she gave such a beating that at the hospital they counted 82 contusions on my body. Even as a child I attended the Central American church; I began teaching Sunday school at age 12. When I was 14 some youth from our church began attending El Calvario church, and shared their experience of speaking in tongues. ... I also received the gift of tongues after much prayer. After these experiences our church split, and about sixty of us left. Along with my husband Mario Méndez I am a member of the first graduating class of the Biblical Institute of El Calvario church.

Mario and Leonor Méndez

speaking people of the church, since Spanish-speaking ministers could not communicate in Kekchi.[24]

This situation eventually led to the establishment of two Mennonite conferences. The Evangelical National Mennonite Church of Guatemala became the independent coordinating body for the 23 Kekchi Mennonite churches that were in existence in 1980. By 1980 the Evangelical Mennonite Church of Guatemala organized itself as the conference for the Spanish-speaking Mennonite churches. Eastern Mennonite Missions along with the Washington-Franklin Mennonite Conference related to both Guatemalan conferences, both of whom had legal jurisdiction, recognized by the Guatemalan government.

The Eastern Pennsylvania Mennonite Church formed in 1968 when a group of bishops, ministers and deacons separated from the Lancaster Mennonite Conference. The new church took a conservative stand on divorce and re-marriage, the use of the prayer veil and un-cut hair for women, forbidding radio and television and participation in organized sports or attendance at public schools. Ministers were unsalaried, chosen by lot, and the use of automobiles was discouraged. The new church organized the Mennonite Messianic Mission which carried mission work to British Columbia, Guatemala, the Bahamas and Paraguay. The first missionaries to Guatemala arrived in 1972, settling in the town of Varsovia in the department of Quetzaltenango.[25]

Initial work involved visiting homes, handing out tracts and holding worship services in the missionaries' homes. In 1977 a church came to be located in La Victoria, attended also by people from La Cumbre, located 1,000 feet higher than La Victoria. A church opened in La Cumbre in 1980. The home congregation has a strong presence of North American families involved in agriculture, who worship and sing in English. In other congregations, although the Guatemalan members speak Man, church services are conducted in Spanish, using traditional hymns translated into Spanish.[26] A school has been established in La Cumbre where children from these churches receive primary and secondary education. The schools are not recognized by the state; the teachers are Mennonite members of the church.[27]

The Mennonite Air Mission began in 1972 thanks to Harold Kauffman, missionary with the Conservative Mennonite Fellowship. Kauffman wished to reach the people of the interior who had no road access. He bought his own airplane and obtained a license to fly it. A base church was established near Guatemala City, from which 10 congregations were founded throughout Guatemala. By 1980 Kauffman was working together with several other leaders: five Guatemalans had been ordained ministers, one a deacon, and 14 more as lay leaders. The Mission had also established a medical service with missionary nurses and teachers to teach in schools that were established. By 1987, Mennonite Air Mission churches numbered 180 members.[28]

The Church of God in Christ (Holdeman) began its work in Guatemala in 1977, when the decision was made to help in the reconstruction of the country following the devastating earthquake of 1976. By 1981 two churches had been established in Barrio el Golfo in El Progreso. This mission maintains a close relationship with the Church of God in Christ of Mexico, using the hymnal published by that church as well as other religious literature provided by the church in Mexico.[29]

The Mennonite presence in Guatemala is widely varied in nature and practice. Five different Mennonite mission organizations were active in Guatemala up to 1980: the Conservative Mennonite Fellowship; Eastern Mennonite Missions (supported by Washington-Franklin Mennonite Conference); Eastern Pennsylvania Mennonite Church; Mennonite Air Mission; Church of God in Christ. Each of these organizations represents a different ideological strand of the North American Mennonite tradition, and the churches founded reflect these distinctives. In addition, Mennonite mission efforts have been directed to both the indigenous population in the highlands as well as the Spanish-speaking population elsewhere, further varying the nature of Mennonite churches in the country. And finally, in some cases churches formed in other Protestant traditions – predominantly pentecostal in orientation – found a home among the Mennonites, as was the case of the Casa Horeb church. The result is a lively mix of Mennonite ecumenism, an ethnic, linguistic and cultural quilt of Mennonite faith and practice.

Anabaptist-Descended Churches in Nicaragua (1966-1979)

Nicaragua, a beautiful country of lakes, rivers, mountains and volcanos, is the largest country in Central America, covering an area of 139,000 square kilometers. It borders Honduras and El Salvador in the north, Costa Rica in the south with the Altantic and Pacific oceans to the east and west. The Spaniards first arrived in this territory in 1523.[1] In his first contact with the people governed by the Chief Nicarao, Fr. Diego de Agüero baptized more than 9,000 native people.[2] The next fifteen years of Spanish rule were a virtual genocide. Bartolomé de las Casas testified that the 1,500 persons sent from Nicaragua as slaves to Panama and Peru perished in the brutal work of the mines.[3] Another important witness to the history of the colony of Nicaragua was bishop Mons. Antonio de Valdivieso, who bravely denounced the wars, tyrannies, injusticies and genocides the Christians imposed on the native peoples. He was assasinated in 1550 in the city of León by the sons of Rodrigo de Contreras, who was then governor of Nicaragua.[4]

The Caribbean coast – described already in 1502 by Christopher Columbus – never was conquered, in spite of repeated attempts in the seventeenth and eighteenth centuries.[5] The region known later as Mosquitia was populated by indigenous groups who lived by hunting and fishing, and would not abide the agrarian and urban life lived in the rest of the country.[6] The first African inhabitants came to the coast as a result of the sinking of a slave ship in 1650. The Atlantic coast was not evangelized until the nineteenth century under English influence, after the emancipation of the slaves in the British Empire in 1833.[7]

With the assassination of César Augusto Sandino in 1934 at the hands of General Anastasio Somoza García, a period of extended military dictatorship began that permitted the United States to control finances and investments.[8] General Somoza became wealthy during World War II by taking possession of extensive properties owned by Germans who were expelled from the country.

The Cuban revolution had a great impact in Latin America. In Nicaragua, Carlos Fonseca Amador founded the Sandinista Front for National Liberation (FSLN) in 1961 and began promoting a guerilla war, based in the mountains of central Nicaragua. A small popular current supported the actions of the FSLN against the Somoza regime initially. Beginning in the mid-1960s, Fr. Ernesto Cardenal developed an important movement of primitivist painting in the Solentiname archipelago of Lake Nicaragua. The art, music and poetry of Solentiname reflected the brutality of repression and called for participation in the struggle against the oppressive regime.[9] The devastating earthquake of 1972 which left Managua in ruins initiated the decline of the Somoza dictatorship, when international aid intended for the suffering was pocketed by the dictator.

Ernesto Cardenal reflects on the 1972 earthquake

Let us not cry for these ruins,
but rather for the people...
But the people are immortal.
They emerge smiling from the morgue...
At midnight a poor woman gave birth to a child,
without a roof over its head
And that is hope.
God has said: "Behold, I make all things new."
And that is the reconstruction.

Other events that contributed to the downfall of the Somoza regime included the assassination of the critical journalist Pedro Joaquín Chamorro in 1978 and the indiscriminate bombing of the Nicaraguan population by the National Guard in the same year. The military triumph of the FSLN came in July, 1979. In contrast to Cuba, hardly any Protestant pastors fled the country following the overthrow of the Somoza regime.[10]

In the 1920s Baptist churches had been founded in six major cities, but the Pentecostal churches that came to the country in the 1950s eventually formed a block that assumed leadership and control of Protestantism in the country. The Evangelical Alliance formed in 1960 and came into conflict with the Somoza regime. In reply to a letter from the Evangelical Alliance, Somoza threatened to remove the constitutional right of the laity to speak.

The first Anabaptist presence in Nicaragua came with the missionaries of the General Conference of the Brethren in Christ (BIC). The BIC movement, which formed in 1780 in the United States, had Anabaptist roots but under Pietist influence, emphasized the experience of conversion and a personal relationship with God. By 1945 the BIC had initiated evangelistic work in Africa, India and Japan. Later this work was extended to Latin America, with missions in Cuba, Nicaragua, Venezuela and Colombia.[11]

In 1965 Pearl and Howard Wolgemuth were the first BIC missionaries sent to this new field.[12] Eventually the Wolgemuths established a work in the town of Esquipulas.[13] The Wolgemuths developed a simple method of evangelization: they used a Jeep that had a generator to power two lamps, a megaphone and a film projector. They would begin projecting a film, and soon there would be 100 to 150 people there to watch. The Jeep was also used to transport people to worship services and Sunday schools. There soon were baptized members in Esquipulas. From the start the Wolgemuths concentrated on educating and preparing young people for leadership in the church,[14] but also opened a clinic in Esquipulas to look after the medical needs of the poor in the community. By 1968 and the baptism by Howard Wolgemuth of sixteen adults and six youth on the shores of Lake Masaya, more than 100 people were attending the Esquipulas and Schick churches; the mission effort was vital and growing by expanding into neighboring communities.[15]

Following the devastating earthquake in 1972, the BIC participated in the relief efforts of the Nicaraguan Protestant aid organization CEPAD (Council of Protestant Churches of Nicaragua) in addition to continuing to expand pastoral and evangelistic efforts. In 1981, Roy V. Sider attributed the rapid growth of BIC churches in Nicaragua to the following factors: 1) An integral ministry that served the social needs of the Nicaraguan poor, especially through the clinics. Four churches were founded as a direct result of that service. 2) Social assistance to the poor was maintained throughout the earthquake and the years of civil war. 3) Communal work with international aid organizations provided food in times of civil emergency. 4) Agricultural projects enabled 100 families to support themselves. 5) Families living times of great crisis, because of the war, sincerely searched for God. 6) Growth was clearly a blessing from God.[16]

In the midst of a revolutionary situation of increasing violence, the BIC missionaries prepared the way for a takeover of the church by national leaders. When the Musser family left Nicaragua in December 1979, in the midst of particularly fierce fighting between the FSLN

Reflections of a Sunday School teacher in the BIC church of El Arroyo

What are the results of war? We all know what they are, and great efforts are made to prevent them. But in reality, there will not be peace on earth until there is peace between humanity and God. .... Since Adam and Eve, human pride has given rise to all kinds of disobedience, crimes, wars, corruption and blasphemies, for which reason God sent his only-begotten Son... Christ is the Prince of Peace, the mediator between God and humankind. ... Christ said: "I have come that you may have life, and have it in abundance" (John 10:10) Why can humanity not experience this life? Why are so many youth in the cemeteries? Simply because, as the Bible says, "the wages of sin are death, while the gift of God is life eternal in Christ Jesus, our Lord."

and Somoza forces, the leadership of the BIC church of Nicaragua was already in the hands of national leaders.[17]

In 1966 the Evangelical Mennonite Conference Board of Missions (EMC Canada) sent its first missionaries to Nicaragua.[18] Alfred and Doris Friesen located in Managua, collaborated with the local Bible Society, and began worship services in homes of interested persons in the Francisco Morazán neighborhood of Managua. By 1969 there were active women's and youth groups, with many youth sent to biblical institutes for preparation to serve in ministry. This led to the construction of the First Mennonite Church in March, 1970. When the Friesen family was forced to return to Canada in 1974 for health reasons, the pastorate was taken over by Caytano Calderón. At the time of the insurrection in 1979, this congregation was the largest and most dynamic in the country, under the pastoral leadership of Lorenzo Romero.[19]

The church in La Paz de Carazo began at the initiative of missionaries Lester and Darlene Olfert, who began their work in Nicaragua in 1970. By 1972 the church had elected Salomón Torres and Antonio Salazar as congregational leaders.[20] By 1978 the La Paz church had 73 baptized members with an attendance of 168 persons. The congregation had numerous and active youth engaged in evangelism, Christian education, music and sports, as well as extending the mission of the church to the town of Las Cruces and San José de la Gracia. In the 1970s, under the leadership of the Olferts, churches were planted in the city of Granada, the town of Colama, and the Managua neighborhood of La Trinidad.[21] In addition the congregation located in Managua extended evangelistic efforts to a poor settlement known today as Ciudad Sandino, where a small but active congregation took shape, with a strong youth group, choir, and women's organization. The small church functioning in San José de la Gracia came to be pastored by EMC missionaries. This latter town was the scene of heavy fighting during the insurrection; its church remained without a pastor when the EMC missionaries posted there decided to leave the county in June, 1979. Donald and Elizabeth Plett assumed leadership of the church there shortly after the FSLN victory, in August, 1979.

The founding of EMC churches in Nicaragua was accompanied by community development work. In 1972 the first VS youth arrived to work in literacy, health and agriculture projects. After the earthquake hit Managua, five volunteers worked with CEPAD's program for feeding children and also worked with church youth, a program which ended for lack of leadership when the volunteers left the country in 1974. Members of the Fraternity church, however, continued to collaborate with CEPAD. EMC missions also worked in health, founding four clinics under the leadership of Doris Friesen.[22] In 1978 the focus shifted away from using registered nurses from the north, to the training of local health promoters. The work of clinics was a positive factor in developing the broader work of the church.

In 1973 the Fraternity of Evangelical Mennonite churches of Nicaragua was organized, with the legal status of the organization confirmed by the government early in 1974.[23] The

Elizabeth Vado's memories of the war

La Paz was close to the city of Carazo, and there were frequent bombings, which made it necessary to take refuge. It was also a rural location through which "the boys" passed (as we called the FSLN guerillas in those days). I remember one time when 25 of these "boys" came through, and we made a meal for them in our house. Then they left. They were armed. They would come at dawn and pass the day under the shelter of trees at the edge of the field. In those days one had to keep one's mouth shut. People were afraid of the National Guard, who were terrible, and so they sympathized with "the boys." … My parents, who were pastors, also suffered at the hands of the National Guard, because it was thought that they were in league with the guerillas. … Some pastors of the Fraternity were arrested, among them Francisco Cano and, I believe, Filadelfio Cuadra, who has since died. So my father was also "on the list." The National Guard once broke into our home, but all they found were Christian materials, including the Bible. They looked everything over and left more satisfied. Another night they surrounded the house and removed only my father. Who knows what they talked about, but he was returned to us. We lived with this tension as children and adolescents. It was a time when one lived on faith and conviction. This is why Anabaptist history makes such an impression on me; there are many things that are similar in that history to what we lived in the time of insurrection. … We used to dig pits in our houses where we would take refuge during the bombing.

Arnulfo Vado and family

Monte de Sión church of the Fraternity of Evangelical Mennonite churches, Managua

Testimony of the pastor Patricio Salvador Mora Mercado

I accepted the Lord in 1977 at the age of twenty years, after hearing a sermon. I decided to serve and follow Him. In 1979 I was not yet a pastor, but I was emerging as an evangelist. This was when the revolution was emerging and the youth were much aware of political events. I also helped the revolution, handing out protest literature; I was part of the church, and we could hide the materials there. At that time the Christian youth were stronger, and involved in the struggle. The triumph of the revolution included many Christian youth, but on the other hand, we served the Lord more. I was aware of many massacres and tortures on the part of the National Guard. I would go, Bible in hand, to dialogue with the Guardsmen and ask permission to speak with the prisoners, because the youth were there. I would encourage them to have faith in the Lord. Thank God, the Guard always respected me and gave me permission to preach the Gospel. I believe this was my biggest contribution, because I spoke with the political prisoners and evangelized inside the jails.

statutes and aims of the Fraternity were established in 1973, among which the purposes of the church were stated as 1) preaching the Gospel of our Lord Jesus Christ. 2) Promoting and maintaining fraternal unity among the churches of Jesus Christ. 3) Cultivating the spiritual and physical health of people in its cultural aspects of good and healthy habits. 4) Cooperating with other Protestants in this country to promote the Gospel and the well being of the society in which we live.[24]

The Nicaraguan mission work of the Mennonite Conservative Conference of Ohio began with Vernon and Dorothy Jantzi. They came to Costa Rica to learn Spanish and began doing literacy work full time.[25] Seeing the needs in Nicaragua, the Jantzis moved there in 1968 to head up the literacy program of the Protestant churches of that county (ALFALIT), joined in that work by three VS workers who were to be engaged in community development and evangelization.[26] While Vernon Jantzi promoted literacy work throughout the country, often in collaboration with biblical institutes of other denominations, VS workers became involved in wide-ranging projects, from helping people with community gardens, health promotion through clinics, agrarian reform, building latrines, constructing buildings, building potable water supplies, giving vaccinations and doing nutrition work.[27] By 1972 there were eleven VS workers in Nicaragua, working in diverse communities.[28]

The year 1973 was seen by the Mennonites as a year of hope and reconstruction for Nicaragua, for they saw that the disaster of the earthquake had led many people to an encounter with Jesus. In some meetings of CEPAD there were as many as 2,500 people in attendance, faced with a huge sign that read "Jesus Christ is our Hope." This hope was evident also in the children, in the new congregations that began to emerge, in the prayers to God for strength to carry out the voluntary service work, and in thanksgiving that God was making hope possible.[29]

Beginning in 1978 the political situation in the country grew tense. The government was being attacked by demonstrations and guerilla activity. The missionaries believed that their mission work could be affected by this situation, and requested prayer on the part of the churches in the north.[30] At the same time, they recognized that there were business people who, along with the poorer people and the FSLN, were also in agreement with the struggle against the Somoza regime.[31]

Josefa Ruíz Manzanares and Verónica Arguedas Ruíz, members of the Fraternity of Evangelical Mennonite churches

Evangelization work and founding churches grew out of the community service of VS workers and literacy work. In Teustepe in the department of Boaco, VS work led to the coming of missionaries in 1974 which was extended to neighboring villages in 1976 and 1978.[32] Mission work in Managua began in 1973, when Elam and Doris Stauffer came to work in a suburb of the city called Colonia de las Américas and established the *Casa de Oración* (House of Prayer) church.[33] As had been the case in Boaco, VS workers had already established a presence in this neighborhood doing community development, building latrines, distributing food and giving practical testimony to the love of God. This neighborhood already had a high percentage of people who had worshipped in Protestant churches, and interest was heightened by the large evangelistic campaign of Luis Palau in 1975.

In November of 1975 José and Teresa Matamoros assumed the pastorate of this church. The first converts under their pastorate were Nicolás and Rosibel Largaespada, Luis Gutiérrez and Chéster Perez, who became deacons in the church.[34] Nicolás Largaespada and Luis Gutiérrez were ordained pastors in November of 1977, becoming the first national pastors of this conference. By 1978 this congregation numbered fifty active members. For their part, the Stauffers began a

Pastors of the Evangelical Mennonite Church of Nicaragua

small church in the Altamira neighborhood of Managua where they lived; by 1978 this church was also under the leadership of national pastors.[35]

Mission work in Puertas Viejas, a town located fifty miles from Managua and accessible from Teustepe, began in 1977. With the help of CEPAD, VS workers built a clinic here. Church services and Sunday Schools began to be held in the VS house located in the town and attendance soon reached 75 persons. The clinic came to serve fifty persons daily, offering prenatal services, care of sick children and vaccinations. In this way a church emerged in this place.[36] In the community of Río Blanco in the department of Matagalpa, VS work led again to the founding of a church: the *Rey de Reyes* (King of kings) church, beginning in 1975. This community was geographically in the midst of the civil war that eventually overcame the country, with incursions by guerillas demanding food, and the increasing presence of soldiers from the National Guard.[37] Towards the end of 1978 a baptism of eleven people was held in this small but growing congregation.[38]

In September, 1977 a meeting was held to establish the Mennonite Conference of Nicaragua with the participation of fourteen delegates and the pastors of the four member congregations.[39] The institutionalization of these Nicaraguan churches marked an impetus for growth of Mennonite churches, especially in the department of Zelaya South, where three churches were established, along with a church in the Managua neighborhood of Villa Libertad.

Memories of Pastor José Matamoros from the time of the Revolution

I saw many things as the year 1978 approached. I saw young men from the church killed. One time we found a young man thrown into a pathway. He was a youth from the church... his throat had been slashed. The family called me to minister to them. Another youth was taken by the National Guard and beaten with rifle butts; they stuck him into a military truck and took him away. He disappeared, but later returned again with a large scar on his face. He had been tortured, and the guard took him for dead and threw him next to a pile of bodies at the Malecón, near the beach of Lake Managua. When he regained consciousness he found himself on top of a heap of cadavers with a wound to his head. ... One late morning someone knocked on the door of my house, and through my window I saw a military jeep and military men. And I thought "Now is the time.. they've come to arrest me for something. I wonder what happened." When I opened the door a captain in the army asked if I was the pastor. When I said yes, he said "I am Manuel, husband of [blank], and I've come to ask you a very special favor." ... He said "look, we're losing this revolution, and I have to flee with my wife. Please help me by sending my family to Costa Rica; help me with a contact there... I'm going to flee in a military airplane to Honduras. Furthermore, I want you to pray for me." He knelt down in my living room. I put my hands on his head and invited him to accept Christ into his heart. And he did. He accepted Christ and prayed with me. I lived through many things like this with both sides in the conflict.

Brethren in Christ and Mennonite presence in Nicaragua, arriving from North America in the tumultuous decade before the Sandinista victory in 1979, needed to negotiate the extreme political tension of an indigenous revolution supported by the socialist world (Cuba, USSR) and opposed by the United States. Nicaragua was experiencing extreme material and spiritual hunger on a geo-political stage. In this context, BIC and Mennonite missions worked to feed and heal both body and soul, and encouraged the nationalization of their churches. The establishment of national conferences helped give autonomy to the Anabaptist-descended churches in Nicaragua.

III

Moving into the Twenty-First Century: (1979-2009)

Introduction: Moving into the Twenty-First Century: (1979-2009)

The three decades from 1979 to 2009 have seen dramatic shifts in the political, social and economic realities of Latin America, with significant regional and national differences. The religious context has also shifted dramatically in these decades for all Christian churches. The long-term historical impact of these changes becomes more difficult to assess, the closer one gets to contemporary events. Nevertheless, a brief overview of regional developments provides a necessary framework for understanding the latest chapter in the story of Anabaptist-descended churches in Latin America.

Social, Political, Economic realities, 1979-2009

The Latin American bishops who met at the Second Vatican Council recognized that their region shared a history and a common set of problems. The Latin American bishops concluded at Medellín, Colombia (1968) that the endemic poverty, inequality and injustice that ran through Latin American society was in fact *structural* growing out of social, political and economic systems entrenched in colonial times and maintained since then. The church, said the bishops, should lead the way in changing the sinful structures of society.

Looking back after more than four decades, the bishops' analysis still expresses fundamental truths: poverty, inequality and injustice in Latin American society remain stubbornly endemic and structural, and Christians are still called to respond to the human needs of the masses of people living in the region. Nevertheless, the models for changing structural inequalities have shifted significantly since the bishops' pronouncement at Medellín, for both the church and the nation states of the region.

The decade of the 1980s brought a fundamental shift in the Cold War thinking that had dominated world events beginning already in the late 1940s. The Cold War era was characterized by global maneuvering between East and West, with the Communist bloc supporting revolutionary movements (and the occasional shooting war: e.g. Vietnam), countered by a Western bloc that fought back, often by supporting "law and order" military regimes overtly, covertly and economically. Latin America was caught in the middle, as proxy battles between East and West were carried out on Latin American soil, with many thousands of Latin American victims.

The progressive weakening of the Soviet bloc in the 1980s, culminating in the dramatic fall of the Berlin wall in 1989, the reunification of East and West Germany in 1990 and the formal end of the USSR in 1991, signalled changes in U.S. interest and policy and changes for Latin America as well. As the 1990s progressed, U.S. intervention in Latin America became more indirect and economic in nature, as opposed to directly political and military, with some exceptions. In Latin America there was a move towards a variety of civilian, elected representative governments. As the new millenium began, Latin Americans increasingly voted for civilian leaders and as they voted, increasingly elected liberal or "leftist" civilian governments, in protest of globalist free trade policies and increasing economic hardship.

Political changes in the Southern Cone countries in the 1980s ran parallel to global changes, although a cause and effect relationship is not obvious. In Argentina the military dictatorship and its "dirty war" of clandestine disappearances of civilians of the 1970s and early 1980s came to an end in 1983, following Argentina's defeat by Great Britain in the Falklands/Malvinas war. The country subsequently moved to democratically elected civilian governments. Uruguay likewise moved from its military rule of the 1970s and early 1980s to representative government; competing political parties contested an election in 1985. Brazil also moved to civilian rule in 1985 for the first time since the military took control of that country in 1964. In Chile, where a CIA-sponsored coup overthrew the democratically-elected president Salvador Allende in 1973, democracy returned in 1990. Finally, in Paraguay the longest-ruling Latin American dictator, Alfredo Stroessner, was ousted in 1989 and elected, civilian government was re-established. The general direction of these changes in the Southern Cone countries of Latin America, all falling within the decade of the 1980s, was remarkably similar in moving away from military dictatorships toward democratic forms of government.

Countries in the Andean region followed the same trend. In Peru, long-term military rule (1968-1980) ended with democratic reforms, interrupted by Alberto Fujimori's self-declared dictatorship in 1992 but resuming again in 2001 with presidential elections. In Bolivia, a coup in 1964 kept the military in power through convulsive times, a period that ended in 1982 with civilian governments being elected since then. In the 2005 election, Evo Morales won the Bolivian presidency with a convincing majority to become the first indigenous president of that country. After 19 years of military rule (1960-1979), Ecuador also returned to elected civilian governments, although the stability of these governments has remained a problem. Colombia's version of democracy – a system of power-sharing between its two major political parties – has managed to avoid direct military rule since 1958. Nevertheless, the Colombian military continues to be a major force in Colombian life, receiving massive U.S. aid for "internal security" and the "war on drugs." Military and paramilitary groups continue to fight multiple guerrilla groups. This instability provides a context in which drug trade flourishes, which funds the warring factions and intensifies violence.

Venezuela (included here among the "Andean" countries for convenience sake only), has had a functioning democratic system since 1958. Hugo Chávez, elected president in 1998, has consolidated power through re-elections and referendums which now allow him to run for office as many times as he wishes.

Politics in the Caribbean region played out against the backdrop of the Cuban revolution (1959), with the United States intervening militarily here and there to "prevent another Cuba," as in the Dominican Republic in 1965 and Grenada in 1983, or exercising quasi-colonial control, as in Puerto Rico. Military invasion or direct control was a secondary response, however, with preferred U.S. policy being the isolation of Cuba and support for "law and order" governments. This support could range from tacit approval of the long-running Duvalier dictatorship in Haiti ("Papa Doc" and "Baby Doc" Duvalier, to 1986) to economic support of former British colonies that gained their independence in this period (Jamaica, 1962; Trinidad, 1962; Barbados, 1966; British Guyana, 1966; Grenada, 1974; Belize, 1981).

Although the presence of Cuba made the Caribbean an area of particular interest to the U.S., it was the political situation in Central America that resulted in direct military and political intervention by the U.S. in the 1980s and 1990s. The 1979 victory of the FSLN in Nicaragua over U.S.-supported dictator Anastasio Somoza triggered alarm in the U.S., and the region became the focus for proxy interventions from both East and West. Beginning in 1981, the U.S. government clandestinely helped organize and support an invading "Contra" army in Honduras against the FSLN government of Nicaragua, against the orders of its own Congress, eventually even selling arms to Iran (secretly and illegally) and using the proceeds of these illegal sales to fund the Contra army. Honduras, which had no guerilla movements of its own, allowed the U.S. to use its territory for military maneuvers and arms drops. In El Salvador and Guatemala, the U.S. government countered the active guerilla movements of the 1980s with direct support of the military governments of those countries, ignoring the massive human rights abuses that were being committed in the name of anti-Communism. The 1980s were a period of overt and clandestine violence in Central America, with thousands of people killed, "disappeared," maimed and displaced.

By 1990 the "Communist crisis" in Central America was over. The FSLN government had been displaced, and Violeta Chamorro was elected president of Nicaragua in that year. By 1992 the conflict in El Salvador had come to an official end, and in Guatemala an uneasy democratic process moved forward in 1986. By 1991 the collapse of the USSR meant the end of direct economic and military aid to Cuba. With the end of Cold War and the withdrawal of Eastern Bloc aid to revolutionary movements, the focus of U.S. policy in all of Latin America became less overtly political.

The political chain of events in Latin America as a whole, and particularly in different regions and countries, posed serious questions for Anabaptist-related churches. Do Anabaptist Christians participate in political processes, and if so, how should they participate? For the last three decades the options for church members have run the spectrum from an apolitical standpoint, through support and participation in democratic movements in society, to limited support of revolutionary movements. These options were more starkly put for some than for others, depending on country or region. In Central America, avoiding revolutionary violence was not an option; the only question was how to respond to that reality as Anabaptist Christians. In the Southern Cone and many Andean countries, where military dictators were giving way to the popular pressure to democratize, there were openings for church people to actually participate in political processes as Christian citizens. In the following chapter some selected examples will be given of how Mennonite and Brethren in Christ churches did in fact respond to their changing political world.

Social and Economic realities, 1979-2009

Beginning in 1982, Latin American countries faced what has come to be called the "debt crisis," fueled by the sharp rise in oil prices in 1973 and the availability of inexpensive capital on world markets. Latin American countries borrowed huge sums of money, at variable rates of interest, and within a decade found themselves in trouble. Interest rates rose to historically high levels in the 1980s at the same time as Latin American export incomes fell with the collapse of commodity prices on world markets. It was a deadly combination. By 1983, sixteen Latin American nations were either facing default or were re-negotiating their massive loans with global financial institutions. In 1983, Mexico, Brazil, Venezuela and Argentina owed a collective 176 billion dollars to international banks.

The Intenational Monetary Fund (IMF) and the World Bank played major roles in the negotations that followed, giving aid tied to internal "economic reforms" in given countries.[1] Argentina, for example, followed IMF policies by cutting funding to health and education and at the same time privatizing national resources. The results were not positive, whether because of the terms of the loans or internal mis-management is still debated. In any case, the Argentine economy completely collapsed in 2001, and the country defaulted on its international loans. By the next year, an estimated 60 percent of Argentineans were living below the poverty line.

The causes and results of the economic crisis in Latin America are argued by experts, but there was an undeniable decrease in the standard of living for the majority of people, generating a grass roots suspicion of globalization, international markets and international financial institutions. The result politically has been a general shift toward the political left, even as Latin American economies slowly recover from the disastrous situation of the 1980s and 1990s.[2]

The economic facts of life of the past three decades have had an impact on Anabaptist-related churches and church members. The support of pastors and church institutions became a critical issue, particularly for churches newly-independent from mission board support, with a membership that was struggling to survive. Churches lost many educated and able members to emigration as many moved North to better their families' educational and economic situation. For those who remained, it was clear that as Christians they needed to respond to the increasing poverty, hunger and displacement that were evident in their neighbors' lives. What should the church's response be to economic forces that seemed to lie outside of the control of the church? In the chapter that follows, some selected testimonies will be given of Anabaptist-related Christians' struggle to maintain their witness in the midst of the economic crises of the past three decades.

The Religious Reality in Latin America: 1979-2009

In 2005, Latin America was home to an estimated 490 million Roman Catholics, nearly half of the world's Roman Catholic population. Nevertheless, a significant majority of Roman Catholics have been and remain nominal Catholics, not actively involved in the practice of their religion. The reforms of Vatican II set out to address this situation with the encouragement of lay participation, the celebration of the mass in vernacular languages and making the Bible available in the vernacular. One result was the emergence of Liberation movements, which developed their distinctive Liberation Theology. For liberationist Roman Catholics, salvation meant liberation from social, political and economic oppression. Liberation thought had affinities with socialist political thought and at times, identified closely with particular political movements. Vatican resistance was not long in coming, and by the 1980s, liberationist seminaries were being closed and radical bishops and archbishops replaced with more conservative men.

The collapse of the USSR ended utopian understandings of socialism, and coincided with efforts from the Vatican to move the church in a traditionalist direction. Nevertheless, liberation theology has not disappeared, and may be gaining strength as political sentiment leans to the left again. In Brazil, where Liberation Theology was strong in the 1980s, the movement remains strong among Roman Catholics. The *New York Times* reported around 80,000 base communities and almost a million liberation Bible study groups in Brazil in 2007.[3]

At the same time traditionalist Catholics have also made gains, with strong support from Rome and its present pope, Benedict XVI. Still, the Roman Catholic church in Brazil and elsewhere has lost many members in the past decades. Benedict acknowledged as much in his 2007 visit to Brazil, when he called on the bishops to be "courageous and effective missionaries." According to Brazil's census, only 74 percent of Brazilians identified themselves as Roman Catholics in 2000, down from 89 percent in 1980.[4] The decline in Roman Catholic church membership seems to be a continuing trend.

By contrast, the decades from 1979 to 2009 have seen a steady increase in Protestant church membership in all Latin American countries, with the most dramatic increases coming in Brazil, Central America and the Caribbean. According to one source, Guatemala has the highest percentage of Protestants (40 percent of the population in 2005), followed by Nicaragua, Brazil, Costa Rica, Panama and Haiti (15 to 16 percent), with most other Latin American countries counting Protestant church members as between 2 and 8 percent of the total population.[5]

Focusing on the decline of Roman Catholicism and the growth of Protestantism in these decades, however, is missing the most dramatic religious dynamic for Latin American Christians, and that is the amazing growth among pentecostal and charismatic Christians. The Pew Forum on Religion and Public Life, citing the World Christian Database, reports a large and growing pentecostal movement that cuts across denominational lines. In 1970, pentecostal and charismatic Christians numbered just 4.4 of the Latin American population; by 2005, this figure had risen to a surprising 28.1 percent of the population. This figure includes not only officially "Pentecostal" denominations, but also charismatic Christians in the Roman Catholic church and in non-Pentecostal Protestant denominations.[6]

The tremendous growth in pentecostal and charismatic Christianity in recent decades is changing the religious landscape in Latin America, as denominational allegiances seem to become less significant. The long-term historical significance of this trend is still unknown. Will pentecostal and charismatic Christians be called to unity, or to further division? How will pentecostal and charismatic Christians respond to the political, social and economic realities they are experiencing in their respective countries? How will the Anabaptist-related witness be shaped by the pentecostal wave that is sweeping Latin America?

It is undeniable that the general political, social and religious trends – barely outlined above – have given a distinct nature to the Anabaptist-related churches in Latin America. Some of the historical responses of these churches have been noted in previous chapters, and will be noted in the following as well. As Mennonite and Brethren in Christ churches have lived out their Anabaptist-rooted faith in the unique Latin American world, they have pondered, changed, shaped and expressed their Christian witness in unique ways. Their testimony continues to speak to Christians of all cultures.

Glimpses of Anabaptist-Related Communities in Latin America (1979-2009)

The previous chapters have presented a brief historical overview of the pilgrimage undertaken by Latin American Anabaptist-descended churches and communities from 1917 to 1979. In this final section, rather than offering a detailed overview of these communities by region, we will rather point to some of the notable developments and challenges that characterize this most-recent historical period. These thematic observations will confirm once again the pilgrim character of Mennonite communities and Anabaptist churches of Latin America, churches that are always on the road, moving from one place to another, establishing new communities in other countries, always with the goal of walking faithfully in the footsteps of Christ.

New mission fields and Mennonite migrations

From 1979 to 2009 Anabaptist congregations were established in three Latin American countries where there had been no Mennonite or BIC presence before, and significant expansion took place in many other countries that already had an Anabaptist presence. The following provides just a partial overview of these developments.

Ecuador

Many different Mennonite Brethren missionaries came to Ecuador to work with the radio station "Heralding Christ Jesus' Blessings" (HCJB), also known as the Voice of the Andes, supporting primarily the German-language programs.[1] In 1979 the Conservative Mennonite Conference initiated missionary projects in Ecuador working with MCC

313

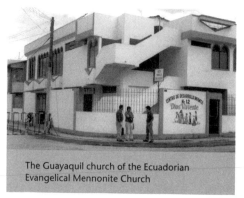

The Guayaquil church of the Ecuadorian Evangelical Mennonite Church

in distributing donated food to different areas of the country.[2] In 1980 the first CMC missionaries arrived in Guayaquil and established a church in a place called Atarazana. The Rosedale Mennonite Mission also worked with MCC in Manta on the Pacific coast in response to massive flooding, building houses and latrines. The first Rosedale missionaries came in 1982, and three new members were baptized on the Murciélago beach two years later.[3] The work expanded to Guayaquil in 1987.[4] In that same year the Ecuadorian Evangelical Mennonite Church was founded. Beginning in the 1980s, mission work in Ecuador included the participation of the Solís and Villalta families, sponsored by the Costa Rican Mennonite conference (CIEMCR), the Mennonite church of Ecuador and Rosedale Mennonite Missions.[5]

In 1992 the Mennonite Board of Missions (MBM) of Elkhart, Indiana collaborated with the Federation of Indigenous Evangelicals of Ecuador (*Federación Ecuatoriana de Indígenas Evangélicos*: FEINE)[6] by sending theological education workers to that country.[7] The work that

Indigenous students in a course taught by César Moya in partnership with FEINE, 2007

was begun by Mauricio Chenlo and his wife Sara was continued by César Moya, his wife Patricia Urueña and their children in a partnership involving their home church *Iglesia Cristiana Menonita de Colombia*, Central Plains Mennonite Conference and Mennonite Mission Network, the successor agency of MBM. Along with their work of theological education among the indigenous churches, they have established a church in Quito made up of Ecuadorians and Colombian refugees. The Moya family has also done ecumenical work on justice, peace and economic issues with the Latin American Council of Churches.[8]

Courses taught by the Moyas led to the formation of an Anabaptist study group in Riobamba in 2003. Although the membership and leadership of this group has changed over the years, a visit to Central Plains Mennonite Conference (USA) churches by Raul and Ivette Escobar and another couple in 2007 fostered a vision for a full-fledged church.

Patricia Urueña and César Moya

With the encouragement of the partnership, the church began weekly meetings during Lent of 2009. Daniel and Beatriz Escobar were invited by the church to serve as pastors with support from Don and Jan Rheinheimer of Mennonite Mission Network. Beatriz had attended evangelical churches for over 30 years and Daniel, who is a lawyer and native of Chimborazo, earlier had worked as an advisor to the bishop of Santa Cruz in Chimborazo in the legal process of returning land to indigenous families. Three years ago Daniel had a cranial operation and survived in a miraculous way. His personal encounter with Christ and an invitation from his brother led him and Beatriz, six months later, to this newly forming Mennonite church where they share leadership with other Ecuadorians.[9]

Venezuela

Five Anabaptist-related groups have been established in Venezuela; each one is small and has a unique history. According to Mennonite World Conference statistics, there were a total of 725 Mennonite church members in the country in 2006.

Two groups were founded by Eastern Mennonite Missions. In 1978, EMM sent the Puerto Rican couple José and Agdelia Santiago to do mission work in Caracas for a period of three years. Pastor Harry Satizabal, member of the Mennonite Brethren church of Colombia, emigrated to Venezuela in 1979 and worked as an electrician for a period of eight months. During this time he got to know the Santiago family, and began working with them. The first church was founded in San Bernardino, near the childrens' hospital. It was called *Jesucristo: puerta del cielo* (Jesus Christ, doorway to heaven). Two more congregations were founded later, the first in Charallave[10] and the second in

Cua. Harry Satizabal established an institute for the training of pastors which began in 1981 with eighteen young people enrolled.[11] The resulting Council of Evangelical Mennonite churches in Venezuela (*Concilio de Iglesias Evangélicas Menonitas en Venezuela*) numbered 3 churches and 70 members in 2004. Also founded by EMM, the Shalom Evangelical Mennonite Church (*Iglesia Evangélica Menonita Shalom*) had two churches with 109 members in 2004.

The two Chinese-speaking churches in Venezuela make up the Evangelical Chinese Mennonite Brethren Church (*Iglesia Evangélica China de los Hermanos Menonitas*). These churches have their roots in outreach efforts made by the Pacific Grace MB Church in Vancouver, British Colombia, Canada, when that church sent associate pastor Miller Zhuang to Venezuela on an outreach mission. The two resulting churches had a combined membership of 115 in 2004. The Venezuelan Association of Biblical Churches (*Asociación Venezolana de Iglesias Bíblicas*) is related with the Fellowship of Evangelical Churches. The Association had 2 churches with a combined 120 members in 2004. Finally, the Evangelical Church of Brethren in Christ in Venezuela (*Iglesia Evangélica Hermanos en Cristo Venezuela*) had three churches with a combined 145 members in that same year.

The Anabaptist-related churches in Venezuela maintain close contact with the Mennonite Churches of Colombia (IMCOL) and have a keen interest in pastoral and leadership education. The Council of Evangelical Mennonite churches in Venezuela established a basic level seminary program that had graduated 54 students by 2004.[12]

Chile

After the military coup in Chile in 1973, many Chileans emigrated to Canada. Among them was Jorge Vallejos and his wife Rut. In Chile, Jorge had been a labor leader and held a post in the Ministry of Agriculture in the government of the overthrown president Salvador Allende. In Canada, Jorge and Rut and other Latin American residents found a church home in the Holyrood Mennonite Church in Edmonton. In the early 1980s the Hispanic community in Edmonton was large, numbering around 10,000 people, of whom half were Chilean.

The long-time Latin American missionary, John Driver, visited the Edmonton community to affirm the nonresistant witness, for the Latin American community was not entirely convinced of the biblical foundations of this position. Vallejos had an evangelistic vision and travelled to other cities, such as Vancouver, Winnipeg, Toronto and Montreal, in order to plant churches. In addition to his ministry with the Hispanic congregation in Edmonton, Jorge Vallejos became the pastor of a new congregation in Calgary. Here the idea was born to take the Anabaptist vision back to Chile, reconnecting with friends and family in the evangelical churches where he had participated earlier.[13] In order to help pursue this possibility, the Edmonton Hispanic church named Nancy Hostetler to accompany Jorge Vallejos back to

Pastor Jorge Vallejos

Chile; she invited Carol Martin on this journey. They reported a very warm welcome from the brothers and sisters in Chile.[14]

In 1983 Keith and Nancy Hostetler and their family were sent by the Mennonite Broad of Missions to serve in Chile, to be involved in Bible teaching and planting new churches. In 1985 this relationship ended, but by 1989 a group of churches had established the Evangelical Mennonite Church of Chile (*Iglesia Evangélica Menonita de Chile*: IEM), continuing their relationship with Mennonite Chileans in Canada.[15] In 2009 this conference numbered about a dozen pastors and congregations, with approximately 800-900 baptized members. With the migration of members, two churches have been planted in in Argentina and Uruguay. Two of the Chilean churches are made up of the Mapuche people in Araucanía and Mañjuco. Pastoral work includes biblical instruction, vocational instruction, musical instruction and

Worship at the 2007 assembly of the Iglesia Evangélica Menonita de Chile (IEM)

dance. These churches work in places of great need, particularly with drug addicts, many of whom have been in prison or live on the streets, and also have notable programs for helping boys and girls.[16] The pastoral leadership of IEM also recognizes the need for training new leaders through a Mennonite Biblical Institute. The congregations engage in vigorous evangelism both inside and outside national borders, conduct marriage encounters and engage in prison ministries. In 2006 and 2009 Titus Guenther returned to provide short-term Anabaptist teaching and links to the wider Mennonite church family.

In the early 1990s the teaching ministry of Titus Guenther and Karen Loewen Guenther, workers for the Mennonite Board of Missions (MBM) and the Commission on Overseas Mission (COM)[17] left a favorable impression on the Chilean students Carlos Gallardo and his wife Mónica Parada. Carlos and Mónica worked as pastors of the congregation in Concepción called *La Puerta del Rebaño* (The Door of the Sheepfold), which was founded by fine arts professor Carlos Salazar in 1986. Carlos and Mónica also pastor a Baptist congregation in Chiguayante near Concepción.[18] *La Puerta del Rebaño* has been supported by the Witness program of Mennonite Church Canada and its U.S. counterpart, the Mennonite Mission Network, primarily with the offering of Anabaptist courses.[19] John Driver, the instructor for some of these courses, noted that the *Puerta del Rebaño* church offered an exciting understanding of the social gospel, where the church was experienced as "not as a hierarchy, but as a community."[20] Another connecting point for the *Puerta del Rebaño* church is a sister church relationship with the Mountain Community Church of Palmer Lake, Colorado.[21]

In 1985 the Mennonite Christian Center (*Centro Cristiano Menonita*) opened in Santiago, to serve as a meeting place and distribution point for Anabaptist literature. This initiative was strengthened by the presence of the Guenthers and deepened significantly through the teaching ministry of Omar Cortés Gaibur, a Chilean pastor and professor, originally supported by COM/MBM. Omar returned to Chile in 1997 after a time of study and interaction in Canada. During the next decade, Omar's teaching role at the Baptist Seminary in Santiago helped articulate an Anabaptist identity, shaping leaders with a vision for shaping churches as communities and witnesses for peace. This led to collaborative work between the Union of Evangelical Baptist Churches of Chile (UBACH), the Mission Network and Mennonite

Church Canada. Beginning in 2007 UBACH established the Christian Center of Resources for Peace (*Centro Cristiano de Recursos para la paz*: CERCAPAZ), and in 2008, UBACH and Mennonite Church Canada entered into a sister church relationship. In the words of UBACH, these relationships "strengthen our common historical and doctrinal identity in the Anabaptist movement."[22]

Finally, it is worth noting the mission program in Patagonia, Argentina which has collaborated in the planting of a new church under the leadership of Wanda Sieber, Marlene Dorigoni and Waleska Villa in the Chilean province of Valdivia. Chile is an example of a country where Anabaptist intitiatives have developed and grown internally as Chileans have embraced Anabaptist faith and practice. This has led to multiple Anabaptist connections within the region and beyond.

Paraguay

The past 30 years have seen a notable expansion of both Mennonite Brethren and Mennonite (MG) churches into the Spanish-speaking and indigenous Paraguayan communities, as well as into the growing Portuguese-speaking Brazilian immigrant community.

By 1984 there were 27 Spanish-speaking MB churches in Paraguay, with around 1,000 members. In that year the Spanish-speaking "Evangelical Conference of Paraguayan Mennonite Brethren" (*Convención Evangélica de los Hermanos Menonitas de Paraguay*) gained the support

Enlhet children from Betania church, near Yalve Sanga, Paraguay

of the Board of Missions and Services (BOMAS) for an ambitious program of evangelization and church planting. By the year 2000, the
Conference numbered 69 churches with 3,000 members, 27 pastors
(12 full time) and 50 church workers. While at the beginning of the
collaboration, BOMAS covered 90 percent of the financial costs, this
had dropped to 40 percent by 2001, and had disappeared altogether by
2005, when the Paraguayan conference covered all of its own costs.

The emergence of the Evangelical Mennonite churches of Paraguay
(MG) was noted in a previous chapter, as well as the shared participation in the Mennonite Committee for Evangelical and Social Action
in Paraguay (COMAESP). This evangelical initiative, born in the German-speaking colonies, permitted the development of mission work
among the indigenous population and Spanish-speaking Paraguayans.
The first Spanish-speaking Paraguayan pastor was Victoriano Cáceres,
pastor of the Mennonite Church of Itacurubí de la Cordillera.

In 1986 conversations began between pastors Julio César Melgarejo,
Carlos Altenburger, and Secundino Morales with the aim of creating
the Spanish-speaking Paraguayan Evangelical Mennonite Conference
(*Convención Evangélica Menonita Paraguaya*: CONEMPAR).[23] In 1989
great organizational changes took place, for the German-speaking conference mission committee COMAESP saw the urgency of permitting
the formal organization of CONEMPAR, to which the majority of Spanish-speaking churches chose to belong. In this same year, work with
the indigenous churches in the Chaco was handed over to the *Menno
Indianer Mission* (MIM). Now successfully established, CONEMPAR is
led by an executive committee of seven members, an executive secretary, an advisor and the presidents of the five departments where there
are churches. In addition, there are commissions for work with women,
youth, education, mission and finances. After a multi-year process of
integrating more of the Spanish-speaking Chaco churches into the
conference, in 2008 CONEMPAR reported 24 churches and 25 church
plants, with a total of 1,751 members and 2,907 participants.[24]

Some further evangelization efforts should be noted, in order to
give a slightly fuller picture of the evangelistic outreach of Mennonites
in Paraguay in recent decades. Beginning in 1971 a large number
of Brazilian immigrants (an estimated 350,000 or more) settled in
Paraguay, primarily in the eastern part of the country. The presence of
so many "brasiguayos" led to evangelization efforts, in Portuguese, by
Mennonites in these communities. Some churches have been estab-

lished, namely the MB churches in Coronel Toledo (40 members in 2005), Santa Rita (100 members), Ciudad del Este (60 members) and Filadelfia (52 members in 2005).[25] A prison ministry in the Tacumbú jail in Asunción has resulted in the founding of an unusual church: the Liberty Church of Mennonite Brethren of Tacumbú (*Iglesia Libertad de los Hermanos Menonitas de Tacumbú*) with a fluctuating prison membership of between 600 and 200 members in 2005. In addition, a chaplaincy for business people began officially in 1991, and continues to the present. Approximately 2,000 people were involved in this program in 2005.[26] Several Paraguayan Mennonite groups also sponsor and maintain a radio station (OBEDIRA) which broadcasts 24-hour Christian programming. Efforts to spread the Gospel to all of Paraguayan society remain vigorous.

Perú

Piura is a region located on the northeastern coast of Peru, bordered on the north by Ecuador and the region of Tumbes, to the south by the region of Lambayeque, to the east by the region of Cajamarca and to the west by the Pacific Ocean. The coasts of Piura were adversely affected in 1983 by the "el Niño" phenomenon. MCC responded by sending volunteers and economic help to the inhabitants who had lost their homes and crops and who urgently needed medical assistance and food.[27] Subsequent to this, Mennonite Brethren congregations were planted in Sullana, Vichayal, el Indio and Chato Chico. Formal worship began in 1985 and ten years later these churches organized the Mennonite Brethren Church of Peru.[28] The Mennonite Brethren began a missionary work in the city of Trujillo in 1994[29] and in Lima in the year 2000. At the time of this writing the Colombian pastors José Manuel Prada and his wife Esperanza Rodríguez are leading a congregation in the city of Lima.[30]

Another work began in Cuzco, Perú toward the end of the 1970s by the Eastern Mennonite Board of Missions of Lancaster, Pennsylvania.[31] Work began in a small town called Lucre, where the first public baptism took place in 1990. The baptism was interrupted by the inhabitants of the place, who rained stones on the celebrants.[32] The Gospel was preached and churches established also in San Jerónimo de Angostura, Huacarpay and in the community of San Francisco. In 1999 the Evangelical Mennonite Church of Peru (*Iglesia Evangélica Menonita del Perú*) was founded.[33] In 2008, the Peruvian church numbered approximately 1500 members in around 20 congregations.[34]

Bolivia

In the last two decades, Bolivia has become the preferred Latin American destination for German-speaking conservative Mennonites. From 1980 to 2007 a total of 53 new colonies have been established in the provinces of Pando, Beni and Santa Cruz. These new colonies originated mostly from the internal division of other Mennonite colonies in Bolivia itself, but settlers have also come from Belize, Paraguay, Mexico, Argentina and Canada. In 2007 there were 30,618 members (adults and children) in these new colonies.[35]

During these decades the two Spanish-speaking conferences have also continued to grow and to develop deeper Anabaptist commitments, demonstrating in the Bolivian context that Anabaptist Mennonites are not a cultural community, but rather a church community with a distinct theological identity.

Cuba

As noted above, the Brethren in Christ began their work in Cuba in the 1950s. In spite of very difficult years after the departure of the missionaries, the BIC churches were officially recognized by the government and have managed to grow and expand in the intervening

Félix Rafael Curbelo, long-time BIC leader in Cuba, shortly before his death, December 13, 2009

years. In 2008 there were a reported 154 BIC congregations with around 5000 members in two provinces.[36]

In 2008 a new Mennonite mission work began in Cuba when pastor Alexander Reyna Tamayo, his wife Aisha Pérez Ramos and their children began a new organization known as the Mennonite Church of Cuba (*Iglesia Menonita de Cuba*). Alexander Reyna and his family had earlier worked as pastors in the Evangelical Missionary Church (*Iglesia Evangélica Misionera*).[37] In 2004 Alexander got to know Janet Plenert and Jack Suderman of Mennonite Church Canada, when they offered courses on the Anabaptist tradition at the Free Evangelical Church in Havana and the Orthodox Church of God in Holguín. With the agreement of the Evangelical Missionary Church, Alexander Reyna made contact with Mennonite Church Canada and created this new organization. It still is not officially recognized by the Cuban government, and continues its work in small home cells. It has a membership of approximately 120 persons in the provinces of Santiago de Cuba, Holguín, Gramma, Villa Clara and Cienfuegos.[38]

Brazil

The Portuguese-speaking Mennonite churches of Brazil have experienced significant growth within Brazil and have also extended their reach to Africa, with mission efforts of their own. In 1982 the Mennonite Center of Theology (CEMTE) was formed to carry out the leadership training program of the AEM (*Associação Evangélica Menonita*). Until its closing in 2005, CEMTE instructed leaders through distance-learning techniques with extension centers for meeting together. By 1986, the AEM had over 1,000 members in 25 congregations in five states of Brazil. The basic course of CEMTE had 173 students in 1987, and more advanced courses were developed over time.

In 1998, the AEM began a program of international outreach, sending a family to Portuguese-speaking Mozambique. The mission, called *Junta Menonita de Missões Menonitas* (JMMI), is coordinated by a Board which acts as a liaison between the Brazilian churches and the missions abroad. A number of Brazilian workers have served the Mennonite churches in Mozambique and Albania. The AEM also promotes a national mission program called "Pronam" to plant churches in Brazil. In 2006, Brazil was home to 8,756 Mennonites in 92 congregations: AIMB had 881 members in 6 congregations, COBIM had 5,000 members in 40 congregations, AEM had 2,500 members in 40 congregations and the Holdeman Mennonites had 375 members in 6 congregations.

Adriane Pereira Nascimento, Brazilian missionary in Mozambique, with a children's choir

As this brief overview of new and emerging work demonstrates, the Anabaptist presence in Latin America continues to grow, most often in organic ways, as established communities and mission boards respond to opportunities. The last two decades have seen the establishment of communities in Ecuador, Venezuela and Chile, countries where there had been no previous Mennonite or BIC presence. Notable growth has taken place in Paraguay with the emergence of Spanish-speaking Mennonite churches and organizations, and in Peru with the opening of new mission fields among Spanish-speakers and Quechua communities. The settlement of conservative German-speaking Mennonite communities in Bolivia has significantly increased the Mennonite presence in that country, and the emergence of new Mennonite ecclesial organizations in Cuba is an example of missionary growth in countries that already had an Anabaptist presence. Finally, the active international mission efforts of the AEM churches of Brazil are witness to the completion of the missionary circle: from churches founded by mission efforts now come indigenous national and international mission efforts.

Responses to Political Reality: Central America and Paraguay

The radicalization of the Sandinista revolution after the 1979 triumph over the Somoza military regime initiated a new pastoral and theological reality for Mennonites in Nicaragua. The departure from Nicaragua of missionaries from the Rosedale Mennonite Mission was the result of a mistake on the part of the Sandinista leadership. It revived memories of the Cuban revolution in 1960s, when North American missionaries left the island in the midst of the radicalization of the Cuban revolution. This led Mennonites to deep reflection on the Latin American theology of liberation.

An important event took place during the CAMCA (Central American Anabaptist Mennonite Consultation) meetings in Nicaragua in 1981. The focus of this meeting was a paper by Mennonite theologian Laverne Rutschman titled "An Anabaptist Analysis of the Theology of Liberation." Rutschman attempted to uncover the interconnections between the situation of poor and marginalized people in Latin America and the social, pastoral and theological options presented by the sixteenth-century Anabaptists. At the same time, the attempt was made to develop a position that took its departure from Anabaptist nonviolence. It was in this context that the Mennonite pastor José Matamoros wrote

> Peace is built on the foundation of justice. We cannot expect to have peace where there is injustice. For this reason I affirm that we should not only repudiate violence, but even more, we should repudiate the injustice that precedes violence. ... There are examples of activists for nonviolence, such as Gandhi, Martin Luther King Jr. and Dom Helder Camara, who have sown the seeds of a great movement for peace which also has been supported by people of all creeds.[39]

Although the Nicaraguan Mennonite and BIC churches managed to gain exemption from military service only for pastors and theological students, the Anabaptist-descended churches did manage to give a faithful peace testimony of their active and nonviolent faith in the midst of the Sandinista revolution, which lasted until 1989.

The Mennonite Central Committee was also visibly present in Nicaragua, working along with CEPAD in the reconstruction of the country. MCC also worked with the Ministry of Agrarian Reform in building irrigation systems, helping refugees displaced by the war, and in community development projects in rural communities, working in conjunction with the Brethren in Christ, the Evangelical Mennonite Conference, and the Fraternity of Evangelical Mennonite Churches.[40]

A Latin American Anabaptist meeting took place in Guatemala in June, 1981 under the theme "Nonresistance. How to live in a socialist society."[41] The meeting brought into focus the need to interpret the relationship between church and state from an Anabaptist perspective in the context of a region brought into turmoil by the triumph of the Sandinista revolution in Nicaragua, military repression in Honduras, El Salvador and Guatemala, and the military resistance of these governments against Salvadoran and Guatemalan guerilla movements. A central question was: How can one accept the political and economic changes brought to the area by the socialist revolutions, without at the same time falling into an unconditional support for one social system or the other?

It was also in this same year, in light of the concrete situation in
El Salvador and Guatemala, that the Mennonite church of Colombia,
remembering the martyrdom of Monseñor Romero,[42] made the following statement:

> The people of El Salvador and Guatemala need our solidarity
> urgently, (they need) our voices, denouncing the constant
> violation of their rights to life, to self-determination, and
> their right to determine their own futures. Every day the
> army, the police forces and paramilitary forces murder farm-
> ers, workers, students, young people, catechists, reporters,
> professors, indigenous people and priests; in Guatemala,
> two Protestant pastors have been murdered. Nevertheless,
> the United States continues to send military advisors and
> weapons... Liberation is not being permitted.[43]

A later meeting of Latin American Mennonite delegates in Antigua,
Guatemala in May 1984, was held under on the theme "The church
witnesses to Central America with Hope." This meeting heard the cry
of Guatemalan pastors and Mennonite leaders who gave witness to
the injustices suffered by the Kekchi and other indigenous people of
Guatemala in the face of the relentless attacks and massacres of the
Guatemalan military forces, and the indifference of the majority of
Protestant churches.[44] Gerald Schlabach called clearly for Mennonites
to be a prophetic community:

> Do not the children who are attacked in Nicaragua, the
> children terrorized in El Salvador, the hungry indigenous
> children of Guatemala deserve the right to reach an age
> when they can decide whether or not they are going to serve
> God? ... God needs to raise up persons who will carry out
> the prophetic ministry that the church is not fulfilling.[45]

In his address, Guatemalan pastor Gilberto Flores Campos force-
fully called Mennonite churches to bring peace and justice together,
to evaluate the existing situation, to develop a strong national leadership and to elaborate an Anabaptist pastoral approach to Central
America.[46] The result of these cries, protests and prophetic messages
were ecclesial initiatives for making an Anabaptist testimony present

in Central America, particularly by means of theological reflection and pastoral and educational institutions such as SEMILLA (Anabaptist Latin American Seminary: *Seminario Anabautista Latinoamericano*), as well as the practical work of MCC.

There was more than one Mennonite position in the face of the revolution and the uprising of Central American people in the 1980s, but critical spaces were opened in which to debate issues from an Anabaptist perspective of nonresistance in an extremely difficult social and political situation.

An important Mennonite contribution in the first half of the decade occurred when 22,000 Salvadoran refugees settled in camps in Mesa Grande and Colomoncagua, near the Honduran border with El Salvador. Many Salvadoran refugees suffered violence at the hands of their country's army. The Salvadoran Flora Fídaz, 21 years of age, tells how her mother and two sisters were first raped and then murdered by Salvadoran troops. Later her seven nephews (aged three months to six years) were strangled by these same soldiers. Pax Christi documented the murder of 2,000 Salvadoran refugees in the first half of 1980 alone.[47] It was in this context that the Honduran Evangelical Mennonite Church along with MCC, the United Nations High Commission for Refugees, Doctors Without Borders, Caritas, Catholic Relief Services and the Evangelical Committee for Development and National Emergencies (CEDEN) took up a pastoral position in defense of the refugees. Several leaders of these organizations risked their lives many times in order to do this work.[48]

Arnaldo Mejía (far right), one of the workers from the Honduran Mennonite Church who worked with Mesa Grande families, improving their housing

Mennonite church members in Honduras also found themselves in tension with Nicaraguan counter-revolutionary forces who came to the Honduran border with Nicaragua. The Honduran Mennonite Church, along with the Committee for Human Rights of Honduras (*Comité de Derechos Humanos de Honduras*: CODEH) denounced the occupation by counter-revolutionary forces of the town of Moriah, on the border with Nicaragua, where a Mennonite church was occupied and local homes were destroyed; in addition, these forces kidnapped the pastor and four members of the church.[49] In 1982 the Honduran government decreed obligatory military service. The Mennonite Church, along with Quaker leaders, communicated its nonresistant position to the Honduran congress and expressed its readiness to provide alternative service in hospitals, emergency help, disaster aid. Although churches gave initial leadership, civil society sought change as well, and in 1994 a constitutional amendment established voluntary military service in peace time.

The political situation in Paraguay presented a radically different situation to the Mennonite churches of that country. In 1979, when Central American countries were plunged into revolutionary situations, Paraguay was still ruled by Alfredo Stroessner who had seized power in a coup in 1954. Stroessner's rule had not posed problems for the German-speaking Mennonite colonists, who had enjoyed a positive relationship with the dictator. When Stroessner was overthrown in a coup in 1989, the country moved into an uncertain time of "democratization." Mennonites responded by participating actively in the shaping of a new constitution for the nation (adopted in 1992). The four points they lobbied for were included in that constitution: separation of church and state, preservation of marriage and the family, religious freedom, and conscientious objection to military service.[50] This experience opened the door to direct political participation; the election of Cornelius Sawatsky as governor of the province of Boquerón and of Heinz Ratzlaff as federal deputy soon followed.[51]

While opinion among the Mennonites of Paraguay is still divided between those who wish Mennonites to remain "the quiet in the land"

Nicanor and Gloria Duarte at the MWC assembly, 2009

and those who favor a principled participation in the political process, the reality is that a significant Mennonite participation in Paraguayan political life has continued and even grown. When Nicanor Duarte was elected president in 2003, on an anti-corruption platform, he appointed several Mennonites to key cabinet posts.[52] The dangers of political participation for Mennonites, as well as the good that could be done, continue to be debated. One historian has written of this recent political involvement, "It is too early to say how history will assess the contribution made by Mennonites."[53]

The stories told here provide just two glimpses of the widely-varied experiences of Anabaptist-related churches, as they give testimony to their Anabaptist faith in the midst of radically-changed political landscape of Latin America in the three decades from 1979 to 2009.

Spiritual Renewal

Renewal by the Spirit has been experienced in many different Mennonite churches in Latin America. In the 1970s pentecostal and charismatic movements swept through Central America, as noted in previous chapters; in the 1980s these spiritual currents came to the Mennonite churches of Uruguay with the missionaries Anita and James Martin, who opened a clinic where they ministered the Holy Spirit and inward healing. This theological and pastoral current was implemented by followers of the Martins, such as the pastors Hugo and Leticia Moreira and pastor Beatríz Barrios. Pastor Nelson Colina, a union worker who lived in exile in Argentina during the Uruguayan military dictatorship and who had pastored at Bethel Mennonite church in Montevideo, also experienced renewal in the Spirit. It was his view that a person who spoke in tongues was not necessarily filled with the Holy Spirit, for even demons are able to speak in tongues. It was his view that a person should be liberated, forgiven and healed inwardly of all evil influences. This inner healing would be affirmed by the fruits of the Holy Spirit, which are peace, humility, love and temperance (Galatians 5:22-23 and Efesians 5:9).[54]

The spiritual renewal movement was strengthened by pentecostal preachers, whose influence permeated Mennonite churches. A clear example of this was the preaching of Puerto Rican evangelist Yiye Avila in Paraguay in 1983. Pastor Andrés Verón testified that by participating in Avila's campaign he was permitted to understand that "the experience of the Holy Spirit is not simply a theory." He also participated the following year in the campaign of the Argentine evangelist Carlos Annacondia[55] and declared "sometimes we have lost the warmth of the Spirit, because nothing happens: there are no tongues, no visions. But then a moment of maturity arrives and the Holy Spirit begins to speak in another way.[56] Pastor Máximo Ramón Abadía, who was president of the Mennonite Brethren of Paraguay at the end of the 1990s, collaborated closely with the evangelistic campaign that Carlos Annacondia carried out in Paraguay. The theme of "casting out of demons" was entirely new but in his view, the participation of Anabaptist churches in these pentecostal experiences allowed the Anabaptist churches of Paraguay to be transformed and to grow numerically, as well as leading to unity with Pentecostal, Baptist and other churches.[57]

Mennonite Church leaders in Colombia have also recognized the importance and the impact of the charismatic movement for their churches. Héctor Valencia affirmed that

> in the past years the Mennonite church has been strongly impacted by charismatic groups. Virtually all of our churches have something of the charismatic movement, some in a more extreme form than others, some more pentecostal than others. The influence came through congresses in which our pastors participated, of which meetings and movements of healing were particularly influential. I don't know if this has been positive or negative. The pentecostals feel impelled to preach, to evangelize and share the word with others. But at times I see that this remains at the level of external rituals. In some of our churches there is more of a tendency to pentecostal ritual than there is to express the very essence of the Gospel. [58]

Gustavo Angulo, another Colombian leader at this time, also affirmed that some churches had had a major pentecostal influence and charismatic renewal, but others had renewed their worship style while still preserving a certain order and tradition. It was his view that the church could not at the same time reject charismatic renewal and also accept new liturgical and worship forms.[59]

Some problems and divisions have occurred in Mennonite churches because of charismatic and pentecostal tendencies. A case in point is that of the pentecostal Colombian pastor Fabio Gómez, who took Jaime Caro's place as pastor of La Mesa church after 1995. Fabio Gómez emphasized the doctrine of the Holy Spirit and did not wish to follow the traditional Anabaptist orientation of the church. His leadership proceeded to divide the congregation in half, and Fabio Gómez left to form a separate church, which in turn also divided. He later had to leave town, for people now knew him and no longer wished to listen to him.[60] César Moya, former executive secretary of IMCOL, has noted that members in the Mennonite church come from very diverse church backgrounds. Along with charismatic and pentecostal influences can also be found influences from conservative Catholicism, liberationist Catholicism or conservative Protestant currents. At least half of the members of the Mennonite church in Colombia come from other churches, with the other half coming initially because of the influence of friends or family members.[61]

In the 1990s the Puerto Rican Mennonite Conference (*Conferencia de Iglesias Evangelicas Menonitas de Puerto Rico*: CIEMPR) was also shaken by continual internal divisions. One of the fundamental causes of these divisions, in addition to personality conflicts, was the pentecostal character of some churches who had come under the influence of preachers such as Jorge Raschke and Yiji Ávila. A further divisive element was lack of agreement on the Puerto Rican identity of the Conference. Although some wanted the Conference to be independent, the Assembly of 1994 decided to begin the process of joining the Conference of Mennonite Churches of the United States. Some had wished to continue as members of the Evangelical Council of Puerto Rico (*Concilio Evangélico de Puerto Rico*), which was more ecumenical, open to dialogue with the Catholic church, and also took a critical posture in questions of the role of the state, such as opposing the presence of U.S. Marines on Víequez island. The pentecostally-influenced Mennonite churches in Arecibo and El Buen Pastor church in Hatillo decided to separate from CIEMPR and formed the Evangelical Mennonite Mission of the Caribbean, Inc. (*Misión Evangélica Menonita del Caribe, Inc.*).

The first Anabaptist communities in Europe in the sixteenth century had a theology, biblical interpretation and pastoral practice shaped by a central understanding of the working of the Holy Spirit.[62] In the view of this writer, one of the fundamental tasks facing Mennonite churches in Latin America today will be the recognition of this theological inheritance based in the Holy Spirit, without this emphasis leading to the ignoring of other elements central to Anabaptist identity, such as a critical stance vis-a-vis the state, a theology and practice favoring the poor, a biblical hermeneutic of nonresistance, and toleration of various ways of understanding the profound mystery of God's work in the world.

Organizational difficulties for Mennonites in Latin America

One of the challenges facing Anabaptist-descended churches in Latin America is the creation of organizational structures that foster unity and solidarity among all churches. When national churches began to grow, the general tendency was to organize local churches by region, such as occurred with the Mennonite Brethren in Colombia and the Evangelical Mennonite Church in Costa Rica. Urban regions automatically have greater access to economic resources than do rural areas, and the churches located in these respective areas are correspondingly wealthy or poor. In some cases these disparities have led to tension and conflict between regional groups. In Colombia, the regional church groups had their own leadership structures, and this led to regional churches having little sense of responsibility for the churches outside their region. A suggested structural solution has been the establishment of a federation that would encourage interrelation between the regions.[63]

In other places, such as in the Conference of Evangelical Mennonite Churches of Costa Rica, the process has worked in reverse, from relative centralization toward fragmentation. In this relatively small conference, some pastors have wished to become more independent of the convention. They not only expressed their desire to form their own organizations, but also have gone behind the backs of their sister churches and begun to do so. This has weakened the Mennonite Conference, particularly when these leaders set out to take control of local church properties in the name of their own organizations. Organizational structures can either encourage or obstruct the unity of the church, and this requires care and discernment in the creation or modification of these structures.

It is also a fact that very often Mennonite organizations, in their zeal to form their own congregations or programs, ignore other Mennonite organizations that already exist in their region or country. In part, this tendency is rooted in the fragmented nature of Mennonite churches in North America. In this writer's view, it would be more fruitful for Anabaptist-descended Latin American churches to focus on structures that unify, that encourage mutual love, that foster support and affection between rural and urban churches and between those who have unequal economic means. It would be most helpful if all Anabaptist-descended associations and federations would see themselves as parts of a large family, where the Anabaptist vision is shared, and where brothers and sisters can place their talents and gifts at the service of others.

Leadership training and education

There have been significant efforts at pastoral and leadership training among the Anabaptist-descended churches of Latin America in the past three decades which have strengthened the local leadership of, the Latin American churches. At the seminary and university level, developments in Paraguay are groundbreaking. Both CEMTA (MG) and IBA (MB) joined the Evangelical University of Paraguay (*Universidad Evangélica del Paraguay*) in 1994, and received accreditation by the Paraguayan government to provide theological training at the university level. Their practical pastoral and biblical seminary programs continue as well, to the benefit of the churches. The churches of Central America have been served by the SEMILLA program, which began in 1984. While the Paraguayan institutions are primarily residence programs, SEMILLA concentrates on teaching by extension, and takes courses to students. SEMILLA's offices are based in Guatemala City, but its program focuses on combining distance education (independent study) with short travelling seminars offered in the home countries of the students.

In Colombia, pastoral training and education has been carried forward by the IMCOL churches through the Biblical Mennonite Seminary

John Driver, popular SEMILLA professor, in 2007

of Colombia (*Seminario Bíblico Menonita de Colombia*: SBMC) and by the Mennonite Brethren through the Center for Ministerial Development (*Centro de Desarrollo Ministerial*: CDM). And, in Brazil the AIMB, COBIM, AEM and other groups have cooperated to form the Fidelis University, a fully accredited educational institution. Fidelis University opened in 2005 with a bachelors program in theology and post-graduate studies in pastoral ministries. Classes at Fidelis are offered at night in the Colégio Erasto Gaertner in Boqueirão, Curitiba. The Colombian and Brazilian programs follow a more centralized model.

The institutions mentioned above are vastly outnumbered by the Biblical institutes, which almost all educate by extension. Many conferences sponsor their own Biblical institutes, with varying levels of academic rigor. A unique model is the congregationally-based biblical education program that has been operating in Argentina since the 1970s. The goal of the United Program of Biblical Education (*Programa Unido de Educación Bíblica*: PUEB) is to educate leaders for the church, but also to raise the level of biblical literacy for lay persons, so that they are enabled to minister within their local congregations. In 2008 there were 565 students enrolled in PUEB programs for the whole of Argentina.

The training of leaders at all levels remains a high priority for the Anabaptist-descended churches of Latin America, and efforts to further theological education are ongoing. In 2007, 45 Latin American educators and theologians met for a consultation at SEMILLA in Guatemala, on how better to share resources and collaborate together, marking an important way forward for the Latin American churches.[64]

Participants, Theological Consultation, 2007

Interpersonal relationships and leadership

One of the aspects still needing attention in Latin American Mennonite churches is the question of personal relationships. When difficulties arise among church leaders the tendency is for a division to occur, such as happened in the Bethel Mennonite Brethren church in Colombia. This problem is exacerbated by the desire for leadership of a church. There are pastors who depend on the church for their salaries and, as time goes by, they dedicate themselves to full-time pastoral work – although full-time, paid pastors remain the exception in Latin American Mennonite churches. Sometimes churches consider concluding the employment of their full-time pastor; but pastors who have become accustomed to a pastoral salary need the economic support of the community. This situation calls for a serious study of pastoral models, as well as the matter of pastoral pensions and their family situations when they reach the age of retirement.[65] Churches also have to plan their work in such a way that they continue to encourage the participation of the youth and the renewal of church leadership.

It has not been easy to prepare the next generation of leaders for Mennonite churches in Latin America. Leaders from rural areas have gone to the cities to study and never returned. Others have received scholarships to study in the United States or Canada and then have been recruited to pastor Hispanic churches in those countries. Those who have formal education have also taken advantage of the opportunities education provides, and have migrated to the cities or to the North. This has created a "brain drain" where Mennonite educational efforts have often not created the new local leadership sought – although Mennonites in other regions or countries have received the benefits. This has been the case in all Latin American countries where there is a Mennonite presence.

This situation raises several important questions: How should Mennonite and BIC church in Latin America prepare leaders so that they serve the local communities that need them? How will these churches address the issue of migration, both into urban areas and toward the United States and Canada? How can they maintain a balance between the local work of ministry and missionary work in other countries?

The leadership of women

Women played important leadership roles in the emergence of sixteenth-century Anabaptism in Europe. There were pastors, prophets, teachers and numerous martyrs who, along with their husbands and families gave witness to their faith in Jesus Christ under the most adverse conditions.[66] The great persecution, which resulted in ca. 3,000 Anabaptist martyrs, led the Anabaptists to withdraw from society. Many families fled to Moravia and the Low Countries and established communities of mutual aid that shared goods, distancing themselves from society. This withdrawal later led to migrations toward Prussia, then Russia and later to the United States and Canada. These later communities, however, organized themselves around a patriarchal leadership.

The first North American mission societies usually sent couples and their families to Latin America to do pastoral work, but as has already been seen, female missionaries and converts played an important role in the organization of women's groups, in evangelization, the organization of Sunday schools and in economic initiatives for purchasing land and churches. The first missionaries commonly emphasized I Corinthians 11:1-16 as a key text, describing how women were to remain under the authority of men and to remain silent in the congregation. Recognized pastors were exclusively men. Nevertheless, as the struggle for the equal rights of women, workers and farm laborers grew, and laws were passed in Latin America allowing increased participation of women in politics, social and economic life and union movements, this also had an impact within Mennonite churches themselves.

The call within Mennonite churches to consider women as leaders began in the 1980s. One of the first discussions of this issue took place at the CAMCA meetings in 1984 in Honduras which met to focus on "The role of Christian women in the churches of Central America."[67] This was followed up the next year, when the CAMCA meetings in Costa Rica had as its theme "The ministry of women." In her reflection, Alba Elena Castillo of Guatemala began with words taken from the universal declaration of human rights (1948) which states "all men are born free and equal in dignity and rights. They are endowed with reason and conscience and should work with one another in a spirit of fraternity." She reminded those present that when the declaration used the word "men" it was referring to all persons, masculine or feminine. Alba Elena Castillo concluded citing John 8:36: "Therefore, if the Son sets you free, you will be free indeed."[68] The Guatemalan pastor Leonor Méndez surveyed the Bible from a feminine perspective, concluding that in spite of the patriarchal culture of the Old Testament, nevertheless there were women judges and prophets as well as others who participated in the social and political life of Israel, not to mention the many positive feminine images reflecting God's activity in the world.[69] A third reflection focused on Jesus' treatment of women, particularly the central role played by the New Kingdom in which God liberates us from oppression because we are members of his family. Jesus changed the rules of his day and provided a new perspective on the relationship of men and women.[70]

Women are developing leadership roles in Latin American churches, above all in the indigenous and Spanish-speaking churches. In the German-origin immigrant Mennonite communities from Canada or the United States, which have profoundly patriarchal structures, such leadership has not been possible. To take only one case in point out of many possible examples, in Puerto Rico women have taken up important pastoral roles, in the face of the crisis experienced by the Conference of Mennonite churches in the 1980s, as deaconesses and pastors. The opening to women leaders can also be seen in the Colombian Mennonite church, whose General Assembly received a request for the ordination of a woman to the pastorate in 1988. The following year the executive committee signed a resolution affirming the right of women to be ordained to the ministry. In Costa Rica, María Rodríguez became the first national female pastor towards the end of the 1980s. Although the statutes of the church had no regulations concerning women assuming the pastorate, her long commitment to her church in Christian education and her pastoral contributions in the Mennonite churches of the province of Heredia led to the community requesting her pastoral services. In spite of her advanced age, Doña María has dedicated many years of her life to pastoral ministry, with great success.

Today we find that the pastoral ministry of women is recognized and put into practice in virtually all the Latin American countries where there are Mennonite and BIC churches, although in some cases this ministry is not recognized by ordination, and practices vary by conference. The ministry of women has been strengthened by the theological education of women in universities and in the theological educational centers such as the Mennonite Biblical Seminary in Bogotá and SEMILLA in Central America.

For Latin American women leaders who attended the MWC assembly in Bulawayo in 2003, the encounter with African women theologians presented a great challenge. From this experience grew the "Movement of Latin American (women) theologians" (*Movimiento*

Alix Lozano (Colombia) and Rebecca
Osiro (Kenya) at the MWC assembly
in Paraguay, 2009

de teólogas latinoamericanas) which, with the support of the Global Gifts project of MWC and the help of Mennonite regional associations, has held meetings in Venezuela (2004), Mexico (2005), Costa Rica (2006), Guatemala (2007) and Uruguay (2007).[71] When the assembly was held in Asunción, Paraguay (2009), 120 Mennonite women from all Latin America met to reflect on the theme "The liberating message of Jesus for women today." Their declaration, read at one of the main worship services of the assembly, made clear their commitment to follow Jesus and to build his Kingdom. They committed themselves to promoting

> a liberating system that breaks the molds and stereotypes of a patriarchal system that excludes women, toward an integral movement led by the Holy Spirit; to walk together in the strengthening of an Anabaptist education and re-reading of the Bible through the eyes of women; to consolidate this movement encouraging the sharing of gifts, exchanging our stories, and participating in theological education and regional meetings.

The declaration concluded by quoting the words of Peter 1:3: "Blessed be God the Father of our Lord Jesus Christ, who according to his great

African and Latin American women
sing on the bus on the way to the
MWC assembly in Asunción

mercy has led us to rebirth for a living hope, for an incorruptible inheritance, pure and undefiled, reserved in heaven for you. Amen."[72]

If this historical trend continues, the increasing leadership of women in Mennonite and Brethren in Christ churches of Latin America will undoubtedly strengthen the witness of Anabaptist-related churches in the region.

Toward a peace theology

The 1970s and 1980s were years of extreme political violence in Latin America, with a hidden "dirty war" taking place in southern cone countries (Argentina, Chile, Uruguay) and open and covert warfare endemic in Central America. The situation has called for a response from Anabaptist-descended churches.

The Mennonite church in Colombia, a country in the midst of social upheaval, with its history of civil war and a present reality shaken by drug traffic, guerillas, the Army and paramilitary groups, has become a pioneer in Mennonite efforts to develop a peace theology. Peter Stucky, one of the best prepared pastors in Mennonite pacifist traditions, said in 1996:

> Our hope is the Kingdom of God. The Kingdom is a gift. It is our hope not only for Colombia, but for the whole world. When we are based in this vision, we live in the here and now. Certainly the here and now anticipates the future. The Kingdom of God has a communitarian connotation. The Kingdom of God cannot be grasped with rituals or practices. The Kingdom of God is a way of living projected towards society; it is an ethic for life, where justice and peace live together.[73]

The *Justapaz* program was founded by the Mennonites in Colombia in 1990.[74] The Mennonite lawyer, Ricardo Esquivia, was director for many years.[75] Prior to founding *Justapaz*, as a result of his commitment to peace, Ricardo left his legal work and the part-time work he and his wife were doing with

Ricardo Esquivia

the Mennonite church, and together with their children, moved to a small town on the Atlantic coast called San Jacinto. They believed that a commitment to peace should be more than theoretical. The problem was that drug traffic had begun in force. Esquivia began nonviolence work with neighbors and local political organizations. This caused difficulties with the army; later the paramilitaries came and killed some of their neighbors. The Esquivia family received death threats, at a time when after the death threat, the paramilitaries would arrive at dawn. For this reason, the Esquivia family left that same day, at 4 AM, moving first to Cartagena and later to Bogotá.

In the face of the reality of violence in the country, the Mennonite church saw the need of working for peace: to open a space for education concerning nonviolence, to teach conciliation and human rights by means of work carried out by the church itself. In this way the church hoped to carry out its mission of carrying forward the values of the Kingdom of God. As the church set out to do this in concrete situations, it began learning how to do it. The church grew stronger as it worked. *Justapaz* reached out from the Mennonite church to the member churches of CEDECOL and from there, to Colombian society as a whole. *Justapaz* became a part of the "Assembly of Civil Society" which coordinated initiatives nationally. In 1999, Ricardo Esquivia was executive secretary of that assembly. The assembly was attempting to create a bridge with the government in an organization called National Peace Council (*Consejo Nacional de Paz*).

Establishing *Justapaz* was difficult, even in the Mennonite churches, for many thought that Mennonites should not be involved in such matters. *Justapaz* came to be only because of the support of a small majority of members in the general assembly of Mennonite churches. Nevertheless, with the passing of time *Justapaz* gained more and more acceptance within the churches. By 1999 it was thought that at least 80 percent of Mennonites were supporters of the initiative. Through *Justapaz*, Mennonite leaders came to participate in the National Peace Council, in the municipal councils of peace, in the municipal councils of human rights, and in the Councils of Displaced Persons (*Consejos de Desplazamiento*). In Cundinamarca there were 116 municipalities open to its work, and on the north coast, in Montes de María, *Justapaz* worked in 8 municipalities. This work for peace was carried out by means of centers of reconciliation, where the attempt was made to bring people together through reconciliation, without recourse to violence. Reconciliation centers were established in La Mesa, on the Atlantic coast and in the city of Cali.

Something similar happened in CEDECOL. In the beginning there was a suspicion that these peace initiatives were Communist-inspired. But by developing the theme of Christian liberty, it was possible to begin teaching conscientious objection. A Seminary for the education of Peacemakers was formed and opened to the public; at one point 180 young people were registered. At first the army gave room to this initiative. When the first 15 young people were trained, there was no problem, but when the numbers grew, the military began legal action and orders were received to shut down the church seminary. An international campaign managed to prevent the closing of the seminary, and later the Constitutional Court upheld the legality of this peace initiative. For these reasons, the army spread the rumor that Ricardo Esquivia had killed a Catholic priest, a falsehood that was published in the national newspapers. The situation became most difficult for the Esquivia family, for they had to re-locate continually and had their lives uprooted. In 1998, Ricardo received yet another death threat.[76]

> One of the things that I have learned from the conflictive Colombian situation is that it is a demonstration of what Latin America is going to be, and some people do not see this. Here in Colombia we have all the conflicts of the 21st century: drug traffic, arms traffic, poverty, we have all the aspects of liberalism and corruption. We hope to create an Anabaptist World Network of Justice and Peace, a request made to Mennonite World Conference, because it is important to work for peace now in a system that is in decay. It is necessary to offer a voice of hope to the world. That is why we also worked in Central America with this peace initiative.
> **Ricardo Esquivia**

In June, 2007 the offices of *Justapaz* were broken into. Two computers were removed which contained information on persons and churches active in the struggle for peace and dignity, as well as information on persons in Protestant churches who have been victims and witnesses of human rights violations. In spite of such a difficult situation, in which persons risk their very lives,[77] *Justapaz* has not abandoned its efforts to promote nonviolence and the constructive resolution of conflicts, and it continues to offer education for peace. *Justapaz* continues collecting documentation which allows for the certification of human rights violations suffered by members of Protestant churches. This activity is carried out by the Mennonite Church in partnership with other Christian churches and human rights and other organizations which share these goals.

Work for peace has been carried forward by Anabaptist-related churches throughout the region, not always as dramatically as in Colombia, but with important results nonetheless. The response of Mennonite and BIC churches peace churches in the revolutionary atmosphere of Central America has already been mentioned, as has the educational work of CERCAPAZ in Chile. In Central America an important educational initiative began with the establishment in 1997 of REDPAZ, the "Regional Network of Justice and Peace" (*Red Regional de Justicia y Paz*). REDPAZ, supported by MCC and other international organizations, is working to establish a lasting and sustainable peace by helping transform human relationships. As of 2009, it had graduated 120 Central American students with a diploma in "Peace Culture and Conflict Transformation." In addition, REDPAZ offers courses and workshops in conflict mediation and resolution for the home, school and church.[78]

The testimony of those who continue to work for peace in conflictive situations, at times at great personal risk, reminds us of Jesus' words: Blessed are the peacemakers, for they shall be called children of God. (Matthew 5:9).

Latin American Anabaptist Organizations and Mennonite World Conference

The relationship between Latin American missions and Mennonite churches moved forward in 1968 when the first Latin American Mennonite Congress was held in Bogotá, Colombia. The Congress met under the theme "For a Strong and Vigorous Mennonite Church." The aims of the meeting were outlined as follows:

• to provide an occasion for representatives of Mennonite churches to get to know each other, and become aware of the work that is being carried out.

• to consider the needs and problems of the church and to see what projects can be worked at mutually, such as literature, publications, etc., avoiding duplication of efforts, personnel and economic resources.

• to receive inspiration and technical help for a ministry to extend and strengthen future work in Latin America.[79]

Since this first meeting a series of congresses have been held, which included the Fourth Latin American Mennonite Congress held in 1978 in San Antonio, Texas under the theme "Anabaptist Christian Education."[80] Although a commission was named here to organize the next gathering, the recommendation to continue meeting regionally won the day. The Central American Anabaptist Mennonite Consultation (CAMCA) was organized already in 1974, and continued meeting every year thereafter.[81]

The Mennonite churches of the Southern Cone did not begin meeting until 1981, when representatives met and discussed the theme "The position of nonviolence and the church's work of rec-

Delegates to the first CAMCA gathering, 1974

onciliation" based on presentations by John Driver.[82] The 13th Anabaptist congress of Southern Cone churches was held in Uruguay in 2007. It considered the topics of "The role of women in the church" (John Driver)[83] and "The family of God" (Dionisio Byler).[84]

A consultation of Latin American Mennonites was not held again until 1986 when "The Mission of the Church" was considered in the city of Antigua, Guatemala.[85] This gathering aimed to "affirm the church in its mission in the face of the challenges of society and the modern world."[86] Since then six more Latin American consultations have been held, the last in Mexico in 2002 which considered the topic of "Anabaptist leadership in Latin America."[87]

The last region to organize itself has been the Andean region, which includes Colombia, Venezuela, Ecuador and Peru. Following a smaller gathering in 2002 in Ecuador, the second Andean Anabaptist Congress was held September 2004 on Isla Margarita, Venezuela, with 85 participants from Venezuela, Colombia and Ecuador, and fraternal visitors from Bolivia, Canada and the U.S. Delegates from Peru unfortunately were unable to obtain visas. The theme was "Restoring in love from a holistic Gospel." Women present gathered for their first Andean women's meeting, considering the topic "Women of the Bible."[88]

The region which has faced the most organizational difficulties, because of its colonial history, political complexity and its many languages, has been the Caribbean region. At the last MWC assembly in Asunción, Paraguay (2009), Caribbean representatives expressed the need to organize themselves as a distinct region. Once this takes place, all Latin American regions will have been properly organized in order to be able to consider together common matters of interest, be they ecclesial, political, cultural or pastoral.

Mennonite World Conference, Mennonite Central Committee and other mission agencies have helped with financial and personnel resources in many of these events, which have continued to strengthen Latin American Anabaptist identity. The regional meetings are where profound theological, social and pastoral reflections take place. These have guided and strengthened leaders and Anabaptist communities, especially in times of military dictatorship, economic crises, ecological disasters and social revolutions.

The two Mennonite World Conferences held in Latin America should also be mentioned. The first, held in Curitiba, Brasil in 1972, introduced fundamental changes which led to a better ethnic balance in the leadership structure of MWC. The second MWC assembly held in Latin America took place in 2009 in Asunción, Paraguay. This assembly had 6,000 registrants of whom half were from Latin America. The Latin American caucus that meets at the MWC assemblies has become an important place where representatives of Mennonite churches can meet to decide leadership posts of important commissions which deal with issues such as Peace and Justice, missions, theological education, ecumenical relations, the Global Mennonite History project and many other concerns and matters that are important for the world-wide church.

The multi-ethnic character of Latin American Anabaptism

The recent MWC assembly held in Asunción in 2009 gave testimony to the multi-ethnic character of Latin American Anabaptism. In Paraguay there are Mennonites of German and Dutch background, as well as Spanish-speaking Mennonites and Guaraní, Toba, Enlhet and Nivaclé indigenous Mennonites. The Enlhet communities of Yalve Sanga[89] in Paraguay as well as the evangelical Tobas[90] in Argentina are aware of their history, and have begun recording their memories, myths, customs and their vision of God. Other indigenous peoples such as the Emberá-Wounaan in Panama have also begun to systematize their cultural inheritance in writing and art, and in this way to affirm their cultural and spiritual identity. Today the Scriptures have been translated into these indigenous languages and many others, such as into Kekchi (Guatemala), Trique (México), and Garífuna (Honduras), as well as into Bri-brí (Costa Rica).

There was a time when indigenous peoples were described as "pagans" by Mennonite missions.[91] Today the great richness of their ancestral spirituality has been recognized, and the whole continent is being called together to participate mutually in the effort to follow after Jesus Christ. In the midst of economic poverty, the Mennonite communities of indigenous and African descent share with us the wealth of their history, culture and spirituality. It is by means of their histories and myths, buried in the depths of the jungle, the oceans, the rivers, rocks and fields, that they exhort us to protect and watch over mother earth. Their visions and dreams help us see the disorder brought to creation by economic systems designed only to protect the interests of transnational corporations and the small minority that control them.[92]

A beautiful sign of fraternity and unity in the midst of diversity was the visit of brothers and sisters from indigenous peoples such as the Metis and Ojibwe (North America), the Quechuas (Perú), Kekchis (Guatemala), the Emberá and Wounaan (Panama) to the lands of the indigenous people of the Paraguayan and Argentine Chaco after the MWC assembly in Paraguay.[93]

This desire to learn from one another and to place our talents at the service of the rest is how the

Reflections of Alina Itucama of Panama

It doesn't matter where we are from, as indigenous people we have a lot that unites us. ... As a Wounaan indigenous woman, [this trip] has inspired me... The word of God, the Bible goes beyond cultures. We have to be wise to preserve cultures, traditions and customs that edify our faith and our lives, and to understand the message of the word through them. Our call is to be an indigenous church in the light of the word because we are created in God's image as Wounaan people.

Our non-indigenous brothers and sisters need to know and understand our customs, traditions and beliefs about God the creator because we are a very different culture with a worldview different from that of the western world. There will always be differences between indigenous and non-indigenous people, no matter how Christian we all are.

We have Christ as a model. He divested himself of his divine prerogatives to be incarnated among people, eating, living and walking together with them, learning and teaching. This teaches us that we need to adapt to the communities where we arrive to share or visit, in order that there can be a good understanding of the word of God.

I give thanks to God for the opportunity that was given me to get to know and to learn from brothers and sisters in the visit and during the MWC assembly. I give thanks also to the brothers and sisters who helped achieve this purpose. May the Lord bless them.

Alina Itucama sings a Wounaan song during the indigenous gathering in Paraguay

great ethnic variety of Mennonites in Latin America can nourish the Anabaptist community. In this way our efforts to be God's instruments in creation can become reality, a creation that looks forward to its liberation with labor pains, such as we groan and sigh for the redemption of our bodies (Romans 8:18-25).

The challenges of following after Jesus Christ

More than eighty Mennonite secondary school students in Paraguay were trained as "servants of peace" for the 15th MWC assembly in Paraguay in 2009.[94] Approximately 800 youth delegates to the World Youth Summit of the assembly, representing diverse countries of Africa, North America, Asia, Europe and Latin America, came to the conference after having done previous study in their churches. In their inquiries, the youth were supposed to define "serving" in their own words, and to describe what "serving" meant in their own lives. Angélica Rincón Alonso of Colombia explained "serving" as "collaboration, love, solidarity, humility, solutions, compassion, gifts and talents, and sharing."[95] Following after Jesus Christ today means taking on the task of serving with love, solidarity, humility and compassion.

In this book we have come to know a part of the historical pilgrimage of Mennonite communities and Anabaptist churches, as they have walked the paths of Latin America. We have made the words of the poet Machado our own: "traveller, there is no road; the road is made by walking." Our desire should be to continue following the Master. The hour is nearing when the sun is at its zenith, and like the disciples of Emmaus we yearn for the "stranger" to fill our hearts with new hope. As followers of Jesus, we are facing many challenges at the beginning of this twenty-first century. "None can know Jesus Christ, unless they follow after Him" said the Anabaptist leader Hans Denck. As the Latin American Anabaptist community, we have decided to follow Jesus Christ. From the depths of our hearts we cry, through tears and joys, "The day is coming to a close; stay with us!" (Matthew 24:13-32).

Appendix 1

Mennonite and BIC membership, by country and region (2009)

Southern Cone

Argentina	5,522
Brazil	11,058
Paraguay	32,217
Uruguay	1,442
Total Membership	**50,239**

Andean Region

Bolivia	18,848
Chile	900
Colombia	3,031
Ecuador	1,050
Peru	986
Venezuela	538
Total Membership	**25,353**

Caribbean

Bahamas	34
Belize	4,129
Cuba	3,373
Dominican Republic	5,682
Grenada	46
Haiti	3,382
Jamaica	686
Puerto Rico	520
Trinidad/Tobago	270
Total Membership	**18,122**

Mesoamerica

Costa Rica	1,784
El Salvador	620
Guatemala	14,301
Honduras	17,789
Mexico	29,277
Nicaragua	11,342
Panama	537
Total Membership	**75,650**

Total Latin American Mennonite/BIC membership (2009): **169,364** in 26 countries.

[*For more detailed information see www.mwc-cmm.org*]

Abbreviations

AEM Mennonite Evangelical Alliance (Argentina) (*Alianza Evangélica Menonita*)

AEM Mennonite Evangelical Alliance (Brazil) (*Aliança Evangélica Menonita*)

AIHMC Association of Mennonite Brethren Churches of Colombia (MB, after 1970s) (*Iglesias Cristianas Hermanos Menonitas de Colombia*)

AIMB Association of Mennonite Churches of Brazil (Portuguese) (*Associaçâo das Igrejas Menonitas do Brasil*)

AIIMB Association of Mennonite Brethren Churches of Brazil (German) (*Associação das Igrejas Irmãos Menonitas do Brasil*: now united with Portuguese churches in the *Convenção Brasileira das Igrejas Evangélicas Irmãos Menonitas*)

ALFALIT International organization promoting literacy (founded 1961, in Costa Rica)

AMA Amish Mennonite Aid (Plain City, Ohio)

ASCIM Indigenous-Mennonite Association of Cooperative Services (Paraguay) (*Asociación de Servicios de Cooperación Indígena-Menonita*)

BIC Brethren in Christ

BOMAS Board of Missions and Services (MB, Hillboro, Kansas, 1966; became *Mennonite Brethren Mission and Service International*: MBSI)

CAMCA Central American Anabaptist Mennonite Consultation (*Consulta Anabautista Menonita de Centro América*)

CBIHM Brazilian Conference of Mennonite Brethren Churches (Portuguese). Now united with churches of German descent in the *Convenção Brasileira das Igrejas Evangélicas Irmãos Menonitas*)

CDM *Centro de Desarrollo Ministerial* (Center for Ministerial Development)

CEDEC Evangelical Confederation of Colombia (Ecumenical: became CEDECOL in 1989) (*Confederación de Evangélicos de Colombia*)

CEDECOL Evangelical Confederation of Colombia (*Confederación Evangélica de Colombia*)

CEDEN Evangelical Committee for Development and National Emergencies (*Comité Evangélico de Desarrollo y Emergencia Nacional*)

CEMEB Evangelical Mennonite Center for Biblical Studies (Argentina) (*Centro Evangélico Menonita de Estudios Bíblicos*)

CEMTA Evangelical Mennonite Center of Theology Asunción (Paraguay: MG) (*Centro Evangélico Mennonita de Teología Asunción*)

CEPAD Council of Protestant Churches of Nicaragua (*Consejo de Iglesias Evangélicas Pro-Alianza Denominacional*)

CERCAPAZ Anabaptist Christian Resource Center for Peace (*Centro de Recursos Cristianos Anabautistas por la Paz*)

CGIEMH General Council of the Honduran Evangelical Mennonite Church (*Concilio General de la Iglesia Evangélica Menonita Hondureña*)

CIEMB Conference of Evangelical Mennonite Churches of Brazil. See AEM, Brazil (*Aliança Evangélica Menonita*)

CIEMPR Conference of Evangelical Mennonite Churches of Puerto Rico (*Convención de las Iglesias Evangélicas Menonitas de Puerto Rico*)

CIEMCR Conference of Evangelical Mennonite Churches of Costa Rica (*Convención de Iglesias Evangélicas Menonitas de Costa Rica*)

CIEMU Conference of Evangelical Mennonite Churches of Uruguay (*Convención de Iglesias Evangélicas Menonitas en Uruguay*)

CIIMB Convention of Mennonite Brethren Churches (Brazil: Portuguese) (*Convenção das Igrejas Irmãos Menonitas do Brasil*)

CMC Conservative Mennonite Conference (before 1954 called the Amish Mennonite Conservative Conference)

CMF Conservative Mennonite Fellowship

CNHMC National Conference of Mennonite Brethren of Colombia (Mennonite Brethren: 1953 to early 1970s. See AIHMC) (*Conferencia Nacional de los Hermanos Menonitas de Colombia*)

COBIM Brazilian Conference of Evangelical Mennonite Brethren Churches (Union of CIHMB and CBIHM, 1995: *Convenção Brasileira das Igrejas Evangélicas Irmãos Menonitas*)

CODEH Committee for Human Rights of Honduras (*Comité de Derechos Humanos de Honduras*)

COM General Conference Mennonite Church, Commission on Overseas Mission (See also MBMC)

COMAESP Mennonite Committee for Evangelical and Social Action in Paraguay (*Comité Menonita de Acción Evangélica y Social en Paraguay*)

CONEMPAR Paraguayan Evangelical Mennonite Conference (MG) (*Convención Evangélica Menonita Paraguaya*)

COSEC Christian Social Service Committee of the Honduran Mennonite church (*Comité de Servicio Cristiano*)

CPS Civilian Public Service (United States)

CSI Christian Service International (Haiti)

EBEX *Ecole Biblique par Extensión* (Haiti)

EMB Evangelical Mennonite Brotherhood (Paraguay) (*Die Evangelisch Mennontische Bruderschaft*)

EMBM Eastern Mennonite Board of Missions

EMC Evangelical Mennonite Conference (Canada)

EMCDR Evangelical Mennonite Church of the Dominican Republic (*Iglesia Evangélica Menonite en la República Dominicana*)

EMM Eastern Mennonite Missions

FEINE Federation of Indigenous Evangelicals of Ecuador (*Federación Ecuatoriana de Indígenas Evangélicos*) now Council of Indigenous Evangelical Peoples & Organizations: *Consejo de Pueblos y Organizaciones Indígenas Evangélicas del Ecuador*

FSLN Sandinista Front for National Liberation (*Frente Sandinista de Liberación Nacional*)

HCJB Heralding Christ Jesus' Blessings/Voice of the Andes (radio station, Ecuador)

HPI Heifer Project International

IBA Biblical Institute of Asunción (Paraguay: MB) (*Instituto Bíblico Asunción*)

IBM Mennonite Biblical Institute (Honduras) (*Instituto Bíblico Menonita*)

IEMA Argentine Evangelical Mennonite Church (*Iglesia Evangélica Menonita de Argentina*)

IEMCO Evangelical Mennonite Church of Colombia (General Conference) (*Iglesia Evangélica Menonita de Colombia*) now IMCOL: *Iglesia Cristiana Menonita de Colombia*

IEMES Mennonite Church of El Salvador (*Iglesia Evangélica Menonita de El Salvador*)

IEMH Honduran Evangelical Mennonite Church (*Iglesia Evangélica Menonita Hondureña*)

IMCOL Mennonite Churches of Colombia (*Iglesias Menonitas de Colombia*) formerly IEMCO

ISAL   Church and Society in Latin America (*Iglesia y Sociedad en América Latina*)

ISBIM   *Instituto e Seminário Biblico dos Irmãos Menonitas* (Institute and Seminary of the Mennonite Brethren

ITE   Evangelical Theological Institute (MB) (*Instituto Teológico Evangélico*)

JELAM   Latin American Board of Mennonite Broadcasts (*Junta Latino-americana de Audiciones Menonitas*)

MB   Mennonite Brethren

MBMC   Mennonite Board of Missions and Charities (Elkhart, Indiana). In 1971 the name changed to Mennonite Board of Missions (MBM). In 2002, MBM united with COM, the General Conference Mennonite Church Commission on Overseas Mission, and the Commission on Home Mission (CHM) to form two national bodies: "Mennonite Mission Network of Mennonite Church USA" and "Mennonite Church Canada Witness."

MBM   (See MBMC)

MCC   Mennonite Central Committee

MEDA   Mennonite Economic Development Associates

MENCOLDES   Colombian Mennonite Foundation for Development (*Fundación Menonita Colombiana para el Desarrollo*)

MIM   Menno Indianer Mission (Menno Indian Mission, Paraguay)

MG   *Mennonitengemeinde* (Distinct from MBs, the MG often associated with General Conference Mennonites of North America)

MMN   Mennonite Mission Network (See also MBMC)

MMR   Rosedale Mennonite Mission (RMM in English) (*Misión Menonita Rosedale*)

REDPAZ   Regional Network of Justice and Peace (Central America) (*Red Regional de Justicia y Paz*)

SBMC   *Seminario Bíblico Menonita de Colombia* (Biblical Mennonite Seminary of Colombia)

SEMILLA   Latin American Anabaptist Seminary (Guatemala) (*Seminario Anabautista Latinoamericano*)

SEMT   Evangelical Mennonite Theological Seminary (Uruguay) (*Seminario Evangélico Menonita Teológico*)

VMB   United Mennonite Brethren Community (*Vereinigten Mennoniten Brüdergemeinde*)

WBT   Wycliff Bible Translators

Endnotes

Because of space limitations, the 80 pages of citations and sidebar credits have not beeen printed as a part of this volume. The citations are available on line, as are the sidebar credits at the Good Books and Pandora Press websites:

www.GoodBooks.com/LatinAmericaNotes.pdf
www.PandoraPress.com/LatinAmericaNotes.pdf

Contact Pandora Press for a printed and bound version:
33 Kent Ave., Kitchener, Ontario, Canada, N2G 3R2   •   Ph: 519-578-2381

Index